DATE DUE

BRODART, CO.   Cat. No. 23-221

D1599196

GOING FOR BROKE

CAMPAIGNS & COMMANDERS

GREGORY J. W. URWIN, SERIES EDITOR

CAMPAIGNS AND COMMANDERS

GOING FOR BROKE

Japanese American Soldiers
in the War against Nazi Germany

James M. McCaffrey

University of Oklahoma Press : Norman

Also by James M. McCaffrey
This Band of Heroes: Granbury's Texas Brigade, C.S.A. (Austin, Texas, 1985)
Army of Manifest Destiny: The American Soldier in the Mexican War, 1846–1848
    (New York, 1992)
(with John F. Kinney) *Wake Island Pilot: A World War II Memoir*
    (Washington, D.C., 1995)
Surrounded by Dangers of All Kinds: The Mexican War Letters of Lieutenant Theodor
    Laidley (Denton, Texas, 1997)
(ed.) *Only a Private: A Texan Remembers the Civil War* (Houston, Texas, 2004)
The Army in Transformation, 1790–1860 (Westport, Conn., 2006)
Inside the Spanish-American War: A History Based on First-Person Accounts
    (Jefferson, N.C., 2009)

Library of Congress Cataloging-in-Publication Data

McCaffrey, James M., 1946–
  Going for broke : Japanese American soldiers in the war against Nazi Germany
/ James M. McCaffrey.
    pages cm. — (Campaigns and commanders ; volume 36)
  Includes bibliographical references and index.
  ISBN 978-0-8061-4337-8 (hardcover : alk. paper) 1. United States. Army.
Infantry Battalion, 100th. 2. United States. Army. Regimental Combat Team,
442nd. 3. World War, 1939–1945—Regimental histories—United States.
4. World War, 1939–1945—Participation, Japanese American. 5. World War,
1939–1945—Campaigns—Europe. 6. Japanese American soldiers—History—
20th century. I. Title.
  D769.31100th .M44 2013
  940.54'1273—dc23
                                                                        2012042873

Going for Broke: Japanese American Soldiers in the War against Nazi Germany is
Volume 36 in the Campaigns and Commanders series.

Dedicated to the memory of
Staff Sergeant Carl K. Morita,
Headquarters Battery,
522nd Field Artillery Battalion,
442nd Regimental Combat Team,
United States Army

CONTENTS

ILLUSTRATIONS

Preface

When World War II began in Europe in 1939, Carl Morita was a teenaged farm boy with a year's credit toward a degree in pharmacy at the University of Colorado. When the war ended six years later, he was a war-hardened staff sergeant in the U.S. Army, having volunteered for service in the summer of 1941. After the Japanese attacked Pearl Harbor, Private Morita and most other Japanese Americans found that many of their fellow citizens looked down upon them because of their heritage and a presumed—and in almost every case nonexistent—allegiance to the empire of Japan. Morita and the other Japanese American[1] soldiers spent the war fighting the prejudice of fellow Americans as well as the soldiers of Adolf Hitler's Germany.

War Department authorities culled all the Japanese Americans from the Hawaii National Guard after the Japanese attack on Pearl Harbor and grouped them into a single, over-strength battalion designated as the 100th Infantry Battalion (Separate). And then, to further allay suspicions of their loyalty, they were sent to the mainland for more training. Most of the Japanese American soldiers already in the Army, like Private Morita, were transferred into non-combat occupations and dispersed throughout the country. At the same time, anti-Japanese hysteria swept much of the Pacific coast and led to the forced removal of more than one hundred thousand Japanese and Japanese Americans to internment camps farther inland. Against this backdrop of suspicion and veiled racial hostility, Americans of Japanese descent sought some way to prove that they were as American as anyone else. The formation, in early 1943, of an entirely Japanese American combat unit was one result.

At first, almost all of the officers were Caucasians, and the unit drew its senior noncommissioned officers from those, such as newly promoted staff sergeant Morita, who already had time in the army. This outfit, dubbed the 442nd Regimental Combat Team, spent over a year training at Camp Shelby, Mississippi, before shipping out for Italy in May 1944. The 100th Battalion, having begun its training well before the 442nd, had already spent several months in Italy attached to the 34th Infantry Division. The 100th had taken part in the desperate fighting at Cassino and had assisted the breakout from the Anzio beachhead that led to the capture of Rome. When the 442nd Regimental Combat Team arrived it ultimately absorbed the 100th Battalion, and the combined unit continued the tradition of valor already begun.

In the fall of 1944, the combat team sailed to France where, as part of the 36th Infantry Division, it endured the bitter fighting in the Vosges Mountains. Heavy losses resulted in the unit spending the winter in relatively quieter duty along the French-Italian border near the Riviera—an assignment that the men referred to as the Champagne Campaign.

Then, in the spring of 1945, the combat team was broken up. The organic artillery battalion stayed with the Seventh Army for the drive into Germany. The rest of the combat team returned to Italy where it was assigned to the 92nd Infantry Division for the final push into the Po Valley.

The experiences of the men of the 100th/442nd are in many ways common to most other units of similar size. They had to deal with the unforgiving terrain of the Italian mountains and the brutal winter weather in France. They suffered from wounds, from trench foot, from cold, miserable weather, and from downright homesickness just like hundreds of thousands of other GIs. But the men of this unit—the overwhelming majority of whom were born in the United States—had constantly to prove to the American public that they were loyal Americans. Many of them fought their nation's enemies while that same nation held their families in what amounted to prison camps simply because of their ancestry. These men looked Japanese, they enjoyed Japanese food, and many of them spoke Japanese, but they were Americans to the core.

A military unit as celebrated as this one has, of course, drawn the attention of earlier historians, so this is not the first account of its actions. Some previous publications have confined their discussions to one individual battalion within the combat team while others have dealt with the total Japanese American military experience of World War II, which included coverage of not only the 442nd but also those many brave Nisei soldiers who served in military intelligence in the Pacific theater. Others have confined themselves to the infantry elements of the combat team, with little or no mention of the artillery battalion, the anti-tank or cannon companies, or the combat engineers. Some begin their accounts in the war zone, with no mention of how and why these units were formed and no coverage of their training. These books do a commendable job of covering their particular areas, but this book seeks to provide a more comprehensive look at the entire story.

Going for Broke seeks to build upon these previous works to present a more complete story. But it is more than a synthesis of earlier books. This book is the story of the fight these men waged against this nation's enemies and also their battle for acceptance by the people of the United States. It is told, as much as possible, from the perspective of the common soldiers, often relying on their own words.

It is, in part, a social history. Readers will read about the soldiers' initiation into the army routine, their training, the clash of culture within their own ranks—between those men from Hawaii and those from the mainland—as well as between the soldiers and the civilians living near their training bases. These soldiers, many of whom had suffered from the racial insensitivities of Caucasian Americans, also exhibited an interesting reaction to the cultural barriers between blacks and whites in wartime Mississippi. Also described is their interaction with the Italian, French, and German civilians with whom they came in contact.

Going for Broke is also an operational history. It places this unit, as an integral part of three successive infantry divisions, in the greater context of the war effort against Nazi Germany. At the same time it illustrates several cultural confrontations—beginning in the training camps themselves as mainland Nisei learned to deal with unfamiliar traits of the islanders and vice-versa.

A note about sources: Among the many sources consulted while writing this book were those that appear on the Internet. The Internet is a double-edged sword for historians. There is a tremendous amount of schlock and unsubstantiated drivel on the Internet, but there is a large and growing body of solid research material also. Internet sources have been of great value in preparing this book. Some of the former officers of the 442nd have put their reminiscences or wartime letters online. Many libraries have begun to digitize their archival holdings and put them online, thus saving the researcher the cost of traveling to these libraries to view their holdings. Most academic libraries subscribe to JSTOR, which has made available the full-text versions of articles in more than a thousand journals. Many wartime military journals—*Quartermaster Review, Intelligence Bulletin,* and *Field Artillery Journal,* among others—are similarly available in their entireties. The U.S. Army's Infantry School has made available many of the papers written by officer-students in the immediate postwar years, and some of these officers thus wrote about their experiences with the 442nd Regimental Combat Team. A couple of entities have placed videotaped interviews with Japanese American veterans online. The University of Hawaii, for one, has undertaken a program to preserve, through such interviews, the World War II recollections of Japanese Americans, including the memories of a handful of men who served in the 442nd. The Go For Broke National Education Center, founded in 1989 in Los Angeles to promote awareness of the service of Japanese Americans in World War II, has undertaken an ambitious program to record interviews with as many Nisei veterans as possible. As of 2013, the number of such interviews available for online viewing exceeded thirteen hundred.

Acknowledgments

I must thank Charles Rankin, Associate Director of the University of Oklahoma Press, for his support for this project. Chuck has gone to greater lengths than an author has a right to expect to get this book to press and has encouraged me when I needed it. I also wish to extend my thanks to Gregory J. W. Urwin, editor of the University of Oklahoma Press's Campaigns and Commanders series and professor of history at Temple University. Greg has been unstinting in his praise of my work and has more than once given me a little verbal nudging when I needed it to keep going. This book would not have made it to the printed page without their help. Finally, I am grateful for the sharp eyes of copyeditor Steve Weingartner. Any errors still present are entirely my own.

GOING FOR BROKE

INTRODUCTION

"I have been accepted for service in the U.S. Army."

With these words, on a standard form postcard, young Carl Katsumi Morita informed his family back home near Ault, Colorado, that he was on his way to becoming a soldier in the United States Army. By July 1941, many of the world's nations had been at war for almost two years, but the isolationist United States had remained officially neutral.

Relations between the United States and Japan had grown progressively more strained during the previous few years. Right-wing militarists in Japan had gained considerable influence at all levels of that nation's government and armed forces, and they seemed determined to lead their nation to international greatness. They wanted to strengthen the existing monarchy, impose some form of corporate state in place of capitalism, eliminate communism, and expand the Japanese empire to alleviate problems at home brought about by a high birth rate and the lack of arable land and important raw materials, such as oil. The first step toward the creation of Japanese dominance over Asia took place in 1931 when Japanese troops invaded Chinese Manchuria, where they set up a puppet government and renamed the country Manchukuo (country of the Manchus) in February 1932.

By 1937, Japanese military leaders were no longer content with the conquest of Manchuria and began taking the rest of China. Thus began a long and bitter war between the two countries, a conflict that would claim the lives of tens of millions of Chinese before it had run its course.

In Europe, meanwhile, Adolf Hitler had come to power in Germany on a program of restoring that nation to its former greatness and establishing it as a dominant world power. He oversaw the building of his nation's military machine that, on September 1, 1939, invaded Poland. Britain and France quickly honored treaty commitments to this victim of Hitler's ambitions and declared war on Germany, but Poland fell. World War II had begun, and after a brief period of relative inaction during the winter of 1939–1940, Denmark, Norway, Belgium, the Netherlands, Luxembourg, and France fell to the German onslaught.

If Britain fell to Germany, as seemed entirely likely, that would leave the way open for Japanese attacks on Hong Kong and Malaya. While some Americans pushed for an embargo on American oil, others, President Franklin Roosevelt among them, advised against the *implementation* of an oil embargo (that might force the Japanese deeper into southeast Asia looking for oil, and might force them into a war with the United States). Instead, the president wanted to hold out the continued *threat* of an oil embargo.

Even while some Americans, both in and out of Congress, steadfastly believed that their nation would be spared from having to go to war again, the president on September 16 signed into law this country's first peacetime conscription bill after much heated debate. During congressional discussions of this bill, New York Senator Robert Wagner proposed an amendment that guaranteed that all young men, regardless of race or color, would be subject to the draft and would be allowed to enlist as well. Many southern senators, as might be expected, opposed this change because it would allow black Americans to enter the military, but resistance also arose within the War Department because of the number of Japanese Americans that might be affected. Senator Millard Tydings, of Maryland, was only one who noted the supposed danger of having a large number of Japanese American soldiers stationed in Hawaii if war came with Japan. He speculated that most would be loyal to the United States but feared those who were not. "I think we had better leave this element out," he declared, "let the Army run the Army, and not have so many generals in the United States Senate." In spite of such resistance, however, the final bill made no distinction among selectees with regard to their skin color or race. Even at such a crisis time as this, the idea of a military draft was far from overwhelmingly popular. There was much bitter debate in the Congress, and the final vote tally in favor of the bill was only 45 to 27 in the Senate and 232 to 124 in the House. Officially dubbed the Selective Training and Service Act of 1940, this law required every man in the country between the ages of twenty-one and thirty-six to register on October 16, although it was thought that no men over the age of twenty-eight would actually be drafted.[1]

Nor was registration restricted to U.S. citizens. The law required aliens to register, although only those who had begun the citizenship process were likely to be called, and that included foreign military officers in the United States on embassy duty. Failure to do so brought the threat of a $10,000 fine and a five-year jail sentence. A California man notified his draft board that he would not serve in the U.S. military "as long as Roosevelt is dictator of the U.S.A." Mohawk and Seneca Indians in New York stated their willingness to fight if war came, but they were not interested in signing up for a military draft. Similarly, several dozen Seminole Indians in Florida refused to register. Generally, however, young men went through the process with a minimum of disruption. In New York City, a resident of Chinatown enthusiastically gathered up registrants. "I tell them they will get a chance to fight Japan," he reported. "They come with me, quick."[2]

This legislation allowed for the induction of up to nine hundred thousand men per year for one year's military training. Among the first to report for active duty were four national guard divisions that had been federalized, and various other reserve components. The first actual selection of men under the terms of the new conscription law took place on October 29, 1940, and it was fraught with symbolism. Workers had painstakingly put almost nine thousand numbered blue capsules into the same glass container that had been used to select men for the draft in 1917. As in the earlier draft, the number of capsules corresponded to the number of registrants in the country's largest draft board. And just as in that earlier draft, Lieutenant Colonel Charles Morris, retired now, tied a blindfold around the eyes of Secretary of War Henry Stimson so there could be no question as to the fairness employed. Stimson ceremoniously fished a capsule out of the bowl and handed it to a waiting President Roosevelt. The president opened the capsule and slowly read the number written inside—158. That meant that in every draft board in the country, the man with number 158 would be the first to report for a pre-induction physical and, assuming that he proved healthy, induction into the army. One of those men, Harry Bell, was present at the drawing along with his fiancé and his mother. The president and secretary left to attend to more pressing duties, but the drawings continued for another seventeen hours until all of the numbers had been drawn and their sequence recorded.[3]

All across the country young men eagerly scanned the list of numbers in the newspapers to try to determine how soon they would be called. Among the 6,175 men holding number 158 were a newspaper reporter in Cleveland, a zookeeper in San Diego, a janitor in Philadelphia, and 4'6" William Giblin, who had portrayed a munchkin in the recent film *Wizard of Oz*. In Boston, a man who held number 158 was the son of a man who had held the first number—number 258—drawn in the 1917 draft. In San Francisco some men formed a 158 Club and hired comedian Bob Hope to emcee a big party at the Sir Francis Drake Hotel.[4]

Having one's number drawn for the draft did not necessarily result in military service. There was a surprisingly large number of draft registrants who found loopholes—deferments—that allowed them to avoid induction. College students, convicted felons, conscientious objectors, men with families, those practicing certain professions, and, of course, those who voluntarily enlisted avoided the draft. And although it was said that draftees "can be blind in one eye, partially deaf in both ears, minus one big toe or two little ones, and still be technically eligible," many were found to be physically unfit for military service. A staffer with the Selective Service System poetically described the difficulty in filling draft quotas:

Ten little registrants standing in a line
One joined the Navy, and then there were nine.
Nine little registrants sitting on a gate
One broke a vertebra, and then there were eight.
Eight little registrants, talking 'bout heaven
One went conscientious, then there were seven.

Seven little registrants, what a strange mix!
One became a pilot, and then there were six.
Six little registrants very much alive
One went and drowned and then there were five.
Five little registrants full of canny lore
One stole a pig and then there were four.
Four little registrants, spry as they can be
One became twenty-eight, then there were three.
Three little registrants, all alone and blue
One fed his relatives, then there were two.
Two little registrants, what can be done!
One went to a psychiatrist, and then there was one.
One little registrant, classified I-A
Physically, mentally, morally okay.
One little registrant to tote a big gun
He got married and then there were NONE![5]

A Japanese American man, when he learned that he held the ominous number 158, decided to go ahead and enlist, but a recruiting sergeant told him that the only assignment open to him was in one of the army's segregated "colored" regiments. He refused and wrote a letter of complaint directly to President Roosevelt. He received a written reply, not from the president, but from Lieutenant General John L. DeWitt, clearing the way for him to enlist. When he once again presented himself, however, army doctors turned him away because of an injury to his trigger finger that he had incurred while working in a civilian butcher shop.[6]

During the spring of 1941, the United States entered into World War II in fact, if not in name. American warships began shadowing German submarines in the North Atlantic and radioing their locations to nearby British forces so they could come in for the actual kill. On May 21, German submarines sank an American freighter, and Roosevelt responded by freezing all German and Italian assets in this country and closing down all German consulates.

The situation in Asia also continued to fester. In August 1940, Japan announced the creation of the Greater East Asian Co-Prosperity Sphere that, in essence, called for Japanese hegemony over all of eastern Asia. This included China, Indochina, Malaya, the Dutch East Indies, India, Burma, Thailand, Borneo, New Zealand, Australia, and the Philippines. On September 27, Japan joined with Germany and Italy in a Tripartite Pact. This agreement recognized each of the signatories' spheres of influence in Europe and in Asia and promised "to assist one another with all political, economic and military means when one of the three contracting Parties is attacked by a power at present not involved in the European War or in the Chinese-Japanese Conflict." Since the agreement also specifically exempted the Soviet Union, it left only the United States as a major party not already involved in the European war or the Sino-Japanese war. None of the members of the Tripartite Pact wanted the Americans to get into the war. In fact, they hoped that the very threats contained in their agreement would keep the United States at bay.[7]

Even while rumors began to circulate in Japan of the possibility of war with the United States, Japanese diplomats sought to avoid such a conflict. In February 1941, Admiral Kichisaburo Nomura came to Washington to try to forestall a possible oil embargo by the United States, and to iron out other difficulties between the two countries. The talks dragged on for months with no progress. Further exacerbating the situation was the fact that the Japanese envoy did not speak English very well and refused to use a translator.

Meanwhile, the Selective Service Act had no immediate effect on twenty-year-old Carl Morita. He would not reach his twenty-first birthday until the summer of 1941, but the law allowed men younger than twenty-one but older than eighteen to volunteer for one year's service, and on March 29, 1941, that is what Morita did. When his longtime friend and future brother-in-law Tomoji F. Uno received his draft notice, Morita decided to go ahead and get his one-year's obligation taken care of too, so he volunteered for the draft. Two days later he sailed through his physical examination in Greeley, Colorado, and on April 9 he received his draft classification of I-A, fit for immediate induction. Three months later, and still two weeks away from his twenty-first birthday, he was on his way to basic training. His family and friends were at the bus station to see him off, and had presented him with a fine new Elgin wristwatch. He, of course, had no idea that he would remain in uniform for more than the required twelve months. Nor could he have known that he would enter combat as a member of a unique military organization that would earn for itself more than just the huge number of individual and unit decorations for valor.[8]

As soon as the draft became a fact of American life, books describing army life began to appear in the book stores, aimed at young men preparing for their year of service. Readers were warned not to bring too much with them in the way of clothing, as the army would provide what they needed. Most of these books agreed that the recruit should bring basic toiletries: a comb, a hairbrush, soap, a toothbrush and tooth powder, and a razor and shaving soap. All of this could fit into a paper bag. Beyond these essential items there was a diversity of opinions regarding what to bring. One source also suggested a few handkerchiefs, a pocket sewing kit, enough stationery and stamps for letter-writing, a wrist-watch, pajamas, tan shoe polish and the accompanying brush or rag, and a change of underwear and socks. A multi-purpose pocket knife, such as those used by the Boy Scouts or in the Swiss army was "almost indispensable." Another book suggested a pair of comfortable shoes, four changes of underwear, six pairs of socks, two bath towels, four face towels, and one woolen blanket. It is not known whether young Carl Morita had read any of these books or not, but the photo of him and twenty other selectees that appeared in the *Greeley Tribune* as they waited for a bus to take them to basic training shows only a small bag by his side. It is un-likely that he carried anything beyond the basics.[9]

After a week of processing at Fort Bliss, Morita boarded a train for the West Coast. By the morning of July 16, the train had reached Ash Fork, Arizona. It stopped there so the passengers could get off and eat breakfast. The brand new soldier also used the time to hunt up a picture postcard of a Zuni pueblo, which he sent home to his dad with a quick message. Three hundred miles later it was dinner time, at Barstow, California, and once again Morita wrote a quick message on the back of a postcard showing Enchanted Mesa, New Mexico. The final stop, at least for the young men headed into the army, was Camp Roberts, near San Luis Obispo, California. In less than a year, a small army of workers had turned over forty-two thousand acres of rolling pasture into a functioning army training camp that included 188 miles of roads, 437 street-lights, four one thousand-foot water wells, three 630,000-gallon water storage tanks, three one thousand-seat theaters, an eleven hundred-bed hospital, and enough two-story wooden barracks to hold almost thirty thousand troops.[10]

Morita spent his first days at the camp getting acclimated to army life. He sent his civilian clothing home upon drawing his government-issue uniforms. The army provided him with seven pairs of undershorts, nine undershirts, six cotton handkerchiefs, and eight pairs of socks. On top of that, he received three pairs of cotton and two pairs of woolen trousers, two worsted and two khaki shirts, two neckties, two pairs of canvas leggings, two uniform coats, an overcoat, a raincoat, three pairs of shoes, one pair of gloves, and two complete denim work uniforms. And as if that was not enough of a burden to carry back to his barracks, he also received a razor (with five razor blades), a shaving brush, a hair comb, and three towels.[11]

Clerical and mechanical aptitude tests took up about two and a half hours one morning, followed by sanitation and hygiene lectures that stressed the importance of twice-a-day tooth-brushing and semi-weekly baths and changes of underwear. He also heard the first of the required semi-annual "Sex Morality" lectures, where a medical officer laid out the grim effects of untreated venereal disease, and a chaplain discussed the morality of engaging in wanton sex. Sometimes these sex instructors attempted to get their message across with a little levity near the end of the lecture by saying something like: "Flies spread disease, so keep yours buttoned."[12]

Morita's high test scores, a result of his year in college and his mechanical aptitude, sent him to the field artillery. His living arrangements for the next couple of months consisted of a steel cot, with the requisite mattress and bedding, on the first floor of a barracks that held the sixty-two other men assigned to Battery D, 55th Field Artillery Training Battalion, 12th Field Artillery Training Regiment. Each barracks had toilet and shower facilities for the men as well as a small kitchen.[13]

Individual training began, as it had for more than a century and a half, with the School of the Soldier. Here Morita and the other recruits learned the basics, the absolute basics, of conducting themselves as soldiers. A contemporary army manual used an entire paragraph to instruct the proper way to stand at attention.

> To take the position of attention[,] place your heels together and on the same line. Allow your feet to turn out equally, forming an angle of 45° with each other. Keep your knees straight but without stiffness. Draw your hips up under your body slightly. Keep your chest up and your shoulders back. Do not allow one shoulder to be higher than the other. Keep your arms straight without stiffness, and hanging at your sides, in such a way that your thumbs are always along the seams of your trousers. Turn the backs of your hands out away from your body and allow your hands and fingers to cup naturally. Always keep your eyes straight to the front. When standing properly[,] the weight of your body will be divided equally between the heels and balls of both feet. When assuming the position of attention, bring your heels together smartly and audibly.[14]

The fledgling soldier also learned how to salute properly and, perhaps more importantly, whom to salute and when to salute. Having mastered the mechanics of this movement, the novice realized that *every* commissioned officer of *every* service rated a respectable salute. Therefore, he had to learn the distinguishing rank insignias of officers not just in the army, but in the navy and marine corps as well.

The next lesson dealt with marching. The new soldiers quickly learned that when they received the command to march, they did not simply shamble off in the proper direction at whatever pace seemed comfortable. First of all, they learned that a soldier always begins marching with his left foot, and that he must then regulate his speed of movement with everyone else who was marching. The instructor called the marching cadence to keep the men in step. When an officer wanted his men to move faster he ordered that they march in "quick time." This meant taking 120 steps per minute, each of which covered thirty inches, and moving the man along at almost three-and-a-half miles per hour. At "double time," the men lengthened their steps to thirty-six inches and their speed to 180 steps per minute. At this rate they were almost running, and were covering ground at better than six miles per hour. Private Morita, who stood only 5'4½" tall, really had his work cut out for him just to keep up with the taller men.[15]

In mid-September, Morita and his fellow trainees underwent gas mask familiarization training. Various poison gasses—chlorine, phosgene, mustard, and others—had caused countless casualties during World War I, among them an Austrian corporal named Adolf Hitler. There were several attempts during the 1920s to outlaw the use of such gasses. In 1922, the United States, along with France, England, Japan, and Italy, signed such a treaty. It was to go into effect as soon as all five nations ratified it, but France never did. Three years later, the United States signed the Geneva Protocol that sought to achieve the same end, but this time the U.S. Senate failed to ratify it. Nevertheless, every U.S. president from Warren Harding to Franklin Roosevelt had stated that the United States would abide by its conditions anyway. "Whether or not gas will be used in future war is a matter of conjecture," stated General John Pershing, commander of the American Expeditionary Forces in the First World War, "but the effect on the unprepared is so deadly that we can never afford to neglect the question."[16]

As Private Morita and his fellow trainees learned the rudiments of soldiering they may not have had time to follow world events, but the United States would find itself embroiled in war before the end of the year. Mindful of the possibility of war, army authorities decided to use the huge influx of soldiers serving under the Selective Training and Service Act to stage what they hoped would be realistic large-scale maneuvers in August and September. Held in central Louisiana, these war games pitted two field armies against one another in a series of tactical problems designed to test, among other things, the utility of continuing the use of horse cavalry and the use of paratroops. Nineteen divisions furnished the nearly four hundred thousand troops who took part in these exercises, and as they "fought" over the woods and swamps the realism was enhanced by the deaths of some two dozen men. One was struck by lightning, another succumbed to a snake bite, a few drowned, others died in vehicle accidents, and five perished in a plane crash.[17]

National Geographic Magazine published an article in the summer
of 1941 that introduced its readers to modern military training
and attempted to illustrate how the thousands of new, one-year
soldiers were progressing. "In the other war I saw guys sent up
front who'd never even fired a gun," reported a grizzled veteran
of World War I. "Now," he continued, "a rookie barely stumbles off
the train that brings him to camp before we shove a rifle into his
hands and tell him to commence shooting." Apparently, however,
those in charge of training at Camp Roberts had not read this article because two months into his training Private Morita wrote to
his father: "I hope they let me shoot a rifle soon."[18]

By that time, the U.S. Army was phasing out the infantry rifle
that had seen it through World War I and began introducing a
newer model. Both rifles fired the same .30-caliber cartridge. The
Model 1903 Springfield rifle, however, was significantly slower to
load and shoot than the modern M1 rifle designed by John Garand. In order to shoot the Springfield, the soldier had to lift up
on a bolt handle on the right side of the rifle and pull it three
or four inches toward the rear. Then he loaded five cartridges
into the weapon's internal magazine through the opening thus
created. Upon pushing the bolt forward it took the topmost cartridge and fed it into the firing chamber. When the soldier then
turned the bolt handle downward his rifle was ready to fire. Then,
after each round he fired, he again raised the bolt handle and slid
it toward the rear. This action plucked the fired shell casing out
of the rifle, and when the soldier pushed the bolt forward again
the next round entered the chamber. It only took a second or
two. The nine-pound M1, however, was semi-automatic. That is,
once the soldier had loaded an eight-round clip and charged the
weapon, all he had to do to fire was pull the trigger. There was no
bolt to operate. The force of some of the gas generated by the explosion of the cartridge worked the rifle's mechanism such that it
ejected the spent cartridge case automatically and inserted a fresh
cartridge into the firing chamber. A soldier could fire his M1 just
as fast as he could pull the trigger. This gave the American soldier
a decided advantage because, at least until late in the war, he was
the only soldier on the battlefield with such a weapon.

Next, recruits learned to disassemble their rifles for cleaning. In some training camps, instructors staged competitions among the troops to see who could disassemble and/or reassemble a rifle the fastest. Unfortunately, this sometimes led to parts becoming damaged due to hurried misalignment or other causes, and the 1943 drill regulations specifically prohibited such drills, saying that in addition to possible damage to the weapons, these speed drills served "no useful purpose." Blindfolded assembly drills did, however, have some value because a soldier could conceivably have to tear down his rifle and put it back together again on some moonless night on the battlefield.[19]

Some soldiers approached rifle training with some experience. Those who had hunted, or who had participated in some form of Reserve Officers' Training Corps (ROTC), either in high school or college, had at least a rudimentary knowledge of marksmanship. For others, however, army training represented the first time in their lives that they had ever even held a firearm. Rifle training, then, had to begin with the very basics. The first thing that the instructors taught was how to aim the rifle with precision. All three elements of sighting—the target, the front sight, and the rear sight—had to be in precise alignment for the rifle's bullet to hit the target.

The second step in this preparatory training was to introduce the recruits to several different firing positions. The men learned how to properly align their rifles' sights while standing, while kneeling, while sitting on the ground, and while lying prone. Part of the training in this step also involved proper breathing. Something as simple as drawing one's breath properly had a major influence on holding the rifle on target. Even a shallow breath caused movement in a man's body, so it was necessary to fire the rifle while not breathing. This, obviously, must be a learned behavior. The instructors taught the men to draw in a breath when they were ready to shoot and then let some of it out. That way, their body could remain motionless for a few seconds without depriving itself of necessary oxygen.

The third step of instruction was to teach the men how to pull the trigger. This, on its face, seems almost too obvious to require any instruction, but most men, without this instruction, tended to jerk the trigger rearward when they fired. This often resulted in the shooter flinching and in a slight movement of the barrel, which displaced the point of impact of the bullet. And the farther away the target was the greater was the amount of miss. In battle, if the target—an enemy soldier—was within twenty or thirty yards such displacement was of little consequence. But the farther away the target was the greater the likelihood of a complete miss. So instead of jerking the trigger, the shooter was instructed to squeeze it with a uniform pressure so that he would not know precisely when the rifle would fire—until it did. He was less likely to flinch and throw off his aim if he could be taught to squeeze the trigger instead of jerking it.

Finally, after perhaps a week of such preliminaries, the soldiers were ready to go to the rifle range to try to put into practice what their instructors had been teaching them. Starting at a distance of only twenty-five to thirty yards from the target, they gradually advanced to the two hundred-, three hundred-, and five hundred-yard ranges. There was a spotter, safely protected by a large earthen berm, for each target. Whenever a shot hit his target, he raised a disc on the end of a pole and placed it over the hole so that the shooter and his instructor could see where his round had hit. But woe be to the soldier whose shot missed the target altogether. The spotter then raised a red flag—known as "Maggie's drawers"—and waved it back and forth in front of the target. (The origin of the term "Maggie's drawers" seems to be a bawdy song called "Those Old Red Flannel Drawers that Maggie Wore.")[20]

As Private Morita neared the end of his basic training he expressed interest, as so many other young men of the time did, in the U.S. Army Air Forces. He had already made inquiries about the enlisted pilot program. "I don't think I'll be satisfied till I know for sure whether I'm eligible as a flyer or not," he confided in a letter home. In the very next sentence he expressed an amazing amount of naiveté about the workings of the military when he wrote: "Perhaps, I'll join the parachute corps next, if I don't like where I'm sent."[21]

On October 6, Private Morita finished artillery basic training. Now he was a real soldier, although he still had not had the opportunity to qualify at the target range with a service rifle. A few days later he was off to his first real duty station. He went to Fort Lewis, Washington, south of Seattle, where he joined Battery D, 146th Field Artillery Battalion. His monthly pay also increased from the recruit's $21 per month to the $50 per month of the private soldier.[22]

CHAPTER ONE

PEARL HARBOR AND AFTER

"I was on K.P. I heard about it on the radio. I was devastated."

While Private Morita settled in to his new surroundings at Fort Lewis, the undeclared war in the North Atlantic escalated when the USS *Kearney* lost eleven men to a German U-boat attack in mid-October 1941. President Roosevelt responded: "America has been attacked. The USS *Kearney* is not just a Navy ship. She belongs to every man, woman, and child in this Nation." Two weeks later a German submarine sank the USS *Reuben James* with the loss of 115 of its crewmen, and now the president gave the navy shoot-on-sight orders with regard to German submarines. Hitler had to be very careful not to draw the United States into the war, at least not until after he had defeated Great Britain and the Soviet Union. He may have remembered that that was a mistake made by the Germans in World War I. Accordingly, German submarine commanders received orders not to engage American naval vessels unless it was a matter of self-defense.[1]

Even as events in the North Atlantic seemed more and more likely to entangle the United States in the European war, events in the Pacific delivered the ultimate spark. By early September 1941, Japanese leaders had decided to declare war on the United States, Great Britain, and the Netherlands unless diplomatic progress was made in getting the United States to rescind its embargoes and other economic sanctions within six weeks.

Still the Japanese did not regard war as inevitable, and in early November 1941 a second Japanese envoy traveled to Washington to assist Ambassador Kichisaburo Nomura in continuing negotiations. Nevertheless, in case the talks proved unproductive the Japanese would be ready to go to war by early December. On

November 7, the two Japanese officials proposed a plan that called for American acceptance of Japan's dominant role in Asia, but Secretary of State Cordell Hull rejected this plan out of hand. A couple of weeks later, the Japanese set forth another plan. According to its terms, the United States and Japan would share the mineral resources of the Dutch East Indies and, except for Indochina, both nations would promise not to send any troops into Southeast Asia or the South Pacific, and U.S.-Japanese trade would be reopened without the burdensome embargo on oil to Japan. As soon as there was peace in China, the Japanese would withdraw from Indochina (assuming, of course, that in the meantime the United States stayed out of China).

Secretary Hull also rejected this plan and instead proposed a three-month truce, during which time the Japanese would pull out of southern Indochina and the United States would resume limited oil shipments to Japan. Prior to formal presentation of this proposal, Hull showed it to several Washington-based representatives of other nations with interests in the region. They were unanimous in their disapproval, saying that it contained no provisions for China's continued existence, and that if China pulled out of the war altogether it would make thousands of Japanese troops available for service elsewhere. This proposal, therefore, was never sent on to Japan.

On November 26, a ten-point proposal *was* presented to the Japanese, but it was not much more conciliatory than the earlier one. Under its terms Japan was to end all military operations in China and Indochina and leave those countries, and extend diplomatic recognition to the Nationalist Chinese government headed by Chiang Kai-shek. Further, Japan was to effectively pull out of the Tripartite Pact with Italy and Germany and join some sort of multilateral non-aggression pact in East Asia. The United States in return would unfreeze Japanese assets in this country, restore trade with Japan, and help stabilize the Japanese currency. The United States would also attempt to end extraterritoriality in China. Secretary Hull knew when he sent this proposal that the Japanese could not possibly accept it. He also knew that it would now be only a matter of time before Japan and the United States were at war.

At this point, Japanese military planners believed that their *only* option was war with the United States. The oil embargo had forced Japanese forces toward the Dutch East Indies to get the oil they needed to continue their conquest of China. They regarded the American embargo, as well as other economic sanctions, as unnecessary provocation. The United States had set the stakes for peace too high. Japan had either to withdraw from China or go to war with the United States. Withdrawal was completely out of the question. Japan had invested too much time, treasure, and lives in the China venture to pull out now.

Private Morita, meanwhile, finally got a chance to go to the shooting range. Perhaps his new battery commander decided that all of his men should have at least some proficiency with firearms, even though they would not likely be called upon to use them unless an enemy was about to overrun their battery's position. Thus Morita finally got a chance to shoot something smaller than a 105mm howitzer, but it was not to be the standard infantry rifle. Instead, he qualified as a marksman with the .45-caliber semi-automatic pistol that had been the army's standard handgun since before World War I. Within less than a week, the United States was at war.

In the pre-dawn hours of Sunday, December 7, 1941, the ships of a Japanese naval task force that had left Japan almost two weeks earlier prepared for action in the waters north of the Hawaiian island of Oahu. The aircraft carriers turned into the wind to launch a variety of aircraft including dive bombers, torpedo bombers, high-altitude bombers, and fighters. American radar operators on Oahu detected the aircraft when they were still 140 miles out, but so complete was the surprise that American military authorities thought them to be a flight of American bombers due in from the mainland. At five minutes to eight, the attack began and America was *in* World War II.

Japanese targets were the American naval base at Pearl Harbor and the military airfields nearby. Eight battleships, the pride of the Pacific Fleet, were moored in two rows close together alongside Ford Island in the middle of the harbor. Fighters and bombers were parked in clusters at Wheeler Army Airfield and at Hickam Field to make it easier to defend against saboteurs. Japanese pilots found these arrangements almost too good to be true. Attack plans also called for the employment of five small, two-man "midget" submarines of the Imperial Japanese Navy. Launched from larger submarines positioned just offshore, they were to submerge and enter the harbor before the aircraft arrived. Then, when the air raid began, they were to launch torpedoes at American warships from close range and escape the harbor to rendezvous with their "mother ships."[2]

The attack was devastating! Eight American battleships were destroyed or badly damaged, as were several cruisers, destroyers, and other vessels. Almost all of the 350 American airplanes at Oahu were destroyed on the ground. Approximately twenty-four hundred Americans died and another one thousand were wounded. Japanese losses in the two-hour raid were all five midget submarines, twenty-nine airplanes, and fifty-five men. That same day (December 8 in territories west of the International Dateline) other Japanese forces struck at targets elsewhere in the Pacific, including, notably, the Philippines, Thailand, Malaya, and Wake Island.

Only a week earlier, many Americans conceded that war with Japan was just a matter of time, perhaps only weeks or even only days away, but most assumed that hostilities would commence in the Philippines or other American possessions far west of Hawaii. This attack, therefore, came as a complete surprise and caught American military authorities unprepared to defend against it.

The attack came as a shock to area civilians, including Japanese Americans and resident nationals. One Japanese American man had gotten up early that morning to help his father work on their garage roof, and it was from there that they both saw the clouds of smoke rising above the harbor. At first, like many others watching that day, they thought the military was conducting extremely realistic drills or war games. And then they glimpsed the solid red balls painted on the undersides of the attacking planes—the Rising Sun emblem of Imperial Japan. "How I hated the Japs for bringing this [war] upon us!" he later recalled, unconsciously using a racial epithet that would be thrown at him before long. Another Japanese American, already serving in the U.S. Army, remembered that his reactions "ran the gamut of shock, bewilderment, anger, shame, and sorrow. But mostly he recalled feeling a "deep anguish and despair because the land that I had been taught to honor by my parents had committed an act of war against the country that I loved." Another remembered how, in the days immediately following the attack, "I kept asking myself: 'Why the hell did the Japanese want to do something like that?' I never once thought of myself as anything other than an American."[3]

Some of the attacking planes flew so low that those on the ground could see the expressions on the pilots' faces. Home on a weekend pass after less than a month in the U.S. Army when the attack occurred, another Japanese American "saw the face of the Japanese pilot in his fur-lined helmet, looking down at us through his goggles." The flier looked "calm and confident. Maybe this was his way of displaying his arrogant superiority, or perhaps he was communicating to us not to worry, that all would be okay." Another had a similar experience. He and his sister had jumped into their car and were hurrying to their parents' home when a Japanese plane strafed the road. The car was not hit, but they could see the impacts of the bullets on the ground alongside as the plane roared overhead. Turning onto another road, they soon saw another plane bearing down on them from the front. Some instinct caused him to crane his neck and stick his head outside the car as the plane approached. "I guess he didn't fire at us," he later recalled, "because he could see that we were Asian." What probably saved him and his sister that day more than his Asian features was the fact that the pilot was able to tell that he was a civilian and, therefore, not on his target list.[4]

Many Americans discounted initial reports of the attack as a hoax like the one in 1938 about an invasion from Mars. In that instance, filmmaker Orson Welles had produced a radio program with realistic-sounding news reports about creatures from Mars attacking earth. Based on the H. G. Wells novel *The War of the Worlds*, the broadcast had briefly caused panic among some listeners before it was revealed to be a complete fiction. Many Americans, therefore, wanted to believe that the devastation being reported from Hawaii was just more of the same.[5]

The Japanese planes had scarcely left the skies over Oahu before rumors of an impending invasion began to circulate. Some claimed that Japanese troops had already occupied all of the other islands in the Hawaiian chain and that enemy submarines had surrounded Oahu. Enemy paratroopers were said to have landed on Oahu already, and because most of the full-time soldiers and sailors ashore had their hands full, it was up to the college students in the Reserve Officers' Training Corps (ROTC) at the University of Hawaii to defend Honolulu. Most Japanese American men attending the university were also ROTC cadets, and they responded to the surprise attack like the American soldiers they were training to become, by rushing to report to their duty stations anxious to do whatever they could. The ROTC was immediately reconstituted to form the basis of the recently-authorized Hawaii Territorial Guard. The student-soldiers picked up basic equipment and waited for duty assignments. They drew gas masks and the soon-to-be obsolete World War I-style helmets. Their rifles were the bolt-action Springfields with which they had trained and which were fitted with highly polished bayonets that caught the sunlight during parades. The firing pins, previously removed to prevent accidental shootings, were hastily re-installed and each student-soldier was issued with five rounds of ammunition. Thus armed, they bravely stood to their assigned tasks. "With pounding hearts," remembered one guardsman, "we moved to the south end of the campus and scanned for the enemy. To put it bluntly, we were scared!" Another collegian had only recently demonstrated the mysterious workings of his military-issue gas mask to his admiring family. They "would have been mightily shocked," he later recalled, "if they knew that I didn't know how to load my Springfield '03 rifle with ammunition. . . . The only war training or experience I had came from playing soldier in the corn field as a child." However, neither fear—certainly a rational reaction to the events of the day—nor their unpreparedness kept these young men from carrying out their orders. Soon they were performing guard duty at the electric power and water treatment plants, the telephone exchanges, and Iolani Palace in downtown Honolulu.[6]

The federalization of the national guard back in October 1940 had affected the two Hawaiian infantry guard regiments: the 298th, composed mostly of men from Oahu, and the 299th, with men from the other islands. Of the roughly three thousand men inducted into these units in 1941, about fifteen hundred were of Japanese descent. On the alert for a possible follow-up invasion, they now fanned out along Oahu's beaches. It was on Waimanalo Beach, on Oahu's eastern side, that a Japanese American sergeant and his Caucasian lieutenant came upon an unconscious Japanese naval officer and made him the first enemy combatant captured during the war. Ensign Kazuo Sakamaki had been the commander of one of the five midget submarines that had been part of the Imperial Japanese Navy's attack force. His boat had lost its steering capabilities, however, and had finally drifted toward shore. Not wanting his craft to fall into American hands, he set a demolition charge before he and his crewmate scrambled into the surf. The charge failed to detonate and his companion was drowned in the surf. It was ironic that it was an American soldier of Japanese ancestry who helped to capture this enemy officer.[7]

On the morning of December 7, members of the United Japanese Society of Honolulu had gathered in a theater in Honolulu to award certificates of completion to the eight hundred or so who had completed an emergency medical course. The timing was fortuitous as almost all of them immediately reported to various aid stations around the harbor to help the hundreds of civilians wounded in the attack.[8]

Within hours of the attack, the president of the Japanese American Citizens' League (JACL) sent a telegram to President Roosevelt offering his organization's full support in the war effort. "In this solemn hour," the letter read, "we pledge our fullest cooperation to you . . . and to our country." It went on to say that "now that Japan has instituted this attack upon our land, we are ready and prepared to expend every effort to repel this invasion together with our fellow Americans." A Japanese American student at the College of Puget Sound in Tacoma, Washington, in an address to the student body on December 8, expressed his feelings of shame and anger over what had happened in Hawaii the day before and promised his loyalty to the United States. "Because I believe in America," he said, quoting a recently written Japanese American Creed, "and I trust she believes in me, and because I have received innumerable benefits from her, I pledge myself to do honor to her at all times and in all places; to support her Constitution; to obey her laws; to respect her flag; to defend her against all enemies, foreign or domestic; to actively assume my duties and obligations cheerfully and without any reservation whatsoever, in the hope that I may become a better American in a greater America." In Texas, a recent Japanese American graduate of Texas A&M University declared: "I'm ready to fight for the United States against Japan, even if I have to kill some of my cousins. . . . We're for the United States 100 per cent."[9]

Rumors of Japanese American cooperation with Imperial Japan were rife all along the West Coast and, indeed, throughout much of the rest of the country. In San Francisco, one story went, twenty thousand Japanese were poised for a revolution. Japanese Americans in California, according to another, were in regular radio communication with Japanese naval forces offshore. Every American ship leaving a West Coast port in late January had supposedly been attacked by Japanese ships, and there were alleged to be secret Japanese airfields in Baja California, Mexico.[10]

The Federal Bureau of Investigation (FBI) had, shortly before the attack on Pearl Harbor, assessed the potential for sabotage among California's Japanese and found it to be minimal. "There will be no armed uprising of Japanese," one report read, and any sabotage that did occur would likely be carried out by agents smuggled in from Japan rather than by locals. In fact, in the months immediately preceding the war, Japanese consular officials demanded lists of American Japanese sailing to Japan out of fear that they were being sent by the U.S. government to spy on Japan.[11]

Nevertheless, starting on December 7 FBI agents immediately began rounding up prominent local Japanese residents. In the months leading up to the attack, agents in Hawaii had identified those Japanese that they thought might pose security risks when war came. They were particularly concerned with some of the community leaders—such as Buddhist priests, those who ran schools to teach the Japanese language and culture, and prosperous merchants. On December 7, immediately after the attack, the agents consulted their lists and quickly went into action rounding up these potential Japanese sympathizers. Also targeted in the sweep, which netted 370 suspects by the end of the day, were commercial fishermen, who routinely used two-way radios and who had the mobility to venture out to sea to communicate directly with Japanese warships if they chose to do so. More than a thousand others were rounded up in the days and weeks that followed, and most were destined to spend the war in detention camps on the mainland.[12]

Shortly after noon on December 8, President Roosevelt asked Congress for a declaration of war on Japan, saying that December 7, 1941, would forever be "a date which will live in infamy" because of the surprise nature of the brutal attack on Pearl Harbor. The vote for war was unanimous in the Senate and Jeanette Rankin, pacifist congresswoman from Montana, cast the only vote against war in the House of Representatives. (She had also voted against American entry into World War I back in 1917.) On December 11, Germany and Italy declared war on the United States, and Congress immediately reciprocated.

With the declarations of war on Japan, Germany, and Italy, all citizens of these countries then living in the United States became, by definition, enemy aliens. This did not mean that all, or even any, of these people actively sought to commit sabotage or hinder the American war effort in any way. It was simply the term used to describe their new status. Natives of Germany and Italy who had become naturalized American citizens did not share this label. Natives of Japan, however, were barred by law from acquiring United States citizenship. The Japanese term that described these immigrants was "Issei," which meant the first generation to leave Japan. Their children born in the United States were called "Nisei," or the second generation from Japan, and they had American citizenship by virtue of the fact that they were born in the United States.

Soon after the attack on Pearl Harbor, FBI agents in San Francisco picked up a Japanese American soldier because of his friendship with a Shinto priest. One of the agents wanted to know if he would fight against Japan if his orders were to do so. The soldier, a corporal, calmly assured him that he would—that he was, after all, an American soldier and would serve in any capacity that was required of him. For some reason his answer, or perhaps his unruffled demeanor, did not sit right with the agent. "You sonovabitch," he ranted, "I expect you to say that you will shoot down the Emperor and tear down the Jap flag and stomp it into the ground!" The corporal soon received orders assigning him to the Enlisted Reserve Corps and sending him home. He remained bitter about this treatment for some time.[13]

Anti-Japanese feelings, particularly on the West Coast, had a long history, beginning well before the events of December 1941. In addition to federal law preventing Japanese immigrants from citizenship, some states passed laws that barred them from owning land. Under pressure from such organizations as the Native Sons and Daughters of the Golden West and the Japanese Exclusion League, California legislators in 1920 extended this ban even to the children of Japanese immigrants, who were American citizens by right of birth. In Los Angeles, where anti-Japanese feeling ran high, there were twice as many German-born residents as those from Japan, but there was no such outcry against those of European birth. In fact, California Governor Culbert Olson was so disingenuous as to suggest: "When I look out at a group of Americans of German or Italian descent, I can tell whether they are loyal or not. I can tell how they think . . . but it is impossible for me to do this with the inscrutable Orientals, and particularly the Japanese."[14]

Many Californians resented the economic competition of hardworking Japanese American farmers. The managing secretary of the Vegetable Grower-Shipper Association of Salinas made no pretense that it was anything else when he said: "We're charged with wanting to get rid of the Japs for selfish reasons. We might as well be honest. We do." And: "If all the Japs were removed tomorrow, we'd never miss them in two weeks, because the white farmers can take over and produce everything the Jap grows. And we don't want them back when the war ends, either."[15]

Even the popular photo magazine *Life* gave way to stereotyping in an article it ran just two weeks after the attack. Entitled "How to Tell Japs From the Chinese," it produced "a rule-of-thumb from the anthropometric conformations that distinguish friendly Chinese from enemy alien Japs." The article described the Chinese as typically tall and slender with long legs and very little facial hair. The "Japs," on the other hand, were characterized as "short and squat" with heavy beards and an "earthy yellow complexion." And popular cartoonist Milt Caniff soon produced an eleven-page cartoon, "How to Spot a Jap," for the army's *Pocket Guide to China* that simply reinforced these physical stereotypes. Caniff depicts the Chinese, when walking, as taking manful strides, while the Japanese shuffles along. He also finds differences in their demeanors. According to him the "Chinese smiles easily—the Jap usually expects to be shot and is very unhappy about it—especially if he is an officer."[16]

A Japan-born veteran of American military service in World War I was overcome with shame that the nation of his birth should attack the United States. He had received a certificate of *honorary* U.S. citizenship because of his loyal service to the nation, although he was still barred from outright naturalization. He took the certificate with him when he checked into a hotel in Los Angeles and, clutching the piece of paper that had meant so much to him, committed suicide.[17]

One voice of reason emanating from the halls of Congress was that of Washington Congressman John Coffee, who warned against what he called a mockery of the Bill of Rights. "It is my fervent hope and prayer," he said, "that residents of the United States of Japanese extraction will not be made the victims of pogroms directed by self-proclaimed patriots and by hysterical self-appointed heroes." His plea for tolerance was soon drowned in a sea of racial indignation. Mississippi Congressman John Rankin, who was already known for his anti-Semitic and anti-black feelings, easily embraced the growing phobia directed toward Japanese in this country. And even though perhaps two-thirds of all Japanese in the United States were born here—and were therefore American citizens—Rankin's mind was made up. "Once a Jap always a Jap," he declared. "You cannot regenerate a Jap, convert him, change him, and make him the same as a white man any more than you can reverse the laws of nature. Damn them! Let us get rid of them now!" Fellow Democratic congressman John Dingel, from Michigan, was even more extreme in his views toward Japanese Americans. He had proposed, even before the attack on Pearl Harbor, that the government should hold ten thousand Japanese Americans in Hawaii as hostages to keep Tokyo honest.[18]

In a twisted bit of "logic," California Congressman Leland Ford in mid-January 1942 stated that all Japanese on the West Coast, including U.S. citizens, should view it as their patriotic duty to submit to forced relocation in support of the war effort. Each such person, in Ford's estimation, who "is really patriotic and wishes to make his contribution to the safety and welfare of this country, right here is his opportunity to do so, namely . . . by permitting himself to be placed in a concentration camp." "He should be willing to do it," Ford continued, "if he is patriotic." Most other congressmen and senators from the West Coast states soon embraced this position and sent a letter to President Roosevelt urging him to take steps to remove all Japanese and Japanese Americans from the coastal states as well as the Territory of Alaska. The next day, February 14, 1942, Lieutenant General John L. DeWitt, commanding the Fourth Army and the Western Defense Command, added his opinion when he stated categorically: "The Japanese race is an enemy race" and that over 112,000 such "potential enemies, of Japanese extraction, are at large today."[19]

President Roosevelt responded to the alarmist outcry by signing Executive Order No. 9066 on February 19, 1942. Arguing that the "successful prosecution of the war" required "every possible protection against espionage and against sabotage to national defense material, national defense premises and national defense utilities," this law authorized the secretary of war or his designees to identify areas of the country that were of particular military sensitivity and to exclude any or all residents from those areas. Action soon followed words, as General DeWitt designated the western halves of Washington, Oregon, and California, and most of the southern half of Arizona, as restricted areas on March 2. All enemy aliens—non-citizen immigrants from Japan, Germany, and Italy—had to evacuate this area.[20]

Canada followed suit five days later. Some Canadians were convinced, as per a rather pessimistic Canadian Air Force study, that "Hitler has promised British Columbia to the Japanese when the time comes to carve up Canada." One suggested resolution of the supposed problem was to give every Japanese and Japanese Canadian $1,000 and a one-way ticket to Japan. Instead, however, almost twenty-one thousand Japanese Canadians, 90 percent of whom were Canadian citizens, were moved off the Pacific coast of British Columbia.[21]

Even after the signing of Executive Order No. 9066, however, there was no certainty as to what was to become of the Japanese and Japanese Americans in the designated areas. California Congressman John H. Tolan headed the Select Committee Investigating National Defense Migration, and he and his committee traveled to five major West Coast cities to hear testimony on the issue. Of course the testimony of Japanese Americans overwhelmingly opposed relocation, but their voices were drowned out by the clamor of anti-Japanese prejudice. California Attorney General Earl Warren, for instance, alerted the committee to the "suspicious" incidence of so many Japanese living in areas adjacent to such important features as airports, oil fields, and military camps. It apparently did not occur to him that the reason for this settlement pattern was that the Japanese had gotten there before the airports and military bases were built and before the oilfields had been discovered. He also found it unsettling that none of the dozens of district attorneys and sheriffs with whom he had consulted had received any reports from California-born Japanese in their areas of any subversive or disloyal activities within the Japanese community. This suggested to him a devious and tight-lipped conspiracy. He was not willing to believe that the lack of reports meant simply that there was a corresponding lack of such suspicious activity.[22]

A few people pointed out to the committee that there had been absolutely no instances of sabotage perpetrated by Japanese or Japanese Americans in the United States. Congressman Tolan merely echoed the sentiments of Attorney General Warren and many others in positions of authority, however, when he said that the very absence of such incidents was proof that they would occur in the future. "So far," he responded to a questioner in Portland, "there are no cases of sabotage; that is, generally speaking. Well, there weren't any in Pearl Harbor, either, were there, until the attack came. There wasn't any sabotage; it all happened at once. In other words . . . if the Pacific Coast is attacked, that is when the sabotage would come, with the attack, wouldn't it?"[23]

One Japanese American announced a desperate proposal to avert wholesale relocation. Under his plan, army officials would enlist enough Nisei men to form an infantry battalion to be used to fight the Japanese enemy in the Pacific. And as a guarantee of the soldiers' loyalty, the federal government would hold their parents hostage until they returned. Government officials quickly turned down the offer. The formation of such a "suicide battalion" would have been a public relations nightmare and would have fed Japanese propaganda claims that the United States was involved in a race war against them. There was also the more practical issue of identity problems. What would prevent Caucasian soldiers, for example, from shooting what they perceived to be enemy infiltrators in American uniforms? And what, by the same token, would prevent enemy soldiers from acquiring and donning American uniforms and actually infiltrating friendly lines?[24]

Those subject to the relocation orders had the option of voluntarily removing to the interior of the country. If all had been able to do so the federal government's active role would have been relatively minor, but only a tiny percentage of West Coast Japanese had any contacts with anyone in the interior states to whom they could apply for aid in relocating. Many of the evacuees were farmers or small-scale businessmen who were unable to find any job opportunities away from their home states; as a result, the government's role quickly expanded.

Government authorities established more than a dozen assembly centers in the coastal states—most were in California—where evacuees could be kept under watch until they were able to work their way inland or, as it turned out, more permanent facilities could be built to contain them. County fairgrounds provided the most likely sites because they were close enough to cities to provide the basic amenities of life and also set apart from these same cities so that soldiers could maintain a vigilant surveillance on the new inhabitants. Thus, nine of the assembly centers were located at fairgrounds, two at race tracks, one at a former Civilian Conservation Corp camp, and one at the livestock exposition hall in Portland, Oregon.

The evacuation took place on rather short notice. The first evacuation notices appeared in various locations in and around the Japanese neighborhoods on March 2, 1942. They instructed each Japanese family to designate one of its members to report to a control center and register each member of the family. Each family then received a registration number and was told when it should be ready to leave. Sometimes these families had a few weeks' notice, but in other instances they only had a few days. Farmers and business owners were forced to sell out or make arrangements with their non-Japanese neighbors to take care of their possessions until they returned. Others had to sell homes and possession, often at ridiculous prices. These forced sales resulted in considerable economic hardships. One family, for example, had to sell an automobile for 60 percent below market value and a truck at an 85 percent loss. One Issei woman was so outraged at the way many Caucasians hovered around waiting to buy her beautiful Oriental pottery for next to nothing that she chose instead to smash it all to pieces before their astonished eyes.[25]

A few families thought that if they delivered themselves to the assembly centers they would be allowed to bring more than just a couple of suitcases each. One such family had a flatbed truck that they loaded up with possessions before driving to the center at Pomona. When they reached the gate, however, they were told to park the truck, grab whatever they could carry, and enter the camp. They tied a tarp down over the remainder and dutifully reported to the camp. For the next few days they were able to look wistfully through the fence at their truck and belongings, but then, one day, it was gone, and they never saw it or their other possessions again.[26]

Workmen installed makeshift partitions in horse stables to turn them into living quarters at the assembly centers at race tracks, like Santa Anita, Tanforan (near San Francisco), or Pomona, They also built barracks in the infields. Adjusting to such living conditions was extremely difficult. These quarters were generally without kitchen facilities or plumbing, and the furniture usually consisted of not much more than an army cot with a straw-filled mattress for each member of the family. At Santa Anita, workers had swept out the stalls and put down an inch-thick covering of asphalt for a floor. The new residents quickly found that, especially on hot days, the legs of the government-issued cots soon sank completely through the gooey stuff. At Tanforan, even after dosing the stables with lye, the pungent aroma of horse manure and urine remained. "These stables just reeked," remembered one of the new inmates of his stay at the Tanforan assembly center. "There was nothing you could do. The amount of lye they threw on it to clear the odor and stuff, it didn't help. It still reeked." Another described his family's new home at Tanforan in similar fashion. "Dust, dirt, and wood shavings covered the linoleum that had been laid over manure-covered boards, the smell of horses hung in the air, and the whitened corpses of many insects still clung to the hastily whitewashed walls."[27]

Those families lucky enough to arrive at the assembly centers and be assigned to the newly constructed barracks instead of the stables found that their living conditions were not much better. One such building, at the Santa Anita racetrack, was about 120 feet long and 20 feet deep. Each family's room contained an army cot for each inhabitant and a bare light bulb for illumination at night. During the day, light came in through two small windows in the back and one in the front. The buildings had no ceilings, but were open all the way to the roof, and the partitions between each family's quarters stopped about eight feet above the floor, ruling out any sense of privacy. There were no kitchens and no bathrooms in the barracks. All of the inmates ate in centralized mess halls and used one of the six latrines scattered about the camp.[28]

Back in Colorado, the Moritas were one of about twenty Japanese families in and around the farming community of Ault, some sixty miles north of Denver. Even the most rabidly anti-Japanese had little reason to move them into the camps. It was not likely, after all, that any would-be Japanese collaborator would have much luck using a flashlight to signal Japanese submarines off San Francisco from the top of Pike's Peak. Still, there were new rules regulating travel that were downright ludicrous. For example, someone driving from Ault down to Denver crossed through three counties along the way. "Before we could travel," one of Private Morita's brothers later recalled, "we had to notify the Sheriff of each county, two weeks in advance, informing them of where we were going, the route we were to take, how long we planned to stay in Denver, and the address where we planned to stay."[29]

Meanwhile, in Hawaii, there was opposition among some of the islands' residents to letting the young Japanese American guardsmen wear their uniforms and carry loaded rifles. They feared that, in the event of an actual Japanese invasion, the guardsmen might find their loyalties wavering between the land of their ancestors and the land of their birth. Finally, on January 21, 1942, authorities disarmed them and disbanded the Hawaii Territorial Guard. Many of the guardsmen expressed stunned bitterness. "All of a sudden they kick you in the ass," one remembered. "And this is when you say the hell with them. You get the feeling you don't want to do nothing. . . . I was just bitter against the people and the system that wouldn't trust me." The situation was, recalled another, "worse than Pearl Harbor. We could accept the fact, by then, that Japan was our treacherous enemy. But to have our own country, in its most extreme time of need and danger, repudiate us, there was something more than we could take. There was no depth to which our emotions sank. The very bottom had dropped out of our existence."[30]

"At the time we were released," remembered a very disappointed collegian, "I was very naïve to think that the crisis had passed, that they just didn't need us any more. But evidently Washington gave orders to kick us out. The next day, in a glaring newspaper headline, I read, 'Volunteers For Hawaii Territorial Guard Needed.'" Another blow to their morale came in the form of a rumor that the Nisei thus culled from the national guard regiments were going to be interned on the island of Molokai, the island to which nineteenth-century lepers had been exiled.[31]

Barred from performing military service, at least temporarily, most of the men returned to their college studies or looked for jobs. About 130 of them, however, hatched a plan about a week later that would allow them to continue proving their loyalty. If they could not serve their nation with rifles on their shoulders, perhaps they could do so with picks and shovels instead. They drew up a petition addressed to Lieutenant General Delos C. Emmons, the commander of the Hawaiian Department, in which they expressed both their disappointment in having been dismissed and their willingness to serve their country in any capacity whatsoever. "Hawaii is our home; the United States, our country," the letter read. "We know but one loyalty and that is to the Stars and Stripes. We wish to do our part as loyal Americans in every way possible and we hereby offer ourselves for whatever service you may see fit to use us."[32]

The men's appeals reached the sympathetic ears of the commander of the 3rd Combat Engineer Battalion at Schofield Barracks, Colonel Albert Lyman. Lyman's family had been in the islands since his grandfather arrived as a missionary in the mid-nineteenth century, and he was the first man born in Hawaii to graduate from the U.S. Military Academy. It was through his intercession that the former guardsmen were able to serve in a quasi-military capacity attached to the army engineers. They formed the basis of an auxiliary company attached to the 34th Combat Engineer Regiment. "We didn't care how menial the work was," remembered one of the men who had been so bitter, "as long as we could help."[33]

When deciding on a name for their unit, they settled on one that combined their status as university students, their desire for Japanese defeat, and their willingness to work, and called themselves the Varsity Victory Volunteers. They generally wore civilian work clothes, but in order to have some sort of distinctive insignia one of the men designed an emblem that showed an eagle with outstretched wings surrounded by stars. This emblem soon appeared over the left breast pocket of their shirts, and some men soon sported a patch consisting of a dark "V" on a light background on the left front pocket of their trousers.[34]

The Varsity Victory Volunteers displayed the marvelous recuperative powers that many young men have by engaging in various sporting activities in their free time. They formed their own basketball and barefoot football teams while three of them played on the regimental baseball team (and two of these men played on the University of Hawaii football team in the fall of 1942). Dozens of them fought in Golden Gloves boxing competition, and three of the fighters won their weight classes at the All-Schofield Boxing Championships. In the evenings or on Sundays, professors from the University of Hawaii visited the men and taught college-level courses in such diverse subjects as literature, philosophy, history, mathematics, psychology, and physical education. One popular course, taught by a pair of professors, was called "Post-war Worlds." Another was "Religion and Literature," in which the two dozen students read and discussed five different books over the course of six weeks. Choices included Stephen Crane's *Red Badge of Courage*, Theodore Dreiser's *Sister Carrie*, Edith Wharton's *Ethan Frome*, Willa Cather's *Death Comes for the Archbishop*, Thornton Wilder's *The Bridge of San Luis Rey*, and James Cabell's *Jurgen: A Comedy of Justice*. Some men, however, preferred other outlets for their free time activities. Like the man who used the space beneath his bunk to make his own illicit alcohol.[35]

Although technically civilians, they received army pay and got their work assignments from army officers. They took up residence in three two-story barracks and had a fourth set aside for their mess hall and offices. And, just as a rifle company in an infantry regiment separated its members into squads, these men divided up into work gangs. Each gang had a foreman who supervised the dozen or so workers under his immediate charge. Reveille sounded at 6:15 every morning, and by 7:30 they were working. They worked eight hours per day, with only Sunday being a day of rest. Over the next several months, they erected half a dozen warehouses, strung untold miles of barbed wire, and quarried tons of rock. Other work gangs were employed in a cabinet shop crafting all manner of office furniture, from chairs and desks to bulletin boards and trophy cases. They even built a reviewing stand so visiting dignitaries could watch soldiers parade by.[36]

At the time of the Japanese attack on Pearl Harbor, Carl Morita was just one of several thousand men of Japanese ancestry in the U.S. Army, and not just those in the Hawaii Territorial Guard and the Hawaiian National Guard but at bases on the mainland. In most cases, these men did not suffer any immediate repercussions. Their fellow soldiers seemed to realize, even if most Americans on the West Coast did not, that they were Americans not Japanese.

There was at least one exception, however, and that was at Jefferson Barracks, Missouri, just south of St. Louis. There the thirteen Japanese American soldiers were locked up in a military jail for, as they were told, "protective custody." They were allowed out for meals and for regular periods of exercise but always under guard. And for fear that some might escape, a soldier always announced a count whenever they left or re-entered their cells. "Thirteen Jap prisoners," he would call. The inmates found this particularly painful. "We were not 'Jap prisoners,'" one recalled. "[W]e were American GIs."[37]

Then, at about the same time that President Roosevelt signed the necessary papers that allowed the army to begin relocating Japanese American civilians away from the West Coast, army officials also began discharging Japanese American soldiers or removing them from combat units and reassigning them to menial jobs in the nation's interior where, it was assumed, any possible loyalty to Japan could not manifest itself in serious sabotage. Early in March, Selective Service System officials arbitrarily reclassified all young men of Japanese ancestry—even those who were American citizens—as enemy aliens unqualified for military service.

At Fort Lewis, Private Morita finally began to experience some of the anti-Japanese hysteria that swept the West Coast. That Sunday in December he had been in the mess hall on kitchen police (KP) duty when he heard on the radio of the Japanese attack; and he, like most Americans, "was devastated." His fellow soldiers knew him for what he was—an American just like them—and did not treat him any differently than before the attack. But on February 20, 1942, Morita received transfer orders. With his battalion preparing for service in the Pacific as part of the 41st Infantry Division, he and all other Japanese American soldiers in the division, were reassigned. Morita went to an infantry unit newly arrived at Fort Lewis: Company K, 138th Infantry Regiment, 35th Infantry Division. Three and a half weeks later, on March 16, he was transferred again as the 138th prepared to deploy to the Pacific theater. His new duty assignment took him off of the West Coast and all the way to Fort Sam Houston in San Antonio, Texas, where he processed papers in the base reception center for newly arriving recruits.[38]

"We had no guns, no combat duty, no training," recalled a soldier who was sent to Fort Sill, Oklahoma, with some two hundred other Nisei soldiers who had been segregated out of their pre-Pearl Harbor units. "They had me fixing trucks, while the others cleaned latrines, served as orderlies for the colonel, and supplied food to the different units. And we did this for more than a year."

Another man at Fort Sill decided that, inasmuch as army officials apparently did not trust him to be a proper soldier, he would make it easier for them to justify such a misplaced opinion. His subsequent actions earned him a lot of time peeling potatoes on KP duty, and in one instance his boss, the head cook, admonished him to make sure that the peeled spuds were completely free of eyes. The unhappy soldier then used a mechanical peeler to follow these instructions. When he finished, the five- and six-inch potatoes were completely free of eyes, but had been whittled down to only an inch or two in diameter. A college-educated Nisei serving in a combat engineer unit suddenly had his work assignment changed drastically. He was assigned to clean the manure in the stall of a general's riding horse. A Nisei soldier stationed at Fort Ord, California, with the 7th Infantry Division when the Japanese attacked received orders sending him to Rockford, Illinois, to show orientation movies to recruits coming in from the Chicago area. "I felt angry and depressed," he said, "but what could I do?"[39]

And even after the Japanese American soldiers had moved away from militarily sensitive areas, officials still expressed doubts about their loyalty. Fort Riley, Kansas, was the home of the army's horse cavalry, and there was still a large number of horses quartered there at the outbreak of the war. Nisei soldiers were assigned to keep the stables clean. However, on April 25, 1943, Easter Sunday, they found themselves herded together into various out-of-the-way barracks buildings, warehouses, even the distant rifle range, with no explanation. These mysterious circumstances were only intensified when the men in one of these barracks noticed through a window that other soldiers outside—Caucasian soldiers—had set up a .30-caliber machine gun and had it pointing directly at the barracks. The mystery was solved a short time later when President Roosevelt, visiting the camp, whisked by in his motorcade. "Here we were," one of them ruefully recalled, "U.S. soldiers, in uniform, citizens, but they still didn't trust us." Nisei soldiers mowing grass at Fort Leavenworth, Kansas, were not allowed to mow within twenty feet of the post headquarters. The men believed that it was because of some fear that one of them might glimpse some classified documents through the building's windows.[40]

Most of the reassigned troops settled into their new jobs without too much grumbling. Some believed that their ethnicity not only kept them in menial jobs but also prevented them from promotions (although there were complaints from Caucasian soldiers at Camp Grant, near Chicago, that Nisei soldiers were being promoted instead of them). This was not the case, however, for Private Morita in Texas. On August 18, 1942, he proudly informed his brother that he had just been promoted to technician 5th grade. The army instituted three technician ranks in early 1942 to recognize the contributions of men with special skills—radio operators, truck drivers, and others. Morita's new rank was designated by a pair of chevrons and a block letter T in the angle beneath them. (A technician 4th grade wore three stripes over the letter T, and a technician 3rd grade's insignia was that of a staff sergeant but with a T between the three stripes and the single rocker.) Morita informed his family that his new rank was "equivalent to a corporal, but a corporal outranks me. . . . We are called corporals . . . and draw corporals [sic] pay." Ordinarily modest and reserved, the young soldier jubilantly signed this letter: "(Corporal) Carl K. Hot Dawg! Morita."[41]

Discharging Japanese American soldiers or transferring them to posts in America's midsection posed special problems for such troops in Hawaii. When the Hawaiian National Guard was federalized in response to the new draft law, Japanese Americans were conspicuously under-represented in its ranks. Whereas the islanders of Japanese ancestry made up over 37 percent of the total population of Hawaii, only about 2 percent of the guardsmen were Nisei. This changed when the Selective Service boards began processing men to fill the guard regiments to their authorized strengths, as approximately half of the three thousand men inducted prior to the start of the war were Nisei. General Emmons had already dealt with the Japanese Americans in the Hawaii Territorial Guard by disbanding that organization and then reconstituting it with all Caucasian members, but he could not as easily dismiss the Nisei in the two national guard regiments.[42]

Many of the newly arriving troops from the American mainland brought with them preconceived notions about the loyalty of Hawaii's Japanese Americans. When an officer told a Japanese

American preacher that he did not trust him because of his ethnicity, the man of the cloth gave the newcomer a blistering dressing down: "If you can not trust a Christian pastor, I wonder whom
you can trust. I am not ashamed to tell you that I am Japanese.
I was born on Kauai, educated in American schools and I don't
know anything but the American way of life. As a high school kid,
I became a Christian over my mother's protest. If you can not
trust me, sir," the preacher finished, "I think you ought to be man
enough to shoot me." Fortunately, the Caucasian officer was chas-
tened and did not take the preacher up on his offer.[43]

After more reinforcements from the mainland arrived in Hawaii, General Emmons found a solution to his problem. On May
12, 1942, he recommended that all of the Japanese American soldiers in the two guard regiments—officers and enlisted men—be
replaced by non-Japanese. "We were stripped of our arms and sent
to Schofield Barracks," remembered a disappointed soldier. When
authorities disarmed them, he thought that they "were going to be
a labor battalion with no arms and ammunition." Instead, he and
the other Nisei from the 298th and 299th Regiments were transferred into the newly-created Hawaiian Provisional Battalion on
May 26, 1942. Emmons hoped that this new unit would be sent to
the mainland. From there, the army might do with these men as it
saw fit, but at least they would be out of the islands and out of General Emmons' area of responsibility. Army Chief of Staff General
George C. Marshall approved the plan, and on May 28 ordered it
to be implemented as soon as possible. Within a week the Hawaiian Provisional Infantry Battalion was ready to sail.[44]

The War Department was willing to train Japanese Americans
as combat soldiers, but was still reluctant to entrust commissions
to such men. So virtually all of the officers appointed to the new
unit were Caucasian or, as the islanders referred to them, *haoles*.
Lieutenant Colonel Farrant L. Turner, who had earned a set of
captain's bars in France during World War I, had been the executive officer of the 298th Regiment, and he wanted to lead the new
unit. Turner, although a haole, was born in Hawaii in 1895 and was
well acquainted with island people and island ways. However, his
boss, Colonel Wilhelm A. Anderson, told him that he was too valuable to let go and recommended someone else for the leadership

role. The decision, ultimately, was up to the chief of staff of the Hawaiian Department, Brigadier General J. Lawton Collins, and he disregarded Anderson's advice and selected Colonel Turner. It was a fortunate choice for all concerned.[45]

By the end of May, the war against Japan had seen some interesting developments. On April 18, Lieutenant Colonel Jimmy Doolittle had led an air raid of sixteen B-25 medium bombers on Tokyo itself, and on May 4–8 a fierce naval battle had taken place in the Coral Sea, not far from Australia, that had seen the Japanese fleet turned back in defeat. Now, as final preparations were being made to ship out the Nisei soldiers from Hawaii another major naval battle was taking shape near the island of Midway. A Japanese victory there might result in another enemy attempt on Hawaii, and this time the attackers might come with a ground invasion force. On June 5, 1942, men of the ad hoc Hawaiian Provisional Battalion began moving from Schofield Barracks to the docks with almost no advance notice to the men or their families. In fact, the men were not allowed even to make one last telephone call to their families and tell them that they were leaving.

Rumors, of course, were rife among the ranks. None of the men knew where they were headed, and many believed that they were simply being shuttled out of the way and would spend the rest of the war in a mainland detention camp, just like so many of the West Coast Issei and Nisei. This thought gained credence when they learned that they were to leave all of their weapons behind. Orders, however, were very explicit. Even though the troops were to leave their weapons behind, they would receive new ones after they arrived at their stateside training camp. General Marshall also directed that "adequate information on this subject should be made available to personnel of unit in order to prevent any feeling that the men are being disarmed and sent to the mainland for internment which is definitely not the War Department's intention." As is often the case, however, such word did not filter its way down into the enlisted ranks.[46]

The battalion boarded the SS *Maui* at Honolulu. The *Maui* was a twenty-five-year-old Matson Lines steamer. At just over five hundred feet long and almost sixty feet wide its rated capacity was 1,650 passengers. This was more than enough space to embark the 1,432 soldiers, especially since they were leaving behind most of their equipment, but they shared the vessel with some military dependents who were evacuating back to the mainland. In spite of the uncertainty of their future, the men reverted back to their happy-go-lucky island ways, and ukuleles, playing cards, and dice soon emerged from their personal baggage. These Hawaiian Japanese were inveterate gamblers, often risking large amounts of money on a single throw of the dice. They called it "going for broke."

Three other transports—also carrying military dependents back to the mainland—accompanied the *Maui* on its journey east, along with some escorting naval vessels. The ships' captains altered course by about fifteen degrees every twenty minutes or so to discourage any enemy submarines that might be lurking in the area, and on June 9 navy blimps appeared from the east to escort the ships for the last few miles. These airships made excellent platforms from which to spot any enemy submarine activity. The next day the *Maui* glided beneath the Golden Gate Bridge and docked at Oakland, California. As soon as the ship reached the dock, the men on board noticed something that they had never seen before—Caucasian men doing hard physical labor as stevedores. Back home no self-respecting haole would stoop to such common labor. This was the first, although not the last, incident relating to race that would open the eyes of the island boys.[47]

Army officials had decided to re-designate this over-strength battalion—it had six companies instead of the usual four—as the 100th Infantry Battalion (Separate). Some of the men were concerned that the "Separate" designation might mean that they were going to be used in some sort of non-combat capacity—perhaps as a labor battalion. To the army, however, the designation simply meant that the 100th Battalion was not yet part of any regiment or other large unit. The men used some of their idle time to ruminate on their new designation—the 100th Battalion—and soon came up with an interesting variant. Since the Hawaiian word *puka* means "hole," and since their numerical designation contained two such holes—the zeroes—they began to refer to their unit as the "one-puka-puka." The 100th was not the only battalion in the army whose members were all of the same ancestral stock.

The 99th Battalion was predominately Norwegian, the101st was Austrian, and the 122nd was Greek. But it was to be the 100th that would become the most famous.[48]

Not wanting to alarm the West Coast locals about the large number of Japanese men in American uniforms, officials hustled them aboard three separate trains as soon as they debarked in Oakland and told them to keep the window shades drawn so no one could see inside the cars. Most of them had never been to the mainland, and the lure of the unknown was just too tempting for them to leave the shades down entirely. Many were struck by the vastness of the land through which they traveled. Others made use of their time by gambling at craps or poker or by singing Hawaiian songs accompanied by the almost ubiquitous ukuleles. There were necessary stops along the way that provided more novel experiences for these men from the islands. Red Cross volunteers—"Donut Dollies"—at a stop in Colorado were surprised, for example, at how well these "Chinese" soldiers spoke English.[49]

Their trains were bound for Camp McCoy, in southwestern Wisconsin. Shortly after crossing into that state their trains stopped at a station which the Nisei took to be their final destination. Several training sites were proposed—all of them well off the Pacific coast. Camp Guernsey, Wyoming was the farthest west. It sits on the North Platte River in the southeastern part of the state and is about equidistant from Cheyenne and Casper. The other two camps were in the Midwest. Camp Leonard Wood is in the Ozarks of central Missouri, and Camp McCoy, in southwestern Wisconsin. The trains finally reached their destination, southwestern Wisconsin. The soldiers were apprehensive about what they saw when they finally halted. Looking out the windows they saw barbed-wire fencing running parallel to the tracks. It seemed to some as if the rumors had come true. They were going to be interned! "For half an hour," recalled one man, "we sat silently in our seats, thinking only of the worst." Then before any orders could arrive confirming these fears, the train slowly backed up and switched onto another track to continue its journey. This brief pause had occasioned much sober reflection among the men on board, but they soon breathed sighs of relief, and after a short time they arrived at Camp McCoy.[50]

Located approximately thirty-five miles east of La Crosse and close to the town of Sparta, Camp McCoy had first been used as a training camp in 1909. Named for two local men, a father and son, who had enjoyed distinguished military careers, it encompassed over sixty-one thousand acres by early 1942. One section of the camp, the fenced area spotted by the Hawaiians, was indeed used as an internment camp both for Japanese and Germans. About a month before the 100th arrived, most of the inmates had been transferred to other camps. One of these was none other than Ensign Kazuo Sakamaki, the midget submarine commander who had washed ashore on the coast of Oahu the day after the attack on Pearl Harbor.[51]

Colonel Turner wasted no time in organizing his command for combat duty. On paper, an infantry battalion's major elements were four companies—not six—each commanded by a lieutenant colonel. Turner oversaw the addition of a medical section, a service section, a transportation platoon, and a service company to the six rifle companies that formed the backbone of the battalion. These additional elements also required more commissioned officers, so Turner requisitioned a dozen second lieutenants. It would be very helpful, he suggested, if these men had spent time in Hawaii and were, therefore, likely to understand island ways. More than half of the new lieutenants met this requirement. They had spent varying amounts of time in Hawaii before the war as corporals or sergeants before attending Officer Candidate Schools and earning their commissions.

One thing that had not occurred to Colonel Turner when requesting new officers, however, was the fact that even though most of these men had served in Hawaii, their attitudes toward the islands and the islanders were not always positive. They, like many other soldiers stationed on Oahu during the late 1930s, had often referred to that island disparagingly as "the Rock." They also, commonly, looked down upon the various Asian cultures in the islands. Within a short time, the determined Hawaiians were able to demonstrate how misplaced such cultural biases were and win over their new commanders. One of the freshly commissioned officers, a man who had already spent more than two decades in uniform, soon found himself admitting: "I'd rather have a hundred of these men behind me than a hundred of any others I've ever been with."[52]

One of the new officers, Second Lieutenant Kurt Schemel, had no prior experience with Japanese Americans, and he expressed disappointment at finding himself in the midst of such men. "My God," he lamented, "I didn't know I was getting into this!" Colonel Turner, who of course had the man's service record in front of him, gently asked him if he had not been born in Germany. "Yes, sir," Schemel replied, "in Berlin." These words were barely out of his mouth before he realized what Turner was getting at. Some people, because of *his* name and ancestry, would question *his* loyalty to the United States just the way that many doubted the Japanese Americans. "If you'll have me," he quickly informed the colonel, "I'll be glad to join this outfit."[53]

Another of the newly minted second lieutenants was Young Oak Kim, of Korean heritage. His assignment to the unit probably represented a well-intentioned but uninformed decision that, since he was of Asian descent, the 100th Battalion was the perfect place for him. It apparently did not occur to the officer making the assignment that Korea had been a virtual colony of Japan since 1905, and that the administration of the colony was anything but enlightened. There was a lot of enmity in Korea toward the Japanese. When Lieutenant Kim arrived for assignment, Colonel Turner immediately saw the possibility for friction, and told Kim that he would begin processing orders for his transfer immediately. "I don't want to be transferred," said Kim. "I am an American and all the soldiers [in this unit] are American. We are all fighting for the same cause." Turner allowed him to stay but cautioned him that if he and the men did not get along he would be transferred. Lieutenant Kim proved to be somewhat of a taskmaster, but his personal bravery and outgoing personality soon made him a favorite of all those with whom he came in contact.[54]

Because of the uncertainty over how the Japanese Americans would be received by the locals, Colonel Turner warned them against going into town alone. Sometimes, however, they just could not avoid confrontation. One night three of the men went into nearby Sparta, where they were confronted by six men from the area.

"This is not a place for 'Japs' to come," one of the locals growled.

"No 'Japs' came here," replied one of the soldiers, adding: "We have never seen such a thing as a 'Jap.' Are there any 'Japs' around here?"

"You're a 'Jap,'" the man said. "If you don't understand, I'll teach you."

"We are not 'Japs,'" said the soldier; "we are Japanese Americans." But the linguistic subtleties were lost on the civilians, and two of them rushed at the soldier. Using judo, of which he was a master, the soldier quickly convinced his assailants that they had accosted the wrong group of men.[55]

The training at Camp McCoy was not particularly taxing at first, and the young soldiers found plenty of time on the weekends to visit Sparta, as well as other nearby communities. They quickly located Sparta's two movie theaters as well as the best places to grab a hamburger and a beer. When some of them began to imbibe a little too much of the latter, Colonel Turner reacted more like an amused father than as a military disciplinarian. He told the assembled men that it was of no use trying to drink all the beer in Wisconsin because there were several breweries in the state whose production would easily stay ahead of their consumption.[56]

Soon the men began going farther afield to satisfy their geographical curiosity. The larger town of La Crosse, on the Mississippi River, was within easy hitchhiking distance from camp, but some men found this method of travel too slow and unpredictable. Instead they hired taxis to make the seventy-mile round trip! La Crosse, in addition to the usual run of eating and drinking establishments, also offered the Trocadero, a large dance hall with a revolving stage. The men could also patronize the Play-Mor Alleys to bowl a few games, or they could ride a steamboat up and down the river from the town.[57]

Hitchhiking was a popular way to get around for the boys from Hawaii, especially since, unlike Caucasian soldiers on the mainland, none of them was able to bring their own automobiles to camp. And the locals were also typically quite willing to offer rides to young men in uniform. One morning in August, for example, four Nisei soldiers (who had dubbed themselves the "Four Musketeers") extended their thumbs together and were soon all piling

into an automobile headed for Madison, the state capital. The
driver had business there that day, and the men took him up on
his offer to give them a ride back later that afternoon.[58]

And while there was some initial curiosity among the civilians
about these rather exotic-looking men in uniform, relations between the townspeople and the soldiers was usually very upbeat
and positive. No doubt the locals, most of whom had never before
seen Japanese in the flesh, were pleased that these men did not resemble in the least media caricatures, common at the time, depict-
ing them as bespectacled, bandy-legged, and buck-toothed. Other
stereotypes, less insulting perhaps but equally inaccurate, were
also dispelled. Some locals expressed surprise, for example, that
the Japanese American soldiers spoke English; others asked them
whether the straw huts that they lived in leaked when it rained.[59]

A free dance lesson was offered to the soldiers, and it was quite
popular. Most of the men had not even talked to a woman since
they left Hawaii, let alone actually touched one. "When a young
lady put her hand on my shoulder and pulled me close to her,"
one man recalled, "I could smell the fragrance of her perfume.
The music seemed distant and I was dazed, unaware of what I was
to learn." The close proximity to living, breathing women was too
much for some of the men, who soon exhibited obvious signs of
physical arousal. This was, of course, quite embarrassing to them
and to their dance partners.[60]

At least some of the young women in Sparta and the surrounding countryside seemed drawn to these men with their lilting
pidgin and stories of the Pacific paradise that they called home.
Real romance blossomed in some cases, with marriages the result.
Sadly, one such new groom discovered that his wife had apparently married him only because of the amount of money in his
savings account. Before he was completely penniless, he divorced
her.[61]

The 100th Battalion had Camp McCoy pretty much to itself
until the end of November, when the 2nd Infantry Division arrived for winter training. The division had come from Fort Sam
Houston, in San Antonio, Texas, where it had been stationed
since the end of World War I and where Private Morita was employed shuffling papers. Friction was almost immediate. It only

took an ill-considered comment or two from the newcomers about "Japs" to lead to physical confrontations. The Nisei generally held their own in these fights, often using judo against the larger but less skilled Caucasians. Sometimes, however, the white soldiers ganged up on individual members of the battalion, and when Colonel Turner heard about these incidents he exploded and went straight to the commanding general of the 2nd Division to complain. After that, both groups kept to themselves.[62]

In October 1942, a contingent of sixty-seven men from the 100th Battalion left Camp McCoy for Camp Savage, Minnesota. Army authorities had selected them, because of their proficiency in the Japanese language, to attend the Military Intelligence Language Training School there. The country was in desperate need of men who could translate captured Japanese documents and who could listen in on enemy communications. The prevailing belief, at least in some circles, that Japanese Americans were not to be trusted because of their fealty to the emperor was undermined by the fact that only a small percentage of the men at Camp McCoy had the required language skills to attend the school.

That same month, three officers and two dozen enlisted men from Company B were selected for other specialized, albeit undisclosed, training. On October 31, they boarded a transport plane at an airfield near Camp McCoy and departed on a journey to an unknown—at least to the enlisted men—destination. Shortly after takeoff, the aircraft's pilot informed his passengers that they were welcome to come forward, two or three at a time, to visit the cockpit and ask any questions they might have. The men soon determined that the plane was heading in a southerly direction, and one man finally just came out and asked the pilot where they were. The pilot, forbidden from divulging such information, could only tell them that they were "somewhere over the United States." Several hours into the flight the plane landed to refuel, and the men read "Memphis" on the side of one of the gas trucks, thus confirming their suspicions as to the direction of travel.

Finally, the plane landed at Kessler Field in Biloxi, Mississippi. The men exited directly from the plane into canvas-covered trucks, driven right up to the door of the parked aircraft. After a short ride they were deposited at an out-of-the-way pier on the coast and taken by boat to Ship Island, a fairly desolate place located about twelve miles from the mainland. There they discovered that they were to be quartered in wooden barracks next to a dilapidated structure known as Fort Massachusetts. Built by the army in the early 1860s, the fort had once housed as many as eighteen thousand troops but had stood empty for the past forty years. The men immediately formed a good impression of their new home, finding the island's sandy beaches and warm salt air very much to their liking—and far preferable to the winter weather that would soon descend on Wisconsin. But they still did not know why they were there.[63]

They soon found out. As it happened, the U.S. Army Quartermaster Corps had decided to use sentry dogs to protect military installations and defense plants against sabotage and had set up a War Dog Reception and Training Center in Virginia. At first more than thirty different canine breeds were accepted for training, but as time went on greater reliance was placed on a few selected breeds such as German Shepherds, Doberman Pinschers, and Giant Schnauzers, among others. Not all the animals were trained as sentries. A few received more specialized training such as the delivery of messages and the detection of mines and booby trap tripwires.

When scattered reports began to come back from soldiers and marines fighting in the Pacific that dogs could sometimes detect the near presence of their Japanese enemies by smell, some of the animals received combat training. It was thought that traditional Japanese food caused a distinctive odor in a person's perspiration and no matter that, by the time an American soldier was close enough to smell a Japanese, he was probably also close enough for the enemy soldier to kill him. Someone in the War Department, perhaps a hunter in his off-duty hours, suggested that dogs be trained to sniff out Japanese hiding places in much the same fashion as English noblemen used hounds to locate elusive foxes. Someone, evidently, also suggested that Nisei soldiers of the 100th Battalion would be ideal for training the dogs.

And so, after enjoying a couple of days of free time, the Nisei soldiers went by boat to nearby Cat Island, a T-shaped island to the west. Unlike the flat and almost featureless Ship Island, Cat

Island featured a swampy, semi-tropical jungle terrain reminiscent of some of the Japanese-held islands in the Pacific. This was where the training was to take place.

The soldiers split up into small groups. At first they hid in the jungle to see if the dogs could track them. Each man carried a container of raw meat, and that might have been what the dogs scented. When the dogs approached, the men lay on the ground with the meat positioned on their throats. They were, at this point, in no danger because the dogs simply ate the meat and licked any residue off the soldiers' necks. The point of this phase of the training, apparently, was to get the dogs thinking about going for the neck.

The next phase of the training was to condition the normally docile dogs to become ferocious. Each dog was chained to a tree while one of the men intentionally mistreated it. Sometimes the trainers used knotted burlap sacks to beat the dogs; sometimes they used sticks. "As a dog lover since childhood," reported one of the trainers, "this seemed so cruel and was very difficult for me to do." Before long, however, the dogs recognized the pattern and growled and bared their teeth upon the approach of the soldiers.[64]

With the dogs thus adequately traumatized and ready to defend themselves against any such future treatment, the training advanced to the next stage. Now, the Nisei soldier wrapped his right arm heavily in burlap and approached one of the dogs, which was restrained by a trainer with a leash. When the trainer gave the dog the command, "Kill!" the animal lunged at the soldier's throat. The soldier used his padded arm to protect himself and allowed the dog to sink his teeth into the burlap until the trainer called him off. The padding was sufficient to prevent bite wounds on the men, but the actions of the powerful jaws nevertheless created the sensation of being pinched by steel pliers.[65]

As the training progressed it became necessary to provide more protection for the soldiers, so they wore padded jackets and pants, hockey gloves, and fencing masks. One of the Nisei soldiers also remembers wearing a knotted rope at his throat. Dog handlers worked half a dozen dogs and would send them against the soldiers in pairs. While one dog went for the knotted rope at the soldier's neck, the other went for his right arm or hand. After a few seconds, the soldier lay on the ground, as if disabled. The dogs snarled at him until the handler called them off. Sometimes dogs that were in the early stages of their training were not as ferocious as the handlers wanted. One such pair of animals, upon hearing the command, "Kill!" simply walked up to the targeted soldier and sniffed him.[66]

These men of Company B eventually moved over to Cat Island to eliminate the daily boat trip. And, since they did not work particularly long hours—the dogs could not be worked for long stretches at a time—they had plenty of free time. The bounty of the sea was available for their taking, and sometimes they went out in small boats to fish, and at other times, when the tide was out, they simply walked out onto the mud flats and foraged for oysters. And during their first three weeks they drank all the beer that had been allotted for their projected three-month assignment![67]

By late January 1943, the training ended and the men returned to their battalion without ever learning whether or not the dogs they "trained" were used or not. The general feeling among the men, however, was that the experiment had been a failure. "We didn't smell Japanese," recalled one. "We were Americans. Even a dog knew that!"[68]

While the dog trainers worked, the days became shorter and the temperatures at Camp McCoy dropped to levels previously unknown to the islanders. At first there was a sense of novelty to the cold weather and snow. The GIs built snowmen and learned to ice skate. But their training schedule soon began to include tent camping, and this was not a welcome development. Not surprisingly, when they received word on December 31 that they would be leaving Wisconsin in a week, they were greatly relieved. They were headed to Camp Shelby, in Mississippi. And although they were sorry to leave all the friends they had made in Wisconsin (one soldier was sure that every one of the soldiers had made some kind of romantic connection with the local girls), they looked forward to warmer temperatures.[69]

Camp Shelby had been activated to train soldiers going to France for the Great War in 1917. Named for a renowned Indian fighter, Revolutionary War officer, and first governor of Kentucky, it was located just south of Hattiesburg, Mississippi, within the De Soto National Forest. Immediately after the war all but four of its more than twelve hundred buildings were demolished, and the camp was allowed to fall into disrepair. Reclaimed in 1934 as a training camp for the Mississippi National Guard, it once again became a federal facility in 1940. Thousands of civilian workmen soon set to work rejuvenating the camp. Operating with a budget of $24 million, they built eighteen hundred new structures and laid out and graded 250 miles of roads. The camp, along with additional acreage that the government leased for training purposes, soon covered almost twelve hundred square miles and was home to as many as one hundred thousand soldiers at once.[70]

When the men arrived at this new training site they had a considerable amount of re-acclimating to do. Gone was the cool climate of Wisconsin, replaced by the Mississippi heat, along with an abundance of ticks, chiggers, poison ivy, and snakes. The six-legged chiggers were especially irritating. They burrowed their heads under the skin of their victims and feasted on their blood. One's natural instinct, when attacked by one of these parasites, was to pull it off immediately. This, unfortunately, only exacerbated the problem because it left the pest's head in place to fester. Some men found relief by applying fingernail polish remover to the site, thereby closing off the chigger's air supply and suffocating it. Others got good results from a commercial treatment available at the PX called SCAT. Snakes were another matter. The islanders had absolutely no experience with such reptiles, and many of the men saw them as interesting creatures that should be handled and examined at close range. The problem, of course, is that some of the snakes were poisonous. Rattlesnakes were fairly easy to identify because of the warning sound they made as they prepared to strike. Coral snakes, on the other hand, were much smaller and beautifully banded with color. Their venom is the most toxic of all American snakes. Adding to the confusion was the fact that there were non-poisonous snakes that had similar markings. If a soldier encountered one of these colorful serpents in the forest he could always fall back on a little ditty that woodsmen had known for years: "Red and yellow can kill a fellow, but red and black is a friend of Jack." Simply put, if the creature had alternating red and yellow bands, it was a poisonous coral snake; if it had alternating red and black bands, it was a non-poisonous king snake.[71]

In addition to the unfamiliar insects and reptiles in Mississippi, the men also encountered a very different social climate than had prevailed in Wisconsin. The novel presence of these distinctly Asian-looking men in a society that was rigidly divided between black and white led to some "interesting" confrontations between the citizens of Hattiesburg and the soldiers. One man remembered the eyes of the locals fixed upon him and his buddies as if they were animals in a zoo.[72]

The 100th Battalion was attached to the 85th Infantry Division upon arrival at Camp Shelby, and once again it was necessary to explain racial terms. When an officer at division headquarters inquired of Colonel Turner if he had gotten his "Japs" to camp all right, the colonel quickly set him straight about the use of that particular word. "Sir," he bristled, "my men are not 'Japs.' That is a term of opprobrium we use for the enemy. My troops are Americans of Japanese ancestry serving in the American Army." The other officer was somewhat taken aback, and Turner continued: "We'd like to have it understood that we don't want [that term] used before our men."[73]

The Hawaiians took part in large division-size maneuvers, or war games, beginning in March. A certain level of realism was accomplished by having the men march some twenty-five miles from Camp Shelby into the adjacent De Soto National Forest. The weather was cold and rainy, giving the men some indication of what they would encounter in Italy and France. They barely had time to recover from these war games when they were on the move again. They moved out in early April, this time by motor vehicle instead of on foot, and maneuvers included several other divisions besides the 85th.[74]

CHAPTER TWO

BIRTH OF THE 442ND

"I feel that I have proven my ability & loyalty now."

While the men of the 100th Battalion were earning the friendship and respect of most of those with whom they came in contact at Camp McCoy, a War Department committee soon began considering various options with regard to the best use of the other Nisei soldiers, like Private Morita, who were scattered across the country. The committee's report, issued on September 14, reflected a tremendous racial bias against those of Japanese ancestry and strongly advised against the use of Nisei soldiers in any capacity. The report declared the Nisei to be "a distinctive class of individuals, so marked by racial appearance, characteristics and background, that they are particularly repulsive to the military establishment at large and the civilian population." And notwithstanding the lack of even a shred of evidence of disloyalty, the report stated that the "lone fact that these individuals are of Japanese ancestry tends to place them in a most questionable light as to their loyalty to the United States." Assistant Secretary of War John J. McCloy and Chief of Staff General George C. Marshall disagreed.[1]

The forced relocation of more than one hundred thousand Japanese and Japanese Americans was, of course, the most obvious manifestation of American racism. Government officials soon found out how widespread this was when they tried to find locations to build permanent relocation camps. Idaho governor Chase Clark made no secret of how he felt. "I want to admit right on the start," he said, "that I am so prejudiced that my reasoning might be a little off, because I don't trust any of them." He finally allowed evacuees to enter his state, but only under severe restrictions. To keep them from putting down roots he wanted a law that would forbid them from buying any land. And he wanted federal authorities to return them all to the West Coast as soon as the emergency was over. "If the Army has the right to bring the Japs into Idaho," he said, "then certainly it has the right to take them out." Wyoming governor Nels Smith promised that any Japanese brought into his state would soon be "hanging from every tree." When authorities set up a couple of camps in Arkansas, that state's governor, H. M. Adkins, made it clear that he did not want any of the internees on work release programs to work on a federal dam in his state. "When you refuse an American to work in the war effort, thereby hindering production in any way," reacted one of the incarcerated Japanese Americans, "you are a saboteur, and a saboteur of the worst kind." He then directed his comments toward the governor and the racially segregated society of the American South. "And if it is your fear that we might get involved in your messy social system, then banish that fear, for we are too intelligent, too well educated, and too Americanized to have any part of it."[2]

Colorado's governor, Ralph Carr, was the only one of the western governors whose states were being considered for internment camps to welcome them, much to the detriment of his own political career. "If we do not extend humanity's kindness and understanding to these people," he said, "if we deny them the protection of the Bill of Rights, if we say they may be denied the privilege of living in any one of the 48 states without hearing or charge of misconduct, then we are tearing down the whole American system. If Colorado's part in the war is to take 100,000 of them, then Colorado will take care of them."[3]

By October all of the assembly centers had been shut down and their residents transferred to one of the ten hastily constructed relocation camps, a government euphemism for what most of the inhabitants referred to as concentration camps. Two camps were in Arizona: Gila River was about fifty miles south of Phoenix on part of the vast Gila River Indian Reservation, and Poston was similarly located on the Colorado River Indian Reservation in the lower Sonoran Desert. Near Amache, Colorado, about 140 miles east of Pueblo and only fifteen miles from the Kansas state line was Granada. Twelve miles northwest of Cody, Wyoming, along the Shoshone River, was Heart Mountain camp. Residents there could see the landform for which their camp was named, rising over thirty-four hundred feet above the surrounding terrain eight miles away. A camp sited in the high desert fifteen miles north of Twin Falls, Idaho, was called Minidoka, even though the town of that name was fifty miles away. Topaz, Utah, 140 miles southwest of Salt Lake City, was another camp. Two camps were located in eastern California: Manzanar, in the southern Owens valley, 220 miles north of Los Angeles and 250 miles south of Reno, Nevada; and Tule Lake, thirty-five miles southeast of Klamath Falls, Oregon. The two easternmost camps were in southeastern Arkansas: Jerome, 120 miles southeast of Little Rock, near McGehee, and Rohwer, about twenty-seven miles north of Jerome. The western camps were all located on fairly unproductive land, often home to mesquite trees, creosote bushes, cactus, and sagebrush. Only the Arkansas camps proved fertile, and even then the residents had to clear away a lot of brush and timber before being able to plant crops in the boggy former swampland.

The physical layouts of these camps were all very much the same. They were laid out like small villages, with intersecting streets and blocks of long, narrow, one-story barracks covered in black tarpaper and partitioned into family living quarters. Each family was assigned one room, measuring about twenty by twenty feet. Some were slightly larger and others were smaller. None of these barracks had cooking, bathing, or toilet facilities, the residents being required to eat in centrally located mess halls and tend to their other needs in common latrines. Barbed wire fencing surrounded the camps and elevated guard towers, complete with machine guns, were spaced around the perimeters.

The government did not spend much time or money furnishing these dwellings. Most families arrived to find a simple army cot with sheets, pillow, and blanket for each person (sometimes with a thin mattress and sometimes not), a pot-bellied stove for heat, and a bare light bulb hanging from the ceiling. As time went on, many of the inmates rounded up scraps of wood and were able to knock together small tables, chairs, and other items. At Topaz, the dust was almost stifling during certain times of the year. "It was almost fascinating," one former resident remembered years later, "to be indoors with all the windows closed and yet see large, suffocating puffs of dust blow in over the [door] sills." In winter icy blasts of wind replaced the dust coming through the cracks in the walls. Some of the more enterprising residents excavated down eight or nine feet inside their quarters where they could be cooler in the summer and warmer in the winter.[4]

Although most of the inmates at these camps stoically accepted their plight, others did not. There was a considerable amount of pro-Japan sentiment in the internment camp at Jerome, Arkansas, where some of the inmates believed that Japan would ultimately win the war. Such feelings were generally more evident among the Kibei—those who had been born in the United States but who had gone to Japan for some or all of their schooling before returning to America. At Manzanar, for example, about a dozen young Kibei formed an organization known variously as the Manzanar Black Dragons or sometimes the Patriotic Suicide Corps. They posted leaflets—in Japanese—at various places in the camp warning the inmates not to help the American war effort in any way. And when some of the people began manufacturing camouflage netting for the army, the Black Dragons encouraged the children in the camp to throw rocks at them.[5]

With internment an accomplished fact, West Coast fanatics quieted down, and the inmates in the camps for the most part resigned themselves to their fate. On September 14, 1942, a board of officers in the War Department published a recommendation that a limited number of Japanese American men be recruited into the army as translators or interpreters, but that other than these relative few none should be allowed to enter military service. The recommendation cited what these officers saw as widespread distrust of the American people toward Japanese Americans as the reason for this prohibition. Lieutenant General Lesley McNair, commander of Army Ground Forces, supported this decision in spite of recommendations to the contrary by various officers in the intelligence branch, who pointed out that the Nisei represented a not inconsiderable manpower pool that was not being utilized.

Halfway around the world, the Japanese gleefully pointed to internment as proof that the United States was waging a race war.

Elmer Davis, director of the Office of War Information (OWI), believed there was a rather simple way to counter such racist propaganda. He disagreed with the War Department committee's assertions concerning the perfidy of resident Japanese and Japanese Americans and, in a letter dated October 2, 1942, he urged President Roosevelt to allow Japanese American men to volunteer for the army and the navy—contingent, of course, upon their passing individual loyalty examinations. Employing a down-home tone, Davis reassured the president that "competent authorities . . . say that fully 85 percent of the Nisei are loyal to this country and that it *is* possible to distinguish the sheep from the goats." Roosevelt was favorably disposed to Davis' suggestion and forwarded it to Secretary of War Henry Stimson for his study and suggestions.[6]

Assistant Secretary of War John J. McCloy urged his boss to support the suggestion. "I believe the propaganda value of such a step would be great," he wrote, "and I believe [the Nisei] would make good troops. We need not use them against members of their own race, but we could use them for many useful purposes." Stimson agreed, stating that to do otherwise simply based upon their race was wrong. Rounding up Japanese Americans into the relocation camps, he went on, was enough. Further support for the idea came from one rather unlikely quarter. General Emmons, in Hawaii, had been the one to authorize the discharge of all the Japanese Americans in the Hawaii Territorial Guard in January 1942, and in the following month expressed his support for a plan to evacuate one hundred thousand Japanese Americans from Hawaii to the mainland because of his concerns about their loyalty. Over time, however, his thinking had undergone a complete metamorphosis. He had seen the hard work of the Varsity Victory Volunteers on defense projects on Oahu, and he knew how well the men of the 100th Battalion were progressing in their training at Camp McCoy. He now wholeheartedly endorsed the formation of an all-Japanese American combat unit. "I am confident," he declared, "[that] these men will give an excellent account of themselves in the European theater."[7]

In spite of this high-level interest, neither the employment of Nisei soldiers already in the army in meaningful duties nor the resumption of enlistments for such men was a foregone conclusion.

There was still a considerable amount of opposition. General John L. DeWitt, for one, had had no change of heart and continued to distrust all Japanese and Japanese Americans. "It makes no difference," he believed, "whether he is an American citizen; theoretically he is still a Japanese, and you can't change him . . . by giving him a piece of paper." Some members of congress were even considering wholesale revocation of citizenship for people—the Nisei—who were born in this country. In spite of such opposition, however, the plan moved forward.[8]

The proposed acceptance of Japanese Americans into the army once again raised certain questions. The first was whether to simply revert back to assigning them to existing units as had been the case before the war, or whether to form a segregated—all-Nisei—unit. The use of such an ethnically based unit would not have been new. African American soldiers in the U.S. Army served in segregated units with—for the most part—Caucasian officers. The so-called Buffalo Soldiers of the post-Civil War era earned martial honors against the Plains Indians, and in World War I the "Harlem Hellfighters" of the 369th Infantry Regiment added luster to this record. And almost all of the soldiers in the army's 12th Infantry Division (also known as the Philippine Division) were Filipinos.

There were advantages as well as drawbacks to each option. Treating these men no differently than Caucasian soldiers and randomly assigning them to existing units certainly would simplify the necessary paperwork. But reverting back to this prewar routine might mean that some Nisei would be assigned to combat units ultimately headed for the Pacific. Since all such units must necessarily stage from West Coast ports it meant that their Nisei members would be in violation of the spirit of Executive Order No. 9066. Of greater concern to many, however, was the problem that such use might create among African American soldiers, who had served in racially segregated units since the Civil War. Integrating Caucasian units with Japanese American soldiers might prompt blacks to call for the same action in their behalf.

Some favored segregating the Nisei for the simple reason that they still had doubts about their loyalty, and having them all concentrated together would make it easier for officials to keep an eye on them. This would, of course, also strengthen the concept of a segregated army and head off protest from African Americans.

Among Japanese Americans some, at least at first, favored the first option—feeling that it would indicate full equality with the white soldiers. Others pointed out, however, that any individual heroic deeds of Nisei soldiers in integrated units would not as likely be noted by non-Nisei media. If instead, however, all the Nisei served together their accomplishments would stand out and easily be recognized. And such service would, it was hoped, demonstrate to the government that Japanese Americans were as loyal as any other group of people within the nation and that internment, therefore, was wrongheaded.

The arguments in favor of a segregated Nisei unit won the day, and on the first day of 1943 General Marshall approved the creation of the new unit. Some felt that such soldiers should be relegated to labor battalions or assigned to other non-combat roles in the same manner that most black soldiers were used. Perhaps they could be sent to Britain to help unload transport ships. Marshall's announcement, however, was that these men were to be combat soldiers—not laborers. The new unit was to be a somewhat self-contained organization, reminiscent of the nineteenth-century military legions, which combined infantry, cavalry, and artillery. This one would consist of the three infantry battalions that normally make up a regiment, augmented by a battalion of field artillery, a company of combat engineers, and a medical detachment. The army assigned the numerical designation of the 442nd Regimental Combat Team to the new outfit. This, to some of the Japanese Americans, seemed like an unfortunate choice of numbers since the word for "four" and the word for "death" are both pronounced in the same way in Japanese. Having *two* fours in the designator seemed to suggest to some that the outfit was headed for bad luck.[9]

The organization of each infantry battalion began with the squad. Effectively the basic "family" of the infantry soldier, the squad was determined to be the largest unit that one man could effectively control with voice commands and without having to rely on radios or runners. Ideally, a twelve-man rifle squad consisted of a sergeant as the squad leader, a corporal as his assistant, and ten riflemen. The assistant squad leader was authorized to carry a Model 1903 Springfield rifle that could quickly be fitted with a grenade launcher. Of the ten other members of the squad, seven carried M1 Garand rifles. Another man carried a .30-caliber Browning Automatic Rifle (BAR). Heavier than the M1, this .30-caliber weapon used detachable twenty-round magazines and served as the squad's machine gun. A BAR gunner who held the trigger down could burn through an entire magazine in just a few seconds. The remaining two members of the squad were an assistant BAR gunner and an ammunition bearer, each carrying a .30-caliber semi-automatic carbine. One wire cutter, one axe, three pick mattocks, seven entrenching shovels, one pair of field glasses, and two compasses were distributed among the members of the squad.

Three squads composed a platoon and four platoons—three rifle platoons and one weapons platoon—a company. A second lieutenant commanded each of the three rifle platoons. Assisting him were a staff sergeant and a platoon guide (who held the rank of staff sergeant), two messengers, and five riflemen. While on the march, each platoon was entitled to the use of two small vehicles to transport extra ammunition and other baggage. Each driver carried a BAR.

A first lieutenant commanded the fourth platoon—the weapons platoon—and was allotted a staff sergeant and two messengers. This platoon was broken up into a mortar section and a light machine-gun section. A staff sergeant commanded each section, with a messenger to help him stay in contact. The mortar section had three five-man mortar squads, each built around a 60mm mortar and commanded by a sergeant. Similarly, a sergeant was in charge of each of three light machine-gun squads, each built around a tripod-mounted, .30-caliber air-cooled Browning machine gun.

Just as four platoons constituted a company, four companies comprised a battalion. The first three companies in every battalion were rifle companies and the fourth was a heavy weapons company. The latter was armed with six heavy mortars—81mm—and four water-cooled, .30 caliber, Browning heavy machine guns.

Three such battalions formed the backbone of an infantry regiment—in this case the 442nd Infantry Regiment.

Twelve companies, designated by letters A through M, except for J, constituted a regiment. (The reason for the absence of a "Company J" goes back at least as far as the eighteenth century. In those days before typewriters, when all written communications were by hand, it was often difficult to distinguish a cursive upper-case "J" from a cursive upper-case "I." Therefore, in order to avoid confusion that could prove catastrophic on the battlefield, military leaders decided not to have a "Company J.")

Traditionally, infantry regiments were folded into divisions, which also contained field artillery battalions and other types of combatant units, and usually numbered about fifteen thousand men. By World War II, however, the exigencies of modern warfare sometimes required smaller units than divisions to accomplish certain tasks, but the tasks themselves required more firepower than was available to a stand-alone infantry regiment. This led to the implementation of regimental combat teams, with each containing an organic field artillery battalion, a company of combat engineers, an antitank company, a cannon company, and a medical unit.

In the case of the 442nd, there was something else to consider, and that was the number of Nisei men eligible for military service. To create an entire division would require, in addition to the original fifteen thousand men, an additional number, perhaps up to fifteen thousand more, to be on hand to replace anticipated losses.

The organization of the combat team's artillery component—the 522nd Field Artillery Battalion—took place on February 1, 1943, under the command of a thirty-year-old attorney from Florida named Lieutenant Colonel Baya M. Harrison Jr., and followed standard guidelines. The battalion had five batteries, which were analogous to companies in an infantry battalion. Batteries A, B, and C (Able, Baker, and Charley in military parlance) were the firing batteries, and each was equipped with four 105mm howitzers and a number of .30- and .50-caliber machine guns. Headquarters Battery was the administrative heart of the battalion, and Service

Battery took care of routine maintenance of vehicles, and the transportation and distribution of food and ammunition. There was also a sixteen-man medical detachment.

The news that the government had decided to raise an all-Japanese American combat unit met with mixed reactions from Caucasians. A former California state senator thought it was the "saddest thing that has happened in this war." Many Japanese Americans saw the formation of the combat team as an opportunity for them to prove individual, as well as group, loyalty by enlisting. Many others were bitter over the entire internment process and resolved to have nothing to do with the war. A Manzanar inmate, who had already demonstrated his loyalty to the United States by serving in the army during World War I, was particularly incensed at the treatment his country now saw fit to impose upon him and thousands of others. He swore that rather than volunteering again he would "become a Jap a hundred per cent and never do another day's work to help this country fight this war." Mississippi Congressman John Rankin still held out some hope that the men in this new regiment would be used as labor troops.[10]

Regardless of the tasks assigned to this new unit, authorities were in virtually unanimous agreement that it would not be posted to the Pacific theater. The arrival in that theater of men of Japanese ancestry wearing American army uniforms could lead very easily to serious problems. Enemy soldiers might infiltrate American lines fairly easily if they were dressed in American uniforms, and GIs and marines might mistake them for Nisei troops and not challenge their presence. On the other hand, if such infiltration did occur it might soon lead to nervous American soldiers mistaking the Nisei for enemy intruders and shooting them before asking any questions.

Nevertheless, planning for the new unit began immediately. There were already a large number of Japanese Americans in the army, in addition to those in training with the 100th Battalion at Camp McCoy. Many were men whose numbers had come up in the draft in 1941, and even into early 1942. Therefore they had all had, by this time, at least a year of training, and the decision was made to build the combat team around a cadre of such men. The officers, for the most part, would be Caucasians, as in the African American units.

The original plan for filling out the regiment was that the bulk of the enlistees would be mainland Japanese Americans—about three thousand of them—and the rest—about fifteen hundred—would come from Hawaii. Recruiting on the mainland was slower than anticipated, however. Many young men of military age were reluctant to volunteer to fight for a country that had put them and their families behind barbed wire fences and machine-gun towers. Others were concerned about what might happen to their families after they had left the internment camps. With no such similar circumstances in Hawaii, however, there was a rush of island boys to be a part of this unique outfit. Mitsuru Doi claimed the distinction of having been the first man inducted into the new unit, but approximately ten thousand others tried to enlist, and the quota was quickly oversubscribed. Then, because of the slow reaction on the mainland, officials opened up Hawaiian recruiting to allow another thousand men.[11]

When one man, standing just 4'9", tried to volunteer an officer told him to go home, that he was just not big enough for the army. He was determined, however, and got back in line. He soon reached the same officer, who by this time had inspected dozens of men and apparently did not recognize him. When the officer asked him his height and weight he boldly claimed that he was 5'2" and that he weighed 115 pounds. "Next," said the officer, waving him on. Another volunteer knew his eyesight was below average, so he somehow got a good close look at the eye chart and committed it to memory so he could "pass" it. So cursory were the physical exams by this stage of the war that one inductee was convinced that the examiners would accept anyone so long as "they couldn't see through our heads." A Caucasian soldier, in a different unit, was convinced that the eye test only consisted of making sure the recruit had two of them.[12]

Some parents presented their sons with traditional Japanese amulets called *omamoris* to protect them while they were away. Other men entered the army under the protection of *senninbaris*, or "thousand-stitch belts." These good-luck charms were very popular in the Imperial Japanese Army, and a fair number of Japanese

American soldiers also wore them under their uniforms. These sashes were usually white, about six inches wide, with each of a thousand red decorative French knots sewn in by a different woman's hands. One man remembered the belt that his mother sent him from Rohwer Internment Camp. Made from an unbleached rice sack, it had a picture of a tiger painted on it, along with the thousand knots. In this case, however, each of the knots was *not* tied by a different woman. According to custom, a woman born in the Year of the Tiger—which occurred approximately every twelve years in Japan's lunar calendar—could tie one knot for each year of her age. Therefore a fifty-three-year-old woman, born in the Year of the Tiger 1890, could tie fifty-three knots instead of just one. This soldier wrapped his senninbari in protective cellophane and carried it with him throughout the war. Another man faithfully wore the belt that the women of Manzanar presented him when he left to join the army, until he was wounded over a year later. Medical personnel removed it from him to better treat his wounds, and he never recovered it. Even so it had, perhaps, served its purpose; he was still alive.[13]

Among the eager island volunteers was eighteen-year-old Daniel Inouye, a pre-med student at the University of Hawaii who was engaged in volunteer work at an aid station. He was somewhat miffed when, after passing the physical exam, he was not immediately notified to report for duty. Fearing that he might have somehow missed out on his opportunity to enlist, he hurried to his draft board. "I'm not leaving here," he said, "until I find out why I was rejected and whether I have any chance at all of getting in." The people at the draft board patiently informed him that his volunteer work and his school work made him too valuable to go into the army, where he would likely become a mere foot soldier. He was not to be denied. "I'd appreciate it if you gave me about an hour," he said. "Then if you will call the aid station and the University, they will tell you in both places that I've given my notice to quit by the end of the week." The stunned draft board official tried to dissuade the young man but could not. "I don't know whether it's right or wrong," the determined young man continued, "whether I'd be doing more good here or in the service. I just know that if there's any way in which I can humanly get into the army, I'm going to do it." Two days later he received a telephone call from the draft board informing him when and where to meet the bus taking recruits to Schofield Barracks for the beginning of their training. He was the second-to-last man taken before Hawaii's quota was met. His father counseled him as he prepared to report for duty. "Whatever you do," he sternly told his son, "don't bring dishonor to the family. This country has been good to us. We owe much to the country; even if it means dying for it."[14]

Not every young Japanese in Hawaii shared this young man's enthusiasm to sign his name on the dotted line when the new organization was announced. When a local police officer addressed about a hundred Nisei workers in a gym on Oahu and told them that they "must volunteer" to prove their loyalty, his message fell flat for some in the audience. Some felt insulted. "I was born an American," Ron Oba remembered, "was educated as an American. I went to American school, I spoke American. As an American, I [felt] loyalty is a given. So why should I be put on the spot to prove my loyalty?" Nevertheless, he ultimately gave in to peer pressure and enlisted.[15]

The Hawaiians came forward to enlist for some of the same reasons that many other American soldiers volunteered. Patriotism. Excitement. Peer pressure. Some men enlisted merely to escape the boredom of their civilian jobs. "People talked about having volunteered out of patriotism," remembered one man, "but frankly we were so bored we would do anything to get out of the monotonous life we had then." And according to another, "Loyalty was secondary. I volunteered to get the hell out of the pineapple field and to go to the Mainland." A student at the University of Hawaii volunteered because he felt that he had no other choice. "I got an F in English [class] and joined the Army to save face."[16]

The volunteers, whatever their motivations might have been, assembled at Schofield Barracks and began their introduction to the military. They were housed in pyramidal canvas tents that housed eight men each. They received bolt-action Springfield rifles and uniforms, underwent testing, and did all the other things brand new recruits do. Nearby civilian tailor shops did a brisk business altering uniforms to fit the smaller-than-usual GIs. The small size of these men presented problems to the army's quartermasters, who had to keep them supplied with clothing. Many of these men wore shirts that measured only 13½ inches in the neck and had sleeve lengths of just twenty-seven inches. Similarly, it was not uncommon to see twenty-six-inch waists and twenty-seven-inch inseams on the trousers. There just were not enough uniforms in those small sizes to outfit all the recruits, so they received clothing that was much too big for them and, as a result, certainly did not present much of a military appearance. Many of the men pressed their mothers or sisters into emergency service altering their garments into some semblance of a reasonable fit. Boots and shoes, however, presented an insoluble problem. One man wore a size 2½ EEE shoe, which was virtually unobtainable in quartermasters' stocks. Instead he had to make do with size 8 and stuff the toes with padding. The only articles of issued clothing that fit one recruit were his belt and his necktie.[17]

They received identification tags—dog tags—that contained their names, their newly issued army service numbers, their blood types, the names and addresses of their next of kin, and their religious preferences. It was this last item that caused some problems. Many of these men were Buddhists, but the list of acceptable religions to be noted on their dog tags did not include Buddhism. The only choices were C (for Catholic), P (for Protestant), and H (for Hebrew, or Jewish). Nor was the army prepared to furnish these men with Buddhist chaplains. When one of the many Buddhist volunteers asked that his identification tags be so marked he met a scornful reply from a Caucasian officer. "Let me tell you that we don't have a Buddhist religion in the American army," the officer replied. "Pick another one." He then chose Protestant, and when the officer asked him why he selected Protestant, he said: "Because I protest!" The angry officer then assigned him to latrine duty.[18]

One of the new recruits, perhaps caught up in the patriotic fervor to volunteer for the army, began to have second thoughts about enlisting. He had a wife and three children, after all, and if he died in the army it would work a terrible hardship on them. Still wanting to serve his country, however, he looked about for a safer occupation than infantry rifleman and soon volunteered to work in the kitchen, even though he did not know the first thing about cooking. Desperate, he sought the help of his friend Ron Oba, whose only acquaintance with cooking came from his stint as a busboy in a Honolulu restaurant, to teach him how to cook. Somehow the two of them managed to produce a batch of non-lethal pancakes the first morning, and after that they both learned "on the job."[19]

After in-processing at Schofield Barracks the volunteers rode the train into downtown Honolulu on Sunday, March 28. They then marched to Iolani Palace, the former residence of Hawaii's last monarch, for a going-away celebration. Unlike the rather furtive leave-taking of the 100th Battalion from Oahu the previous May, over fifteen thousand friends and family members of the new volunteers gathered on the grounds of the palace to honor the eager young volunteers about to head for training on the mainland. There was the expected round of speech-making by local dignitaries and well-wishing from the families and friends of the fledgling soldiers. Some volunteers from the Big Island had only recently arrived on Oahu and did not yet have uniforms. They took up position at the rear of the formation, but many of the civilians, not realizing who they were, jostled past them to get closer to the men in uniform. An editorial in the local newspaper labeled this event "a demonstration such as, perhaps, only Hawaii could furnish, but it was a demonstration of value to the entire nation." And then it was off to the docks.[20]

With well-wishers lining the streets, the new soldiers shouldered their rifles and their heavy duffle bags and headed for the docks. The men were not allowed to stop along the way for a final good-bye kiss from a loved one, but were hurried along by military policemen. Many of the men resented the manner in which they left the island. Army trucks could easily have been provided to carry the men's heavy bags and allow them to march along the street with at least a modicum of military bearing. Instead they struggled along, trying to manhandle duffel bags that were almost as big as they were. It is uncertain whether this was due to some logistical oversight in arranging transportation or if it was thought of as a good toughening-up exercise, but some of these men had real difficulty completing the trip with their full duffel bags. This was a decidedly *un*military parade!

The SS *Lurline*, a former Matson Lines luxury liner, had been converted to troop-carrying duties and was set to convey the new volunteers to the mainland. Before the war, as many as 240 tourist-class passengers could share the ship with up to 475 first-class travelers. The latter could enjoy the *Lurline*'s spacious cabins that, according to company literature, were "implicit with every imaginable comfort." Or they might book one of the ship's deluxe suites, each of which was said to be "a repository for that trinity of necessities—beauty, comfort, and utility." Indeed, the brochure continued, it "would be difficult to create or imagine a more distinctive, beautiful quarters." Of course, such grand accommodations were long a thing of the past by the time the *Lurline* began carrying soldiers for Uncle Sam. The once-roomy staterooms now contained enough bunk beds for a dozen men.[21]

As had been the case when the 100th Battalion had made this trip the year before, there was plenty of gambling on board. In addition to the farewell money that families had bestowed on their sons, many of these young men had spent the previous year or so working long hours at civilian jobs and earning a lot of overtime pay. Craps appeared to be the most popular game, and it was not unusual to have several games going at once with as many as thirty men participating in each. One onlooker recalled that "twenty-dollar bills just covered the floor in these games."[22]

Recruitment was slower on the mainland. Many men in the internment camps refused to volunteer, thinking it the height of hypocrisy for the government that had imprisoned them and their families to now think that they would jump at the chance to risk their lives for that very government. Many thought the camp's young men were foolish to fight for the United States when that country showed so little respect for Japanese Americans. The initial reaction of one of the Minidoka inmates, was: "Up your ass, Uncle Sam!" He pointed out the obvious fact that while Japanese Americans were rounded up wholesale and put in what amounted to prison camps, there was no corresponding large-scale imprisonment of German Americans or Italian Americans. In addition to that, he commented, "we were told to prove [our loyalty] with our blood! I certainly had no incentive to serve, much less die for this FDR brand of democracy." In spite of his bitter feelings, however, he later volunteered. Many of the volunteers faced the mockery, and even physical assault, of the other internees, who thought they were foolish to volunteer. A teacher at Poston had to listen to the taunts of some of the young men who were his students when he decided to enlist. He was able to achieve some level of satisfaction later, however, when some of them showed up as drafted replacements for the 442nd in Europe.[23]

CHAPTER THREE

TRAINING

With the decision having been made to raise and train a Nisei regimental combat team, it now remained to decide who would do the training. Almost all of the officers were to be Caucasian. This was due in part to the small number of Japanese American officers already in the service. And in part it was due to the same race attitude that dictated that black soldiers should have white officers. Many of the officers, particularly the lieutenants, reported to Camp Shelby straight from Officer Candidate School and probably had less overall military experience than many of the sergeants.

Others, like Lieutenant Colonel James M. Hanley, had several years of reserve service. He was assigned as an instructor at the Infantry School at Fort Benning, Georgia, when he received word of his transfer to the infant 442nd Regiment. Having grown up in North Dakota, it is unlikely that Hanley had had any interaction with Japanese Americans before arriving at Camp Shelby. In fact, when he informed his family of his new assignment the general response was: "Why, you can't speak Japanese."[1]

The regiment's first commanding officer was six-foot Lieutenant Colonel Merritt Booth, a forty-three-year-old West Point graduate. Early in his career he had served in an exchange program with Japan whereby he commanded a platoon in the Japanese army. He was fluent in both written and spoken Japanese and seemed to be a good choice for his new assignment. He had only just arrived at Camp Shelby, however, before new orders sent him to Washington to work in military intelligence. His replacement was Colonel Charles W. Pence, who had been an outstanding athlete at DePauw University before leaving school to join the army during World War I.[2]

It was decided to use some of the five thousand or so Nisei already in the army to form the basis of the training cadre for the new unit. This would have a double benefit. It would cull existing Nisei soldiers from the various army camps where they were often performing menial tasks, and consolidate them in one place. Second, the new soldiers would probably respond well to instructors who were also of Japanese ancestry and who already knew something about military life.

The men who formed the training cadre, both officers and enlisted men, began to arrive at Camp Shelby as early as February 1, 1943. Six men from Camp Barkley, Texas, were the first to report and were soon assigned to the artillery battalion that was to become part of the combat team being formed. When they stepped off the train they were alone. There was no one there to meet them and show them where to go. Finally, the railroad station agent tracked down Colonel Hanley, the only officer in residence, and he came to the station to welcome the new men. Gradually, over a period of time, the rest of the training staff arrived. They came from camps all over the country. By the middle of the month these men began learning how to teach and lead other soldiers.[3]

Colonel Harrison and the other nine original officers of the artillery battalion were all Caucasians, as were an additional twenty-two newly commissioned officers who arrived before the end of the month. The original ninety-six enlisted cadre men, however, were all Japanese Americans who, like T/5 Morita, were already in the army when the war started. Now was their chance to be soldiers again! Morita, who was soon promoted to staff sergeant, was one of only eight or ten enlisted men who had received any previous artillery training, but for the past year he had been performing administrative work at Fort Sam Houston in San Antonio and needed brushing up. There was not much time before the arrival of fresh recruits, so the initial training of the cadre was arduous.

Often overlooked, or at least underappreciated, in the study of warfare is the work of the combat engineers. Yet without the commitment, hard work, and bravery of these troops, the infantry would often be unable to do its job at all. The combat engineers assigned to be part of the 442nd RCT formed the 232nd Engineer Combat Company, and it boasted one of the few Nisei officers in the combat team. Captain Pershing Nakada, a graduate engineer from the University of Nebraska, was named for General John Pershing, under whom his father had served as an orderly during World War I, and he immediately set to work training his men.

Not only did the two hundred officers and men assigned to this company receive regular infantry training, they also had to learn how to locate and deactivate enemy land mines, and to place their own mines in areas most calculated to cause significant damage to the enemy. They had to learn how to build many types of bridges, from pontoon bridges for hasty river crossings to steel or timber bridges strong enough to hold up to heavy vehicular traffic. They had to acquire expertise in demolitions so they could, when the situation demanded, destroy these same types of bridges, as well as enemy roadblocks and other obstructions. They would need all these skills later.

By the middle of April, the living quarters assigned to the 442nd Regimental Combat Team were ready for occupation. They were far from luxurious. One of the early arrivals thought they resembled chicken huts. Instead of the two-story wooden barracks buildings such as those at Camp Roberts, the men took up residence in what were called hutments. These structures were approximately square in floor plan with wooden walls up to about three or four feet from the ground and wire mesh screens from the top of the walls to the eaves. The roofs were canvas.[4]

On the 13th, the first of almost twenty-seven hundred Hawaiian recruits began arriving. For most of them, never having left Hawaii before, it was a great adventure, and they were anxious to see and experience what the American South offered, such as alligators and snakes. Because there are no snakes native to the islands many of the new arrivals eagerly anticipated seeing one, although one man indicated that he would likely run in the other direction if he did. Another man seemed almost disappointed that not only were there no snakes in his bed, there were none in the entire barracks. One day a soldier in the 3rd Battalion nonchalantly strolled into camp holding a half-dead snake by the tail. It was a coral snake, quite colorful but extremely poisonous. Whereupon the battalion commander, Lieutenant Colonel Sherwood Dixon, decided to play a joke on the men that would also, he hoped, teach them an important lesson.[5]

Somehow the colonel came into possession of a six-foot rattlesnake—dead. Since his battalion was scheduled for a long practice hike that day he had his driver take him out ahead of the column. Near a bend in the road he and his driver coiled the dead snake so that it looked like it was about to strike from behind a bush. They even propped open its mouth with small sticks. They then lounged against the jeep waiting for the troops to arrive. "Eight hundred men plodded down the road in column of twos," recalled Colonel Dixon a few years later, "and as every pair came around that bush they nearly stepped into a rattlesnake's mouth that looked as big as an alligator's. In perfect cadence they twisted and jumped a yard to the left, looked quickly and sheepishly over at us, not wanting us to think they were 'chicken,' and then hustled right on down the road. . . . After that I never saw a soldier carrying a snake by the tail."[6]

By early April most of the recruits had arrived in camp, although some were still in transit—including three from Alaska. On the 15th, Colonel Pence formally welcomed the assembled men of the 442nd to Camp Shelby. "You men have more than an opportunity," he informed them. "You have a challenge. If there is any one lesson the history of America has taught, it is this: That the rights of American citizenship must be defended before they can be enjoyed fully."[7]

The new arrivals took up the challenge of citizenship in another way too. Not only were these soldiers putting their lives at risk for the good of the country's war effort, they were also putting their money where it would help. Within a short time of their arrival at Camp Shelby, Nisei recruits bought war bonds with a face value of more than $100,000. Over the next several weeks more recruits arrived, many of them having volunteered from their temporary homes in the internment camps, and by May 10 basic training began in earnest.[8]

The army sometimes seemed to assign men almost by whimsy. One man remembered arriving at Camp Shelby with five other recruits and asking for assignment to the combat engineers, but there were no vacancies there. The artillery battalion, however, had three immediate vacancies, so the six men were lined up and the three tallest went to the artillery! Another man, with a degree from Princeton University's School of Public and International Affairs, found himself assigned as a surgical technician. Even though he lacked any training for the job, the army further assigned him to teach others. He got through it by studying a topic on his own at night and then parroting it back to the ten or twelve men under his instruction the next day. "There I was," he said, "teaching them while I was teaching myself."[9]

Ironically, Ron Oba, the former restaurant waiter from Hawaii, wound up in the kitchens at Camp Shelby. Perhaps army officials, like his friend, calculated that his experience as a busboy qualified him as a cook also. At the army cooking school the curriculum was apparently tailored to where the students were stationed rather than to the needs or desires of the soldiers themselves. For example, this Japanese American from Hawaii learned to prepare such traditional Southern dishes as hominy grits, rutabaga, liverwurst, mutton, yellow squash, black-eyed peas, corn bread, brussels sprouts, rhubarb, and pig corn. His first attempt in the kitchen did not go as well as the pancakes he had helped turn out back at Schofield Barracks. During his first day on the job, the head cook told him to make gravy from scratch. When Oba asked for instructions, the cook simply told him to check the manual. But the manual was not very helpful to one so completely unprepared for kitchen work. The book defined gravy as the juices and fat that come out of meat when it is being cooked. "For a brown gravy," the guide instructed, "flour is added to the[se] drippings and fried until brown. Then meat stock, water, or milk, is added, a little at a time, and stirred continuously until the desired thickness of gravy is had." The head cook added to the manual's rather vague instructions by telling his novice to add some butter, flour, salt, pepper, and water. Oba duly added these ingredients, but the water was cold and caused the flour and butter to separate and float to the top of the growing mess. He had to throw it all away and start over again.[10]

Many Caucasians, both within the regiment and without, had trouble pronouncing some of the Japanese names. Royce Higa heard his name mangled as "High-Gah," and Lloyd Hoshide became "Horse Hide." And a hospital orderly in Italy could not figure out how to pronounce Ben Tamashiro's name so he substituted that of a famous Russian general named Timoshenko (although it is difficult to see how this was any easier to pronounce). And when Richard Oshiro received a Silver Star medal for gallantry, the Caucasian officer who pinned it onto his shirt pronounced his name "O'Shire," whereupon another officer standing nearby congratulated him and told him how pleased he was to see an Irishman being decorated with a Silver Star.[11]

For at least some of the men, this was not a new phenomenon. Yeiichi Kuwayama, a 1940 graduate of Princeton before he was drafted, had a first sergeant who continually stumbled over the pronunciation of his name. In exasperation, he finally simply called him "Kelly."

A California Nisei remembered when one of his elementary school teachers in Stockton, California, told the class that she had trouble pronouncing the Japanese names and instructed those children to go home and come up with more English-sounding names. Because his father admired Ford automobiles, he took the name "Henry." When another man's father arrived in Hawaii as part of a group of common laborers, immigration officials had difficulty pronouncing their Japanese names. And in the same way that Ellis Island agents often shortened or Anglicized Eastern European names, Hawaiian officials entered them all under the name "Tojo."[12]

The Caucasian officers at Camp Shelby had their task made even more difficult by the fact that large numbers of men had the same surnames. There were, for example forty-six men named Nakamura, including three who also shared a first name; forty Tanakas, three of whom had identical first names; thirty-three Yamamotos, and thirty-one Matsumotos. Sergeant Morita's lineage was also well-represented with over two dozen men answering to that name. One newly minted Caucasian second lieutenant, who had never met anyone of Japanese heritage until he arrived at Camp Shelby, worried that some visiting officer of high rank might require him to name every man in his platoon. To his good fortune that never happened. He admitted that he would have been completely lost if it had.[13]

When the men in the Hawaiian contingent of the new regiment reached Camp Shelby, there was an immediate problem. They had assumed, quite understandably, that some of them would be promoted to the noncommissioned officer ranks when the various companies and battalions were formed. Many of them had brothers or friends in the 100th Battalion who were wearing stripes, but their situation was not the same. Most of the men in the 100th were already in one of the activated national guard regiments when the war began. They had already undergone basic training, and some of them, having proven themselves, had been rewarded with promotions. But the recruits for the 442nd were, for the most part, without any formal military training. Some, it is true, had served briefly in the Hawaii Territorial Guard and then in the Varsity Victory Volunteers, but most were starting their military lives from the very beginning, and they quickly learned that most of the leadership positions were already filled—with mainland Nisei. The cadre was made up of men who usually had more than a year of training behind them. In time, as the new arrivals gained training experience, there would be promotions for them.

A mainland Nisei whose fair complexion earned him the nickname "Whitey" was taken aback by the behavior of the Hawaiians he met at Camp Shelby. "They would squat on the floor," he recalled many years later. "[T]hey'd go barefoot because they weren't used to wearing shoes. They seemed extremely rude and crude in their language." On the other hand, a Hawaiian artilleryman said that the islanders "felt so damned insecure and intimidated because [the mainlanders] spoke better than we did." The men from the mainland spoke mainstream American English. To the Hawaiians, many of whom who had grown up in plantation villages where only the owners and overseers spoke that way, the mainland Nisei came across as haughty and stuck up. When the islanders conversed, on the other hand, they were almost unintelligible to the mainlanders because of the manner in which they spoke.[14]

The style of language—pidgin—that many of the islanders spoke has a long and interesting history. Native Hawaiians probably first heard the English language spoken when Captain James Cook and his British crewmen came ashore in the islands in 1778, but it seems unlikely that this brief exposure had any lasting effect. As time passed, however, Hawaii became a convenient stopping place for traders sailing from North America to China and back again. In Hawaii they could replenish their stocks of food and fresh water before beginning the next leg of their voyage. Language experts theorize that English-speaking traders in the Chinese ports—along with Portuguese merchants who had long preceded them—introduced a vastly simplified form of language to the area so they could do business with one another. The rudiments of this language of business—or *pidgin*, as the Cantonese pronunciation sounded to western ears—eventually made its way eastward to Hawaii.[15]

American missionaries began to arrive in the islands in the 1820s and, along with introducing the natives to Christianity, they also began to teach them English. Interestingly, members of Hawaiian royalty were entranced by this new method of communication and eagerly embraced it. By 1855, there were ten English-language schools in Hawaii, and by the end of the century English had become the official government language and was the instructional language in all the schools. By that time too, however, large numbers of people had begun immigrating to Hawaii to work in the cane fields, and had brought their languages with them. The greatest numbers of these workers came from China (forty-six thousand) and Japan (sixty-one thousand). During the first decade or so of the twentieth century, seventeen thousand Portuguese, six thousand Puerto Ricans, eight thousand Spaniards, and eight thousand Koreans added to the mix. And, finally, some 120,000 Filipinos arrived by about 1930, adding three more languages—Ilocano, Visayan, and Tagalog. These newcomers often worked and lived in close proximity to one another on the sugar plantations, and it became necessary for them to learn to communicate. The pidgin that resulted incorporated not only some of the words from the various languages but the syntaxes as well.[16]

One of the idiosyncrasies of Hawaiian pidgin is the common use of the word "stay" to indicate ongoing action of some kind. For example, a Hawaiian might inquire of one of his companions: "Where you stay go?" To an outsider, this seems to be contradictory gibberish, but the speaker simply means: "Where are you going?" Another frustrating example is the use of the word "get" in place of "to have." A mainland Nisei from Philadelphia experienced a slightly unsettling introduction to pidgin when he reported for KP duty in the mess hall at Camp Shelby. When a deliveryman arrived with a load of ice, he yelled at the mess sergeant: "Do you want any ice?" The sergeant, an islander, yelled back: "Stay get!" What he meant was that he already had enough. All that registered with the young soldier, however, was the word "get," so he had the man proceed with the ice delivery. "The sergeant," remembered the recruit, "gave me hell when he found out that I had told the iceman to bring in the ice."[17]

Other differences also manifested themselves between the two groups. The Hawaiians came from a culture where Japanese Americans made up a significant percentage of the population. They did not, therefore, experience the overt discrimination that some mainlanders did. They were able to develop a group identity that was characterized by a happy-go-lucky, one-for-all-and-all-for-one attitude. This was reflected at Camp Shelby by their free-spending ways. They often received money from home and were not shy about spending it. If one of them wanted to go with a group to the PX for beer but had no money, he went anyway. He knew that someone in the group would buy beer for him. Then, when he had money, he repaid the favor. If a Caucasian soldier got into a fight with an islander at the PX, or anywhere else, he quickly found himself facing every Hawaiian in the place.

The mainland Nisei came from a culture where Japanese Americans were a distinct minority. Many of them remarked that upon reaching Camp Shelby they were astounded to see so many Japanese faces in one place. Some of them had faced open prejudice because of their ancestry. They learned early in life that the smart, safe thing to do was to go along to get along. They kept to themselves and did not want to make waves. Nor were they as free with their money as the islanders. Of course, many of these men had entered the army from relocation camps. They had no money to spend, and much of what they got from Uncle Sam on paydays went to families still in the camps. The Hawaiians saw this as proof of haughtiness, just like the mainlanders' use of "proper" English in conversation.

The two groups soon took on the aspects of rival street gangs. The mainlanders referred to those from Hawaii as "buddhaheads," a common pejorative for Japanese at that time. The islanders called the mainlanders "*kotonks*," a term with several possible origins. Perhaps the most popular version is that it was the sound that resulted when an islander grabbed two mainlanders and banged their heads together—because their heads were hollow. Or that it was the sound that an empty-headed mainlander's head made when it hit the floor after being struck by a Hawaiian's fist.[18]

Sometimes the islanders picked fights with mainlanders for no other reason than that they were mainlanders. When a new arrival from the internment camp at Amache, Colorado, was being shown to his hut at Camp Shelby by an orderly, he was quite startled by the rude reception he received. "Ey," called out a soldier outside the hut, "you one f—— 'kotonk', eh? No get smart around here or I goin' broke you ass!" When he saw what a startling effect he had had on the new arrival, he continued: "You like say something? I like hear what one 'kotonk' sound like. Wass you name? Wassamatta? You no like me or what?" Before the one-sided discussion could proceed any further, a less confrontational soldier emerged from the hut and berated the troublemaker. "Hey, you mudda f——, beat it!" he demanded. "Why you like make trouble? If you like pick on somebody, pick on me. I take you on any day, brah, an' I goin' lick you! G'wan, beat it!" Then, turning to the newcomer, the smiling soldier said: "Don't mind him, he's one bum, always making trouble. . . . We're only jokin' when we call you guys 'kotonks.' We don't mean anything bad. Come. We go meet da udda guys in da hut."[19]

Many years later, Dan Inouye looked back and laughed about the friction. The mainlanders not only spoke more proper English than the island boys, their Japanese was also better in many instances. "If I were a Mainlander," he remembered, "I would have laughed at some of the pidgin that spouted out of the mouths of these Hawaiians." But if a mainlander *had* laughed at the way they spoke, there would have been a fight.[20]

And the rivalry was not confined to islanders vs. mainlanders. Those Nisei living in mainland cities looked down on those in the countryside, and even among the urbanites those from Los Angeles felt themselves far superior to those from smaller cities such as Seattle. Some of the mainlanders from farther inland also found the clothing styles of some of the California Nisei to be more than a little odd. One of Sergeant Morita's fellow Coloradoans, for instance, recalled that "we didn't hit it off with the California boys because they came in with their 'pachuko' haircuts, those zoot suit jackets, those great big hats and the pants that came down just tight around the ankles. . . . We called the California guys 'Yoggadies.'"[21]

The rivalry between the buddhaheads and the kotonks eventually subsided into good-natured ribbing, but not without some violent confrontations. In one instance, islanders singled out a mainland soldier whom they thought talked down to them. One night, after the lights were out, several islanders from a different hut came into the hut where this man was sleeping and administered a severe beating. When another mainlander tried to help the defenseless man, the gang turned on him too. There was talk that if the friction continued, the regiment might be disbanded and all of the men sent as individual replacements to Caucasian units.[22]

Food could also be a source of friction. The islanders did not get as much rice in their standard army fare as they were used to, but learned that they could trade their potatoes to Caucasian units in return for their rice. They also suggested that everyone chip in a couple of dollars per month so the cooks could buy even more rice than was available through barter. Some of the mainlanders, however, resisted. At one point, army officials asked whether the men in the 442nd wanted to be issued the Filipino ration instead of the standard army fare. This ration had lots of rice, but little meat, eggs, or cereals. This never came to pass. Some men relied on packages from home to supplement their diets with Japanese dishes. For a while, one man received weekly boxes from his father containing such delicacies as squid and abalone in addition to rice.[23]

Training activities at Camp Shelby always received coverage in the Hattiesburg newspaper, and it was not unusual for groups of citizens to visit. When it was learned that several members of the local ladies auxiliary were coming to see the Nisei soldiers, the head cook of Company F decided to honor them with a tasty yellow layer cake with a creamy icing on top. He was gratified to see how popular his cake was, but his mood was ruined when he heard one of the ladies declare that she had never tasted better *cornbread*. How could she have compared his creation to something as coarse as cornbread! He waited until the mess hall was clear of these ladies, and then he unceremoniously threw the remainder of his fluffy confection into the nearest garbage cans.[24]

The degree to which the citizens of Hattiesburg and the surrounding area accepted these rather exotic newcomers varied considerably. Many, already imbued with a sense of racial superiority, regarded them as members of another inferior race. One man had the distinct impression that the local people regarded them as they would animals in a zoo. At the opposite end of the spectrum was a local rancher-businessman named Earl Finch who lived with his invalid mother just outside of Hattiesburg. (Finch was only a few years older than most of the young soldiers at Camp Shelby, but flat feet and a weak heart disqualified him for military service.) Driving through the city one cold, blustery afternoon in April, he saw one of the Nisei soldiers idly killing time outside a drugstore. "This kid didn't look like he had a friend in the world," remembered Finch, "and I invited him [and a friend] to the house for Sunday dinner." After enjoying a typical Southern Sunday dinner of fried chicken, the young men returned to camp and Finch went about his business. But the next evening, when he returned from work, these same two soldiers were sitting in his parlor visiting with his mother. They had brought her a bouquet of American Beauty roses as a "thank you" for the generosity and hospitality that she and her son had shown to them the day before. This was the beginning of Earl Finch's commitment to the Japanese American soldiers. His largesse soon became widely known throughout the regiment, and soon he was staging weekend watermelon parties for as many as a hundred men at a time. He hired busses to go to the internment camps at Rohwer and Jerome in Arkansas to bring back young Japanese American women to be the soldiers' dates at dances he sponsored. He even organized a rodeo for them in the summer of 1943, complete with bucking horses and bulls brought in all the way from Oklahoma and New Mexico to his 542-acre ranch.[25]

A few other civilians went out of their way to be friendly to the trainees. The Young Women's Professional Club in nearby Bogalusa, Louisiana, hosted over two dozen Nisei soldiers on a weekend in early June. A few weeks later more than fifty officers and men spent a weekend in New Orleans where the members of the British Seamen's Club arranged an afternoon swimming party and, after a visit to an amusement park, hosted the visitors at a dance.[26]

The presence of a large number of Japanese Americans at Camp Shelby made for an interesting mix of race relations, as it introduced a third race to the rigidly bi-racial society of Mississippi. The officers told the Nisei soldiers that local society considered them to be white instead of "colored." Therefore, they could patronize the better local restaurants, they could sit in the front sections of buses, and they could use the "Whites Only" drinking fountains and restrooms. When some of the men arranged for their families—wives and children—to relocate to Hattiesburg, however, it added an unforeseen problem when it came time to send the children to school. School boards throughout the South held rigidly to the Supreme Court-approved concept of "separate but equal" schools for black and white students. The schools were decidedly "separate," but they were definitely not "equal" in terms of facilities. The law did not allow any non-Caucasian students to attend the whites' school, and the handful of Japanese American parents refused to send their children to the rundown schools set aside for black schoolchildren. School board officials resolved the impasse by renting a one-room house for the Nisei (actually Sansei—or third generation) students and recruiting the mother of one of them to serve as a teacher.[27]

The Nisei soldiers, many of whom had been subjected to overt racism themselves, were nevertheless stunned at the virulence of black-white relations in the South. "We smoldered inside," one of them later recalled, "because . . . when you've suffered at the hands of prejudiced men, it's almost as painful to be on the other side of the fence." Businesses in Hattiesburg—restaurants and movie theaters, for example—were rigidly segregated. When the GIs went to a movie they quickly learned that they were not allowed to sit in the balcony or, as the locals called it, "nigger heaven," because that was set aside for black patrons only. And since these men rode busses back and forth between Camp Shelby and Hattiesburg, they often witnessed alarming examples of blatant prejudice and physical confrontation. State and local laws required that buses have partitions between the seats to be occupied by white and black riders. The whites rode in the front. The blacks rode in the back. Riders attempting to sit in the "wrong" section could be put off the bus by the driver and face a fine for disregard of the ordinance. Drivers who failed to enforce these restrictions also faced fines, but rare indeed was the driver who did not willingly see that his passengers sat in the assigned sections. At a bus station in Hattiesburg, a Nisei GI witnessed a white bus driver beat a black soldier with a blackjack because the man tried to board his bus when the "black" section was already full. Other bus drivers nearby congratulated the abusive driver and shook his hand in admiration of how he dealt with the issue. Local police soon arrived and took the *soldier* off to jail.[28]

Many were the times that black soldiers headed back to camp after a pass could not get a bus to stop and pick them up because its black section was already full. In one instance, a bus driver physically kicked a black soldier off of his bus, whereupon an outraged—and inebriated—soldier of the 442nd administered a beating to the callous driver. Another time, half a dozen Nisei soldiers were waiting for a bus to take them to New Orleans on a weekend pass. When an elderly black woman attempted to get on the bus before all of the waiting whites had boarded the driver stepped off the bus and knocked her down. "I grabbed the bus driver by the shirt," one of the soldiers later recalled, "and dragged him out of the bus. Six of us kicked the hell out of him for knocking that poor black woman down." When word of such episodes reached camp, the officers assembled the men and told them that they would have to live with the situation as it was, that they could not change the mores of an entire region of the country. After a similar incident a battalion officer simply told the men to "take him behind a building and beat him where no one can see you."[29]

The training schedules often provided the men free time on the weekends, and baseball continued to be as popular at Camp Shelby as it had been at Camp McCoy. There were two distinctive leagues at Camp Shelby, one made up of teams representing units assigned to divisions while unattached units formed the other league. In fact, the Nisei entered two teams in this league, one staffed by the infantrymen of the 442nd Infantry Regiment and the other drawn from the men of the 522nd Field Artillery Battalion.

A Headquarters Battery corporal organized the artillery battalion's team, and its opponents included civilian teams as well as other servicemen's teams. And even though there were plenty of teams within Camp Shelby, the men of the 522nd also traveled to the Mississippi towns of Biloxi, Meridian, and Pascagoula to play. Among the Nisei, the 522nd team beat the 100th Battalion in their only game against one another and also defeated the 442nd team in two out of three games.[30]

The infantrymen of the 442nd, however, ultimately won the league championship and faced the winner of the divisional league, the 273rd Infantry Regiment, in a three-game series to determine the Camp Shelby baseball champion. The two teams split the first two games and met for the championship on October 23, 1943. The 442nd was the home team and got off to a bad start as the visitors scored twice in the top of the first. The left-handed Nisei pitcher settled down after that, eventually striking out eight, and his team scored one run in the third and tied the game in the fourth. And that is how the score stood at the end of eight and a half innings. The first batter in the bottom of the ninth made an out before a pinch hitter singled. The right fielder was next and let the first couple of pitches go by. He then drove the ball over the head of the base runner at first and, indeed, over everyone's head and out of the park for a game-winning, championship-clinching home run. The players were jubilant, and Earl Finch was on hand to add to their celebration with huge trophy that he had bought.

In fact, he had been so sure of their ultimate triumph that he had already had it engraved.[31]

At Camp Shelby, the Hawaiian recruits dominated the lighter weight classes in boxing and included a former bantamweight champion of the Territory of Hawaii and another who held the welterweight title for the island of Maui. But Yukito Umeda probably had the most interesting prewar boxing "career." Only sixteen years old when the Japanese attacked Pearl Harbor, he remained at home in Honolulu and continued to box at the Catholic Youth Organization gym. Officials soon decided, however, that to avoid enflaming ethnic passions more than necessary, Japanese American boxers could only fight each other. Disgusted, Umeda told the boxing team manager that he was quitting the ring. The manager thought it over for a few minutes and then told Umeda that he was no longer Yukito Umeda, Japanese American boxer. Now he was Tommy Wong, Chinese American boxer. He boxed under that name until he joined the 442nd upon reaching his eighteenth birthday in early 1943.[32]

Many of the Hawaiians had grown up swimming in plantation canals or in the surf, so when the opportunity arose to participate in competitive swimming there was no shortage of eager volunteers. Eight of the combat team's best swimmers represented the unit at the Southern Amateur Athletic Union Senior Swimming Championship in New Orleans, where they competed against military as well as college swim teams. They returned to Camp Shelby with the first place team trophy and sixteen other medals, including a second place in the three-meter diving competition. Team wins included both the 225-yard and 300-yard relays.[33]

Although sports provided an outlet for any energy the men might still have after their rigorous training, Saturdays often found Nisei soldiers at the Ritz Café on Main Street where, according to a part-time bus boy, they consumed "rather large amounts of beer." But they were also hungry for female companionship. A few Caucasian women were open-minded enough to see past the racial differences and go on dates with some of the men, but the deeply ingrained racial attitudes in the deep South made such pairings fairly rare. And when one of the men actually fell in love and married a local Caucasian girl, members of the Ku Klux Klan

burned a cross on her parents' lawn. There were Japanese American women in the two internment camps in neighboring Arkansas, however, and the enterprising soldiers wasted little time in
arranging meetings.

On Saturday, May 1, three buses pulled into their training area
carrying almost a hundred of these women, along with a half dozen
chaperones, from the camp at Rohwer for a weekend of parties.
The Station Hospital Medical Detachment Orchestra played for
the dance that night, and whenever the band took a break some
musically inclined Hawaiians (and it seemed as if most of them
were) stepped in. Harry Hamada and the Shelby Hawaiians entertained, as did Herbert Sasaki and the Hawaiian Combateers.
The next day the girls, in groups of four, visited and ate lunch
with the soldiers in two dozen mess halls across the camp before
being treated to a baseball game between the infantrymen and
the artillerymen. There were several reunions between siblings
who had not seen one another in many months, but the champion reunion must have been that of Tsuruko Miyagi and her two
brothers. Mrs. Miyagi had left the islands in 1931 to go to school
on the mainland, where she then married and began a family.
She had never returned to Hawaii. Now, after a dozen years apart,
she met up with Susumu and Minoru Kishaba, her two younger
brothers.[34]

Some of the young women felt overwhelmed, and a little intimidated, by the greatly skewed ratio of men to women. Others,
however, rather enjoyed the odds. One of the girls said that she
had never before felt so popular. Another thought the odds were
extremely advantageous. The situation, she said, made "a girl . . .
feel for once in her life just as popular as heck, there being so
many boys to give her attention."[35]

Meanwhile, the girls at Jerome, the other internment camp in
Arkansas, felt shunned because they had not been invited, so the
soldiers invited a hundred of them for the second such weekend
some seven weeks later. In the interim, however, reports reached
Jerome about the decidedly *un*gentlemanly behavior of some of
the soldiers. One of the soldiers even admitted that the "way the
girls were mauled about on the dance floor was a pitiful sight." By

the middle of the last week before the second scheduled dance, more than half of the slots remained unfilled, so the call went out to the Rohwer girls too. Eighty-three young women finally made the trip, including a few from Rohwer who had gone in May. Obviously, their experience then had not been an unpleasant one.[36]

The visits by the girls from Arkansas' internment camps had proven, in spite of a few negative incidents, generally popular. At the end of July, about three dozen officers and men of the Combat Team's 232nd Engineer Combat Company returned the favor by visiting Jerome. There was the usual well-chaperoned dance on Saturday and optional church services on Sunday morning. The engineers played a baseball game against a camp team in the afternoon and lost 10–6 before heading back to Shelby and another week of training. When it came time for the engineers to host the girls from the internment camps in mid-September they put their technical training to use. In addition to the usual dance on Saturday night and the round of visits on Sunday, the engineers took the girls for boat rides in their river assault boats on the Leaf River, just north of camp.[37]

The young Nisei soldiers found other ways to amuse themselves in their spare time. Beer-drinking and gambling seem to have been among the favorite diversions. A 3rd Battalion man had a unique method of drinking his beer. He wore his raincoat to the PX even though there was no chance of rain in the weather forecast. He explained that he tended to get sloppy when he drank too much, and the raincoat would protect his uniform from spills or other accidents. "By his fifth beer," commented one of his buddies, "his raincoat has done its duty and he's telling me where the army can shove the short-order drills and the ten-mile hikes. I agree with him even without a raincoat."[38]

And among the gamblers, craps seems to have been one of the favorite games. Future U.S. senator Dan Inouye was particularly successful with the dice. Back in Hawaii he had won $800 at Schofield Barracks while he and the other recruits waited for orders to ship out to the mainland, and he continued his winning ways at Camp Shelby. "I cleaned up," he said, averaging $1,500 in winnings every month.[39]

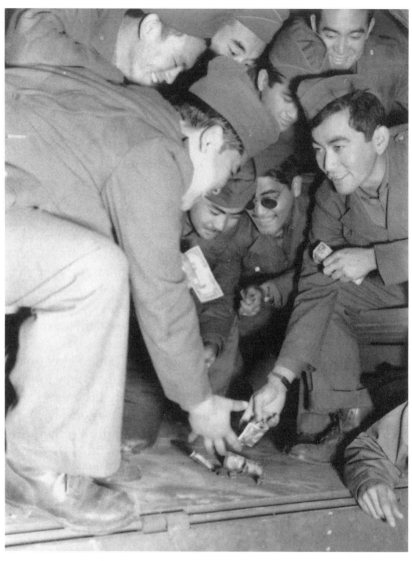

Any flat surface will serve to support a game of craps. Here soldiers use the floor of a truck. Signal Corps photo.

Lieutenant Colonel Sherwood Dixon, commanding the 3rd Infantry Battalion, urged his men to stage weekly talent shows as a way for them to keep busy on the weekends when there were no girls in camp, and each company took its turn. These shows combined singing, dancing, magic acts, and anything else the men could come up with. There were, as one might expect, some instances where things did not go quite as planned. One man volunteered his abilities as an escape artist, but was not as skilled as he had advertised. "The magician," according to the local newspaper, "overestimated his ability to get out of the ropes. Tied up early in the show, he was still writhing in his meshes when the show closed and the audience had departed." Entertainment usually ran to the musical, but one of Sergeant Morita's Colorado friends brought down the house with a striptease act, followed by an all-male chorus line doing the can-can—or trying to—in ankle-length dresses and heavy army-issue footwear. Company K's show on May 26 was probably typical. A member of the Hawaiian Combateers served as master of ceremonies and introduced the Company K Serenaders, who sang "Across the Sea." Next up were the Company K Tumblers, followed by a harmonica soloist. Another soldier demonstrated the latest jitterbug-style dance steps, and one of the officers played his trumpet in the manner of popular bandleader Harry James. Officer participation presented the men with some interesting choices. If they did not respond enthusiastically, they worried, the officers might "reward" them with extra duty. Hoping to obviate such an outcome following the performance of three singing officers from Company L, someone held up a sign to the audience that read: "Clap Like Hell."[40]

No regiment is complete without its own official band, and the 442nd was certainly going to be complete. Auditions began in mid-June, and it soon became apparent that there was no shortage of musical talent among the Nisei GIs from which to form such an organization. The hope was to field forty qualified musicians, some of whom might also double in a thirteen-piece orchestra. Sergeant Harry Hamada, who already had put together the Shelby Hawaiians, had no difficulty in qualifying for the new band. He could play either the string bass or the saxophone. Among the aspirants were at least two other men who had been band leaders before the war. The new band's official name was the 206th Army Ground Forces Band.[41]

The short Nisei soldiers were at a decided disadvantage when it came to marching. It would not have been so bad if their officers had also been Japanese Americans, but the tall Caucasian officers had much longer strides than their men. "We were supposed to walk fast for three minutes," remembered one soldier "then slow down for three, but with our short legs, we were running all the time to keep up with the lieutenant." Another recruit complained that his company commander was so tall that he had to take three steps to every one of the officer's just to keep up.[42]

In addition to calisthenics and road marches that the trainees were subjected to on a regular basis, they also had to traverse an obstacle course to test their physical fitness and stamina. The course was laid out over fifteen hundred feet and was to be completed in no more than three and a half minutes. There was no time for dawdling. The first obstacle was an eight-foot wall that had to be clambered over. Then the trainees had to leap across a trench and weave through a series of pickets before wriggling through a long section of pipe and climbing a ten-foot rope. A five-foot fence was next and then a seven-foot-wide trench that they had to swing across on a rope. On the other side of the trench was a twelve-foot ladder that each soldier climbed up one side and down the other. Then they had to negotiate a one-foot-wide, twenty-foot-long beam elevated seven feet above the ground and then swing hand-over-hand along a fifteen-foot-long horizontal ladder. Finally, they clambered under one fence and over another before sprinting to the finish line. And they did not run this course in shorts and t-shirts, but in full combat gear, carrying a rifle and a thirty-pound backpack.[43]

It could be difficult for the men to remain attentive to the sometimes boring field lectures while squatting on their helmets in the energy-sapping Mississippi heat. Some of the men began to wear dark sunglasses that effectively hid their eyes from their instructors and allowed them to nod off; if, that is, they could maintain their balance on their steel perches. Barney Hajiro, a twenty-seven-year-old draftee from Maui, found that he could get out of some of the training by reporting to sick call with some real or imagined illness. At other times, soldiers' inattention led to comical exchanges, as when a Company I officer noticed a man apparently nodding off. "You are on guard duty," the lieutenant yelled at the startled soldier. "Here comes an enemy battleship, straight at you. What do you do?" Thinking quickly, the man replied that he would sink it with a torpedo. "And where do you get the torpedo?" the officer smugly inquired. "The same place you got the battleship, sir," was the reply.[44]

The training eventually took on a more realistic aspect when machine guns fired live ammunition over the men's heads as they crawled under barbed wire entanglements. The gunners were careful to keep their fire well above the soldiers, but even then accidents sometimes occurred. A bullet apparently struck one of the vertical metal poles to which the barbed wire was fastened and ricocheted downward, inflicting a fatal wound to one of the trainees.[45]

On June 13, after perhaps a week of weapons familiarization training, the Nisei soldiers boarded trucks that took them to the rifle range at Camp Claiborne, Louisiana, to try to put into practice what their instructors had been teaching them. Camp Claiborne, about 220 miles west of Shelby, was not as large as Camp Shelby, but it had plenty of space for all types of weapons training. For two days, the men of the 100th Battalion got in a lot of instructive practice firing their rifles, machine guns, and mortars. One man reported that his twelve-man squad had to share one rifle, which meant that at any given time eleven of the men were merely spectators.[46]

When it came time for the 3rd Battalion to qualify with the M1 the men faced the added difficulty of torrential rains. Nevertheless, all 824 men had to qualify within two days, because after that another battalion would arrive for its turn. By the end of the second day, almost 98 percent of the men had fired well enough to achieve at least the status of marksman. Most of the men who failed only missed the minimum score by a few points, but there were a few men who just could not seem to get the hang of it. "In justice to them," their battalion commander commented, "it must be said they all wore glasses thicker than the soles of their shoes and couldn't see the front sight of an M-1 without a telescope. I don't know how they ever got into the Army in the first place, but I certainly admired their spirit for trying."[47]

One soldier had an added problem. He was left-eye-dominant, and the only way he could shoot at and hit anything was if he shot left-handed. His instructors were insistent that he learn to shoot right-handed, so he rigged up a special pair of shooting glasses to help him. Actually, they were just the cheapest pair of glasses he could find because he did not need any vision correction. Instead, he removed the lens from the right side and stuffed a tissue between the left lens and his eye. That way, he would have to use his right eye to shoot. Ironically, when he reached Italy his officers and sergeants were not so picky about how he shot, just as long as he had a reasonable chance of hitting what he aimed at, so he reverted to shooting left-handed.[48]

During World War II all soldiers received training in the proper use of the bayonet. Handy for opening tin cans or a myriad of other uses, the bayonet rarely saw service as a weapon. A trainee bound for the 94th Division had a bayonet instructor who was fresh from combat in Italy. "One day," he told the men, drawing on his recent experience, "I came around a corner and met a giant of a German soldier who had a bayonet on his rifle too. He grinned and went into the on guard position, ready for a bayonet duel. I grinned, crouched into position, and pulled the trigger. The poor German was shocked at my ethics, but I won the duel." This instructor believed that the bayonet was most useful when guarding prisoners. "It scares hell out of them," he said. "As long as you have ammunition," he told them, "don't consider using a bayonet. If you run out of ammunition, you should first consider running." It was better, according to the old saying, to "run away and live to fight another day."[49]

No one quite knew how the large number of Caucasian soldiers already training at Camp Shelby would react to the influx of Japanese Americans. The camp commander, hoping to prevent hostile confrontations among his command, suggested that the Nisei have their own separate PX so they would not have to rub elbows with Caucasian soldiers when they went for an occasional beer or two. Colonel Pence opposed such a plan, suggesting that it seemed to put some sort of stigma on his soldiers. No separate PX was built.[50]

On July 7, a new training company, designated Company S, joined the combat team, at least temporarily. Its members were Nisei soldiers from the Military Intelligence Service Language School at Camp Savage, Minnesota. They had completed their language training, but before shipping them out to various units in the Pacific, the army sent them to Camp Shelby for eight weeks of basic combat training.[51]

Occasionally, officers from the language school combed through the ranks of the men at Camp Shelby to find more men to train as interpreters and translators for the war against Japan. Applicants who were already fluent in Japanese had the best chance for a transfer. Those men, after all, would require the least amount of preparation for deployment to the Pacific. The language skills of others were not sufficiently high to be useful to the intelligence branch. In fact, out of approximately thirty-seven hundred Nisei soldiers who applied for transfer, only about one hundred possessed the requisite language skills.[52]

Applicants for transfer typically faced an interview with a Nisei sergeant in order to weed out the ones who did not demonstrate a sufficient grasp of the language. In one such interview, the sergeant handed the applicant a book written in Japanese and asked him to read it. The soldier was in over his head. He could not read a single word. "No, this is too hard for me," he replied and handed it back. "Try this one," the sergeant said. "This one is easier." And it was easier, although it was still too difficult for the soldier, and he handed it back also. With the third, and easiest, book the soldier's face brightened momentarily. "I know some of that!" he proudly announced. He finally ruefully admitted that, like many Nisei, he had dutifully gone to Japanese school as a young man but had not really learned much. He probably never thought that it would be of much value to him. "But I'd *like* to go to language school," he implored. "I'm a good learner."

To his great surprise he was accepted for transfer. The required paperwork would take a couple of weeks to process, but he could not help but feel relieved to be transferring out of the infantry and into what he assumed to be a less dangerous situation. For the next couple of weeks he and the others selected with him looked at every road march they made and every foxhole they dug as quite possibly the last of either they would ever have to accomplish. When he finally saw his name posted on the bulletin board with others for transfer, however, he was disappointed. He was leaving Camp Shelby, but he was not headed north toward Minnesota. He was going to Italy to join the 100th Battalion.[53]

Not every man who volunteered for training was accepted. One man, drafted after the 100th Battalion had already gone to Europe and begun to establish itself as a fighting outfit, began to realize the true gravity of being in the army when he saw the lists of casualties from this outfit that regularly appeared in the newspapers. So when a recruiter for the language school came around, he decided that that might be a less dangerous way to serve. The recruiter, in order to test his language proficiency, showed him a piece of paper with a Japanese character on it and asked him if he recognized it. He did not. The trainer showed him several more characters, but he recognized none of them. Finally, he recognized a character used in the spelling of his own name. "Soldier," the recruiter informed him, "by the time we train you, the war will be over."[54]

Although Sergeant Morita spoke Japanese, there is no indication that he ever considered requesting a transfer. Perhaps, like many first-generation Americans, he possessed sufficient knowledge of the language for him to communicate verbally with his parents but not enough to read or write it. Or, again like many other men in the unit, he might have reasoned that he had a better chance of proving his loyalty in combat against the Germans than by translating Japanese messages and interrogating Japanese prisoners, and therefore did not seek such a transfer.[55]

On July 20, 1943, the men of the 100th Battalion paraded for a very special purpose. This was the day they would receive their distinctive unit flag. The members of the unit had agreed to a battalion motto while they were still at Camp McCoy. "Remember Pearl Harbor," was a very fitting slogan for these sons of Hawaii. Also to be emblazoned on the banner was a representation of a particular leaf that was thought to ward off evil and an ancient Hawaiian helmet of yellow feathers. After sending these details to Washington for the official blessing of those who design army heraldry, Colonel Turner was stunned to learn that the design had been turned down. In its place was a picture of a red dagger and the motto, "Be of Good Cheer." He raised such a ruckus that the army capitulated and allowed the original design, and that is what was on the banner presented to the assembled battalion on that hot summer day.[56]

After receipt of its distinctive flag there was little else for the battalion to do to prepare itself for actual combat. The men had been together, training, for over a year. This was longer than the training some units received that had already shipped out. During July, most of the men received ten-day furloughs, and since Hawaii was too far away for them to go to see family members before shipping out, they contented themselves with visiting cities like New York or Chicago.

Almost all of the men signed up for GI insurance policies that would pay their next of kin in the event of their death while in the service. Even some of those whose next of kin were in Japan eventually signed up to have the premiums deducted from their pay. And as all of the last-minute paperwork was nearing completion they also submitted to final physical examinations. A half dozen failed and replacements from the new 442nd Regiment were hastily transferred into their former slots.

At last the day came—August 11—when the men boarded trains to leave Camp Shelby. Two days later they arrived at Camp Kilmer, New Jersey. Named for the poet—and World War I casualty—Joyce Kilmer, this camp was part of the huge New York City port of embarkation for troops going to Europe. The Nisei soldiers did not have long to wait. Orders arrived at midnight on August 20 for the men to proceed to the dock. There they were ferried over to Staten Island to board the SS *James Parker.*

After being aboard all day the men finally saw the New York skyline start to recede along with the sun on August 21. The ship was crowded, and many of the passengers had to take turns sleeping in the limited number of bunks provided. The sea remained calm, helping to cut down on the number of cases of seasickness, and the men spent their idle time playing cards, rolling dice, singing island songs, and just shooting the breeze with one another. Twelve days later, on September 2, 1943, the *James Parker* reached Oran, Algeria.[57]

A few days after the 100th Battalion sailed from New York, a Third Army inspection team arrived at Camp Shelby on August 23 to evaluate the men of the 442nd. Over the next six days the men demonstrated what they had learned. They performed speed marches and engaged in small-unit tactical exercises. They answered questions on such seemingly insignificant topics as the nomenclature of the army gas mask. And inspectors visited their living quarters, mess halls, and supply rooms to make sure that everything therein was up to army requirements. When the ratings were in they showed grades of "Excellent" in physical fitness of the men and "Very Satisfactory" in everything else.[58]

Also at about this time, several hundred new soldiers arrived at Camp Shelby, but they were not there for training. For them, the war was over. They were German veterans of the *Afrikakorps* who had been captured in the waning days of the North African campaign and would now sit out the rest of the war in American prison camps. Clad in obsolete U.S. Army fatigue uniforms of blue denim, with "PW" stenciled on them in several locations in a contrasting color, some of these men were glad to be away from the killing. Many found prison food better than their military rations. "I can hardly manage to eat all the food," a German noncommissioned officer confided to his diary.[59]

With so many young American men in the military during the war, it was difficult to find enough laborers to perform necessary agricultural work. One solution was to employ German prisoners of war at this task. Thus, only about a week after their arrival, Camp Shelby's newest residents boarded trucks on Sunday, September 5, and, along with guards from the 442nd, headed for the peanut fields of southeastern Alabama. Traveling only during daylight hours, the trucks passed through Mobile and then turned northeast, finally stopping for the day at Andalusia, Alabama.

Before beginning the next day's leg of the trip, the American battalion commander, Colonel Hanley, remonstrated with his German counterpart. "I thought these were German soldiers," Hanley remarked. The German officer snapped to attention. "*Jawohl*," he said, "*Deutsch Soldaten.*" Hanley then motioned for him to follow, and they walked over to the area where the Germans had camped the night before. It was covered with litter of various sorts, and the German officer needed no further prodding. He ordered his soldiers off the trucks, and within a very short time they had policed up the area until it was spotless.[60]

The second day's drive brought the convoy to a temporary prison camp on the outskirts of the city of Dothan. Each morning trucks loaded with prisoners rolled out of the camp toward Headland, about fifteen miles northeast of Dothan, or to Newton, some twenty miles to the northwest. Civilian farmers met the trucks and then transported the number of workers that they needed for the day to their fields. Guard details followed in army trucks. The work day ran from about 8:00 A.M. to 4:00 P.M. There was a one-hour lunch break during which time the workers sought to find a shady place to eat the three sandwiches each was provided.[61]

The Germans and their American guards got along very well with one another. The Nisei guarded the German POWs with unloaded rifles—although they had ammunition in their cartridge belts. There was one instance (at least there was *rumored* to have been one instance), where a guard fired his rifle, but it was not at a prisoner. According to the story, one of the soldiers decided to shoot at a crow that was roosting in a nearby tree, but missed it. The Germans, who had stopped to eat lunch, ribbed him good-naturedly about his poor marksmanship. He then handed his rifle to one of them to see if he would have any better luck—and he did![62]

About the only physical altercations that occurred were between the guards. One evening, Barney Hajiro arrived late for the evening meal. The mess hall was closed and the cooks told him he was out of luck; that they were not opening up the mess hall just for him. The hungry, and by this time belligerent, soldier challenged one of the other men to a fight—an infraction that occasioned Hajiro's first court-martial.[63]

Although some of the prisoners were extremely dedicated Nazis, most of them got along fairly well with their Japanese American guards. At the end of each day in the peanut fields the workers marched back into a double barbed wire stockade for the night. The GIs camped nearby. Special Services troops occasionally showed movies at night, mounting a movie screen on the back of an army truck that was positioned so all could see the film. The POWs eagerly crowded up against the edge of their stockade to watch. One night, after the movie was over, some Germans began to sing. And after a beautiful rendition of "Lili Marlene," the Nisei decided to sing one of the popular songs of the day. Colonel Hanley later recalled that the Germans had far outshone their hosts in the music department. "It was pretty bad," he remembered; "the contrast could make a man cry. It was embarrassing."[64]

On several occasions the guards, who had had the benefit of late night socializing, used their days to catch up on sleep while the prisoners worked away. Then, upon hearing the approach of an American jeep, the prisoners would wake their dozing guards so they would not get into trouble.[65]

The Nisei soldiers continued to encounter Caucasians in Alabama who seemed completely unaware that the men before them in uniforms were as American as they were. One of the men met a young college girl and had an interesting conversation with her. He noticed the titles of the school books she was carrying and commented on the fact that one of them was on algebra. Stunned, the coed asked him where he had learned to speak English so well. "Oh, on the way," he innocently told her, "when they told us we were coming to America, we read the book, and tried to learn English."[66]

With the harvest complete the prisoners and their guards headed back to Mississippi, arriving at Camp Shelby on October 3. A sad note attached to all of this was the death in a traffic accident of two members of the combat team's medical detachment on September 16 between Geneva and Dothan, Alabama.[67]

Camp Shelby, indeed most U.S. military bases, provided rather limited opportunities for off-duty entertainment beyond what the PX or local movie theaters might offer. But it was private enterprise, with government urging, that stepped in to alleviate boredom and improve soldier morale. In 1940, long before America's entry into the war, Army Chief of Staff General George Marshall called for measures to make soldier life more bearable, and in early 1941 six separate entities got together and chartered the United Service Organization (USO). Funded entirely by donations, the USO established centers adjacent to military bases all across the country where soldiers could relax in their off-duty hours. These centers usually provided free coffee and snacks and often hosted dances and other social functions intended to combat feelings of homesickness among the troops. Because no individual USO center could handle the huge number of men at Camp Shelby, several smaller centers were established. And, in deference to the well-entrenched racial attitudes of most white Mississippians at the time, these centers were segregated. Four served Camp Shelby's white soldiers and one served its black soldiers; and there was even a separate facility for Jewish soldiers. But the Nisei presented a special problem, being neither white nor black. Ultimately a seventh USO center, dubbed the Aloha Center, catered to them.[68]

The artillerymen finished their basic training on August 30, and many of them began enjoying fifteen-day furloughs in early September. Some of the mainlanders used the time to visit their families in the relocation camps. Others, and in fact most of the islanders, went off in search of excitement. For some it was as near as Jackson, Mississippi, or New Orleans or Chicago. For others the lure of New York City was too much to resist, and they spent their time visiting the standard tourist attractions but also patronizing the Miyako Restaurant where they could eat their fill of traditional Japanese food.

There were some administrative changes to the battalion at about this time. The anti-tank platoon that had been part of the Headquarters Battery was dissolved, allowing the infantry regiment's antitank company to handle all such chores.

By the fall of 1943, army planners finally got around to adding a cannon company to the 442nd Regiment. The purpose of this unit, which by then was being added to almost all infantry regiments, was to provide the parent unit with added organic firepower. There would be times, after all, when the 522nd Artillery Battalion's twelve 105mm howitzers would be unavailable to

Japanese American trainees receive instruction on the 37mm anti-tank gun. Signal Corps photo.

support the 442nd. Cannon Company, as a permanent part of the regiment, would always be on hand with six howitzers of its own.

Cannon Company's commander, Captain Edwin Shorey, faced difficult staffing problems because by the time his company came into existence almost all of the Nisei soldiers with any artillery experience had already become part of the 522nd. He was able to find only one man with prior artillery training. The rest of the men came from the infantry battalions of the 442nd.[69]

Training for the new company was necessarily fast-paced. The men had a lot to absorb if they were to be able to perform on the same level as the men in the artillery battalion. Their training began in early October, and by the 19th they were active on the artillery firing range. A few weeks later, six men went to the Gulf Coast of Texas to undergo training on how to hit moving targets with their jeep-mounted .50-caliber machine guns. The training was very much like that received by army air force gunners, whereby they fired at large sleeve targets towed by low-flying airplanes. They might not ever be called upon to shoot at enemy planes, but there might come a time when such skills could be used against enemy trucks or tanks.[70]

By the time the 100th Battalion had landed in North Africa, the men of the 442nd had undergone four months of rigorous training. During that time over four hundred of them had proven themselves worthy of promotion. When the time came to award the additional stripes, however, the regiment's officers seemed to go out of their way to give the majority of them to men from the islands. For example, of the fifty promotions in the infantry battalions that were announced on September 11, only two went to soldiers from the mainland. And of the forty-one men selected for promotion in the 232nd Engineer Combat Company, only one was a mainlander![71]

At the end of the 522nd's unit phase of training in November, officers from the IX Corps put the battalion through its paces. All of the firing batteries sailed through, with Battery C performing so well as to earn a letter of commendation from the commanding general of the corps artillery. The battalion, as a whole, also met all expectations.[72]

In mid-November Sergeant Morita finally received orders for advanced training. He reported to Fort Sill, Oklahoma, home of the field artillery, on November 18 for communications training. After a couple of days of orienting himself to his new surroundings, Morita and 153 other men from various field artillery battalions reported for their first day of training on Monday, November 22. His classes had barely started, however, when he and others at the post celebrated Thanksgiving with a traditional feast that included turkey and gravy and a list of side dishes that would have pleased many a gourmand. Army officials in all the training camps made an extra effort to ensure that all the men in the unit got special food that day to mark the occasion. The soldiers who were out on maneuvers ate their turkey dinners under field conditions, but the food enjoyed by some of the men back at Camp Shelby was certainly not what most Americans ate that day. Their feast featured not only the traditional turkey dinner, but also raw fish, fried rice, and pickled vegetables to give the meal an island flavor.[73]

Morita and his classmates put in almost forty-eight hours each week in learning their new skills. The first four weeks of schooling were the same for everyone. This included, of course, the basics of communication but also such topics as map reading, camouflage, intelligence, and the workings of the message center. The class then separated into three groups. One group, the wire section, learned the intricacies of laying and maintaining communications wire in combat situations. The other two sections of the class concerned themselves with radio communication. The men in one of the groups—"radio section one"—trained to be radio operators and the others went to "radio section two" where they received more technically-oriented instruction so they would be better prepared to go on to take the Radio Repairman Course. Selection for these advanced courses was very competitive, but Sergeant Morita's performance was such that he was tabbed for radio section two. He applied himself diligently and was honored with a certificate of completion on February 12, 1944. Seven of his classmates had dropped out along the way.[74]

A few days after Sergeant Morita began his classes at Fort Sill, the men of the artillery battalion left Camp Shelby for the Third Army Maneuvers held in western Louisiana from late November 1943 until late January 1944. At various times during this training exercise, the 522nd worked with the 89th Infantry Division, the 97th Infantry Division, and the 86th Infantry Division. The objective of this training was to expose the men as much as possible to combat conditions. They practiced the dozens, if not hundreds, of things necessary for the functioning of a field artillery battalion in action. These included: locating firing positions for the guns; digging in the guns; camouflaging the gun positions; digging individual foxholes or trenches; setting up communications networks, both by wire and by radio; locating and manning observation posts; operating the fire direction center; and then doing everything all over again at a different location.

Putting artillery fire accurately onto a target required complex calculations. Most artillery fire during World War II was indirect; that is, the targets were not visible from the location of the guns. Instead, forward observation teams went into the front lines attached to a particular infantry unit to locate targets. These might consist of enemy artillery positions, columns of armored tanks or self-propelled guns, enemy troop concentrations, and anything else that might hinder the advance of the American infantry. Each team usually consisted of an officer, a scout/rifleman, a radio operator, and another man to carry extra radio batteries. When a team located a likely target, the officer had to plot the target's precise location onto a grid map and then radio this information back to the battalion's fire direction center. He then maintained radio contact until the target was destroyed.

The artillerymen at battalion then plotted the location of the target on their copy of the same map. Precise calculations were then made to locate the target relative to the locations of the guns. This gave a horizontal angle, and even a tiny error in this calculation could result, depending upon how far away the target was, in the rounds landing hundreds of yards off target. The horizontal distance to the target had to be measured with a similar degree of precision, and the elevation of the target compared to the elevation of the howitzers had to be factored as well in order for the gunners to estimate the size of the powder charge needed to propel the rounds to the target.

Usually the forward observer, after radioing the target location back to battalion, would ask the gunners to fire a marking round before loosing the first salvo. Then, when he saw where that round landed, he called in any adjustments needed to bring the guns on target. Of course, for the observer on a battlefield that was being pounded by multiple batteries, identifying the marking round from his own guns was no easy task. So as soon as the gunners pulled their lanyards the observer would hear, "Number one on the way!" Then, when the computed time of flight of the projectile had elapsed, he heard "Splash!" When he saw an explosion at the exact same instant that he heard the word "splash" he knew that was his marking round. If the marking round had been correctly ranged but was off to one side of the target, the observer would instruct the gunners to bring the next round in to the left or right by so many yards. Similarly, if the marking round fell long or short, the observer transmitted the appropriate correction. Two or more marking rounds might be needed for the guns to be on target, a process that usually did not take more than a minute or so. When a marking round struck the target, the observer instructed the gunners to "fire for effect." Then, every gun in the battery—or every gun in the battalion if the importance of the target warranted it—began laying rounds onto the target in what was hoped would be a devastating barrage.

The type of target also dictated the type of fuse to be used on the projectiles. If the target was a group of German tanks, for example, the gunners would apply fuses that detonated upon impact with the vehicles. But if, instead, the target was a massed group of infantry the gunner would use time fuses. These fuses were designed to burst above the ground, thereby spraying the target area with lethal shards of shrapnel. For these rounds to have maximum effect it was imperative that the calculations establishing the distance to the target and the relative elevation of the target be precise.

Soldiers on the receiving end of artillery fire typically dove for cover after the first round arrived. Artillerists therefore sometimes employed the "time on target" method, which was particularly useful against large masses of troops or vehicles. It involved making calculations that allowed every gun in a battalion to hit the same target simultaneously. Sometimes several battalions were tied in with the observer for time-on-target fires, and the results could be devastating for those on the receiving end.

In the event that the forward observation teams could not get close enough on the ground to potential targets, they could take to the air. The battalion, as part of its standard equipment, had a couple of Piper Cub aircraft to be used for spotting likely targets. These aircraft, as one aerial observer wrote after more than seventy combat missions in one, "do not and can not take the place of ground observation but, properly used, they do greatly amplify and complement it." The pilots, all Caucasians, flew the airplanes while observers in the back seats made the necessary calculations when they located a target, and then radioed its coordinates to the battalion's fire direction center.[75]

The weather during the training maneuvers was cold and rainy much of the time, and it was not unusual for the men to have to brush frost off of their sleeping bags when they awoke in the morning. One soldier remembered this time years later as the worst winter of his life, even though he and his comrades would endure worse weather in Europe. Fortunately, the men occasionally received passes to go into the neighboring towns to enjoy whatever they had to offer. And the USO sponsored movies in the camps.[76]

One of the artillery radio operators, a man who had become quite proficient before the war with a ham radio, used his considerable expertise to add a little levity to the maneuvers. He regularly tuned in to the radio traffic of one of the opposing artillery battalions until he became fairly familiar with its routine and the names of its officers. Finally, he got on his radio and called the "enemy" battery, telling its men that their captain had just instructed him to tell them to get packed up and ready to relocate the battery within one hour. This, of course, led to a considerable amount of confusion in the "enemy" battery and some knee-slapping laughter for the Nisei.[77]

Volunteering for service among Japanese Americans was still not reaching the levels desired by the army, so the Selective Service System again reclassified Japanese Americans I-A on November 18, 1943, and began calling them up in January 1944. Infantry battalion training could not wait for new draftees to arrive and began on November 23. This phase of the training presented officers and men with tactical problems that required them to maneuver in larger bodies than before. One of the great difficulties was in controlling the movements of these units through wooded or hilly terrain while remaining in contact with higher headquarters.

The three infantry battalions that formed the regiment began field training on December 13, but Colonel Pence brought them back to the relative comfort of their huts on the day before Christmas. The wives of the enlisted Nisei had spent weeks transforming the Aloha USO Center into a special place for the holiday. On the walls hung paintings of tropical flowers and scenes of the Hawaiian countryside. A large Christmas tree dominated the center of the room, and around it were wrapped packages for the soldiers. There was a program of Christmas carols on Christmas Eve, and on Christmas night the packages under the tree were handed out to the happy soldiers. All of these men, whether from the islands or from the internment camps, were far from home, and many families in Hattiesburg and the surrounding area invited one or two men each to come into their homes and share the holiday spirit with them.[78]

Sergeant Morita and other members of the battalion on detached duty at Fort Sill enjoyed a Christmas dinner that was every bit as lavish as their Thanksgiving meal had been. They were lucky. The artillerymen on maneuvers in Louisiana were subjected to one of the coldest and wettest winters in recent memory, and they spent Christmas on the muddy roads of Louisiana moving to another position. It was almost midnight before the movement was complete, and there were no turkey dinners for most of the men. Camping in ice-covered tents was an unpleasant experience but one that was destined to be repeated when the Nisei GIs reached Europe.[79]

The infantry and combat engineers of the 442nd Regiment were attached to the 69th Division for its D-Series (or divisional) army maneuvers that began in the De Soto National Forest in Mississippi on January 28, 1944. Such large-scale maneuvers usually provided the final training that units received before shipping out for Europe or the Pacific. They lasted twenty-four hours per day, rain or shine, in order to give both commanders and soldiers a realistic experience of what likely lay in store for them. Opposing forces were designated as either the red force or the blue force, and the individuals within those organizations wore appropriately colored armbands for identification.

To add a sense of urgency and realism teams of umpires roamed through the woods and swamps in their jeeps. Each umpire team consisted of an officer, an assistant, a radio operator, and a driver, and it was up to the officer to determine the tactical success or failure of each element based upon the relative firepower of the engaged units. For example, if two platoons, one from the red force and one from the blue force, encountered one another and opened fire—using blanks, of course—the umpire had to decide which side would likely have defeated the other. He did this through a system of weighted values placed upon different weapons. He would count the number of rifles, machine guns, and automatic rifles on each side to see which one had the statistical edge. He then awarded victory to that side and ordered the other side to retreat.

There were limitations as to how realistic these war games could become. During the previous summer, an infantry commander wanted to move his unit but was concerned that "enemy" observers might be able to detect the movement. Therefore, he radioed back to the artillery to fire smoke shells to provide a smokescreen to his front that would shield his men's movements. When the artillery was unable to comply someone suggested that he would just have to pretend that a smokescreen existed where he needed it. This suggestion did little to mollify an already frustrated officer. "How can you pretend you had smoke," he fumed, "when the enemy was sitting there two or three hundred yards away watching your every move?" An umpire with a background in ordnance came to the rescue. He wired several white phosphorous grenades at intervals along a one hundred-yard line between the opposing forces and hooked them up to electric detonators. He then attached blasting caps and fuses to some four-ounce blocks of TNT. Then, holding one of these home-made charges in his hand, he had another man ignite the fuse. He then threw the charge as high and as far as he could. The resulting explosions were fairly good approximations of artillery air bursts, and when he set off the strings of white phosphorous grenades they provided a very believable smokescreen. Unfortunately, the pyrotechnics soon started a grassfire that ultimately burned up about twenty acres of pasture.[80]

The weather during the first ten days of the maneuvers was clear and cold, about what one could expect for that time of year. During this time the 442nd was part of the 69th Division's Blue Force. After the arrival of the 522nd Artillery Battalion, the Nisei soldiers became the "enemy" Red Force, and the weather deteriorated with the addition of rain and wind. These war games consisted of six field problems. In the first three the Nisei acted as part of the parent unit, and in the last three they portrayed an enemy force. During these exercises one of the men from regimental headquarters found a copy of a 69th Division codebook that someone had dropped. It was then an easy matter to generate fake orders that sent various elements of the 69th on all sorts of wild goose chases.[81]

Whenever they had a chance, the men built gasoline-fed bonfires to keep warm. "The redolence of burning pine needles," recalled one man, "was sullied by the smell of scorched woolen sox and charred leather boots as the miserable men crowded the leaping flames." Nor were officers immune to the rough going. "There is nothing as miserable," confided a battalion chaplain to his wife, "as getting up in the morning at below freezing temperature in this god forsaken [*sic*] land . . . to go marching along through the thickets and the jungles through swampland in icy water up to your knees, to ford rivers and run up and down hills"[82]

During these maneuvers an umpire halted the 2nd Battalion as it marched down a country road. He told the battalion commander, Colonel Hanley, to assume that the enemy had planted mines in the road ahead and that he had to figure out how to move his men safely past the mines. He also told Hanley that his men were not allowed to avoid the mines simply by leaving the road and marching through the adjacent fields. These instructions were designed to test how well the officers and men would adjust to rapidly changing circumstances on a battlefield. While the men rested nearby, Hanley pondered the problem. He recalled that his men had just passed a small herd of cows, so he sent one of his noncommissioned officers back to ask a favor of the cows' owner. Soon the farmer appeared with his cattle, driving the animals straight down the middle of the road. When the animals had reached a point about fifty yards ahead of the men, the battalion commander started his troops forward, right behind the cows. The umpire again stopped the column. Had he not made himself clear? he wondered. Again he told the commander that he was to assume that there were enemy mines in the road ahead. Colonel Hanley smugly instructed the umpire to assume that the cows had set off all of the assumed mines that were in the road and had, in fact, also provided the commissary with a considerable amount of fresh beef in the process. And on marched the 2nd Battalion. Such examples of improvisation were, of course, valuable in ascertaining how well individual officers adapted to the fluid conditions of modern battle.[83]

Further frustrating the judges was the tendency of the Nisei soldiers to disregard some of the rules. Those "captured," for example, often found ways to escape and make their way back to friendly troops. Many of those ruled to be "casualties," and therefore out of action, resurrected themselves, snuck away, and returned to their units.[84]

Language confusion due to the Hawaiians' use of pidgin still created communication problems when Second Lieutenant Ralph Potter was trying to lead his mortar platoon in a tactical withdrawal. "Move straight back singly," he instructed his men, "and assemble at the edge of the clearing just behind the hill." This order was met by querulous stares, but no action. "The clearing," he repeated. Still no movement. Soon Potter was shouting, but to no avail. The battalion executive officer, Major Emmet O'Connor, soon appeared and realized, since he had spent considerable time in Hawaii, that the men did not know the meaning of the word "clearing." He suggested that Lieutenant Potter substitute the term "no more trees place" for "clearing." As soon as he did so smiles of understanding appeared on the faces of his troops, and they quickly carried out his order.[85]

Striving for realism meant that the field kitchens were not always able to keep up with the trainees. Thus the men were introduced to field rations—known as C-rations. Army dietitians and food scientists began work before the war on easily portable individual rations for combat soldiers in situations where more conventional cooked meals were unavailable to them. The result was called the C-ration. A day's supply of these rations occupied six metal cans, two of which were to be consumed in each meal of the day. There were ten different entrees, including meat and spaghetti, ham and lima beans, pork and rice, and chicken and vegetables. The second can in a soldier's meal contained one of six different varieties of biscuit, beverage powder, sugar, cereal, and candy. And finally, each meal also included three cigarettes, with matches, chewing gum, salt tablets, a can opener, and toilet paper. And although it was never the government's intent that soldiers should have to subsist on C-rations for more than perhaps a couple of days, men often went for much longer periods of time with nothing else to eat.[86]

The search for a less bulky ration resulted in the K-ration. These were initially developed as a lightweight packable ration to be carried by paratroopers, although they soon were issued to all combat troops. Three separate rations—one each for breakfast, dinner, and supper—fulfilled one day's food requirements. Each meal filled a cardboard box that was sealed with wax to try to keep the contents fresh. The waxed box also served as a source of fuel for cooking the food in the field. The composition of the rations varied. A breakfast meal, for example, would likely include a canned meat product of some sort, a compressed cereal bar, some biscuits, some instant coffee, sugar, and a fruit bar. The dinner box could contain a can of cheese spread, biscuits, a candy bar, and a powdered drink mix. The supper meal included another canned meat product, the ever present biscuits, instant coffee, and bouillon powder. Every meal also included four cigarettes and matches, a can opener, a wooden spoon, salt, chewing gum, and toilet paper.[87]

The men were sometimes able to supplement their K- or C-rations with home-cooked meals of fried chicken and biscuits. Several artillerymen came upon a farm house with a sign on the front porch advertising fried chicken, so they stopped for a meal. This "restaurant" was far from being a full-fledged dining establishment, however, and the proprietor told them that if they came back in a couple of hours he would have a fine meal ready for them. He had to kill and pluck a chicken before he could cook it. The soldiers assented, and when they returned later they ate what one decided was the best chicken he had ever tasted.

A couple of other artillerymen had a very different experience. They had wandered lost in the swamps for three days before coming upon a lonely cabin inhabited by a man and woman who had never in their lives journeyed more than thirty miles from that spot. The famished soldiers asked the woman if she could fry a chicken for them, for which they would gladly pay. Unknown to the men, this woman had never prepared fried chicken, although she had seen pictures of people obviously relishing its taste. "After about two hours," one of the men recalled, "the lady came in with two scrawny drumsticks and two biscuits." When they asked where the rest of the chicken was, she told them that she had thrown it away. The picture she had seen had shown folks eating only the drumsticks, and she thought that those were the only edible parts on the bird. But what she served seemed to defy the very meaning of the word "edible." "We couldn't cut, bite, or chew the chicken it was so old and tough," the soldier remembered. And then, to top it off, the well-meaning—but incompetent—cook offered the men chicory coffee that was, according to one of them, "so strong that it would melt a spoon." Somehow they choked it down and then, unwilling to offend the woman's generosity, they told her how good it tasted, whereupon she insisted on refilling their cups.[88]

Occasionally, the men of the combat team resorted to the age-old military pastime of living off the land by stealing food from the local population. And sometimes officers participated, or at least turned a blind eye toward, illicit foraging for food. Once, after an all-day training march, a sow and her nine offspring strolled unconcernedly through the site of a battalion headquarters. The battalion commander shouted at the pigs in hopes of scaring them off, but to no avail. Several of the footsore soldiers soon forgot how tired they were as visions of freshly cooked pork filled their thoughts. Unsheathing their bayonets, they quickly seized and dispatched the piglets and then went off in pursuit of the fleeing sow, weapons in hand. Observing their antics, the colonel turned to his second in command and said, "You are my witness. I did my best to keep them [the pigs] out. . . . If they enter our bivouac area in direct disobedience to orders, they do so at their own peril." Due to the rapid reaction of his men, "the invasion had been repelled."[89]

The artillerymen were barely back at Camp Shelby long enough to clean up their uniforms and gear before joining the rest of the regiment in the D-Series (or divisional) army maneuvers in Mississippi's De Soto National Forest. At the completion of these maneuvers—the 442nd Regiment had "defeated" two of the 69th Division's three regiments—the Nisei soldiers again returned to Camp Shelby. The exercises had been helpful in teaching the men tactics, although the officers had probably benefitted more from the experience than the enlisted men. One of the latter broke down simple infantry squad tactics to its most basic element. "Make sure that you know where the enemy's at," he explained many years later, "and you find something in between him and you that will keep him from killing you, and you get in position where you can kill him. That's it. Plain and simple."[90]

While they were in the field they missed out on the visit to Camp Shelby of famed actress, author, and comedienne Gypsy Rose Lee. On her way to Hollywood to begin filming *The Belle of the Yukon* with Randolph Scott, she stopped at Camp Shelby on Sunday, January 30. During her tour of the camp she visited mess halls, the reception center, the station hospital, and seven other venues (theaters and service clubs) where she entertained the soldiers with a steady patter of jokes and double entendres. A former striptease artist, she drew upon that part of her life when talking with the soldiers. "You know, in one of my acts," she told them, "I talk about my books; in another act I talk about my play; and in a third act, I get right down to BARE FACTS." Her audience loved it.[91]

The soldiers spent the next few weeks polishing their abilities to work as members of one large combined arms unit comprising infantry and artillery. There was also more testing in order to convince higher authorities that these units were, indeed, ready for deployment to a war zone.

CHAPTER FOUR

TRIAL BY FIRE

For most of the first year of American involvement in the war against Nazi Germany, the army air forces (AAF) carried the combat burden. Bombers based in England raided targets in German-occupied countries and against Germany itself as military planners in the United States rushed to train soldiers and provide the necessary manpower for land warfare.

On November 8, 1942, while the Hawaiians at Camp McCoy were being introduced to cold-weather training, Allied troops, most of them Americans, landed along the northern coast of Africa, all the way from French Morocco in the west to Algeria in the east. These forces were to jointly drive east across Algeria and Tunisia to link up with British forces advancing toward them from Egypt—in the process eliminating the Axis presence in North Africa. The conquest of North Africa would make the Mediterranean safe for Allied shipping headed to and from the Pacific, and it would demonstrate to the Soviet Union that its American and British allies did not expect it to wage the war against Germany singlehandedly.

The untested American soldiers facing the battle-toughened Germans and Italians got a vicious introduction to warfare in North Africa. They experienced heavy losses at places like Kasserine Pass in Tunisia before ultimately, after six months, forcing the surrender of a quarter million Axis troops in May 1943. By that time, American bombers, flying from African airfields, had begun to raid targets in Italy and central Europe, including the valuable oil refineries in Romania.

Following victory in North Africa, Allied planners immediately set to work preparing an invasion of Sicily. Allied control of that island would further ensure safe passage of Allied shipping moving between Gibraltar and Suez. At the same time, planning was moving forward for an invasion of Europe through northern France. This planning had important repercussions for the troops deployed along the northern coast of the Africa. The Allies did not have, nor were they likely to acquire, enough ships and landing crafts to adequately support both the invasion of France and any similar amphibious assaults anywhere else.

Nevertheless, on July 10, British and American forces, using the resources that were available, began landing on the southeastern coast of Sicily. By that time the fight had begun to drain out of many of the Italian units, but there were sufficient German forces there to resist the invasion with some vigor. The American Seventh Army under Lieutenant General George S. Patton moved west along the southern coast, while General Sir Bernard L. Montgomery's British Eighth Army moved in the opposite direction. Both armies faced fierce resistance before linking up at Palermo, on the north coast, on July 22.

By then, the invasion of France had been postponed into the following year, thereby leaving the forces in the Mediterranean theater a window of opportunity in which to use available shipping to mount an attack elsewhere. The big question was: where? Several locations offered possibilities for success. Some American strategists looked toward the islands of Sardinia and Corsica. Success there would further enhance the safety of sea travel within the theater, provide airbases closer to other enemy targets, and serve as a springboard to an invasion of southern France. Perhaps such an invasion of the European mainland could be accomplished in conjunction with the proposed cross-Channel assault from England.

British military leaders countered with a proposal to invade the Balkans, although such a move would first necessitate securing airfields in southern Italy from which to support the operation. Success in the Balkans would disrupt Germany's supply of certain raw materials, such as oil, copper, and chromium, from that part of Europe. An attack there might also draw significant German forces away from the Russian front, thereby easing the enormous burden on Soviet forces and, perhaps, keep the Soviet Union in the war.

Both options had their disadvantages. Sardinia and Corsica, planners believed, could be conquered in a relatively short time and with minimum cost. The loss of these two islands was, however, not of great consequence to the Axis powers. Furthermore, Allied occupation of these islands would alert the enemy that the next move would likely be against southern France, thus giving the Germans time to move reinforcements to the threatened area. Pursuing this particular strategic option would also put a tremendous strain on the available resources for moving and landing large numbers of troops. There just were not enough shipping resources to support two invasions of France—one from England and one from the Mediterranean.

Invading Europe through the Balkans also presented difficult problems. Such a move would require amphibious landings both in Italy and in the Balkans. Assuming success in both instances, Allied forces would then have to create and protect an extremely long logistical life line to subsist themselves.

A third scenario, and the one ultimately adopted, was to invade southern Italy and move northward. This would necessarily tie up numerous German divisions, thereby preventing them from going either to the Eastern Front to battle the Russians or to France to repel the coming invasion there. Allied control of airfields in southern Italy furthermore would mean that enemy targets in Austria, Romania, Czechoslovakia, and southern Germany would be within reach of heavy bombers. Finally, an invasion might be the final impetus needed for an increasingly war-weary Italy to pull out of the conflict altogether. On July 25, Italian King Victor Emmanuel III deposed Benito Mussolini and replaced him with Maresciallo d'Italia Pietro Badoglio. Badoglio immediately assured his German allies, and the rest of the world, that the departure of Mussolini in no way indicated any loss of resolve on the part of the Italian government to stay in the war.

Once the decision had been made to invade Italy, the most important question to be answered was just where in Italy the landings should be made. From the eastern end of Sicily it was but a scant few miles across the Strait of Messina to that section of Italy known as Calabria, the "toe" of the Italian "boot." If the Allies landed there, they could then move overland toward Naples on the west coast. Travel would not be easy, however. The mountainous terrain and primitive road network would make movement by a large body of men, along with their tanks, trucks, bulldozers, and other cumbersome equipment, extremely difficult.

Another option was to land somewhere farther north in the hope of interposing between enemy forces retreating northward from the southern tip of Italy and Rome. Various ports along the coast offered advantages. Naples was one, but it was too far north. The site chosen for the landing had to be close enough to Sicily to allow fighter-bombers based there to cover the landing.

Planners ultimately selected Salerno, on the lower west coast of Italy, because of its good port facilities and because it was the farthest port city from Sicily that could be covered by fighters flying out of bases there. The use of aircraft carriers would have allowed an invasion closer to Rome, but they were needed to prosecute the war against Japan. Further recommending Salerno as a target, however, was the presence of a large airfield at Montecorvino, just a few miles inland. Allied progress in Italy would be immeasurably assisted by its capture.

Meanwhile, after debarking from the ship in Algeria and once again feeling solid ground under their feet, the men of the 100th Battalion motored to Fleurus, a few miles west of Oran, where they were to be quartered. The campsite, which previous residents had dubbed "Goat Hill," was hot and dusty and had an overabundance of pesky sand fleas. The potable water provided by army engineers was barely drinkable, due to the heavy amounts of chlorine in it to kill germs. Luckily, there was plenty of locally produced wine within a short distance of camp. The soldiers quickly discovered that they could obtain French money for the purchase of wine, and anything else, by selling some of their equipment to the locals. In each soldier's gear, for example, was an unbleached white muslin mattress cover, which could double as a body bag in the event of his death. There was enough fabric in each of these to produce a robe for the Arab lucky enough to own one. Some Algerians also traded for the soldiers' blue denim duffel bags. With two holes cut in the bottom, a bag made an acceptable pair of baggy pants with a drawstring closure at the "waist."[1]

The Nisei soldiers once again encountered alien cultural traits, although this time they were far more radical than what had been apparent in Mississippi. An officer who had arrived in North Africa several months earlier thought that "Oran must be the Singapore of the Mediterranean . . . with a heterogenous [*sic*] population that lends . . . a cosmopolitan and colorful atmosphere." Guidebooks warned Americans against flirting with local women. "Never stare at one," they cautioned. "Never jostle her in a crowd. Never speak to her in public. Never try to remove the veil. This is most important. Serious injury if not death at the hands of Moslem men may result if these few rules are not followed." And, the booklet continued, if an American found himself in a situation that might result in a fight, that local men were pitifully inept when it came to boxing. Instead, it warned, they "fight with knives, and they are probably a lot better at it than you are."[2]

GIs who had been there for a while even warned the new arrivals to remove any finger rings because Arab thieves would not think twice about cutting off a man's finger to get his ring. In fact, a street urchin even stole an American battalion commander's field jacket from the back seat of his moving jeep![3]

The new arrivals quickly discovered that the level of hygiene exhibited by the Arab segment of the population was considerably lower than that to which they had grown accustomed in the United States. One man recalled walking through a street market and marveling at the goods offered for sale. He noticed a vendor wave his hand over some "odd black things" and they immediately changed color, becoming much lighter. And then he realized that the shopkeeper had merely chased off the countless flies that covered everything in the market.[4]

Even though the men of the battalion were now, technically, in a war zone, the bitter fighting that had raged in North Africa was over. Colonel Turner still did not know how his troops were to be employed until he visited headquarters in Oran on the day after their arrival. A colonel at headquarters, who had spent time in Hawaii before the war and knew Turner personally, suggested that his troops might patrol the rail line that connected Oran with

Casablanca. Theft by local tribesmen along the line had reached serious levels, but perhaps employing an infantry battalion to keep watch would resolve the issue. Turner declined. He and his men had not spent more than two years training only to become railroad policemen.

Instead, the battalion was assigned to the 34th Infantry Division. The 34th was originally made up of national guard troops from Iowa, Minnesota, and the Dakotas, and had come into federal service a few months before the attack on Pearl Harbor as a result of the 1940 Selective Service Act. It was the first American division deployed to meet the Germans in World War II. Landing in Northern Ireland within eight weeks of the beginning of the war, the 34th took part in Operation Torch, where it suffered 4,254 casualties. One of the division's original battalions, the 2nd Battalion of the 133rd Infantry Regiment, was detached and used as a headquarters guard for General Dwight D. Eisenhower in Algiers, so the Hawaiians were assigned to assume its former position within the division. Major General Charles W. Ryder welcomed the untested troops to his division, and the commander of the 133rd Regiment informed his officers to instruct their men as to the background of their new comrades. "They are not Japanese," he cautioned, "but Americans born in Hawaii. . . . And tell your men not to call them Japs, or there'll be trouble."[5]

The island soldiers only had a couple of weeks in Africa for final training before heading for Italy. Part of this time was spent in acquiring knowledge from "lessons learned" by the other men in their new regiment. But there was time for recreation as well. The 133rd Regiment's baseball team had recently lost to another team from within the division, and the 133rd's coach was happy to learn that there were some extremely good players in his regiment's newest battalion. He soon drafted a few of them onto his team and avenged his earlier loss. The Nisei ballplayers, however, saw no reason to continue to contribute their best athletes to the regiment's team and quickly formed a battalion team. In a game against the regimental team, the Nisei coasted to an easy 26–0 victory.[6]

Following Mussolini's ouster as the de facto head of the Italian government, King Victor Emmanuel surrendered Italy to the Allies unconditionally on September 3, 1943. On that same day, the

British Eighth Army crossed over from Sicily to the Italian mainland. Six days later, the American Fifth Army began landing at Salerno. Not all of the huge Allied military force that had grown throughout the North African and Sicilian campaigns was available for the invasion of Italy. General Eisenhower detached seven entire divisions—three British and four American—as soon as Sicily was secure and ordered them to Britain where they became part of the force being put together for the invasion of France scheduled for the early summer of 1944.

General Mark Clark, commanding the Fifth Army, had seen combat in North Africa, but neither he nor his two corps commanders, Lieutenant General Sir Richard L. McCreery, commanding the British 10 Corps, and Major General Ernest J. Dawley, commanding the American VI Corps, had ever participated in an amphibious landing.

The invasion beaches lay just south of Salerno, and planning called for the British 10 Corps to go in on the left and the American VI Corps to land on the right. In addition to the British 46th and 56th Infantry Divisions, the British corps also contained two British Commando units and three American Ranger battalions. The 10 Corps was to drive inland north of the Sele River and capture the road and rail center of Battipaglia and the Montecorvino airfield as quickly as possible. It was also to seize the passes leading northward through the mountains toward Naples.

The American 36th Infantry Division spearheaded the VI Corps' operation. Landing south of the Sele River; its goal was the high ground overlooking Salerno from the east and south. The 45th Division would wait on the ships, ready to come ashore as soon as there was room for it in the VI Corps' lodgment, and the British 1st Armored Division was similarly set to reinforce the 10 Corps. In the meantime, the American 3rd Infantry Division and the 82nd Airborne Division remained in Sicily awaiting further developments, and back in North Africa, the 1st Armored Division and the 34th Infantry Division were available when needed. Air cover was not as extensive as originally planned because a large number of previously available bombers had also gone to Britain in preparation for the bombing campaign that was intended to soften up German defenses prior to the invasion of France.

The landing began early on the morning of September 9, 1943. Many GIs, who had just learned of the Italian surrender, thought the landing would be easy. Some, in fact, were concerned that, having spent so much time and effort training and preparing for combat, they were to be denied the opportunity to prove themselves in battle. Even with the Italian army no longer a threat to the Allies, however, there were more than enough Germans in the country to make things unpleasant for them. The mountainous terrain, the rapidly approaching rainy, winter weather—and the swiftly flowing rivers—added to spirited German resistance to make Allied progress toward Rome slow and bloody.

The invasion caught the Germans with fewer defensive troops in the area than they would have liked, and the Allies got ashore with light casualties. But congestion on the beaches hampered the unloading of supplies and reinforcements, and the Allies were slow to expand their beachhead as a result. This gave the Germans enough time to bring reinforcements to the scene, and they soon began to create significant difficulties for the Allies.

On September 13, *General der Panzertruppen* Heinrich von Vietinghoff, the German commander, learned of a gap between the two Allied corps and assumed that it was an indication of an imminent withdrawal back to sea. In fact, American planners had considered consolidating their position by evacuating one of the corps ashore and using it to reinforce the other, but abandoned the idea as posing too great a risk. Vietinghoff immediately launched an offensive that nearly succeeded in eliminating the Allied beachhead. By the end of that day, however, the 3rd Infantry Division in Sicily had boarded ships bound for the invasion site, although it would take several days to reach the mainland. More immediate reinforcements came from the skies that night as thirteen hundred paratroopers of the 82nd Airborne Division dropped onto a landing zone along the beach from an altitude of only eight hundred feet. Another twenty-one hundred paratroopers landed the following night. By the night of September 15, General Clark was confident enough to declare that the beachhead was secure and that there would be no retreat.[7]

Vietinghoff soon changed his mind about German chances for victory as British troops from the Eighth Army neared Salerno

from the south. *Generalfeldmarschall* Albert Kesselring, Vietinghoff's superior, finally agreed with this assessment and ordered
southern Italy to be abandoned. Vietinghoff's role in the German
withdrawal was to establish a temporary defensive position that
ran from Salerno on the west coast to Foggia on the east coast
until stronger positions could be established farther north. In
spite of this strategic setback, General Vietinghoff was moved to
announce that: "Success has been ours. Once again German soldiers have proved their superiority over the enemy."[8]

On September 17, the German high command finally saw the
futility of trying to hold onto Naples and ordered its evacuation
in favor of the stronger positions farther north. It was important
that the retreating army destroy anything that the Allies might
use to pursue it. General Kesselring instructed Vietinghoff that
his men were to take all means of motorized transportation with
them when they left the city. That meant trucks, buses, and private
automobiles. Anything related to the transportation industry that
they could not take with them they were to destroy, including the
Alfa Romeo automobile factory. This level of destruction was to be
expected in time of war to deny one's enemy the use of anything
of military value, but much of what they destroyed made the city
uninhabitable for its civilian residents too. The Germans demolished hotels, university buildings, water reservoirs, power plants,
food storage facilities, and canning factories. Then they left powerful bombs in some of the rubble that were timed to explode
days, or even weeks, later.[9]

The next day, General Clark ordered his Fifth Army to wheel
to the left and head up the west coast of Italy. The 10 Corps remained as the army's left flank and advanced upon Naples. The VI
Corps, bolstered by the addition of the 3rd Infantry Division and
under its new commander, Major General John P. Lucas, swung
into the mountainous interior where it had the dual responsibility
of maintaining contact with the 10 Corps on its left and with the
left flank elements of the British Eighth Army on its right.

Progress through the mountains would have been difficult for
the VI Corps even in peace time. Roads were often narrow or nonexistent, and the retiring Germans did as much as they could to
impede the Allies' progress. Just between the villages of Paestum

and Oliveto, for example, they demolished more than two dozen bridges. Using prefabricated bridges where they could and building entirely new structures where they had to, combat engineers worked hard to keep the troops in motion. Major General Lucian K. Truscott, commander of the 3rd Infantry Division, recognized the value of these sometimes overlooked troops when he declared that the most valuable weapon in the American arsenal was often the bulldozer. A week later, however, the 3rd Division came to a halt when it encountered three destroyed bridges with a combined length of three hundred feet. Even where there were no bridges to rebuild progress up and down the mountains was very slow.[10]

The steep mountain trails were difficult for individual soldiers to navigate. But for those men whose task it was to bring up food, water, and other supplies the trails were absolutely treacherous. Some farsighted 3rd Division planners had brought pack mules and their civilian handlers along with them from Sicily, and they proved quite valuable. General Clark soon had officers scouring the countryside to obtain enough such animals to equip each division in the Fifth Army with three hundred to five hundred mules. Finding enough suitable animals was not easy. The retiring Germans also recognized the usefulness of such beasts and took along as many as they could. Then, to prevent the Allies from making use of any that were left, the Germans slaughtered all that they could not use. Army purchasing agents traveled to as far away as Sicily, Sardinia, and even North Africa, to find mules. Ultimately, mules were shipped, along with their necessary equipment, all the way from the United States.[11]

Meanwhile, the 34th Division prepared to land as soon as the beachhead was secure. Thus, two of the division's three infantry regiments, the 135th and the 168th, sailed from Mers El Kebir for Italy on September 17 with the expectation that they would experience an orderly debarkation at Salerno's docks. These two regiments were barely at sea before officials in Italy realized that, because of all the wreckage still remaining in the harbor at Salerno, unloading these troops was not going to be as rapid or as smooth as had been hoped. Dockworkers in Oran had made maximum use of all available space when loading these ships, as if

A member of the 522nd Field Artillery Battalion receiving some mule-handling tips from a member of the Italian 11th Pack Mule Company. Signal Corps photo.

they were heading to normal docking facilities instead of heading for a hostile shore. This meant that items such as rifle ammunition might be stowed in several different places on board instead of all together. Upon unloading, therefore, a great deal of time was spent in sorting out all the different classes of cargo and distributing them to the proper places.

Because it was vital to get as many combat-ready troops ashore in the shortest possible time, and because the ships carrying these two regiments could not be unloaded with the necessary speed, word was sent back to Oran for the 133rd Regiment, along with the newly attached 100th Infantry Battalion, to come to Salerno at once. In just forty-eight hours, the four ships designated for this movement were combat-loaded, with every element of cargo in discreet locations, and at sea. The ships moved with urgent speed and arrived in the harbor at about 8:00 A.M. on September 22, just a few hours after the ships carrying the other two regiments had arrived. The harbor, although still clogged with the wreckage of sunken ships, was busy nonetheless. Navy destroyers laid down a smoke screen along the beach to make it more difficult for Germans to observe the landing, and Allied planes flew overhead to discourage what was left of the Luftwaffe from attacking the troops as they went ashore.[12]

The men of the 100th Battalion clambered over the sides of the SS *Frederick Funston* and down the cargo nets into the waiting landing craft for the final run into shore. Other troops had secured the city before their arrival, but landing was still not without its difficulties. Many of the regiment's landing boats made it all the way onto the beach where their passengers emerged onto the sand without so much as wet boots. A few others, however, grounded on sandbars before reaching the beach. Nevertheless, the ramps on the fronts of the boats came down, and the men aboard exited into the water. One craft grounded on a sandbar about 150 feet from the beach, and when the men on board hopped into the water they discovered it to be neck deep on many of them, while others had to swim toward shallower water. Soon, however, they all managed to get ashore where they followed carefully marked trails to avoid encountering unexploded ordnance and land mines.[13]

One of the men going ashore groused about having to carry a bolt-action, model 1903 Springfield rifle that had a grenade launcher attached to the end of the barrel. His instructions were that he use it to destroy any enemy tanks he might encounter, although he doubted whether he could even take out a jeep with it. When he finally entered battle he took advantage of the first opportunity to "trade in" his Springfield, picking up an M1 rifle lying next to a dead GI and leaving the Springfield in its place. Later, he exchanged the M1 for a lighter M1 carbine in the same fashion. Later still, he traded the carbine to an Italian partisan in exchange for a 9mm Beretta semi-automatic pistol.[14]

The entire regiment was ashore within twelve hours. While most of the 100th Battalion marched to a campsite about six miles from the beach, orders arrived that temporarily detached its two supernumerary companies, E and F. Fifth Army had selected these two companies to stay near the port to guard an ammunition dump and a landing strip.[15]

While the 10 Corps fought its way through the mountain passes west of Salerno, General Clark assigned other goals to the units of the VI Corps. He saw the village of Avellino, about thirty miles east of Naples on Highway 7, as being of great strategic value. Its possession by the Allies would give them an avenue into the German flank at Naples. Clark ordered the 3rd Division to assault the town over the mountains, and instructed General Ryder to send his 133rd Regiment to occupy the village of Montemarano, about ten miles east of Avellino, but on the same road. Pursuant to these orders, the men of the 133rd Regiment clambered into the backs of dozens of 2½-ton trucks and began the circuitous movement on the rainy night of September 26.[16]

The weather was not the only hindrance to rapid movement. The mountain roads were narrow, and the retreating Germans had destroyed many of the bridges along the way. The convoy of trucks finally arrived the next night at a point about six miles east of Montemarano. The next day the command passed through the position of the 45th Infantry Division and moved around Montemarano to the northwest. There was still no contact with German soldiers, but the engineer troops were busy locating and removing land mines along the way.

Italian civilians welcomed the Americans and were eager to help them. Some had apparently watched the Germans planting mines and had since marked their locations. One man approached some Company B men with information that a German soldier was nearby and that he was anxious to surrender. An officer took a few soldiers to where the man was concealed, and, after relieving him of his Luger pistol, brought him back to camp. He was understandably surprised to see that his captors, although wearing U.S. Army uniforms, had very Asian faces. He made the same assumption as to their ancestry that many American soldiers did, and that was that they must be Chinese. He knew that Germany and Japan were allies so when he learned the true ethnicity of his captors he perhaps began to wonder if Japan, like Italy, had surrendered to the Allies only to then join the coalition against Germany.[17]

This was also the day that saw the first shedding of blood by a member of the 100th Battalion, although it could have been much worse than it was. When a passing jeep rolled over a mine some of the resulting shrapnel struck a man in the face. His wounds were only superficial, but the next day saw the first of what soon became a very long list of Nisei soldiers killed in action.[18]

On September 29, British General Sir Harold R. L. G. Alexander, commanding the Fifteenth Army Group, and therefore General Clark's boss, decided to give the Fifth Army more freedom of movement. He told Clark that his right flank no longer needed to maintain contact with the British Eighth Army and could move forward. Clark then altered his battle instructions to reflect his army's new autonomy. The 3rd Division's goal was still Avellino, which General Lucas, commanding VI Corps, called "the key to the situation." The 133rd Regiment's assignment changed. It was to cut one of the roads leading north out of Avellino toward Benevento in order to help prevent the escape of Germans from Avellino.[19]

Company B led the 100th Battalion's advance that day, and at about mid-morning one of the platoons rounded a bend in the road and immediately ran into a firestorm of German machine-gun bullets. Enemy mortar and artillery fire began landing on the road to add to the confusion. Sergeant Shigeo "Joe" Takata, armed with a BAR, took the lead in attacking one of the machine-gun nests, but a piece of shrapnel soon cut him down. With the steel fragment in his head and his life rapidly draining away, he was able to point out the locations of the enemy gunners before he died. He was the battalion's first combat fatality, but he would be far from the last. Before that day was even over another member of the battalion lay dead and seven others had been wounded.[20]

It is unlikely that any amount of controlled, stateside training can really prepare a man for actual combat, and this was made apparent very early. One man likened his feelings in combat to what one would feel upon walking into a very dark room that was filled with rattlesnakes. "You don't know if you'll get bitten or not," he mused. "But you're very scared and very careful."[21]

But if any Germans thought that the Nisei soldiers would be an easy enemy to dominate, they were quickly disabused of that notion. Later that day, German tanks and infantry had the 100th Battalion pinned down. GIs used bazookas to immobilize one of the tanks, but its crew continued to fire its main gun and machine guns. A Caucasian officer then watched one of the Japanese Americans work his way up close to the tank and force a hand grenade in through the driver's vision slot, thus ending the tank's usefulness. "Quite a feat," the officer later wrote, "for their first time in battle!"[22]

Even after all the training these soldiers had undergone, it required the dangers of actual combat for some lessons to sink in. During the 100th Battalion's first week in combat it became necessary for some men in Company B to cross over a slight rise. The platoon commander realized that any German nearby would be able to see each man as he crossed the knoll because he would be backlit by the sky, so he told them to crawl over the hill. One man, however, disregarded this advice and walked upright. He was immediately hit in the leg by a German bullet. When his lieutenant asked him why he had disregarded the order to crawl, the soldier replied that he did not want to get his uniform dirty.[23]

All across Italy, enemy troops continued to fight delaying actions until German engineers and Italian laborers could complete construction of strong parallel lines of defenses farther north. The first of these, known variously as the Reinhard Line or, more commonly, the Bernhard Line, extended roughly west to east from a position on the Italian coast about fifty miles north of Naples.

On October 1, British soldiers skirted the eastern edge of Naples and continued northward in pursuit of the retiring Germans, and the next day American forces entered the city to stay. On that same day, troops of the British Eighth Army began to occupy Foggia and the surrounding airfields on the east side of the country. And on October 2, other British forces made an amphibious landing at Termoli, on the Adriatic Coast.[24]

By now, the Allies had accomplished a great deal in Italy. They occupied airbases that were well within bombing range of Germany itself. The almost simultaneous evacuation of German troops from Sardinia and Corsica gave the Allies another possible staging area for the invasion of southern France. And nineteen German divisions were tied down in Italy, and therefore unavailable for use in northern France against the planned cross-Channel Allied invasion.

The 133rd Regiment was in the vicinity of San Giorgio del Sannio on October 2 when orders arrived directing it to capture the ancient walled city of Benevento, a few miles to the northwest. A heavy pre-assault bombardment by the attached 125th and 151st Field Artillery Battalions helped pave the way into the city with only moderate American casualties. Some of the men celebrated their victory with the contents of a distillery that they found in the town. The combination of adrenalin, alcohol, and the release of pressure that followed the fighting was not easy to control. One man, after having fortified himself with liquid bravado, proceeded to shoot at the glass and ceramic insulators atop all of the electric poles in his vicinity. His company commander called him to account the next day, and the man readily admitted his transgression. "Capt[ain]," he confessed, "I'll take the blame for everything that happened in Benevento last night, except blowing up the bridge, those damn Krauts did that!"[25]

In early October, Hitler sent two more divisions of troops to Kesselring with a restatement of orders to hold in place. Nevertheless, work was already underway farther north to build another set of defenses in case the Allies proved able to overpower Kesselring's position. It was imperative that Kesselring hold for six months at the very least, nine months was preferable, so that the new defenses could be completed.[26]

By October 9, General Clark was anxious to get his Fifth Army across the Volturno River before the Germans had time to make such a crossing too costly. Choreographing such a movement, however, required considerable effort. The tentative plan called for the 3rd Division to cross the westward running river just upstream from Capua at the same time that the 34th Division crossed to its right. The big question was whether the 45th Division, on the Army's extreme right, could protect these crossings by moving down the valley of the Calore River just above its junction with the Volturno. The 45th Division began moving immediately. The

Calore Valley, while lightly defended, presented the tired soldiers with difficult terrain.

An hour after midnight on October 13, American artillery began blasting enemy positions north of the Volturno while soldiers of the 3rd Division prepared to cross the river. (Interestingly, this was the day that Italy declared war on its former ally, Germany.) German artillerists, mortar men, and machine gunners were quick to respond, knowing that the American barrage was probably a precursor to an infantry crossing. Nevertheless, the Americans came on, and by that afternoon, in spite of losses, had five battalions across.[27]

At about the same time that 3rd Division troops began crossing the river, the men of the 34th Division's 135th and 168th Infantry Regiments also eased into the water farther east after only about fifteen minutes of divisional artillery preparation. Some of the men crossed in rubber boats and others waded part way and swam part way. The current was swift, and the crossing was difficult, but German armed resistance was surprisingly light. The troops of the 3rd Panzer Grenadier Division assigned to that sector had not yet all arrived from their prior posting, and those who were there had not had much time to prepare their positions.

General Ryder hoped for a respite after getting his infantry across the river. He wanted his engineers to have time to build bridges that would support tanks, truckloads of supplies and reinforcements, and other heavy vehicles before ordering his men forward. This was a luxury, however, that the war effort could not afford. The 135th and 168th Regiments were still the two forward elements of the 34th Division, and they pushed forward against stiffening resistance.

By the middle of October the 100th Battalion had reached Bagnoli. As it trucked through one small Italian village, local children delightedly threw apples to these "Chinese" soldiers who had come to liberate them from the Germans. It was also at Bagnoli that Companies E and F finally rejoined the battalion. And it was at about this time that General Ryder authorized the distribution of divisional shoulder patches to his newest battalion. The insignia of the 34th Division reflected the unit's heritage. During World

War I, the 34th Division trained in New Mexico and soon became known as the Sandstorm Division. In 1918, one of its members with artistic abilities submitted the winning entry when a contest was held to come up with a distinctive insignia. His original design showed a bleached buffalo skull superimposed upon a clay Indian jar. The final version showed a red bull's head against a black background in the shape of a pottery jar.[28]

The three American divisions on the east flank of the Fifth Army's line met heavier enemy resistance as they moved north from the Volturno. The town of Dragoni became the focus of the 3rd Division and most of the 34th. On October 18, General Ryder sent the 1st Battalion of the 133rd Infantry around to the northeast of the town to capture a bridge that spanned the upper reaches of the southerly flowing Volturno, so it could not serve as a German escape route. The Germans were a step ahead of them, however, and blew up the bridge after retreating across it.

Shortly after midnight on October 20, the 100th Battalion waded across the Volturno near the wrecked bridge and entered the bombed out village of Alife. The 133rd Regiment's new objective was the town of San Angelo D'Alife, about seven miles to the northwest. Panzer grenadiers were dug in with their machine guns along the way and had seeded the approaches with land mines. To add to the difficulties of any American unit trying to reach the town, German artillery observers in the surrounding hills were poised to call in heavy fire. Any attacking force would have to try to get through this valley at night in order to minimize direct fire losses.

Company A of the 100th Battalion led off the attack just after dark on October 21, avoiding roads and moving across country. The men made slow but steady progress for a few hours, but then, about 10:30, the Germans discovered their presence in the valley and loosed a storm of fire. Within minutes thirty Company A men were out of action, ten killed and the rest wounded. More men were hit as the battalion remained pinned down and the men tried to extricate themselves from this brutal killing field. By dawn, the survivors of Companies A and B had pulled back and moved to the outskirts of Alife, where Company C joined them later that afternoon.[29]

During the predawn hours of October 22, the Nisei soldiers started off again headed toward a critical road junction south of San Angelo D'Alife, while the 3rd Battalion moved toward a similar target somewhat closer to the town. As the 100th Battalion moved through a flat area, German artillery and small arms fire erupted from the Matese foothills nearby, causing a near panic among the men. One newly encountered weapon that was particularly frightening for the slowly advancing infantrymen was the *Nebelwerfer*. This six-barreled rocket launcher's projectiles whistled through the air with such an eerie sound that those on the receiving end nicknamed these guns the "screaming meemies." When an American replacement officer in a nearby unit first heard these rockets he asked a soldier what the noise was. The tired GI said: "It is Hitler's pipe organ playing 'The Purple Heart Blues.'"[30]

Also hindering the 100th Battalion's advance that day were the first enemy tanks that the Nisei had encountered. They knocked one of them out with a bazooka, and an artillery observer flying overhead in a single-engine airplane was able to call in accurate artillery fire that damaged five others, but there were still enough left to cause considerable anxiety in the American ranks before they retired. German resistance that day prevented both battalions from reaching their objectives.[31]

During the night of October 23–24, San Angelo d'Alife's defenders evacuated that town, as well as nearby Raviscanina, and fell back toward the north. As the 1st Battalion of the 133rd entered the village, the men of the 100th Battalion scaled the heights of nearby Hill 529. This real estate was taken at a considerable cost. Twenty-one of the 133rd Regiment's fifty-nine killed were from the 100th Battalion, and sixty-seven of the 148 wounded were also Nisei. From October 25 until the end of the month the 100th acted as the division's reserve force. This gave the men time to rest and refit before the next push.[32]

A wounded German prisoner being treated by a 100th Battalion surgeon registered astonishment, as had an earlier captive, to see Japanese men in American uniforms. This time, however, the Nisei played upon his fears and "admitted" that they truly were from Japan and that that nation had indeed switched sides in this war, leaving Germany alone of the original Axis powers.[33]

Also during this rest period the 100th Battalion experienced a leadership change. Authorities had apparently decided that Colonel Turner, who was pushing fifty years of age, was too old to stand up to the rigors of active campaigning and had decided to send him home to a less physically demanding job. He had been almost a surrogate father to many of the young Hawaiians, and they were sad to see him go. Turner's most likely successor was Lieutenant Colonel James Lovell, but he was in the hospital recovering from shrapnel wounds, so the executive officer of the 133rd Regiment's 3rd Battalion, Major James J. Gillespie, took over the 100th Battalion.[34]

November opened with the 100th Battalion still in a reserve role but on the march toward the northwest. And even though the unit was not in direct contact with enemy troops, a combination of strafing German fighter planes and well-aimed artillery continued to thin its ranks. About midnight on November 3–4, the battalion, as part of a regimental movement, began crossing the Volturno River, yet again. The water was cold that time of year, but the depth seldom reached the waists of the troops. The goal was the village of Santa Maria Oliveto and the hills that overlooked the town from the west, but first the men had to traverse an area some fifteen hundred yards across that was thick with German mines and booby traps. "Once across the river," remembered a soldier in the 133rd, "the mine fields were hell, trip wires were tripped, flares lit the sky and men seeking cover were caught in minefields as mortar and artillery shells rained down upon them. They soon found themselves in a hell of flying shrapnel and exploding mines. Soaked to the skin and shivering from the cold, they moved forward hoping some of them would reach their objective alive." Nearby artillery observation teams were able to plot the bloody progress of the advancing Americans by listening for the explosions of enemy mines. Among the dozens of men who fell victim to these devices was Company C's German-born Lieutenant Kurt Schemel, who had at first been so reluctant to serve in the Nisei unit. He was the battalion's first officer to be killed in action.[35]

By dawn, the battalion had successfully forded the river and moved a couple of hundred yards nearer Santa Maria where it spent the day hunkered down and awaiting further developments. Those developments came the next day when Major Gillespie received orders to have two of his companies attack three hills west of Santa Maria. Companies E and F began the movement by marching westward to get around behind the hills and not be exposed in the open fields to the south. As the forward elements neared the village of Pozzilli, they spotted an American soldier rather nonchalantly walking toward them. He identified himself simply as "Thompson" and said he had left his parachute unit in Naples without permission. Apparently the pace of the war there was too slow and boring for him, so he decided to come snoop around at the front to see what excitement he might find. He reported that there were no Germans in Pozzilli, but that they had left behind lots of mines and booby traps. He then led the Nisei to the base of the hills that were their objectives.[36]

By this time it was 4:00 P.M., and darkness was approaching. An officer from Company E led a group of volunteers to probe for mines and mark out a safe trail for those who would follow. Looking for a way to alert the men to the presence of the mines, they decided that toilet paper would be relatively easy to spot, even in the dark, and used it to mark a safe trail through the minefield.[37]

Companies E and F, leading the battalion through the danger zone, had safely progressed through most of the mined area when someone realized that the machine-gun sections from Company D, who were next in line, had halted for some reason. Thompson, the errant paratrooper, went back down the trail with two other men to usher the rest of the battalion forward before the Germans discovered them. Explosions soon revealed that the toilet paper markers were not as effective as had been hoped. Thompson had inadvertently tripped a mine and was ripped apart by the blast. When those nearby searched his body they could find no identification on him, not even the standard issue identification tags. It was almost as if he had never existed.[38]

The sounds of the mines exploding had not unduly alarmed the Germans on the tops of the hills, so the battalion pushed on. Several hours later the men crested one of the hills and took the enemy there by complete surprise. The last thing the defenders had expected was an attack from the rear. The victors immediately set to work digging foxholes in preparation for the counterattack which they were sure would follow. By the time the sun rose on the morning of November 6, two other hills had been taken with scarcely any resistance.[39]

When the German counterattack finally came it was directed against Company F. During the ensuing firefight, an officer and two men from Company D moved forward looking for a vantage point from which to direct mortar fire down upon the enemy. These men never wavered, even in the face of fierce enemy fire. Finally, however, after about two hours a German artillery round burst above the men and killed them. Desultory firing went on over the next couple of days, and on the 11th the battalion abandoned the hills.[40]

On November 13, during a respite from the fighting, Companies E and F, the two extra companies in the battalion, were skeletonized by distributing most of their personnel among Companies A, B, C, and D to replace heavy combat losses. Even with the infusion of these men, the four companies were still well below authorized strength. Seventy-eight officers and men had been killed or fatally wounded and another 239 had suffered injuries since the battalion's arrival in Italy.[41]

When a man was wounded there was a certain chain of events that was set in motion to effect his treatment. The first responsibility for his well-being rested with himself. Every soldier carried a first-aid packet that contained a bandage and some anti-bacterial sulfanilamide (or sulfa) powder to sprinkle into a wound before bandaging. He also carried a small tin of the same substance in tablet form. (Some soldiers, theorizing that the curative powers of the sulfa pills could be used in other ways, took them as a preventive treatment for gonorrhea rather than report themselves for specific treatment. Thus, when wounded, there were often no sulfa pills available.)[42]

Each infantry battalion carried a number of medical personnel on its rolls to treat the sick and wounded men and to transfer the more serious cases to better equipped facilities than are generally available near the fighting line. A medic was the person whom a wounded man was most happy to see. This aid man applied rudimentary first aid, bandaging wounds and splinting fractures, for example. Next he attached a diagnostic tag to the soldier's uniform that described what medical measures he had taken and whether or not he had administered morphine. Then, if the wounds were not life-threatening, and if the man was able to walk, he would start toward the battalion aid station for further treatment.

More seriously injured men required the assistance of litter bearers. Two of these men could transport a litter patient, but it was always easier with four. Sometimes the litter bearers were part of the battalion's assigned medical personnel, but quite often they were men who were not immediately required to take part in combat. Members of the regimental band, for example, often carried the wounded. Likewise, in rugged terrain like the mountains of Italy where it was difficult to maneuver any vehicle larger than a jeep, members of an anti-tank or combat engineer company provided this often life-saving service. Some men had worse luck than simply to be wounded. As a medic was tending the wound of one Nisei soldier, the injured man was hit again. Then, when the litter bearers hoisted him up for the trip back to the aid station, he was hit a third time.[43]

At the battalion aid station a surgeon reviewed the medic's tag and, if necessary, provided further treatment. He stabilized the patient and, if his wounds were sufficiently serious, prepared to send him further to the rear, to a clearing station. Because battalion aid stations were often not far removed from combat, this transfer might have to wait for a lull in the action. In these cases, the medical personnel made the wounded man as comfortable as possible while they waited for a chance to safely evacuate him by jeep or ambulance.

The mountains in Italy where these soldiers fought and died, however, were often devoid of even the most basic form of road, so it often took much longer to get a wounded man to an ambulance. In January 1944, the 133rd Regiment, to which the 100th Battalion was still attached, used six-man litter teams to move the wounded down a mountain from one relay post to another. Four men always carried the litter while the other two rested as they walked. When they reached the next relay station they handed over their patient to the next team and returned for another. The relay stations were spaced such that each litter team required about two hours to make the round trip. Depending upon the distance covered, it might require several dozen litter-bearers to evacuate each wounded man, and the journey to an ambulance sometimes took as long as fifteen hours. Late in the war, a Nisei soldier found a much quicker way to reach an aid station after he sprained his ankle while clambering up the side of a mountain. Some nearby Italian partisans generously offered the use of their donkey to convey him down to the medical facilities. He gratefully accepted their offer and naturally assumed that one of them would go with him to guide the animal through the minefields that abounded. Instead, however, one of the Italians merely slapped the animal on the rump and sent it on its way. "I thought the donkey and I were destined for donkey heaven," the soldier thought, as he and his mount careened down the mountainside. But they made it safely.[44]

Clearing stations were usually far enough removed from the front to be safe from direct enemy action. And the farther away from the scene of action that a medical facility was, the better prepared it was for more sophisticated treatment. Further examination here might result in the patient be sent further to the rear, to an evacuation hospital. And those requiring amputation or other serious procedures eventually wound up in general hospitals before being sent all the way back to the United States. Ambulatory patients received red corduroy robes to wear over their pajamas when they were out of bed, and these were marked with the letters "M.D." and "U.S.A." for Medical Department, United States Army." Some patients, displaying a macabre sense of humor, insisted that the letters stood for "Many Die, You Shall Also."[45]

Of course, not every wounded soldier survived long enough to reach medical care. In one instance, the 100th Battalion was attacking up a hill but it was slow going, and the men were hugging the ground as they tried to return fire. The Germans began rolling grenades down the hill. The soldiers were able to slap some of them away before they exploded, but one exploded alongside one soldier, shredding his arm from the shoulder down. A buddy rushed to his side to administer whatever aid he could and found

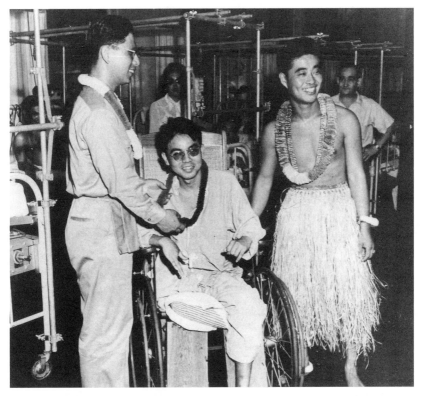

Nisei soldiers brighten the day for one of their severely wounded comrades in a stateside hospital. Signal Corps photo.

the man lying on his back and conscious. The injured man's first concern was whether his face had been torn up by the blast. Then, when assured that his face was undamaged, he noticed what was left of his arm laying across his chest, grabbed it with his uninjured hand, and asked whose arm it was. "Mine," his friend gruffly replied. "Let go so I can work on you." He tried to locate and tie off the severed artery but was unsuccessful. "It had shrunk in like elastic being cut," he recalled. "Soaked in blood, I could not grab it. I got so frustrated, I cried out loud while he died in my arms."[46]

All of the Allied units in the Fifth Army had suffered extensive losses during the campaigning in Italy, and surviving soldiers were near exhaustion. General Clark therefore ordered a two-week stand-down beginning on November 15. Active, offensive infantry operations ceased in order to allow the tired men to refit and rest—although the artillery remained active. Most of that two-week period was one of rain and mud. Inside the tents of the 15th Evacuation Hospital the six inches of mud on the floor had the consistency, according to one observer, "of good, thick bean soup and about the same color." Out alongside the roads the mud was often a foot deep.[47]

On November 18, there was a shakeup in Fifth Army as troop units shuffled around, at least administratively. Major General Geoffrey T. Keyes arrived from Sicily where he had commanded II Corps. With the fighting in Sicily over, however, II Corps was a corps without much in the way of actual soldiers. With Keyes' movement to Italy, however, the 3rd and 36th Divisions became part of a rejuvenated II Corps. The 34th and 45th Divisions remained in VI Corps, along with the newly arrived French 2nd Moroccan Division. These three divisions formed the right of the Fifth Army line, with II Corps immediately to their left.

On November 24, the day before Thanksgiving, Allied leaders in Italy issued new battle orders. The goal was the Eternal City itself—Rome. To reach it, however, Allied troops had to dislodge the Germans, as well as some stubborn Italian units that had not surrendered when their civil government had. The enemy troops were well dug in all the way across the Italian peninsula. The plan was to attack the defenses along the high ground on either side of the entrance into the Liri Valley—the western gateway to the town of Cassino—while simultaneously enveloping Cassino by driving the Germans off the high ground to the north and northwest of that town. The capture of Cassino was crucial. It would unlock a portion of Highway 6, the main road to Rome. The 34th Division's first goal was to capture the area around the town of Cerasuolo, northeast of Cassino to uncover an important road junction.[48]

Cerasuolo, like many Italian towns, was surrounded by hills, the control of which was imperative for any force attempting to hold the town itself. The maps of the area showed that some of these hills had names—Mount LaRocca, Mount Pantano, and La Croce—while others, apparently deemed of lesser significance by the cartographers, were simply identified by numbers—Hill 920, Hill 1017, and Hill 841. La Croce was the objective assigned to the men of the 100th Battalion, but in order to reach it they first had to neutralize the numbered hills previously mentioned.[49]

Officials of VI Corps allotted a full pound of turkey for every one of its troops to celebrate Thanksgiving Day, on the 25th. But despite the purchase of almost four dozen pack animals a few days before the holiday, a lot of men were unable to receive this holiday treat until the next day. By then, much of the meat had spoiled, although some men ate it anyway—and paid the price with diarrhea.[50]

The 133rd Regiment's commander ordered two of his three battalions—the 3rd and the 100th—to begin an attack before full light on November 29. They were to drive the Germans from the hills west of Cerasuolo, while the 168th Regiment attacked Monte Pantano to their left. Of course, as former soldiers the world over will attest, rare is the plan that survives the first five minutes of a firefight, and this was to be no exception. As Companies A and B moved forward, they met unexpectedly stubborn German defenses on Hill 841. They faced rifle and machine gun fire, mines, and mortars. They were so close to the enemy position that it would have been dangerous to call in American artillery fire because without absolute precision some of the rounds would undoubtedly have fallen near enough to the Americans to cause casualties. The attackers had to make do with organic mortars and machine guns only.

Progress up the hill was very slow, and it was a time of individual heroics. A GI in Company A wiped out a German machine-gun crew with his BAR while dodging bullets and grenades. Shortly thereafter an enemy 88mm antiaircraft gun opened up on the advancing soldiers, and he put it out of action by killing most of its crew. But he did not kill mindlessly. At one point in the action he came upon some Germans, one of whom he judged to be not more than fourteen years old. "I couldn't shoot him," he later recalled. "He looked so young." Instead this young German joined a handful of others that the compassionate American had captured. By the end of that particular action this GI had accounted for almost a score of Germans killed in addition to those he captured. Unknown to him, his superiors recommended him for the Distinguished Service Cross. Later, when he was summoned to headquarters, his immediate reaction was to wonder how much trouble he was in, and for what reason. Instead, General Ryder pinned the nation's second highest award for valor to his chest.[51]

Company B also had its heroes that day when a heavily armed party of some forty German soldiers attacked a handful of its men protecting their platoon's flank. A BAR man quickly emptied four magazines—eighty rounds—of ammunition before an enemy bullet disabled his weapon. His squad leader, hearing his calls for help, provided covering fire for him while he found an un-damaged BAR to use and rejoined the action. When this second weapon then jammed, the intrepid soldier picked up an M1 rifle and continued firing until he and his sergeant had killed almost all of the attackers.[52]

The C Company soldiers on Hills 1017 and 920 were also busy. Food and water were in short supply, and re-supply was extremely uncertain. Keen-eyed German observers on nearby hills were alert to any movement down and off Hill 1017 by men going for sup-plies. The only "safe" time to go was at night, and then the ter-rain itself became the enemy as the men had to negotiate rough ground and steep trails to reach the supply points. And it was more difficult going back with their loads of food and water, loads that often weighed as much as fifty pounds.

On the morning of December 1, reinforcements arrived at Hill 1017 in the form of two under-strength rifle platoons and a machine-gun squad from Company E. After the recent transfer of personnel, that was all that remained of that company. These reinforcements led another assault toward the top of the hill, but their efforts were no more successful than the previous ones. Losses were heavy. A platoon in Company C was down to nine men, the highest ranking of whom was a private, first class. Or-ders soon arrived to cease offensive operations for the time being. "This we were glad to do," remembered one of the men. "We dug our slit trenches deeper and got ready for a counterattack and a long stay."[53]

The first counterattack came not from the Germans but from Mother Nature as the temperature dropped and a light snow began to fall. The snow soon turned to rain, and the men passed a miserable night as their foxholes began filling with icy water. More and more of the men began suffering from trench foot as a result of their constant exposure to the winter weather. Resembling frostbite, and also known as immersion foot, it was fairly common during World War I's stagnant trench warfare. It was caused by wearing wet socks and boots for prolonged periods, and cold temperatures only made it worse. Typically, the soldier's feet would begin to swell and become extremely painful to the touch. Trench foot rendered sufferers unfit for combat just as surely as if they had been wounded by bullets or shrapnel.

Medical officers encouraged the men to remove their boots when they had a chance and massage their feet to keep blood circulating. As well-meaning as that advice undoubtedly was, it was virtually impossible to follow. "I would defy that doctor who gave that order," one man mused, "to sit on the front line, in a fox hole with inches of ice water, to take off his boots and massage his feet. You didn't know when the enemy attack would begin, and you had to be ready to run—with your boots on!" The soldiers were also encouraged to change into dry, warm socks whenever they could—daily at least and more often if possible. The problem, of course, was that these men did not have that many extra socks and even when they did put on a pair of warm, dry socks they became cold and wet within a relatively short time.[54]

"When I removed my shoes my feet puffed up," remembered a Caucasian soldier from the 34th Division, "and I was unable to get them back in my shoes again. I left the shoes in the sun for a while to dry out while I examined my feet. They were terribly swollen, bluish-white in appearance and not comfortable, though not really paining as they would later in the hospital. I had a little feeling in them and found it difficult to walk. In order to get my feet back in the GI boots I had to cut them [the boots]."[55]

There was very little treatment for trench foot other than bed rest, which often lasted for weeks and sometimes for months. Sufferers complained of feeling a burning sensation in their feet and being unable to even touch their feet without considerable pain. Many men, after they reached hospitals, slept with their feet in the open because even the touch of a bed sheet caused excruciating pain. In extreme instances, gangrene set in and required amputations of varying extent—sometimes a toe or two, and sometimes the entire foot. Army officials in Naples had commandeered a former school for use as a hospital, and soon there were so many patients there with trench foot that the facility began to be referred to as Trench Foot College. By the following winter, some forty-five thousand GIs were out of action in Europe because of trench foot. This had the same impact on the war effort as pulling three entire divisions out of the battle line.[56]

There is always a danger, when writing about a military unit, of making it seem stronger, braver, or more daring than any other unit. The War Department got this ball rolling with regard to the Nisei troops, even while the war was still going on, with praiseworthy accounts of their actions. Such propaganda, it was felt, would work in several ways. It would elevate the morale of the soldiers in the unit. It would help to alleviate the prejudice aimed at Japanese Americans on the home front. It would also blunt claims from Japan that the United States was waging a race war—claims that had received a considerable boost from the internment program.

Sometimes the well-intentioned praise heaped upon the Nisei unit was a source of embarrassment instead. Late in 1943, for example, the *Honolulu Star-Bulletin* carried the account of a valiant rescue by men of the 100th Battalion of twenty-two soldiers from another outfit who had been surrounded by the enemy. Unfortunately for accuracy's sake, however, the rescue never took place. The trapped soldiers had already escaped by the time the Nisei patrol arrived. "I don't mind being written up for things I did," one of the "rescuers" wrote to the newspaper, "but neither do I want to be glorified for things I didn't do." A month later, another letter appeared in the paper, this one from the battalion's morale officer. "We are just some of the many American soldiers doing our share," he wrote, "not asking for any favor, but the chance to do our share."[57]

By December 4, the 34th Division had suffered eight hundred casualties in advancing barely a mile. The progress of the 45th was only slightly better. On the 8th, General Lucas sent the fresh 2nd Moroccan Division to begin relieving the 34th. Usually in such situations, the relieving troops simply took over the existing foxholes from those men being relieved. These North Africans had not suffered the battle losses that the 34th had, however, and so outnumbered the Americans they were replacing that there were not enough foxholes for them all, and they had to dig more to accommodate themselves. The Americans were aghast at the seeming lack of discipline displayed by the newcomers as they openly used flashlights and casually built small fires—two things the Americans had refrained from doing when so close to the enemy. "The Bosche know we are here," was a typical reply, "why not be comfortable!"[58]

A company of Moroccans finally arrived at Hill 920 to relieve the exhausted Nisei there. These Americans had suffered heavy losses. Companies E and F ceased to exist altogether now as the few remaining men in each of those units transferred into Company C. Companies A and B had been similarly relieved by the Moroccans and the entire battalion was temporarily removed from the fighting front for a much-needed rest. The next morning the cooks dished up a breakfast for the men that most had been dreaming about. The soldiers attacked the ham and eggs, pancakes, mush, and coffee with perhaps more enthusiasm than they had attacked the Germans. They had been subsisting on C- and K-rations for so long that many of them had difficulty digesting "real" food, and diarrhea was the result. That afternoon, trucks arrived to take the battalion back to a better-equipped rest area near Alife.[59]

The men spent the next couple of weeks in the rest area, but they were not idle. They engaged in rigorous physical training, practiced patrolling techniques, and absorbed replacement soldiers into the decimated units. But at the end of every day of training they had access to cooked meals, hot-water showers, and (almost nightly) movies. They received warm wool winter uniforms and new blankets—and a new commanding officer. Major Gillespie had been dealing with stomach ulcers for some time and his health finally reached a point that demanded hospitalization and a lengthy recovery period. Major Caspar Clough, who had already been awarded the Silver Star for gallantry with the 1st Infantry Division in North Africa, assumed the leadership of the 100th Battalion. Several Nisei staff sergeants also received battlefield promotions to second lieutenant during this time.[60]

As Christmas neared the men looked for some way to mark the occasion, some way to try to forget about the war and enjoy what was usually a festive time of year. Some medics gathered up empty food cans from the mess tent and, with a deft use of tin snips, created bits of shiny metal that passed as Christmas ornaments that they hung on a couple of makeshift Christmas trees. Then, on Christmas eve, they went from tent to tent throughout the battalion area singing carols.[61]

The German "Winter Line," as it was called, was finally breached, but it did not seem to bring the war any closer to an end. The Germans simply fell back to their next prepared line, the "Gustav Line." Fifth Army planners believed that with enough constant hammering the Gustav Line, too, would fall, but at a terrible cost. They decided, therefore, to stage an amphibious landing somewhere north of the western end of the German defenses while other units applied frontal pressure to the Gustav Line. They chose the port city of Anzio, about thirty miles south of Rome, as the site for this operation. Once the landing troops were safely ashore one of three things was certain to occur. One: the invaders would move inland and turn south, thereby crushing the Germans between themselves and other Fifth Army forces still arrayed in front of the Gustav Line. Or, two: the Germans would abandon the Gustav Line and move north to avoid just such a situation as this. Either occurrence was welcome to the Allied forces in Italy. Or, three: the Germans would react quickly to the invasion and push the attackers back into the sea.

Both the success or failure of the Anzio landing would have far-reaching consequences. If the landing failed it would mean that the Allies might indefinitely postpone the cross-Channel invasion of France, which was to follow later that spring. If the Germans could *not* defeat the Anzio landing, it would put the Allies that much closer to capturing Rome.

The key to Rome was still the Liri Valley, which angled from southeast to northwest and toward the capital city. General Clark planned to use each of his three corps to gain the valley. The British 10 Corps was to attack and seize the hills guarding the southwestern approaches. The French Expeditionary Corps was to attack the northwestern positions. Then, with the enemy ousted from the overlooking heights, II Corps, to which the 34th Division had been transferred and which temporarily included the 1st Armored Division, was to move up the center of the valley. Plotting these movements on maps—even topographical maps—gave only the slightest indication of how difficult these movements would actually be.

On New Year's Eve the 100th Battalion started back toward the scene of active fighting, marching westward to Presenzano in a snow storm. The Nisei, along with the 3rd Battalion of the 133rd Infantry Regiment, joined up with Colonel Robert T. Frederick's elite 1st Special Service Force on the far right of II Corps to form the infantry component of an ad hoc task force designated Task Force B. Its assignment was to take the key fortified village of Cervaro, which, along with several important hills, guarded the entrance to the Liri Valley.

Under cover of darkness on the night of January 6, the 1st Special Service Force began working its way up the sides of Monte Majo, which it secured early the next morning. The attached battalions from the 133rd Infantry followed the force men onto the hill, and that night the 100th Battalion moved off to capture an adjacent height known simply as Hill 1190. The battalion made no progress, getting lost instead in the fog and unfamiliar surroundings, but succeeded in occupying the hill the next night. Colonel Frederick's force, in the meantime, took an adjacent hill, and the Americans then endured two days of fierce counterattacks before the Germans decided that they had had enough and fell back. They evacuated Cervaro, and on the 13th, Task Force B was disbanded and the Nisei returned to 34th Division control, taking up temporary residence in the village of San Michele.[62]

Farther west the Anzio operation began at about 2:00 A.M. on January 22, 1944. It was, initially, a tremendous success—something definitely not predicted by the results of rehearsal landings south of Salerno a few days before. In those landings, captains of some of the transport ships were hesitant to approach very close to the beaches, so the assault troops spent up to four hours being tossed about in the smaller landing craft trying to reach dry ground. Hardly any of the infantrymen landed where they were supposed to, and rough seas swamped over forty amphibious trucks, sending about two dozen howitzers and anti-tank guns to the ocean's floor. General Truscott was furious. "To land this division at Anzio as it was landed during the rehearsal," he fumed, "would be to invite disaster." He believed that an alert enemy counterattack with forty or fifty tanks would defeat the entire attempt.

Fortunately, the Germans were not the alert enemy that Truscott feared—at least not when the actual landing took place. The Germans were caught unaware, and Allied naval gunfire quickly knocked out the feeble resistance offered by a few coast artillery and antiaircraft guns. In less than twenty-four hours, thirty-six thousand assault troops, or 90 percent of the total, were ashore with their gear and moving inland. The harbor and beaches were soon swept clear of mines and the Allied troops established a line three miles inland with a total loss of only thirteen killed! By the end of the third day ashore the Allies had established an irregularly shaped beach head along fifteen miles of coast and extending inland some seven miles at its deepest. The invaders spent most of the next week bringing ashore the supplies they would need to conduct a prolonged campaign.[63]

But the Germans did not remain idle for very long. They rushed reinforcements to the trouble spot from as far away as France, Yugoslavia, and even Germany. When the Americans attempted to break out of their initial beachhead, they found the resistance *very* tough. After some early success, a fierce German counterattack forced the Americans back to their original line.

Even though the 34th Division was not slated to participate in the landings, it would have its hands full trying to help tie up Germans along the Gustav Line so they could not join the defenders of Anzio. Two days before GIs hit the beaches, the 34th Division was scheduled to act as a ready reserve for the 36th Division as it crossed the Rapido River south of Cassino, near the elevated village of Sant' Angelo d'Alife.

On the night of January 20, two regiments from the 36th Division began crossing the Rapido at three separate locations. The river was not particularly wide, perhaps thirty to fifty feet, but it was too deep to wade and the speed of the current lived up to the river's name. And the Germans added their own impediments. According to one American officer, obviously a Midwesterner, the enemy "had staked out enough barbed wire on both side [*sic*] of the Rapido river to fence in all the farms in Iowa and Illinois." And while the wire slowed the advancing Americans, German mines, artillery, mortars, and machine guns ripped into them. Enemy fire destroyed many of the boats before they even arrived at the river's edge and knocked out bridges as fast as the engineer troops could build them. A few handfuls of troops got across the river, but most pulled back by early morning to wait for the dark of night before making another attempt. The second try was only slightly more successful. Two battalions got across and dug in about one thousand yards beyond the river, but they were subject to brutal German fire throughout the day of the 22nd, and only forty or fifty were able to escape back across the river that night. An officer in a neighboring division wrote: "The attack by the 36th Div. appeared doomed from the start. When daylight broke [its men were] exposed like sitting ducks in the flats and hell took a recess while the Germans took over!" The 36th Division lost almost seventeen hundred men in the two futile attempts to cross the river. The division commander, wrote in his diary that on January 22 "two regiments of this Division were wrecked on the west bank of the Rapido." (Two years later, after the war was over, survivors called upon Congress to launch an official investigation of what it termed the "Rapido River fiasco and take the necessary steps to correct a military system that will permit an inefficient and inexperienced officer, such as General Mark W. Clark, in a high command to destroy the young manhood of this country and to prevent future soldiers from being sacrificed wastefully and uselessly.")[64]

So, while the 36th pulled back to recover and refit, it fell to General Ryder's 34th Division to continue the operation. More specifically, General Keyes directed the 34th to make its attempt farther upstream, where the water was shallower and boats and bridges would not be immediately necessary. Once on the opposite bank, part of the division was to strike straight ahead across Monte Cassino, one of the mountain guardians of the entrance to the Liri Valley. The other part of the division was to swing downstream and drive the Germans out of the town of Cassino, which sits at the base of the mountain. Ryder assigned the task of clearing the town to his 133rd Regiment.

The plan called for the 100th Battalion to form the left flank of the regiment with the 1st and 3rd battalions to its right. The latter two battalions were to neutralize an area known as Monte Villa, where German troops defended about twenty wrecked Italian army barracks, while the 100th attacked the town of Cassino from the north. The first problem facing the men was getting across the river. German engineers worked to make this as difficult as possible. Crossing the river even without the addition of any man-made obstacles was difficult enough, but a concrete wall, varying in height from seven to twelve feet, blocked access to the river. And soldiers who made it over the wall to the opposite shore then faced a steep earthen wall. The enemy made a crossing at this point even more difficult by damming the river downstream from the Americans. This not only allowed the Germans to deepen the amount of water in the river channel itself, but also left knee-deep water and mud in the fields east of the river. And, of course, they had liberally seeded the area with mines.

The operation began about 10:00 P.M. on January 24. American artillery blasted the German defenses in the area for a solid thirty minutes before the infantry moved forward in the dark. Men with mine detectors carefully moved forward and cleared lanes for their comrades who followed. By this stage of the war in Italy, however, the Germans had begun to use mines constructed largely of wood and plastic that the metal-seeking minesweepers could not detect. Some men thus resorted to the most basic type of search. When German fire disabled the mine detector that one man had started with, he laid it aside, got down on his belly, and inched his way forward, carefully feeling for tripwires with his hands. In this fashion he cleared a safe path five feet wide and 150 feet long.[65]

By dawn, Companies A and C had reached the concrete wall along the east bank of the river with only minor casualties. The other two battalions of the regiment had not progressed as far. To the right of the 100th, only a handful of men from the 3rd Battalion had reached the protection of the wall, while to their right the men of the 1st Battalion were still two hundred yards from it. The remaining rifle company of the 100th Battalion, Company B, started forward as a reinforcement but was shredded by

machine-gun fire, mortars, and artillery. Only about a dozen of
the men reached the safety of the wall. The rest sought shelter in
shallow irrigation ditches that crossed the field or by digging into
the mud where they lay.[66]

The battalion commander, Major Clough, was wounded in the
arm, although not seriously. Major George Dewey, the regimental
executive officer, took command of the 100th, but his tenure was
not long. He had orders to advance the battalion across the river
first thing in the morning, so he asked the Nisei commander of
Company A to lead him over the open ground after dark and up
to the wall so he could familiarize himself with the terrain. Major
Jack Johnson and a handful of enlisted men also went along. As
the small party carefully picked its way toward the wall, a German
machine gunner in the hills on the far side of the river randomly
opened fire. He may not have actually seen the men moving
through the field in the dark, but may simply have been spraying
harassing fire in the general direction of the Americans. Nevertheless, his "aim" was good. Both of the senior officers went down,
and as Major Johnson tried to crawl for cover he detonated a mine
that killed him instantly. Major Clough, his wound freshly ban-
daged, again took command of the battalion, but the next morning's attack was cancelled. Instead, Clough ordered Company C to
pull back from the wall.[67]

Safely traversing enemy minefields was often a matter of luck,
but some men from the 133rd Infantry employed a novel way of
improving their chances. They tied long lengths of explosive detonating cord to rifle grenades and fired them into the mine fields.
The grenades flew into the minefields, trailing the cord behind
them. When the grenade exploded it triggered the detonating
cord that, in turn, set off all of the nearby mines, thus creating safe
lanes through the field.[68]

Before dawn on the 25th, General Ryder could see that the
crossing was unlikely to succeed, so he made some adjustments in
his alignment. He shifted the 100th to the north where it became
the right flank of the regiment. American artillery again pounded
the German positions, and during the day each of the American
battalions achieved partial success. After the sun went down again
most of the 133rd was across the Rapido and holding on.[69]

Enemy fire kept the men of the 133rd from making any progress on the 26th, so General Ryder ordered the 135th to cross the river slightly downstream from them to try to take out the German positions. That night only one company of the 135th made it across the water, where it ran into mines, barbed wire, and machine-gun fire.

Next, Ryder ordered his remaining regiment, the 168th, to cross the river and push its way through the 133rd's tenuous position. This attack, however, was to have more firepower. Following a rather standard predawn artillery bombardment two platoons of tanks led the way for the two infantry battalions committed to the assault. Only four tanks successfully reached the far side of the river, and German mines and artillery knocked them out after a few hours. Four rifle companies made it across, however, and by the end of the day had worked their way across an expanse of flat land and up to the top of Hill 213 northwest of Monte Villa. Confusion ensued after a fifth company reached the hill after dark, and three of the companies pulled back across the river before daylight. The other two companies were ordered back, too, and another crossing was made about five hundred yards upstream.[70]

The 168th Infantry launched another tank- and artillery-supported attack on January 29 to recapture Hill 213 and the nearby Hill 56. Tanks from the 760th Tank Battalion led the assault over the river, seven of them crossing before 7:00 A.M. Even with the tanks, progress was slow against determined German resistance. At about 4:00 that afternoon almost two dozen more tanks from the 756th Tank Battalion suddenly sprinted across the river to help out. The fighting in the area was still not over, but the added muscle provided by the armored vehicles hastened things along, and by sunrise on January 30 the 168th Regiment occupied both hills.[71]

Major Lovell returned from his hospital stay to resume command of the 100th Battalion on January 29, just in time to lead it back into action north of Cassino. "I hate to have to do this, Major," the regimental commander apologized ahead of time, "they've [the men of the 100th Battalion] been hit hard already, but I've got to use your fire-eaters in this attack."[72]

On the first day of the new month, General Ryder sent his 135th Regiment west from Hill 213 toward Monte Castellone and the 133rd east against the wrecked military barracks at Monte Villa. After securing the barracks late that night, the 133rd, with tanks from the 756th Tank Battalion, moved down the road the next day toward the town of Cassino two miles away. Enemy resistance was stout.

The 3rd Battalion of the 133rd moved directly on the town from the north, and even with the added firepower of accompanying tanks, the Germans kept them from getting a firm lodgment inside the city. Anti-tank fire from the town and machine-gun and mortar fire from a hill to the west stopped the GIs. Therefore, on the 3rd, most of the attackers swung toward the northwest to try to drive the enemy off these hills. If the Americans could capture this high ground they could make continued German occupation of the city untenable. The first hill, Hill 175, fell, but the enemy continued to pour fire from the ruins of an old castle on top of Hill 193, or, as it was soon dubbed, Castle Hill. It was essential that Castle Hill, looming as it did approximately five hundred feet above the city, be swept clear of enemy forces.

German engineers had had plenty of time to design and build defensive positions in the hills around Cassino, and they had not wasted that time. Using reinforced concrete and steel, they had improved upon nature's rocky defenses. Many of the man-made works could survive massive amounts of incoming fire. Outgoing firepower was also stupendous.

Meanwhile, the 1st Battalion had, with the support of tanks, forced its way into the northeastern edges of Cassino. Urban warfare was vicious. Not only did the Germans have the advantage of occupying the stoutly built stone houses and shops, but they had strengthened them even further with additional steel and concrete. For an American soldier to expose himself in the streets was to invite an almost instant barrage of fire.

One company from the 133rd escorted a tank platoon into the northern edge of the town that afternoon and began clearing buildings one at a time. It was a slow process. As the soldiers approached an enemy-occupied building they poured as much tank and rifle fire into its windows as they could. Then, while the Germans sheltered themselves from this fire, a couple of infantrymen rushed up to the structure and tossed hand grenades into the first-floor windows to finish them off. Others fired rifle grenades into the windows of the upper stories hoping for the same fatal results.[73]

As five American tanks clanked down a narrow street, German anti-tank fire focused on the third one, knocking it out of commission. Its wreckage, in the middle of the column, thus prevented the first two tanks from retreating and the last two from coming to their assistance. After dark, the two lead tanks found a way to extricate themselves, and the infantrymen, now deprived of the firepower of the tracked vehicles, also withdrew.[74]

The 133rd renewed its attack on the town the next day with a fearsome amount of artillery assistance. The 151st Field Artillery Battalion fired almost forty-six hundred rounds into Cassino, but they had little effect on the well-fortified Germans. And on this day the riflemen encountered a half dozen enemy tanks and were forced, once again, to retire.

By February 5, most of the men of the 3rd Battalion had moved off of Hill 175 and into the northwestern corner of Cassino. The 1st Battalion, unsuccessful within the city, moved around to the west and began to assault Castle Hill once more, but neither battalion made much progress.

On the crest of Monte Cassino some fifteen hundred feet above the city stood a huge Benedictine monastery, the Abbey of Monte Cassino. Original construction on this site dated back over fourteen hundred years, and even though it had fallen victim to invading Lombards, Saracens, and Napoleonic French troops it once again stood proudly atop the hill. The monastery was home to about seventy monks and much valuable artwork when the Germans began to incorporate Monte Cassino into their Gustav Line. Allied planners knew what an important place the Catholic Church had in the very culture of Italy and had promised the Italian people to do their best to see that no harm came to the monastery or, indeed, to any other church structures in that nation. The Germans also respected the significance of the building and promised not to station troops inside, even though its geographical prominence made it an ideal location for an observation post. And although the German high command forbade its troops from taking refuge within the solid walls of the monastery, there was no such restriction with regard to the area just outside of these walls. Enemy troops dug in all around the monastery, setting up observations posts and digging gun pits.[75]

The fighting took a staggering toll on all combatants. By the end of the day on February 7, the strength of the three rifle companies of the 100th Battalion was down to only seven officers and seventy-eight men fit for duty.[76]

Before dawn on February 8, the 168th Infantry Regiment attacked Monte Cassino, and a few hours later what remained of the 100th Battalion, under cover of a smokescreen, swept around to the west of Castle Hill in an attempt to neutralize enemy forces on a slightly lower hill, Hill 165. The wind began to shift before the men reached their goal, however, and with no more smoke to hide them they made irresistible targets for German machine guns and mortars on the surrounding hills. Major Lovell went down with a bullet in his chest. He painfully piled rocks in front of himself as a shield against further injury, but was unable to protect his legs. Three more bullets struck him there. A sergeant braved withering enemy fire to run some thirty feet to the wounded officer and then dragged him out of the line of any further fire, thus saving his life.[77]

Meanwhile, an enemy self-propelled gun appeared atop Castle Hill and begun to fire at the exposed men on Hill 165. The Nisei were almost powerless against it until a bazooka man arrived with his weapon. He already had one armored enemy vehicle to his credit as he tried to get close enough to this one for a crippling shot. He finally fired from only about thirty yards distance and knocked one of the vehicle's treads off. This kept it from maneuvering, but it had no impact upon its ability to keep firing. He fired another rocket, only to have it bounce off without exploding. On his third attempt he scored a direct hit. His rocket pierced the vehicle's armor and exploded inside the crew compartment. He had helped to spare his comrades from the vehicle's cannon fire, but now he was the target of dozens of enemy rifles and machine guns. One bullet hit him in the arm, but he crawled into a position of relative safety and waited for dark.[78]

For the next four days, the Nisei soldiers remained dug in on the slopes of Hill 165. They could not move forward because of the intense defensive fire, and they could not move back for fear of being mowed down from behind. Finally, on February 12, they were able to extricate themselves and pull back to a reserve location north of Hill 193. But not everybody got to rest. Company B soon advanced into Cassino to help out the 3rd Battalion.

Tank cannons and 105mm and 155mm howitzers pounded the city into rubble. The relatively new 8-inch howitzers also assisted in the destruction of many buildings. Those that the defenders had reinforced, however, seemed immune to shellfire. One side effect of the use of all this firepower was that the streets were soon filled with the debris of fallen buildings, making it impossible for the American tanks to penetrate farther into the city.

Riflemen used bazookas to blow holes into buildings so they could enter them without exposing themselves in the streets. It was not unusual for a bazooka team to fire as many as nine rockets pointblank at a building's wall in order to create a big enough hole for the men to scramble through—after first clearing the rooms beyond with grenades. They then repeated the process to get into the next building without having to enter the streets. Rockets and grenades were cheaper than human lives, but it was still slow going. Americans only cleared five buildings on February 9, and two more on the 12th.[79]

Casualties in II Corps were so heavy that General Clark decided to take it out of the line as soon as he could find other units with which to replace it. These other units were the British 2nd New Zealand Division and 4th Indian Division, both of which comprised an ad hoc New Zealand Corps under the command of Lieutenant General Sir Bernard Freyberg. Freyberg's goal was the same as Keyes' had been—to destroy German resistance in and around Cassino.

Freyberg assigned the task of driving the Germans off of Monte Cassino to the 4th Indian Division. Its commander, Major General F. S. Tuker, after studying the battlefield situation at length, was

convinced that German troops were using the monastery in violation of previously agreed upon protocol. Proof of such duplicity
was in the report of an Italian civilian who said that he had seen
numerous German soldiers and machine guns inside the building before he left on February 7. Less than a week later artillery
observers from the 131st Field Artillery Battalion swore that they
saw small-arms fire originating in the monastery. General Tuker
declared that military necessity demanded that the monastery
be bombed. Freyberg agreed and began pushing up the chain of
command for permission to do so.

General Clark, and many other high ranking officers, believed
that bombing the monastery would be a mistake. They doubted
that the Germans were actually using the structure since they had
plenty of other observation points on the hill that would serve
them just as well. Also, destroying such a site, with all of its religious and historic significance, would be a tremendous public relations gaffe, and the Germans would still have its rubble
from which to continue fighting against the Allies. On February
13, Lieutenant General Ira C. Eaker, commander of the Mediterranean Air Command, and Lieutenant General Jacob L. Devers,
Deputy Supreme Allied Commander of the Mediterranean Theater of Operations, flew over the monastery in a small observation
plane to see for themselves if the Germans were inside. Flying only
about two hundred feet above the structure, each man said he
saw German soldiers in and around the abbey as well as a military-
type communications antenna. Clark reluctantly assented to the
request for bombardment.

A little before 10:00 A.M. on February 15, the first American
planes arrived over Monte Cassino and began their bomb runs.
By day's end over 250 medium and heavy bombers had unloaded
almost six hundred tons of ordnance onto the mountain top. At
precisely 10:30, 266 rounds of artillery smashed into the building
in a carefully choreographed time-on-target barrage. American
observers reported dozens of German soldiers scrambling from
the wreckage. A later report, however, from an Italian civilian
who had been inside the abbey during the attack, claimed that
there had never been any German soldiers within its walls. The
archbishop declared in a German propaganda interview a few

days later that "until the moment of the destruction of the Monte Cassino Abbey there was within the area of the abbey neither a German soldier, nor any German weapon, nor any German military installation." Because these air raids reduced much of the historic structure to rubble there was no reason now for the Germans not to occupy and make use of the still substantial defenses atop the hill, and they did so. More modest air raids continued for the next several days. The 4th Indian Division had relieved the 135th and the 168th Regiments of the 34th Division and now sought to capture the abbey. Its efforts, however, proved fruitless. It would be some time before Allied troops forced the defenders out.[80]

On February 22, troops from the 6th New Zealand Brigade relieved the last elements of the 34th Division, which had remained in the northeastern corner of Cassino. For the 34th Division, the fight for Cassino was over. It had been particularly costly for the 100th Battalion. Four officers had been killed and fifteen injured, while forty-four enlisted men had paid the ultimate price and 130 others had been wounded. Battalion losses since landing in Italy approached 60 percent.[81]

The division retired to San Angelo d'Alife, and after a few weeks it relocated to San Giorgio del Sannio for a period of rest, refitting, and training. The men enjoyed reading their mail, eating hot food, and taking showers. Unlike most of the other combat units overseas, the pool of possible replacements for the 100th Battalion was racially restricted. Its officers could not simply requisition the needed number of men from the nearest replacement depot; they had to have Japanese American soldiers. Back in Mississippi, therefore, the 442nd Regiment became a source of replacement for the 100th Battalion.

A call went out to the various units within the combat team at Camp Shelby to provide men for immediate deployment to Italy. The natural instinct on the part of the unit commanders was to weed out their less desirable recruits and get rid of their worst troublemakers and misfits. At least one man was certain that that was the practice, and was a little taken aback when his name appeared on a list of replacements for the 100th. "Apparently," he mused many years later, "we [replacements] were noted as the lousiest guys in the 442nd," although he had certainly considered himself to have been a good soldier up to that point. "I wonder why I was picked. . . . They even gave me a good conduct medal."[82]

Some of the combat veterans of the 100th Battalion seemed disappointed to see the arrival of replacement troops. They had hoped that the army would pull their entire unit out of battle and maybe even send it back to the States to rebuild its manpower strength. Obviously, that was not about to happen. The replacements eagerly sought the advice of the men who had already experienced a considerable amount of combat. "If you survive five minutes of war," one of the men learned, "you are a veteran." Another, realizing that there was no better preparation than on-the-job training, believed that if a soldier could survive his first hour in battle he would probably have learned enough there to have a good chance of surviving the rest of the war.[83]

It was about this time, too, that the 133rd Regiment's "missing" battalion, the 2nd, arrived from North Africa. This was the battalion whose place in the regimental structure had been filled by the 100th. But the Nisei battalion did not become an orphan. General Ryder, the commander of the 34th Division, was so impressed with its performance that even though the 2nd Battalion of the 133rd Regiment took over its original slot within the regiment, the 100th remained part of the 34th Division.

At 8:30 on the morning of March 15, while the 34th Division continued training, over 170 medium bombers—B-25s and B-26s—appeared over Cassino and began dropping 1,000-pound bombs into the city. A few minutes later, the first of over 260 heavy B-17s and B-24s arrived to continue the assault. Dust and smoke soon filled the sky over the town, such that bombardiers in many of the later-arriving planes had a difficult time making out the target. As a result, bomb accuracy fell off dramatically. Estimates were that more than two-thirds of the bombs fell outside the city, but about three hundred tons of explosives did hit the target. About two dozen bombers failed to drop their loads at all because of the uncertainty as to what they would hit down below. Hundreds of howitzers and heavier guns added their weight to the raid. By early afternoon, cloud cover so obscured Cassino from the air that 260 heavy bombers scheduled for another raid turned back to their bases, leaving the smaller fighter-bombers to continue the

assault. And for what? Indian and New Zealand troops spent another week desperately fighting through what was left of the town
and trying to dig the Germans out of the rubble of the abbey. And
after suffering two thousand casualties, they were no closer to success than they had been the week before.[84]

At Anzio, meanwhile, the Germans were strong enough by the
end of January to thwart Allied attempts to break out of the beachhead, but three German counterattacks during February were
repulsed, and both sides settled into a stalemate as each sought
some advantage over the other. Part of the Allied plan called for
the transfer of the 34th Division to Anzio, so the 100th Battalion
trucked to Naples on March 24 and the next day boarded LSTs
(Landing Ship, Tank) for the trip up the coast. It was a short trip,
less than eighteen hours, but it was long enough for some of the
island boys to break out their dice. Several curious sailors were
lured into a variation of craps that used three dice instead of two,
and by the time the vessels arrived off Anzio on the morning of
March 26 they had empty pockets.[85]

German artillerists welcomed the new arrivals to the beach with
a bombardment that included shells from a gun many miles away.
Later it was discovered to be not one gun, but two massive 280mm
weapons mounted on heavily reinforced railway cars. Each of
these 230-ton behemoths could fire a 550-pound shell from its
seventy-foot barrel out to a distance of some thirty-eight miles.
The Germans called these guns "Robert" and "Leopold." The GIs,
of course, had no way of knowing what pet names the Germans
had bestowed upon these massive guns, and indiscriminately
dubbed them "Anzio Annie" or the "Anzio Express." The former
nickname was simply a matter of alliteration, but the latter had
to do with the size of shells that issued forth with the sound of a
speeding freight train. A soldier in the 36th Infantry Division said:
"It sounded like a box car flipping end over end through the air
with its doors open."[86]

At Anzio the 34th Division relieved the 3rd Division, which had
spent more than two months in the line. The Hawaiian battalion's
specific role was to take over from the 2nd Battalion of the 30th
Infantry Regiment to the right of center of the Allied position.
The troops rode trucks from the beach to their assigned spot in

the line, where they inherited some stoutly built dugouts from the departing units and soon made themselves as comfortable as possible. The terrain here was vastly different than the mountains from which they had come. And even though they were not at the very front, they quickly became aware that sharp-eyed enemy lookouts were quick to call down machine-gun and mortar fire on any movement that they discerned in the American lines. The only time the men dared to venture forth from their dugouts was after the sun went down for the day.

And it was crowded. The flat plain stretching inland from the beach gave the Germans uninterrupted views of the Allied position as well as clear fields of fire for their artillery. In some respects the beachhead resembled some Old West prairie dog town. In addition to fortified bunkers for the soldiers, underground facilities had been constructed for the housing of headquarters, hospitals, supply dumps, and maintenance shops. The area's high water table meant that it was impossible to dig very deep before flooding occurred. Engineer troops solved this problem by digging down about three-and-a-half feet with their bulldozers for the tents that housed the hospitals and other facilities and then piling dirt and sandbags up around the walls of the tents for added protection. Tankers and artillerymen similarly dug in their vehicles and guns so as to minimize exposure to the enemy.[87]

On April 2, the 100th Battalion welcomed a new commanding officer. Lieutenant Colonel Gordon Singles transferred over from the 69th Division to replace Major Clough, who remained with the battalion as Singles' assistant. Perhaps more welcome than the new commander, however, was the arrival two days later of another batch of replacements. Eighteen officers accompanied the 261 enlisted personnel from Camp Shelby, bringing the battalion's strength to just under eleven hundred men. Two days later they moved up to within a couple of hundred yards of the front and into dugouts and partially demolished farmhouses that dotted the area.[88]

The men spent their days sleeping, writing letters, or just generally whiling away the hours. After dark, they emerged from their places of refuge for various duty assignments. Some men busily filled sandbags, others stood guard, and still others went on combat patrols to try to capture German prisoners for interrogation by intelligence officers. Those who did not have assigned duties spent the time socializing and trying to figure out new variations on army food. They had already arranged with quartermasters to trade their potato ration for rice, and they supplemented that with anything that might even remotely resemble vegetables. They were remarkably inventive. Sometimes "liberated" chickens wound up on their menus.

Some of the men even feasted on rabbit, but with unforeseen consequences. A local physician kept rabbits for experimental purposes. When they began to disappear he had a very good idea about what had happened to them and came immediately to the 100th Battalion's headquarters to complain. When Colonel Singles learned why the doctor had the rabbits he expressed his concern that they might have been injected with something that could have serious, maybe even fatal, effects on anyone who ate one. The rabbits' owner assured him that they were completely healthy, but Singles nevertheless decided that it was time for his men to learn a lesson about respecting civilian property. He immediately put the word out that the recently eaten rabbits had been injected with some serious disease, and that soldiers who had eaten them must report immediately to the doctor in town for treatment. The guilty men, not knowing what horrible affliction they might have contracted, but anxious for the cure, lost no time in visiting the good doctor. They were unaware that the rabbits they had stolen had belonged to him, and they did not learn until too late that the antidotes he administered were strong laxatives. Soldiers being soldiers, however, it is not likely that this lesson discouraged them from foraging in the future.[89]

By this time many of the men had gained access to radios, and during idle time they tuned into English-language Axis radio stations featuring sultry-voiced, American-born female announcers. Rita Zucca, using the radio name "Sally," broadcast from various Italian cities, and Mildred Gillars, calling herself "Midge," originated most of her shows from Berlin. Ironically, it was "Midge" who became popularly known as "Axis Sally" or "Berlin Sally." Nazi propagandists intended for these programs to undermine Allied morale by offering the latest popular American music (to

make the GIs homesick) along with comments about the likelihood that their wives or sweethearts were being unfaithful to them
at home with men not in the service. The songs from home did
make the men a little bit homesick, but they were not impressed
by the propaganda messages. "Her routine drew many snickers,"
remembered a soldier in the 133rd Infantry Regiment, "but her
broadcasts did more to help rather than hinder morale." When
one of the Nisei soldiers commented that he liked the program
because there were no commercial interruptions, another suggested that it was because the German government was the spon-
sor, and it would soon be out of business. These programs seemed
only to inspire the men to do whatever was necessary to get the
war over with and get back home as soon as possible.[90]

Meanwhile, plans had gone forward for a major attack to punch
through the German lines and begin the advance to Rome. One
thing keeping those plans from being implemented was a lack of
intelligence with regard to the German forces in the vicinity of
the 100th Battalion. There was some concern that a German panzer division was in the neighborhood, and if that was so it would
make the breakout more difficult. Large combat patrols of eighty
to ninety men had been going out almost every night trying to
capture prisoners for the top brass to question, but they had
been notably unsuccessful. Young Kim, the 100th Battalion's Korean American intelligence officer, proposed a bold plan to bag a
prisoner.

Kim suggested that a small patrol might have more success than
the larger ones because it would make less noise when it moved.
When he told Colonel Singles just how small a patrol he had in
mind, however, the new battalion commander was aghast. Kim
proposed that only one other man accompany him on this dangerous mission, and Singles immediately refused. Kim was insistent, however, and after two days of obstinacy, the colonel relented
and pushed Kim's plan further up the chain of command. It took
a week to get clearance from Fifth Army headquarters, but finally,
on a night in mid-May, Kim was ready.

His plan was so audacious that it just might work. He figured
that during the day no one would expect such a thing to happen,
so that is when he planned to execute his snatch mission. He would

work his way as close to the enemy's lines as he could at night, even though that is when they would be most alert. Then, when their level of alertness tapered off after sunup, he would make his move.

Kim selected Irving Akahoshi, from the battalion's headquarters company, to accompany him on the most dangerous part of the mission. Two or three riflemen would also go part way in order to give him covering fire with their BARs if that became necessary. Around midnight, the men slipped through previously arranged cuts in the barbed wire and concertina wire that piled up over eight feet high along the front line and into a shallow ditch that was manned only at night. Leaving the riflemen in the ditch, Kim and Akahoshi crawled forward, cradling their Thompson submachine guns as they went. They reached the vicinity of the German ditch after about an hour of very careful crawling. They were so close to the enemy soldiers that they could almost have reached out and touched them. The two Americans then settled in, motionless, for the rest of the night.

Just as the sky started to lighten, the Germans began to pull back toward their bunker. The two Americans watched them go. Their plan was to circle around through a wheat field so as to approach the bunker from the rear. Kim was counting on the Germans relaxing their vigilance, and he hoped that there would be even less of a chance that the enemy would spot the Americans coming in from behind them. When the GIs reached the bunker they would each toss two fragmentation grenades inside. Kim specified these rather than the high explosive grenades because they were not quite as noisy. The walls of the bunker would further muffle the sound and make it less likely that the Germans in nearby positions would hear them. The grenades, Kim hoped, would disable enough of the men in the bunker that he and his companion could grab one of them, even if he were slightly wounded, and make their escape back to friendly lines.

The two Americans approached the German position carefully, trying to locate the enemy soldiers within. When Kim peaked around the front corner and saw two soldiers in a slit trench, fast asleep and snoring, he motioned Akahoshi, who had already loosened the pins on his grenades, to come forward. Kim changed the plan on the spot. They would not have to resort to their grenades after all, and they had a good chance of capturing not one but two Germans. Each of the Americans pushed the muzzle of his machine gun into the mouth of one of the slumbering soldiers. The Germans came awake with a start, but with the gun barrels pushing into the backs of their throats were unable to utter a sound, and soon all four men, captives and captors, were carefully crawling back toward the American lines.

They reached the ditch that served as the nighttime position for American sentries and holed up there for the rest of the day. It would have been too risky to expose themselves, even for the short time it would have taken them to move from this trench to the safety of their bunkers. That evening, around seven, they completed their mission. (Each man later received a Distinguished Service Cross for his actions.) Intelligence officers were able to tell right away, almost without even questioning the prisoners, that there was no German panzer division in front of this part of the line. The insignias on the German uniforms were not those of panzer units. Plans for the breakout could now go forward.[91]

The 100th Battalion shifted slightly toward the northeast, and took over a position previously occupied by the 1st Battalion of the 133rd Infantry. No sooner had the men begun to settle in than one of those brief interludes of humanity interjected itself into the war. The Germans sent a message across to the Americans that there were eight wounded GIs behind German lines, and that they were willing to honor a short ceasefire to allow these men to be retrieved. The battalion's surgeon and its chaplain accompanied the recovery team into the 170-foot wide Mussolini Canal, which, at this time of year, had very little water in it. There, under the watchful eyes of a couple of German soldiers, they found a lieutenant from Company A along with some wounded enlisted men. While the wounded were being tended, one of the German soldiers proposed an extension of the truce to allow his comrades to bury the bodies of a dozen dead Americans near their lines. The American recovery team, however, had no authority to negotiate such a deal and the dead were left where they were. But they were beyond caring.[92]

The breakout from the Anzio beachhead began the next day, May 23, 1944. Within the previous two weeks, units of the British

Eighth Army had penetrated the Gustav Line west of Cassino and had also breached the Hitler Line, a little farther north. As the Germans in that area pulled back toward the north, pursuing American troops along the coast began to link up with their comrades in the Anzio area. The Anzio troops now pushed inland, toward the northeast, hoping to interdict the fleeing German Tenth Army and crush it in a classic hammer-and-anvil operation with the pursuing Eighth Army. To accomplish this, therefore, it was first necessary for the Allies to control Highway 7, which passed about a dozen miles inland from Anzio on its way to Rome. Then, they were to cross a line of hills and block Highway 6, which also led to Rome and was the other major escape route for the Germans.

During the opening days of the breakout, the 100th Battalion remained in reserve. Another 115 officers and men arrived from Camp Shelby on the 24th, and received assignments to various companies whose strength had been seriously reduced. But on May 27, it was back into action as the men boarded trucks and headed for the front. On that day, the 34th Division joined with the 45th Division to attack northward. The objective of the 45th Division, on the left, was the railroad station at Campoleone, while the 34th moved along Highway 7 toward the medieval walled village of Lanuvio. After advancing against light-to- moderate resistance for about a mile and a half, both divisions were halted by increased defensive fire. The assault resumed the next day, but progress was very slow over the next few days.[93]

A little before 9:00 A.M. on June 2, Companies B and C of the 100th Battalion began advancing toward the little village of Pian Marano, almost straight north of Anzio. The Germans, as usual, had prepared the battlefield carefully. In areas that lay outside the range of their machine guns, they placed hundreds of mines. Thus, when the two advancing rifle companies attempted to escape machine-gun fire they found themselves in the midst of minefields. Fighting throughout the day, the battalion finally entered the town early on the morning of June 3 when the Germans pulled back. The heroism of the men of Companies B and C in this fight resulted in the award of ten medals for valor—including six Distinguished Service Crosses. A Company C man, for example, wiped out two machine-gun positions with his BAR, killing or wounding over a dozen German soldiers, and a Company B soldier knocked out several other positions and captured two dozen enemy troops. But the victory, like all others, was not without human cost. Fifteen Nisei were killed and sixty-three wounded.[94]

Later that afternoon Colonel Singles took command of an ad hoc task force consisting of his own 100th Infantry Battalion, two field artillery battalions, two companies of tank destroyers, and a company of chemical mortars. Task Force Singles—as it was designated—was to drive the remnants of the 29th Panzer Group from Hill 435, which overlooked a critical road junction just south of the village of Genzano where the roads from Lanuvio and Nemi merged with the Via Appia, or Highway 7, coming from Velletri toward Rome. If the Germans were to safely escape the Allies coming up from the south they would have to be able to make use of this junction.[95]

The fight for Hill 435 began at 8:30 in the evening, as the sun sank low in the west. As the big guns of the 125th Artillery began plastering German positions on top of the hill, the men of Company A began their assault. There was still a lot of fight left in the veteran 29th Panzer Group, and its machine guns and mortars soon pinned down the advancing infantrymen. Singles then committed his other two rifle companies, B on the left and C on the right. At the same time he ordered the tank destroyers to focus their fire on the top of the hill while the heavy mortars from the 84th Chemical Mortar Battalion dropped smoke shells into the enemy positions. By midnight it was over. The Americans were on top of Hill 435 and fifty German prisoners were headed for the rear.[96]

General Kesselring finally conceded that he had to pull back from the hills southeast of Rome if he was to have any chance of saving his army to fight another day. During the night of June 2 and 3, therefore, German troops began moving out of their positions, their movements masked by a furious artillery barrage meant to keep the Allies at bay. When the artillery finally fell silent, General Ryder pushed combat patrols forward to see what the enemy was up to. Just after midnight, these patrols discovered that Lanuvio was free of German soldiers, and by early the next morning it was firmly in the hands of the 168th Infantry Regiment.[97]

Pushing forward as rapidly as possible through Italian villages, along Highway 7, the amount of civilian damage encountered was appalling. According to a Caucasian soldier in the 34th Division, "the stench of dead humans permeated the air so profusely," in the village of Albano, "that even a gas mask was not a deterrent to the odor. For all the cleanliness efforts of the human being there is nothing more obnoxious than the smell of a human body during decay and here the awful odor of hundreds of them wafted in the air."[98]

The capture of Rome seemed a certainty by this time, and opposing commanders had already decided that the city would not share the fate of Naples. Urban fighting would necessarily see the destruction of a tremendous amount of priceless art and architecture, and both sides had reasons to avoid this. The Allies had already paid a price in public relations with the destruction of the abbey at Monte Cassino and did not want a repetition of that. The Germans knew that if they contested the Allied advance through Rome that much of the Christian world would, quite correctly, place the blame for the resultant destruction on them. Responding to a request from the president of neutral Ireland to guarantee the protection of the Holy City, President Roosevelt announced that the preservation of that city's antiquities was completely in the hands of the Germans. After all, as he pointed out, if there were no German soldiers in Rome the Allies could ensure its protection. General Clark amplified this sentiment when he stated that if the Germans opposed "our advance by disposition and fires that necessitate Fifth Army troops firing into the city of Rome, battalion commanders and all higher commanders [were] authorized to take appropriate action without delay to defeat the opposing enemy elements by fire and movement."[99]

Task Force Singles sped forward throughout the day of June 4 as surviving remnants of enemy units hastened to escape capture. By mid-afternoon, Singles' men were within about six miles of Rome. They were poised to enter the Eternal City as its liberators when orders arrived for them to halt. They then watched disconsolately as the tanks, trucks, and halftracks of the 1st Armored Division rushed by them and into Rome—and into the history books—as the city's liberators. Romans showered the liberating Allied troops with flowers and wine in a joyous celebration. It was rumored that the level of the Tiber River where it flowed through the city increased measurably from the amount of wine-induced urine that the soldiers contributed to it. "Beautiful girls," recalled one GI, "and some not so beautiful, kissed and hugged every soldier they could reach." The 100th Battalion, however, missed out on this.[100]

Many of the men believed that they were once again victimized because of their ethnicity. Nevertheless, they rode through Rome in trucks later that night, but by that time most of the city's revelers had gone to bed. Once through the city the motorcade advanced a few more miles up the coast. Task Force Singles ceased to exist there, and all of the attached artillery units returned to their parent organizations.

The rejoicing in the Allied nations over the capture of this first Axis capital faded quickly. Just two days later, on the morning of June 6, the British Broadcasting Corporation made the following short announcement: "Under the command of General Eisenhower, Allied naval forces, supported by strong air forces, began landing Allied armies this morning on the northern coast of France." The long awaited invasion of Western Europe had begun.[101]

The occupation of Rome brought with it several logistical difficulties. The nearest large port in Allied hands was at Naples, which meant that hundreds of trucks stayed busy hauling vital supplies to the army more than a hundred miles away. It therefore became vitally important to take Civitavecchia, the port that lay about forty miles northwest of Rome and was that city's major outlet to the sea. Civitavecchia was under no such guarantee as Rome had been, and it was vital for the Allies to capture it before the retreating Germans could inflict the same level of destruction as they had on Naples. Of equal importance were the airfields at Viterbo, northeast of Civitavecchia and about the same distance from Rome.

Early on the morning of June 6, the 34th Division began its movement toward Civitavecchia along the coastal highway—Highway 1—while the 36th Division moved north on a parallel road toward Viterbo. The 1st Armored Division sent tanks and self-propelled guns to accompany each of these infantry formations.

The Americans encountered little in the way of opposition as they moved warily forward, and by the end of the day the 34th Division had reached a point about seventeen miles from Civitavecchia. Because the resistance had been so light the column continued forward even after sunset, and by noon the next day the port was in American hands.

General Ryder immediately sent the 133rd Infantry forward on a truck march up the highway toward Tarquinia, about ten miles north of Civitavecchia. Proceeding carefully, the soldiers covered half of the distance by nightfall without any sight of enemy troops. The next day, however, they came upon elements of the newly-arrived 361st Regimental Combat Team of the 20th Luftwaffe Field Division hastily digging foxholes and other defensive positions. Due to faulty intelligence, the Germans were unaware that American forces were so near, and when the 133rd attacked, it took the enemy completely by surprise. The enemy regiment was soon completely shattered and its demoralized survivors streaming northward to escape.[102]

On June 9, the 34th Division went into corps reserve near Civitavecchia after being relieved by the 36th Division.

CHAPTER FIVE

GOING OVERSEAS

"We feel that we are now ready to take our places beside the 100th Inf. Bn."

In February 1944, after a year at Camp Shelby, the 442nd Regimental Combat Team finally received orders to prepare for overseas deployment. The soldiers welcomed this bit of news as it meant that they would finally be able to put their training to use. They would finally join with the 100th Battalion and start proving to Caucasian America that they were truly patriotic. Sergeant Morita's reaction was probably typical. "I'm feeling O.K.," he wrote to his brother, "and chafing a little at the bit waiting to go." He expanded upon this in another letter the same day: "We feel that we are now ready to take our places beside the 100th Inf. Bn." He had completed the last of his communications training at Fort Sill on April 1 and was then assigned to head up the three-man radio section of the artillery battalion's Headquarters Battery.[1]

Actual departure for the seat of war, however, was still a couple of months away, but such a lead time was necessary because even though most of the men in the regiment had spent almost a year in training, a lot of work remained to be done to get them, and the individual units to which they belonged, ready to go.

One problem was making sure that every company, battery, and battalion of the combat team had its full complement of officers and men, and that all personnel were physically capable of functioning in combat conditions. Some soldiers were in the base hospital, too ill to travel. Others were unavailable for immediate deployment because they were receiving specialized training at other camps—such as the field artillery schools at Fort Sill. But since the entire process of getting a regiment or a battalion ready to deploy overseas usually took several weeks to several months, most of these men were able to complete these phases of their preparation and return to Camp Shelby before the 442nd departed.

Further exacerbating the situation was the fact that thirty infantry officers and 325 men had left Camp Shelby as replacements for the 100th Infantry Battalion since the beginning of the year, and even after the 442nd received its preliminary orders to move another ten officers and 155 men were rushed to Italy as additional replacements. The fighting around Cassino and Anzio in Italy took a heavy toll on all units, and there was an almost constant call for the 442nd to send replacements to the 100th. Most of these men came from the 1st Battalion of the 442nd at Camp Shelby, leaving that battalion far below its required strength.[2]

Preparations also included physical examinations again to make sure that none but the healthiest individuals would ship out. These were necessary to cull men who had passed perhaps less stringent examinations upon induction or who had developed conditions during their initial training that disqualified them for combat service. While some men functioned flawlessly at stateside camps, the rigorous demands of active campaigning could prove too daunting for them. In some instances age was the deciding factor, particularly among officers. And psychological screening sought to identify and weed out those who, because of deep-seated trepidations about combat, would be more of a liability than an asset to the regiment.

Adding to the difficulties for the Nisei units was the fact that they did not have the entire U.S. Army pool of manpower from which to draw. All of the replacements had to be Japanese Americans, and there just were not enough of them available. The draft, only recently reopened to Japanese Americans, was only then beginning to provide recruits. And that was with some difficulty. There were still concerns among army officials as to the loyalty of Nisei men being considered for military service. Thus a questionnaire was developed and administered to all Japanese American men of draft age to determine their suitability for induction. There were two questions that caused a considerable amount of anxiety within the internment camps. Question number twenty-seven asked: "Are you willing to serve in the armed forces of the

United States on combat duty, wherever ordered?" The wording of this question left many men uncertain as to just how to answer. Some thought that by answering "yes" they were, in effect, volunteering for immediate service. This was not an attractive option for men still trying to come to grips with the whole internment experience.

The very next question, number twenty-eight, asked: "Will you swear unqualified allegiance to the United States of America and faithfully defend the United States from any and all attack by foreign or domestic forces, and foreswear any form of allegiance or obedience to the Japanese emperor, to any other foreign government, power or organization?" This question also spurred some resentment as, by asking the respondent to "foreswear any form of allegiance or obedience to the Japanese emperor" it seemed to say that there was such an allegiance to Japan that now had to be eradicated. One must remember that virtually all of these draft-age men were native-born American citizens. A "yes" answer to each of the questions would presumably prove a man's loyalty, but not everyone wanted to answer that way. "I paled when I read these words," remembered one man.

> That government had incarcerated me against my will, taken away my freedom, prevented me from getting an education, subjected me to the intolerable humiliation of an interrogation by the FBI, caused me to despair of ever leaving the camps, and now—on top of all this—it was trying to coerce me into pledging my unconditional loyalty to it. I did not want to yield to that kind of oppressive force."[3]

By this time many of the Japanese Americans had been behind the barbed wire of the internment camps for quite some time, and they deeply resented what they considered yet another manifestation of doubt about their loyalty.. It did not require deep reflection to see the gross hypocrisy of the government demanding military service from a group of people that it had so recently mistrusted so much as to imprison them. Some men refused to answer either question, and some answered "no" to one or both questions. Others tried to put conditions on their answers. Yes, they would serve in the armed forces if their families were then released from the relocation camps. Of course, those men who refused to answer the questions at all, or who answered "no" to them, or who tried to answer them conditionally, were immediately labeled as troublemakers. Many were rounded up from the various camps and sent to the camp at Tule Lake where they could be kept under close watch.

In some camps there was a much more open opposition to the draft. At Manzanar, an openly pro-Japan group, calling itself the Black Dragon Society, terrorized those who did not share their feelings. And at Heart Mountain, some of the inmates formed the Fair Play Committee, which urged the young Nisei men to resist induction by refusing to report when they received orders for their pre-induction physical exams. And even though most Nisei draftees duly reported for service, almost 270 did not. Many went to jail after being found guilty of evading the draft, but their prosecutions were not always above reproach. In Idaho, for example, the presiding judge was former governor Chase Clark, who had openly admitted that he did not trust any Japanese Americans. But rather than recuse himself from hearing these cases, his preferred solution to the problem of dealing with such people was to send them all to Japan "and then sink the island." Some of the appointed defense attorneys were not much better. One told a defendant: "I'll be damned if I'm going to help you." Another, referring to his clients as traitors, refused even to sit at the same table with them.[4]

Judge Clark ran a series of trials with almost clocklike precision. After empanelling a jury pool of some thirty-four local citizens he proceeded to hear thirty-three cases in eleven days. He shuffled the jurors to get "new" panels for each trial, but it meant that almost all of them heard at least ten cases during this time, and one man heard fifteen. When a fair-minded defense attorney finally complained that such a practice almost guaranteed prejudiced juries, the judge dismissed his complaint and went on with the proceedings. The "juries" found all thirty-three men guilty, and Judge Clark sentenced each of them to pay a $200 fine and to serve thirty-nine months in prison.[5]

Judge Louis E. Goodman, hearing the cases of twenty-seven draft resisters in California later on, did not share Judge Clark's narrow view and dismissed the charges because of a lack of due process. "It is *shocking to the conscience*," he ruled, "that an American citizen be confined on the ground of disloyalty, and then, while so under duress and restraint, be compelled to serve in the armed forces, or be prosecuted for not yielding to such compulsion."[6]

As Nisei draftees began to arrive, reluctantly in some cases, the combat team's manpower strength grew slowly. Even with the influx, there were not enough men at Camp Shelby to fill out all three infantry battalions. Instead, all personnel shortages in the 2nd and 3rd Battalions were filled from among the ranks of the 1st Battalion. That battalion was then re-designated a training battalion—the 171st—and none of its personnel went overseas with the regiment. Instead, upon arrival in Europe, the 442nd Regiment absorbed the 100th Battalion in order to reach full, three-battalion regimental strength, and the 171st trained and forwarded Nisei replacements as fast as they were needed.

It was a constant problem. Four divisions slated for deployment overseas in the spring and summer of 1944, for example, were short a total of almost twelve thousand men from their authorized fifty-seven thousand. In addition, over twenty-seven thousand of the men who were present were found unfit for various reasons and the divisions had to absorb over thirty-nine thousand replacements to make up the difference and reach full authorized strength. Thus, fully two-thirds of the men in these divisions had not had extensive training together before going overseas.[7]

A second area of concern with regard to preparations for overseas deployment was the level of training of individual soldiers. During the year at Camp Shelby, for example, Japanese Americans again became subject to the military draft and many of those selected reported to Camp Shelby for their training. That meant that by the time the combat team had received orders to move, many of these recruits had only been in camp a short time, and their training was definitely not up to an acceptable level. Nor could Caucasian recruits who were more fully prepared be folded into the team.

The camp hummed with the activity of show-down inspections where every soldier and every unit had to show that their equipment was on hand and in serviceable condition. Whatever had been lost or worn out had to be replaced. This covered everything from the uniform allotments to weapons and other hardware. Quartermasters had to make sure that each soldier had every piece of clothing that was officially specified, and that sometimes made for comical situations. Because the Nisei troops tended to be much smaller in stature than most men in the army, acquiring uniforms that fit properly was very difficult. A great deal of the substitute clothing that arrived was too big, and rather than compromise the entire movement by ordering the correct, and hard to come by, sizes, clerks searched the individual personnel records to locate any soldiers who might have been tailors before the war. Not all of the men thus identified had equal levels of skill. And although most did a competent job, one soldier's cut-down uniform came back to him with such drastic alterations that the sleeves of his coat did not extend past his elbows![8]

To ensure that the soldiers did not go off to war with weapons that were not in the best condition, loads of brand new ones were sent to Camp Shelby. The soldiers would leave the rifles, machine guns, and mortars they had been training with behind for later trainees. This meant, however, that time had to be set aside for the men to go back to the firing range to zero in their new weapons. And some of the replacement troops used this opportunity to qualify with their weapons for the very first time. Many army recruits of the mid-twentieth century were completely unfamiliar with firearms, and yet, in the army their lives would quite literally often depend upon their abilities to fire such weapons and hit what they aimed at. Such weapons familiarity was just as important for artillerymen like Sergeant Morita, who qualified with both the M1 carbine and, earlier, the .45-caliber pistol. There was always the possibility that an enemy attack might actually reach the gun positions of the artillery. In such cases, the gunners had to be able to pick up their rifles and defend themselves. The commander of Battery C took about two dozen of his men to the rifle range for some last-minute qualification firing. By early afternoon all of the men had fired acceptable scores and the exercise was complete.

The officer knew, however, that if they returned to camp so early there would be some other chores for them to perform so he decided to have the men kill some time by continuing to practice. He also decided to sharpen up his own shooting eye and proceeded to fire at the target downrange. The result was the dreaded "Maggie's drawers." He was certain that he was a better shot than that and figured that the carbine's sights must be slightly off. He quickly made an adjustment and fired again. Same result. After a half dozen shots with no improvement, his men let him in on the secret. When he decided to shoot, one of the men picked up the phone nearby and notified the men in the pits that the lieutenant was going to shoot and asked them to wave Maggie's drawers no matter where on the target he hit. Everyone, including the lieutenant, enjoyed the joke.[9]

Other equipment, everything from typewriters to jeeps, had to be securely crated for the long journey, but there were no ready-made packing boxes for such items. Instead, a junior officer who took on the ad hoc designation of "regimental packing and crating officer," requisitioned lumber and nails, and put three shifts of men to work in the motor pool building shipping crates. Coded shipping numbers were then stenciled on all the crates and equipment, and all unit designations were removed or painted over. There was no need to let the whole world know which units were shipping out.[10]

Each soldier also was required to mark every piece of his clothing and personal equipment—belts, canteen pouches, haversacks—with an identifying number. This number consisted of the first letter of a soldier's last name, followed by the last four digits of his army service number. Some men simply used an ink pen to inscribe the number but most appear to have used small rubber stamps with the requisite information. This was more efficient because of the large number of items awaiting marking. Soldiers stamped the number inside the waist band of trousers, the inside of shirt collars, and inside their service caps, for instance. In Sergeant Morita's case, because his service number was 38008451, he marked all of his possessions with "M-8451."

It was impossible, of course, for the Hawaiians to bid farewell to their families in person, but the mainlanders hoped for an opportunity to see relatives once more before heading into the war zone. Army officials, wary that news of the impending deployment would reach the wrong people if men were allowed off base this soon before departure, put extremely tight controls on passes. A man in Company I whose parents were in an internment camp had about given up hope of a last farewell when a friend in the company came to his rescue. Since passes were generally merely typewritten on plain paper, his friend had no trouble typing up a bogus pass, to which he then forged the company commander's name, and the family reunion was able to take place after all.[11]

In mid-April, as their final preparations neared an end and their departure date from Camp Shelby loomed, many of the young soldiers took time for celebrations. Due to the large number of Hawaiian soldiers these parties often took on the semblance of island luaus complete with pigs slowly roasting over hot coals, shrimp, sashimi, and chicken. No group of young men could have a respectable party without liquid refreshments, however, and they were plentiful. The party held by the artillery battalion's headquarters battery, for example, included thirty-five cases of cold beer.[12]

Finally, on April 22, the troops bade farewell to Camp Shelby and boarded passenger coaches that would take them to Camp Patrick Henry, near Newport News, Virginia, and their Port of Embarkation on the East Coast. By the time the 442nd left Camp Shelby there was probably very little doubt as to their ultimate destination. The 100th Battalion was in Italy, and that was where the 442nd would go also. In fact, in a letter to his wife three months before departure one man expressed his certainty by saying that he would have to start learning to eat spaghetti soon.[13]

For two days the crowded troop trains steamed across the South. Inside, decks of cards and pairs of dice made their appearances rather quickly and great sums of money changed hands before the trains arrived at their destination. Not all of the card-playing was for money, however. Some men, whether unwilling to risk their hard-earned pay or perhaps having already lost it, played just to pass the time. Among the soldiers whiling away the time on the train by playing cards was a pair of men, one of whom seemed to win every hand they played. They were only playing to fend off boredom, no money was changing hands, yet the loser grew more and more frustrated at his inability to win even one hand. His seatmate finally took pity on him and explained that from his aisle seat he could read his partner's hands in the reflection of the window glass behind him.[14]

The 442nd remained at Camp Patrick Henry for only a week, about average for units passing through on their way to Europe. During this time the men filled out more forms, received their inoculations against diseases like typhus and small pox that they might encounter, went through gas mask training, and attended to a number of other last minute details. They spent their spare time writing letters home—under strict censorship rules—drinking beer, singing songs, and, for a lucky few, introducing themselves to the female nurses at the base hospital.

Racism again became evident when some of the men attended a dance at the USO club, where hundreds of soldiers sought dances with the limited number of Caucasian girls on hand. Some of the white GIs resented the Nisei asking the USO hostesses to dance, and a fight soon broke out that involved perhaps as many as a hundred men on each side. But the Japanese Americans were not alone. Black soldiers, who had a long, bitter experience of racism at the hands of whites, joined them in the melee.[15]

Finally, on May 1, it was time to go. The men once again boarded a train for the short trip to the dock at Hampton Roads. They carried their rifles with them but left everything heavier, such as mortars, machine guns, and howitzers, behind. An army band welcomed them to the dock with the World War I favorite "Over There" as well as other tunes, and Red Cross ladies plied them with coffee and doughnuts as they prepared to embark. Sometime during the boarding process each soldier received a one-page, mass-produced "letter" from President Roosevelt reminding him that he was a soldier of the United States embarking on a perilous but important journey. "You bear with you," it read, "the hope, the confidence, the gratitude and the prayers of your family, your fellow-citizens, and your President."[16]

The men lined up on the pier in alphabetical order and slowly moved toward the base of the gangplank. A man stationed there had a master check list of all the names of the men scheduled for passage on that ship. When Sergeant Morita reached the checker he heard him call out "Morita," to which the sergeant responded, "Carl K." before passing up into the ship. The same procedure was followed until each man's name had been checked off and he trudged up the gangplank burdened down with his rifle, ammunition, pack, helmet, gas mask, canteen, and a duffel bag or two. At the top of the gangplank a crewmember directed him toward the hold that was to be his home for the crossing. The men did not know exactly where they were headed, only that it would be someplace where they could fight Germans or Italians.

Early in the war large cruise liners, such as the *Queen Elizabeth* and the *Empress of Scotland,* were converted to troop transports, and these stayed in service throughout the war. These ships were big and fast, and could outrun any German submarine, so they usually traveled without any military escort and made the crossing in about a week. Soldiers who had hopes of a genteel crossing when assigned to one of these luxury vessels soon had those hopes dashed. An infantryman crossing on the *Queen Elizabeth* in the fall of 1944 recalled: "There's nothing to say about it except that we were too damned crowded, and our quarters were deep in the belly of the ship. We were so hot that we slept naked and dripped waterfalls of sweat through the thick canvas of our bunks." He also found the food "lousy."[17]

The soldiers of the 442nd Regiment sailed instead on purpose-built ships called Liberty Ships. The original impetus for the construction of these ships—officially designated Emergency Cargo Ship(s)—came from the need to help Britain and her allies in the war against Germany. German submarines were sinking ships at an alarming rate by the spring of 1941, and the United States was the only country not already at war that could reasonably expect to build replacements. Although President Franklin Roosevelt, a man steeped in naval history and tradition, thought they were real "ugly ducklings," they were never intended to win beauty contests, and they proved to be vital to Allied victory. They were constructed from prefabricated modules that were welded together. These construction methods allowed the shipyards to turn them out in record time. The *Johns Hopkins,* for example, was delivered to the navy only two and a half months after workmen in the Bethlehem Fairfield yard in Baltimore laid its keel. The Liberty Ships were not built for great speed, however, so navy warships generally shepherded them across the Atlantic in convoys to protect them from German submarines. The ships carrying the 442nd were part of a very large convoy that was sailing for the European-Mediterranean theater.[18]

The men's quarters were extremely crowded. Canvas bunks were slung from four to six high with perhaps a three-foot passageway between tiers. Only the bunks closest to the ceilings (overheads in naval parlance) had enough light to permit the occupant to read or to write letters. The bunks were so close together that, according to a soldier in the 45th Division: "The only way to stretch out on your . . . bunk was to slither aboard edgewise (there were about fifteen inches of headroom before you encountered the sagging butt of the man above) and kick your barracks bag, which shared the bunk, onto a neighbor's territory. If he was asleep he wouldn't kick it back." The officers' accommodations were only slightly better.[19]

The men were allowed up on deck for fresh air, but there was a limited amount of space available to them. They could lean against the rails, or they could sit on the deck or on hatch covers. The deck and hatch covers were far from clean, however, and cleaning them for the benefit of his passengers was apparently not very high up on the ship captains' lists of things to do. When one captain was asked about the possibility of getting these surfaces cleaned he promised to see to it after the ship had put to sea. One of the army officers on board even offered to have his men do the work if the captain would just supply the necessary mops and buckets. It would give the men something to do with their idle time. The captain declined, however, saying that his civilian crew received extra pay for doing things like that and did not want to forego it.[20]

Being on deck, however, instead of in one of the stifling holds was still popular. One of the infantrymen was captivated by the nighttime sights of the ocean. There were "fluorescent fauna and flora floating by—'lightning bugs' of the ocean, underneath the ship, going by. To watch it was just amazing. We didn't know all these plants and animals had lights and such things. During the day, huge jellyfish and whales would appear."[21]

The vast majority of American soldiers on these ships were making their first such voyages, although the Hawaiians in the 442nd had obviously made at least one earlier trip. As the ships carrying the regiment eased away from the pier and into the Atlantic on the night of May 2, some of the passengers began experiencing the agonies of seasickness. The malady seems to have been fairly widespread, but of differing degrees of severity. Nor was it a respecter of rank. A Nisei officer from Cannon Company must take the prize for susceptibility to seasickness. He experienced symptoms of seasickness as soon as he set foot on the deck of the ship—even though it was securely moored at the dock—and remained queasy for the entire trip. A Caucasian captain, suffering from recurring bouts, was conversing with a fellow officer as he lay on his bunk during a momentary respite from the awful symptoms. Suddenly, with no warning, they heard a loud explosion that was immediately followed by the unmistakable rattle of gunfire up on deck. The seasick officer was too sick to investigate, but his healthier companion rushed up on deck to see what was happening and found that it was simply routine gunnery practice. As he returned to the cabin he decided to play a cruel joke on his ailing colleague. He told him that the first explosion had been that of a detonating German torpedo, and that the ship's crew was valiantly trying to fight off an enemy submarine. This did little to help the captain's spirits. In fact, seeing a potential end to his misery, he turned over in his bunk to face the wall, muttering that he hoped the submarine would succeed in sinking "the damned tub" which was the cause of all his discomfort. Usually, after an initial bout of nausea, the men gained their "sea legs" and made the rest of the journey in good health.[22]

About five days out, the convoy encountered severe weather. The rough seas started a new wave of seasickness throughout the ships. Men who had recovered from initial bouts of motion-induced nausea started all over again, and many men who had escaped the symptoms up to this time fell victim. Sergeant Morita was among this latter group "and stayed sick for 3 days," he told his father in a letter. "After that I managed to look bored for the rest of the trip."[23]

One may imagine the conditions among the enlisted men, in closed holds full of men in close proximity to one another, if even only a few of them were sick. "A slight smell of seasickness hung over the whole ship," one of the travelers recalled years later, "and seemed especially acute in the messes, where the men were jammed elbow to elbow." The clever soldier was the one who quickly jumped into the topmost bunk in a stack. That way there was no danger of a man above him vomiting on him. On some ships there were so many soldiers hugging the rails of the ship and vomiting overboard—feeding the fish—that they could later claim to have gone to Europe "by rail."[24]

A sergeant in Cannon Company savored the fact that he was not seasick when many of the men around him were. He had a simple solution, he told them. All they had to do was to inhale when the ship was on the top of a wave and exhale when it was down in a trough. This seemed to work for him, and he preached it to the other troops. Alas, he finally succumbed. He still touted his method, but said that he had accidentally reversed the order and had inhaled when the ship hit bottom and exhaled when it reached a crest.[25]

A battalion of combat troops taxed the abilities of a Liberty Ship's overworked galley crew to keep up with the demand for food, so meals were limited to two per day on some of the ships, although additional snacks were sometimes available in the evenings. The men stood in line for breakfast, and by the time they had finished eating it was almost time to stand in line again for their next meal. The food seemed to be plentiful, but the menu was not very imaginative. One soldier remembered "an endless river of chipped beef and beans [and] great bottomless jars of apple jelly." Others recalled boiled eggs, toast, and coffee for breakfast; soup and crackers for lunch; and potatoes, rice, and Spam for the evening meal. A Caucasian soldier, who had made the trip the year before the 442nd went over, commented on the difficulties involved in merely getting to the food. "Incredibly complicated routes were laid out between each hold and the soldiers' galley," he recalled, "winding up and down ladders, in and out of passageways, and occasionally popping out onto some odd corner of the deck itself, so that a man in line actually caught glimpses of sea and sky. The dispensation of food was timed and the routes were planned so that if a soldier wanted to eat three meals in a day he was on his feet for at least fourteen hours." Several soldiers were so seasick that they could hardly get out of their bunks, and the only way they survived at all was likely due to kind-hearted comrades who brought them food.[26]

Even the best food, however, sometimes went to waste because the rocking motion of the ships induced seasickness in the men. On the USS *Elbridge Gerry*, an army cook got into the galley and prepared two hundred tasty pork chops for the evening meal, but not very many men showed up to eat. And many of those who did soon found themselves lining the rails of the ship and retching into the sea.[27]

Daily hygiene became problematic on board these crowded troopships. The lavatories—or "heads"—were often quite a distance from the men's sleeping quarters, and it was difficult to keep them clean during the crossing. The urinals were long metal troughs, and they sometimes became slightly clogged when seasick troops vomited into them. When that happened they remained partially filled with stale urine, and then, if the seas were anything but calm, the liquid sloshed from one end of the trough to the other, splashing those unfortunate enough to be standing near the end. "With each rise and fall of the ship," remembered a Caucasian soldier who made the trip a few months later and encountered the same problem, "the urine rushed back and forth. When the flow hit either end of the urinal, it shot six feet into the air, spraying everyone nearby. Urinating became a timing game. Urinate fast at one end and run before the flow returned for another splash. Soon the urine and vomit mix was draining down into our sleeping quarters. The smell caused more men to become seasick. It took hours before crew members fixed the drains."[28]

Maintaining fresh laundry was also a problem for the soldiers. One of the medics on board noticed that the sailors regularly cleaned their mops by tying them to ropes and dragging them in the water behind the ship. It seemed like an easy, and inexpensive, solution to the laundry problem so he tied up a bundle of dirty clothes, tied them to a rope, and dropped them over the side. He apparently had not paid attention to the fact that the sailors were very careful not to leave their mops in the water for too long. When he finally decided to retrieve his bundle of clothing he found every article shredded beyond use.[29]

Fresh water on these trips was at a premium and was only authorized for drinking and cooking. Any bathing that the men wanted to do was done in cold saltwater showers with a special pumice soap that caked up on the men's skins instead of lathering. A 99th Division soldier emerged from these saltwater showers "feeling uncomfortable and dirty," while a member of the 442nd's Cannon Company said that it felt as if his skin was covered with "candle wax and hard cheese." Those who were either too seasick or simply not in the mood to take at least the minimum hygienic precautions sometimes came down with rather interesting conditions. One unfortunate soul spent the entire four weeks at sea without bathing and reached Italy covered with pubic lice, or "crabs," even in his eyebrows.[30]

Officers on some of the ships tried to institute regular periods of exercise for their men. This served the dual purpose of giving the men something to occupy at least part of their time, and to keep them from losing the physical conditioning that they had worked so hard to acquire over the last eight to ten months. It was difficult to keep the men interested in such mundane activities, and the extremely crowded conditions on the decks of these ships also made it very difficult to find room for them.[31]

While some of the men spent their idle time reading novels or fashioning finger rings from silver coins, others preferred to gamble. "In the evenings and during time off in the afternoons," recalled a member of the 522nd Field Artillery Battalion, "the ship was like the Casino of Monte Carlo as thousands of greenbacks changed hands in various games such as crap[s], poker, and blackjack." Down in the holds multitiered poker games were the norm, the dealer often having to distribute cards to players in bunks above and below him and across the narrow aisle. A GI who had made the voyage almost a year earlier was sure that there must have been one overall champion on each ship who wound up with all of the ship's money in his pockets. One of the regiment's chaplains was disappointed on the first Sunday at sea when he seemed to be competing with the card games going on in the hold. Very few of the soldiers came up on deck for services. However, in the spirit of the adage that if the mountain will not come to Mohammed then Mohammed must go to the mountain, the chaplain scheduled the following Sunday's services to be held in the hold instead of on deck. Some of the card players, perhaps shamed by the preacher's actions, decided to pay attention to the service, but after the opening invocation most returned to the elusive chase after money. The chaplain resigned himself to the situation and conducted subsequent services topside. At least the air was fresher there.[32]

Some of the ships in the convoy broke away and headed toward Britain. No one knew it at the time, but the long-awaited invasion of northern France was imminent, and the men aboard these vessels would likely be fed into that operation in fairly short order. On May 20, the remaining ships of the convoy reached the twenty-two-mile-long Gibraltar Strait that was the entrance to the Mediterranean Sea. Looming to an altitude of almost fourteen hundred feet on the left, or port, side of the ships was the Rock of Gibraltar (which many of the men recognized from their high school geography books). Eight miles of water separated the "Rock" from French Morocco on the other side of the strait, giving the men the opportunity to see two continents at the same time. It was about this time, too, that the men learned their destinations when officers began handing out Italian-language phrase books to those who were interested. The army's *Pocket Guide to Italian Cities* cautioned the soldiers about what they might find when they reached Italy. "About the only thing in this booklet that can be guaranteed is the terrain. The rest of it is up to the fortunes or misfortunes of war. Many of the towns and cities described here have been bombed and shelled by us as we approached, and shelled by the enemy as he retreated. And many of them will still show the marks of the destruction visited upon them when these lands were being conquered and occupied by the Germans." This warning probably did little to lessen the soldiers' yearning to finally set foot on solid ground again—war torn or not.[33]

A few of the ships, including the *Elbridge Gerry*, carrying most of the 2nd Battalion, broke away from the rest of the convoy after reaching the Mediterranean and headed for the port of Oran, Algeria, to unload a cargo of ammunition that was needed there. The men of this battalion had much the same reaction to Oran that the men of the 100th Battalion had had almost a year earlier. They found the city dirty and the natives larcenous.[34]

The rest of the regiment went to Augusta, Sicily, but only for a day, and then on to Naples, Italy, arriving on May 29, 1944, after a four-week crossing. Because of limited dockage at Naples the *Johns Hopkins*, carrying the 522nd Field Artillery, sailed on around the heel of Italy's boot and landed some of the men at Brindisi and the rest about sixty miles up the coast at Bari, although not without mishap. Coming into Brindisi, soldiers lined the rails of the deck with all their gear, eager to get onto dry land again as their ship moved carefully through the harbor. The ship's captain, however, approached the dock at too great a speed and instead of gently nudging up against it the ship hit it hard enough to knock many of the soldiers off their feet and send some of their duffel bags tumbling overboard. But at least they were finally getting onto dry land again![35]

Bari was not untouched by war. Back in early December, a German air raid on the harbor resulted in seventeen Allied ships sunk and half a dozen others damaged. Of the seven American ships in the harbor on that day, only one came through unscathed while six were sunk. One of those, the SS *John Harvey*, had been carrying a large supply of mustard gas, to be available for retaliation in case the Germans, as they had done in the First World War, initiated gas warfare. Most of the gas that was released as a result of the bombing blew harmlessly out to sea, but enough remained in the harbor to injure over six hundred people.[36]

The Nisei artillerymen had to make their way from the southeastern coast of Italy to the Naples area, where the rest of the regiment had landed. The most efficient means of transportation available was provided by the Italian railroad system, but the GIs did not think very highly of it. They were loaded aboard the small European boxcars for the trip west. Similar cars in France during the First World War were known as "40 & 8s" because they were sized to carry either forty men or eight horses. The cars still carried the aroma of recent equine passengers.

On June 5, the men of the 2nd Battalion boarded the British ship HMT *Samaria* for the final leg of their trip to Italy. The collision of cultures that had begun when they landed in Algeria continued when they encountered the food on this ship. Their first meal on board consisted of boiled liver and boiled potatoes. The next included whole kippers and oranges. The men were glad that they had not had to transit the Atlantic with such a menu.[37]

CHAPTER SIX

THE 442ND IN ITALY

"So far the war hasn't affected me—perhaps its [sic] because someone I know hasn't got it yet."

The 442nd had not been in Italy long before losing one of its own, but the man's death was not due to hostile causes. On June 2, a truck accidentally struck and killed a Company E soldier, and even though his death was not combat-related it was no less tragic a loss for his family and friends.[1]

Traffic was also a problem for large bodies of troops moving through Rome a few days later. In order to avoid traffic jams, the various elements of the artillery battalion staggered their start times by fifteen minutes. Headquarters Battery led the way just after midnight on June 10, followed, in order, by the firing batteries and Service Battery. Confusion still ensued in the dark, narrow, unfamiliar streets. When an officer in Battery C asked a GI he saw on the street if they were headed in the right direction, the soldier replied: "Beats the hell out of me Buddy, I just got here." Another soldier he asked was just as lost as he was and replied: "That's where I'm going, can I get a ride?" Whoever was leading Battery A got lost and took its seventeen vehicles into a dead-end street. Each vehicle then had to back down the street very carefully, particularly the prime movers that were pulling the guns. Battery C, which started through the city some forty-five minutes after Headquarters Battery, reached Civitavecchia first, while the final vehicles of the convoy did not pull in until five hours later.[2]

On June 11, 1944, elements of the 522nd Field Artillery Battalion, the 232nd Engineer Company, and the 3rd Infantry Battalion of the 442nd Regimental Combat Team linked up with the 100th Battalion. (The 2nd Battalion arrived on June 17.) Shortly thereafter the infantry battalions were combined, with the 100th becoming the first of the three battalions of the 442nd. This decision caused some hard feelings on the part of the men in the 100th. They had already spent eight months in combat and had earned quite a reputation as excellent soldiers. And that reputation identified them as members of the 100th Infantry Battalion (Separate). They did not now want to lose that identity by becoming members of the 1st Battalion, 442nd Infantry. Some referred to the 442nd as a "rookie outfit" whose members would now share in the reflected glory of the 100th Battalion. In the interest of unit morale, authorities decided to let the battalion retain its unique designation, but it was, nevertheless, no longer "separate" but an organic part of the larger unit.[3]

The veterans helped the newcomers adjust to the reality of war. For example, they told the new men how to differentiate among incoming artillery shells. They told them that if they heard a shell that seemed to be whistling that they were probably safe, as that shell was headed for some other target. If, on the other hand, the sound grew rapidly in intensity, like an onrushing freight train, there was no time to lose in finding shelter because that round was going to hit very close by.[4]

Deciding where an artillery round would fall was also on the minds of the gunners of the 522nd Field Artillery Battalion, but they were more concerned with outgoing rounds than with incoming. News of the battalion's high level of training had preceded it to the war zone, and General Ryder seemed particularly interested in observing it in action. The gun crews had achieved quite an enviable record while training in the States. They were able to set up their guns and get them firing in very short order, and they were proud of their reputation. So, while waiting for the arrival of the 2nd Battalion to join the rest of the regiment, the 522nd prepared a demonstration for the general.

General Ryder, along with the artillery battalion's commander and a couple of other artillery officers, positioned themselves on a hillside downrange from the howitzers. The target was a spot that was a comfortable distance away from the observers but close enough for them to see how accurately the shots fell. Unfortunately, new sighting devices for the guns had been issued to the men while they were on the way to Europe, and these instruments operated in an exactly opposite manner to the ones with which they had trained so hard at Camp Shelby. The men had plenty of time on shipboard to familiarize themselves with the new devices, but the demonstration for General Ryder was to be the first time they actually used them. The gunner corporal for number two gun, which was used to fire the registration round, was completely familiar with the new gun sight, having practiced with one often during the long voyage across the Atlantic. When the time came to impress the top brass, however, the sergeant from the first gun ordered him to step aside so he could have the honor. He apparently did not have the same amount of practice time as the corporal and forgetfully rotated the control in the old—and now wrong—direction. As a result, the round fell uncomfortably close to the officers downrange. The sergeant immediately received instructions to shift the point of aim farther to the left, away from the officers. Again, however, he erred, and the second shot came in so close to the general and the other officers that they had to dive for cover.[5]

To say that General Ryder was unimpressed with the 522nd's accuracy would be a mistake. He was impressed—but in a negative sense. The displaced corporal remembered that "instead of impressing the General, we nearly killed him." Ryder ordered Colonel Harrison to load his men back on some ships and take them back to the United States until they were ready—really ready—for combat. The colonel pleaded successfully for a second chance.[6]

While the combat team was so close to Rome, and before it became heavily engaged in the war, passes were made available to as many men as possible. Every day three officers and fifty men got to visit the Eternal City. Some were drawn more toward the opportunities for alcoholic drink than anything else the city had to offer. "Made me see pink elephants with wings flying around the Vatican," one man remembered. "Don't remember my pass to Rome very clearly but I know it was a beautiful place."[7] An army guidebook urged the GIs to see as much of the sights as they could while the government was paying for it, and most of these accidental tourists found places like the Coliseum and St. Peter's Basilica to be architecturally awe-inspiring. One of the combat team's medics thought St. Peter's was almost impossible to describe. "[I]ts

richness and vastness," he wrote, "is enough to make one dizzy."
Sergeant Morita, on the other hand, enjoyed seeing the typical
tourist attractions, but knowing how much money tourists spent
to see them during peacetime baffled him. "Perhaps its [*sic*] the
war angle," he wrote to his brother, "but I'll be darned if its [*sic*]
worth all that to me to see these things."[8]

The men of the 100th also enjoyed some much-needed time
away from combat. For two weeks they engaged in training, replacing worn out or damaged equipment, and relaxing. Two officers and sixty men received five-day passes to the Fifth Army Rest
Center at Porto Mussolini, and each day 10 percent of the remaining men received twenty-four-hour passes to Rome. In the Vatican
City, Pope Pius XII held an early morning audience for Nisei GIs,
and two officers and fifty men from the 100th, along with three
officers and 120 men from the other two battalions of the 442nd,
were selected to attend. For those men who remained in camp,
there were movies and band concerts at night, and swimming in
the daytime.[9]

The rest period ended on June 21, when the men clambered
aboard trucks for the sixty-mile drive up the coast to the 34th
Division bivouac near the village of Grosseto. A few days later a
couple of sergeants from the Anti-Tank Company stumbled upon
two enemy soldiers who seemed anxious to give themselves up.
The prisoners were not ethnic Germans, but Turkomen who had
been pressed into German service. It is likely that they saw the
advance of the American soldiers as a chance to sit out the rest of
the war in a prisoner of war camp instead of continuing to fight
for a cause that was not their own.[10]

The 34th Division had orders to relieve the 36th Division, and
from then on its task was to push the Germans north as fast as possible, and without losing contact with the 1st Armored Division
on its right. Its first tactical objective was the town of Castagneto,
about twenty miles up the coast from Grosseto. The 442nd Regiment was responsible for a four-mile sector in the middle of the
divisional front, while the 133rd Regiment occupied a seven-mile
front on its left, and the 168th Regiment covered the four miles
on the right. The third regiment in the division, the 135th, remained in reserve.[11]

As the newly arrived Nisei soldiers moved into position for their first battle with the enemy they encountered some gruesome reminders of the finality of combat. Here and there lay the unburied bodies—both German and American—of the victims of a recent firefight. The first sight of a dead body is often a great revelation to a young soldier. One of the combat team's medics, a man whose job would soon be to patch up the ripped and torn bodies of his comrades, had a great awakening when he first laid eyes on the fly-covered face of a dead German. "I had naively looked upon war," he said, "as a great adventure; now, it looked horrible. . . . One sobers up real fast . . . staring down in awe and incredulity at all the blood and mess of a jaggedly ripped-open body. War quickly lost its glamour."[12]

The foxholes that the men had cursed back at Camp Shelby now became potential life savers, and there was very little complaining about having to dig. (Even one of the chaplains told his wife in a letter that he would give his right foot to be back at Shelby.) And if a man did not have a proper shovel he used his bayonet, his helmet, his mess kit—anything that would get the job done as quickly as possible. Shortly after arriving in Italy, one of Cannon Company's island boys exclaimed: "I dug so deep I heard Hawaiian music."[13]

Immediately in front of the 442nd Regiment were some hilltop villages all connected by a single road that wound through rugged terrain. It snaked its way southward from Belvedere about half a mile to Suvereto and then switched back about 150 degrees northward toward Sassetta, some four-and-a-half miles away. Early on the morning of June 26, Colonel Pence committed his troops to action. The 3rd Battalion advanced, generally, along the road that connected Suvereto and Sassetta and relieved the 517th Parachute Infantry Regiment. After clearing Suvereto it was to attack Belvedere from the south. The 2nd Battalion, to the right of the 3rd, moved forward to relieve the 142nd Regiment of the 36th Division. Its goal was to cut the road linking Sassetta with Castagneto farther to the north. The veteran 100th Battalion was held in readiness to follow up the 3rd Battalion as needed.[14]

Officers had spent the previous evening poring over maps of the immediate area, but it soon grew too dark to send out patrols for more detailed topographical information. And although the maps made it pretty clear that the men were in for some rugged terrain there were some surprises. Sometimes, for example, deep ravines rendered radio communication impossible. Nor did the maps show the many foot paths and trails that traversed the area. For men moving up at night, as these men were, it became almost impossible to determine whether they were moving in the right direction or not.

The 2nd Battalion moved out at 6:30 A.M. with Company F in the lead and Company E ready to assist. Heavy machine-gun platoons from Company H accompanied each of the rifle companies, and Company G provided flank security on the right. Within an hour, both E and F had moved into the hills east of Belvedere and were making good progress.[15]

The 3rd Battalion did not fare as well. The predawn darkness and the unfamiliar terrain contributed to the battalion becoming lost. By 8:00, therefore, regimental authorities decided to modify the attack orders. All further action was postponed until 9:00 so the affected units could get back on track. Company G moved forward, but Company F was out of communication with headquarters and did not receive the new order until its troops had pushed on and reached the point that had been selected as the battalion's first objective for the day.

The men of Company F moved along both sides of a road that paralleled Cornia Creek, with scouts out trying to make contact with the rest of the battalion. When there continued to be no sign of friendly troops ahead, the company halted in the cover of some woods while the company commander went forward to confer with his scouts. Peering through his binoculars, he spotted enemy soldiers moving down the road in his direction. Their casual demeanor suggested to him that they were unaware of the proximity of his force, so he ordered his scout squad forward to engage them.[16]

The scouts crept forward, using the drainage ditches on each side of the road for concealment, and quickly ran into a buzz saw of enemy fire. If the sudden appearance of American soldiers surprised the Germans, they recovered very quickly. Soon a German tank appeared, supported by infantry. While most of the American riflemen nearby opened fire at the approaching soldiers, one of them took on the tank with rifle grenades until a bazooka team could get in a killing shot. The rifle grenades exploded in front of the tank, but did not stop it. The bazooka, often a very effective tank killer, was out of action because the batteries that powered it were dead. Luckily the GI riflemen had the advantage of being equipped with semi-automatic rifles and carbines, as opposed to the Germans' bolt-action rifles. The Americans thus were able to put out a greater rate of fire than they received and the enemy soon left the road and began moving overland toward the rest of Company F.[17]

Nearby, a machine-gun platoon in support of Company E noticed Company F's predicament and opened fire in that direction. The volume of fire from these machine guns, added to that already being provided by Company F, blunted the German advance in that sector.[18]

In the meantime, a German self-propelled gun joined in the battle, firing directly at the men on the ground. A mortar squad leader in Cannon Company ordered his crew to temporarily abandon its gun and seek shelter. One man, however, seemed determined to stop the heavy fire coming from the German gun and manned the mortar by himself—a truly unequal fight. His first shot, at a range of about four hundred yards, missed the target. He adjusted the mortar for the second shot, which also missed. His third shot was almost perfect, dropping directly in front of the enemy vehicle. By now the Germans had located his position, and before he could fire a fourth and potentially crippling round, a shell from the enemy gun hit his position and killed him instantly. But his mortar fire was not without effect. The German gun crew, perhaps wondering how many other American mortars were about to zero in on them, pulled out of the battle and retreated.[19]

The 522nd Artillery Battalion had moved through the night and arrived near Suvereto just before dawn. Within a couple of hours it was dug in and ready to go to work. Embarrassingly, however, when the first call for a fire mission came in there was a problem carrying it out. When a Battery B gunner rammed a round into the breach of one of the guns he failed to seat it all the way. Looking around he grabbed up a sledge hammer and gave the round a solid whack. And although this was certainly not standard procedure—and in fact was quite dangerous—it worked and the round was soon on its way. The 522nd Field Artillery Battalion's war had begun. It was 6:22 A.M.[20]

By mid-day, the 100th Battalion's brief respite was over. The 3rd Battalion had succeeded in capturing Suvereto, but intense German fire from the vicinity of Belvedere made any further progress impossible. Neither Colonel Singles nor his company commanders had had time to make a proper reconnaissance of the area over which they must move, but they hastily studied the available maps to glean as much perspective as they could.

Singles inserted his command between the 2nd and 3rd Battalions. The 100th Battalion moved across a road that led east out of Suvereto at noon and began climbing toward Belvedere. The men were able to move, unobserved by the enemy, around the east side of the village to a point just to the northwest. From there they were able to observe a fairly strong enemy combined force of infantry, armor, and artillery below them and to the west.

The enemy artillerists were firing their three guns toward Suvereto, unaware that American infantry had taken up a position on their left flank. Not wanting to miss out on such a good opportunity to do the enemy damage, the commander of Company B ordered one of his platoons and several sections of machine guns to move down the slope toward the German guns and take them under fire. The machine guns, along with some 60mm mortars, proved very effective, silencing the German guns within five minutes.[21]

While Company B's heavier weapons were busy with the German artillery, one platoon headed toward the village. One squad went right, one went left, and the remaining squad moved straight into the north end of town. By this time most of the Germans had vacated the buildings, and the GIs soon cleared the village with minimal friendly casualties.[22]

Meanwhile, the remaining rifle platoon of Company B moved toward an isolated farmhouse east of the road connecting Suvereto and Sassetta. As one squad moved cautiously toward the house the other two held back to provide covering fire if it was needed. And it was! A machine gun opened up on the attackers, but one of the

GIs was able to knock it out with a rifle grenade. Other grenades, thrown into the windows of the house, caused those inside to surrender almost immediately. This unassuming dwelling turned out to have been a German company command post and, along with the prisoners, the GIs captured a truck, a pair of half-tracks, and eleven small utility vehicles, similar to the American jeeps.[23]

The Americans did not have time to savor their success, as more Germans advanced on them under the cover of a tank. A three-man bazooka team quickly began working its way to within range of this new threat. For the bazookas to be effective they had to be fired at ranges close enough to penetrate the tank's armor. While one man provided covering fire with his BAR, a bazooka man waited for the tank to come ever closer. He finally fired when the tank was almost on top of him. He destroyed the panzer, but the blast knocked him unconscious and killed the third member of the bazooka team. The German infantry, no longer emboldened by the presence of the tank, began to withdraw under fire.[24]

Farther up the road a motorized column of seventeen small amphibious utility vehicles and a few motorcycles fled north toward Sassetta. To reach that town, however, and any hope of immediate safety, the column had to run a gauntlet of machine-gun fire from Company B. Soon a tangled mass of German vehicles and dead and wounded soldiers clogged the road. The smoke had barely cleared when four enemy troop carriers were sighted moving up the road in the same direction. Two of the drivers were able to steer around the wreckage on the road and escape, but the Americans killed the other two drivers and most of their passengers. "The boys really enjoyed it," recalled one of the Nisei soldiers, "although now when I think of it, it's brutal and inhuman!"[25]

The 100th Battalion continued to make slow but steady progress flushing enemy troops from the occasional farmhouses. In one instance, when a handful of men from Company A fired into a house, they observed enemy soldiers beating a hasty retreat out the back. Unsure whether the house was then vacant, one of the Americans then tossed a grenade in through the front door to flush out any diehards, and three more Germans marched out with their hands held high. But what was even more surprising was that behind them walked three American scouts from the 34th

Division who had fallen into German hands earlier that day and were now rescued.[26]

By late afternoon, the 100th had pushed well past Belvedere and on toward Sassetta, and the 2nd and 3rd Battalions, having endured their baptism of fire, were also moving north. The Nisei soldiers killed 178 Germans that day and had captured eighty-six others. In addition to the enemy personnel who fell into American hands, the GIs also captured or destroyed dozens of vehicles, including two tracked personnel carriers, two antitank guns, two tanks, three self-propelled guns, eight trucks, thirteen motorcycles, and nineteen small utility vehicles.[27]

The 100th Battalion attacked Sassetta the next day about noon while the 3rd moved around to the west until it reached commanding terrain north of the town. The guns of the 522nd Field Artillery Battalion also got into the scrap, firing salvoes at enemy positions that were timed to explode in the air directly above the German troops. This type of fire was much more destructive than if the rounds had exploded upon impact with the ground. The guns of Cannon Company were also busy that day, damaging three enemy self-propelled guns and causing a fourth to retreat.[28]

It was on this second day of combat that an incident occurred that revealed how quickly a man's savage instincts can be aroused in wartime. A sergeant from Company K noticed a small group of GIs near a well casually filling their canteens with water. Knowing that such a cluster of men was an open invitation to any enemy artillery nearby he quickly sought to disperse them—but he was too late. An enemy shell screamed into their midst, hitting the sergeant squarely and ripping him apart. One of the Nisei who escaped injury noticed that two German prisoners seemed to be enjoying the effect of this fire so he shot and killed them both. Such is the dehumanizing impact of war.[29]

As the men from Company A moved into the liberated village they were welcomed by one of their own. A truck driver from headquarters, thinking that the village was already in friendly hands, or perhaps lost and thinking he was in a different village entirely, had boldly driven into the center of town that morning. When German bullets began making impact uncomfortably close to him he realized his mistake, but rather than risk turning his truck around and trying to escape along his original route he abandoned the vehicle and took to a nearby cellar. He was greatly relieved to see friendly faces.[30]

Another surprise also awaited the victorious Americans. The retiring enemy had not taken the time to clean out all the food and liquor shops as they went, and the Nisei soldiers discovered the contents of a well-stocked wine shop and soon dispatched a truck load of spirits to the battalion kitchen. They also "liberated" numerous pigs and chickens and enjoyed a good meal before pushing on toward the northwest and their next objective—the village of Castagneto.[31]

As the 3rd Battalion started toward Castagneto, the 100th moved directly north to secure a vital road junction. In the dark, and over unfamiliar terrain, some of the 3rd Battalion troops stumbled into the German roadblock that was the objective of the 100th Battalion. This surprise assault—a surprise to both the attackers and the attacked—caused the Germans to think that they were about to be overrun, and they hurriedly fell back. In their haste they abandoned yet another tracked personnel carrier and a couple of 81mm mortars.[32]

Enemy tanks were known to be in the area so the men of the Anti-Tank Company were alerted to bring one of their guns into position, ready to fire. When a German tank appeared, at a distance of almost a mile, they eagerly sprang into action even though the tank was too far away for them to have much chance of inflicting a fatal hit. Nevertheless, they soon sent a round in the direction of the enemy armor. The only effect it had, however, was to reveal to the Germans the location of the American gun crew and bring down a considerable amount of artillery fire on it. Generally, however, the men in the Anti-Tank Company found the mountainous Italian terrain particularly difficult (as did German tankers). They therefore soon put their heavy, and useless, weapons into storage and filled in wherever they were needed. They served as riflemen; they carried food up to the rifle companies; they helped carry the wounded back to the aid stations.[33]

Italy's mountainous terrain also dictated a change in artillery tactics. While in training at Fort Sill the pilots of the artillery battalion's two spotter planes had been instructed on the safest way

Pilot and observer prepare to go aloft to find targets for the 522nd Field Artillery Battalion. Signal Corps photo.

to do their job, and that was to fly no higher than six hundred feet, to remain at least one thousand yards behind the front line, and to only remain in the air for only a few minutes at a time. These planes had a cruising speed of only seventy-five miles per hour and would have made very tempting targets for any German fighters in the area. They were also unarmed and without armor protection, so that if they flew over enemy infantry positions it was quite possible for them to be shot down with rifle or machine-gun fire. While these tactics were sound as long as the area of operations was as flat as the Oklahoma countryside, the pilots discovered that they had to get up higher to be able to spot likely targets in mountainous surroundings. A spotter pilot operating in Italy before the arrival of the 442nd Regimental Combat Team reported good results only at elevations well above the prescribed six hundred feet. In the mountains he often flew as high as eight thousand feet. "Now, as we are out over a valley," he reported, "we range from 2,500 to 4,000 feet. Observation is good from there.

One can see any vehicular movement and pick up gun flashes" from enemy artillery.[34]

The Germans learned to respect the presence of these small planes and tried to avoid movement anywhere near the front during daylight hours. And since the pilots relied on the muzzle flashes of German guns to pinpoint their locations, the enemy batteries often remained silent when one of these "grasshoppers" was aloft. "Whenever the . . . plane puts in an appearance," reported a German soldier, "guns are silenced and all personnel . . . remain quiet in the hope of escaping detection and the rain of steel that always follows discovery."[35]

The Nisei soldiers had earned a rest, and on June 29 General Ryder ordered the 135th Infantry Regiment to move forward through the 442nd, allowing the 135th to go into a relatively quiet area to act as the 34th Division's reserve force. The 2nd and the 100th Battalions moved to the recently liberated village of Bibbona, while the 3rd Battalion was temporarily dispatched to Monteverdi to watch for a possible German counterattack on the division's flank.

The temporary respite from combat allowed the men to reflect on their recent experiences. The tension of constantly having to be alert for any sign of land mines or other enemy presence was so great that one man was certain that he had had such a tight grip on his rifle that he must have left permanent fingerprints deeply impressed into its wooden stock.[36]

On their second day in Monteverdi, a 3rd Battalion man discovered a cache of wine that rivaled, or perhaps exceeded that found a few days earlier in Sassetta. The village's previous residents had tried to camouflage it before they evacuated, but they were not able to completely hide the estimated fifteen thousand gallons from the inquisitive Americans. Unfortunately, the parched soldiers were unable to slake their thirsts before orders to move out for Bibbona arrived only thirty minutes later.[37]

The 442nd Regimental Combat Team had less than a week of combat experience when Sergeant Morita expressed to his brother how he was reacting to the experience of war. "So far the war hasn't affected me—perhaps its [sic] because someone I know hasn't got it yet. I've seen plenty of dead, but I look upon them as machines or something. No human interest. Perhaps its [*sic*] best. If it affected me I wouldn't be worth a damn."[38]

In war, as in many other aspects of life, fortune sometimes favors the bold. On July 2, while a few men from Company G checked out a small village they observed some jeeps heading toward the center of town. One of the men strode confidently out into the intersection and held up his hand like a traffic cop, and the vehicles came to a stop. He was then stunned to discover that these were not GIs in jeeps, but German soldiers in their own vehicles. The Germans were just as surprised to see that this traffic officer was not one of their own. Some shots were hastily exchanged, but the Germans soon realized that the town was in American hands and that their only hope for survival was to surrender, and they did just that.[39]

Other surrenders occasionally occurred when least expected. During a brief stop, the first sergeant of the Anti-Tank Company used the time to relieve himself. He laid his rifle down, grabbed up a shovel, and walked off the roadway for a little privacy. A few moments later, he returned to the road with, in addition to his shovel, a prisoner! The German had apparently tired of war and was anxious to turn himself in to the first American soldiers he encountered. Of course, the men in the Anti-Tank Company got quite a kick out of the fact that he had surrendered to an American soldier armed only with a shovel.[40]

The men were not above a little theatrics when it came to convincing reluctant German prisoners to answer questions. Not having any luck prying information from one prisoner, the interrogator raised his voice in feigned exasperation and ordered the prisoner taken outside and shot, making sure that the other captives who were waiting their turns in the next room heard him. The initial prisoner was then taken out of the room and sent on to the nearest prisoner collection points but after he left the building one of his guards fired a shot into the ground. The effect on the waiting captives was to make some of them almost eager to answer questions when their turns came.[41]

The Japanese Americans also showed initiative with regard to keeping their communications secure from enemy eavesdropping. Just as Navajos and other American Indian "code talkers" used

THE 442ND IN ITALY 201

their native tongues to confuse any Japanese listening in to their communications in the Pacific, the buddhaheads in the 442nd employed similar tactics. At one point, a soldier was attempting to send a message when he heard an unusual buzzing sound coming from his radio that was louder than the usual static. The Nisei on the other end must have heard it too, and, suspecting that it was due to a German eavesdropping, the two GIs began conversing in a bewildering mixture of languages and dialects in an effort to confuse their unwanted listener. One man spoke in Japanese, and got a response in pidgin. He responded in a Filipino dialect. The conversation then proceeded with a mixture of Hawaiian, Chinese, Portuguese, Spanish, Italian, and Korean, with a sprinkling of American slang terms and profanity. In this manner, both men understood one another. Another time, a soldier needed a replacement bolt for his Thompson submachine gun, or Tommy Gun, as well as more ammunition. Time was of the essence, so the radio operator called: "Hama hama Tommy gun boltsu, hayaku, eh? And ammo mote kite kudasai." The man on the receiving end of this message knew that it meant "Rush order on a Tommy gun bolt and please bring up some more ammo." It is unlikely, in either of these instances, that any Germans listening in could make much sense of it at all.[42]

The American advance continued, with special importance attached to the capture of the town of Cecina at the mouth of the river of the same name. Two battalions of the 133rd Infantry drew the assignment of clearing the town, but the defenders, members of the 16th SS Reconnaissance Division, put up a vicious resistance. The American attack began before dawn on July 1, and finally succeeded in securing the town the next day. It was a costly battle for both sides. The 133rd Regiment suffered 404 casualties—killed, wounded, and missing—and buried a hundred German bodies.[43]

The men of the 133rd had earned a rest, but the rest of the 34th Division pushed onward. While the attached 804th Tank Destroyer Battalion moved along the narrow coastal road on the regiment's west flank, the 135th Regiment moved along the western slopes of a valley leading north, the 168th went along the eastern slopes, and the 442nd marched through the middle of the valley.

The 442nd's 2nd Battalion pushed enemy troops back from Molino a Ventoabbto and into positions of considerable strength. The defenses of most consequence to these attacking soldiers were on Hill 140. From the top of this hill German observers could, and did, direct heavy artillery fire onto the forces below. To the left, or west, the 100th Battalion came under heavy fire that German observers were directing from the elevated town of Rosignano Marittimo, a couple of miles from the seacoast.

Companies E and G moved against Hill 140 on July 4, but did not make much progress. All but one of the officers of Company G were soon killed or wounded, as they led their men forward into withering small-arms and artillery fire. Because so much of the company leadership was out of action and unable to lead, it was up to the individual soldiers to recognize what needed to be done and to do it. Thus a Company G BAR man moved out a little ahead of his platoon and neutralized a German machine-gun nest at rather long range. Enemy fire soon tore his weapon from his hands so he commenced to throw hand grenades at nearby positions until his platoon caught up with him and he obtained a rifle from a wounded comrade. He and the rest of his company continued to advance, and in their zeal they outdistanced the friendly forces on either side of them. In danger of being surrounded, they began to pull back. In an infantry firefight perhaps the only thing that is more dangerous than advancing against the enemy is withdrawing under enemy fire. The BAR man stayed behind and gave covering fire with his rifle until the other GIs had reached safety. His exhibition of bravery was only one of many that day.[44]

The fighting on July 5 was a virtual repeat of the events of the day before. The 442nd fought grimly all day long to hang onto its positions, and things began to look up late in the day. Elements of the 135th Regiment had entered Rosignano Marittimo and were slowly fighting from house to house and street to street, pushing the defenders out. The Germans had their hands full with the 135th, and this development allowed the 442nd a respite from the five-hour pounding they had been receiving from German guns in and around the town.[45]

That night, beginning about ten o'clock, Companies F and G, moving as quietly as they could, began shifting to their right to get onto the German flank. The Germans on Hill 140 awoke the next morning to find these American soldiers uncomfortably close to their positions. And try as they might, they could not dislodge them. Company H, the battalion's weapons company, brought its 81mm mortars to bear, firing more than twelve hundred rounds into the German lines. Smaller mortars also played a part. A Company F man became a one-man mortar squad that day when he took a 60mm tube, and as much ammunition as he could carry, and crawled as close to the enemy line as he could. Unable to manhandle the mortar's heavy base plate to his forward position, he took off his helmet, set it on the ground, and filled it with dirt. Then he balanced the bottom of the firing tube in the helmet and began to fire. Precision of aim, of course, was practically non-existent, but he was able to drop enough of his rounds into or near the German positions to cause them considerable concern. When he ran out of ammunition, he crawled the two hundred yards back to the American lines and got another load. He kept this up for about twelve hours.[46]

As the 3rd Battalion began pushing along a ridge that ran from Hill 140 toward the west the GIs discovered German bunkers throughout the area, and progress was slow. At one point, a Company K soldier used his Thompson submachine gun to break up a German machine-gun crew before it could do much damage. Of course, his action then drew retaliatory fire, which he also quickly silenced. The Germans then tried to stop him with grenades. One grenade exploded close enough to send shards of steel into his left arm, but his wounds scarcely slowed him. An inspiration to the men in his platoon, he refused evacuation until he saw his men safely in a defensive position. He had killed or wounded over a dozen Germans. Among the Nisei killed this day was Goro Kashi-waeda, whose last-inning home run had sealed the Camp Shelby baseball championship back in October.[47]

That evening the 522nd Artillery Battalion hammered the crest of Hill 140 with high explosive rounds that detonated in the air directly over the German positions. The commander of the 2nd Battalion jumped up and down with glee over the artillery's effectiveness. After almost an hour the barrage lifted, and all three rifle companies of the 2nd Battalion began a concerted assault. Bitter

One of the 105mm howitzers in action in Italy. Signal Corps photo.

fighting continued into the night until finally, at about midnight, the last of the Germans abandoned that portion of Hill 140 that had been the primary objective of the battalion.[48]

The howitzers got so hot from the rapid firing that the gunners soaked burlap bags in cold water and draped them over the barrels to cool them off. This met with only limited success, so some men in Battery B put an empty shell casing into a gun to seal it off and then poured water into the barrel. After a few minutes had elapsed someone opened the breech of the gun and pulled the shell casing out. It was full of boiling water! Another battery was dug in along a creek, and as the guns fired the men tossed the empty shell casings behind them toward the stream. By the time that battery had ceased firing that day the number of shell casings piled up had nearly dammed the waterway. The battalion fired over eighteen thousand rounds during the first week of July and over seventeen thousand rounds the week after that.[49]

So fluid was the action during early July that the artillery relocated four times in one week, firing in support of infantry assaults on enemy positions. During one twenty-four hour period in early July, the battalion unleashed over forty-five hundred rounds. The artillerymen's routine became one of moving, digging the guns in, firing, and then moving again, digging the guns in again, and firing again. "The only thing I got to kick about," Sergeant Morita wrote home, "is being so darn dirty. I really miss clean clothes and a shower."[50]

By dawn of July 7, it was the 2nd Battalion's turn for a rest, as the men of the 100th filed into line to replace them. The rest gave men time to clean, replace, or refurbish their clothing and equipment. And it gave them time to become homesick. "It must be grand in the islands now," the battalion chaplain wrote his wife. "I daydream all day about home—the peaceful evenings, the soft breeze—and the smell of gardenias and ginger always in the air. Here in Italy," he continued, "all we smell wherever we go are manure piles and chicken coops."[51]

But even in the so-called reserve areas the men were not immune to danger. As a hungry soldier investigated a vegetable patch to see what he might be able to add to his dinner he saw an enemy soldier approaching a nearby farmhouse. The German did not notice him so he waited until he was well within rifle range before squeezing off a shot. He missed, and the now thoroughly frightened man took off. But what was more astounding was that some two dozen Germans already in the farm house also scurried out and headed for safer climes. The American was so startled by this mass exodus that he just stood there and watched them run without shooting at them.[52]

It was still dark the next morning when the 100th Battalion began its move toward the northeast from Hill 140 with the 3rd Battalion on its left. While the 100th advanced upon the village of Castellina Marittima, northeast of Cecina, the 3rd Battalion moved to interdict the road running from that village to Rosignano Marittimo, five miles to the west. The men of Company C hoped to capture the heights overlooking Castellina so they could furnish support for their comrades in Company B when they carried out the assault upon the town itself. The quickly moving Nisei were able to gain control of the high ground in relatively short order, but there were still pockets of resistance scattered about.

A couple of German machine gunners had set up their weapon in an abandoned house and were in a position to cause serious problems for the Americans. so a Nisei officer—with the unlikely nickname of "Chicken"—led a squad from Company C to the trouble spot. Rushing the house, they killed one of the gunners and captured the other. The location of the dwelling, however, so dominated the surrounding terrain that it was obvious that the enemy would try to retake it. When the counterattack came, the defenders were ready. The lieutenant cautioned his men to hold their fire until it was impossible for them to miss. The Germans were nearly on top of the house when fire erupted from its windows and doors. Devastated by the volume of fire, those enemy soldiers not hit withdrew. After the Americans also turned back another attack an hour later, the Germans resorted to heavier weapons. If they could not regain this observation post they would at least make it unusable for anyone else. The third assault benefited from the support an 88mm antiaircraft gun doing yeoman's service as field artillery. Four times the 88 scored hits on the now-crumbling structure, but even against such weapons as this the Americans held fast. Finally, in the face of even heavier artillery fire, the lieutenant ordered his men to abandon this exposed position while he remained behind with a BAR to fight off one more attack. As the enemy infantry approached the house it remained silent, and they likely believed that the Americans had all finally vacated its premises. When the lieutenant opened up with his BAR from point-blank range, he shattered not only this belief but their formation too. The surviving Germans had finally had enough. When they withdrew this time, they did not return.[53]

A German infantry company, supported by three tanks, took Company B under fire as the Americans worked their way toward the village. One of the GIs carried his bazooka into a roadside ditch and then moved as far forward as he could, waiting for a chance at a tank. When the first tank had approached close enough, he let loose with a rocket and scored a direct hit. The immobilized and burning tank effectively blocked the road for those behind it. By now, the Americans had called upon the gunners of the 522nd Field Artillery Battalion, and they laid down such an accurate barrage that the enemy soon abandoned the field, leaving Castellina to the advancing Americans. One of the best marksmen from Company B added insult to injury when he began calmly picking off the retreating soldiers. Having dispatched ten Germans at distances up to three hundred yards, he climbed up into the second floor of a house and continued shooting from one of the upstairs windows.[54]

As Companies A and B approached a little cluster of homes along the Pomaia-Rosignano road the next day they came under fierce rifle and machine-gun fire. And although they soon had the houses cleared of enemy troops, Germans occupying an old castle in the hamlet continued to pepper them with bullets. One man stepped forward with a plan to silence the castle. Arming himself with an abundance of hand grenades, he instructed his comrades to use their rifles to keep the enemy soldiers pinned down so he could get closer to the castle without being observed. Under this covering fire he rushed forward until he reached the structure's walls. Then, after catching his breath, he crept as close as he could to one of the open windows and tossed a grenade inside. He then moved around the entire perimeter of the building throwing a grenade into every opening he encountered. He then led a squad of riflemen into the building to mop up the last of the resistance. This attack cost the Germans ten dead and three captured. Sadly, the brave volunteer was among the Americans killed.[55]

By noon on July 12, Companies A and B of the 100th Battalion had reached the outskirts of Pastina, but the German defenders still showed a considerable amount of fight. Once again it was time to call in the heavy firepower of the 522nd Artillery Battalion, and the gunners once again delivered the goods. By the end of the day the village was in friendly hands. That night, the 3rd Battalion moved into the village to allow the tired soldiers of the 100th Battalion to obtain a little bit of rest in a safer area toward the rear. By then, too, the aggressiveness of the Americans all across the Fifth Army front had forced *General der Panzertruppen* Joachim Lemelsen to order his German Fourteenth Army to start pulling back toward the Arno River.

One of the regiment's chaplains, after witnessing combat for the first time, cautioned his wife that it was nothing like the combat in movies or popular fiction. "If you ever see movie actors like

Errol Flyn[n] heroically going through some battlefield with torn sleeves and a submachine gun in his hand," he wrote her, "throw a ripe tomatoe [*sic*] on the screen." Another man probably spoke for many when he was asked, many years later, about his initial reaction to combat. "Well," he said, "in plain language, we were scared shitless."[56]

Men facing death often respond in unlikely ways. When medics brought one man into an aid station no one thought that he could possibly survive. "He was wounded all over," one GI remarked. "Even down to his big toe . . . just blasted with shrapnel." He lay quietly, never crying out in pain. Suddenly, he sat bolt upright, as if to tell a joke. "I'm going to pretend that I'm dead," he declared with a loud laugh. Whereupon he lay back down and died. In another instance, the explosion of a German 88mm shell sheared one man's legs off below the knees. Those near him applied tourniquets to slow the bleeding, but it was quite some time before he could be carried back to an aid station. By then it was dark, and the mangled soldier lay, with other wounded, waiting for his turn on the operating table. There were many wounded, and this man always insisted that the medics treat other men first because their wounds were more severe. By the time it was his turn, however, he had bled to death in the dark.[57]

For the next couple of days, while the 100th Battalion remained in reserve, the 2nd and 3rd Battalions made good progress in hastening the German retrograde movement. With the able support of the 522nd Artillery, the 3rd Battalion took San Luce on the 13th, and the 2nd Battalion captured Pieve di San Luce on the next day. That night General Ryder ordered his 168th Regiment to relieve the 3rd Battalion at the edge of Lorenzano.[58]

By July 15, the 100th Battalion's rest was over, and the 522nd was busy in support of Company C as it encountered German troops a few miles northwest of Orciano. All three rifle companies of the 100th Battalion were together again later that day. The 2nd Battalion was also busy on the 15th, drawing its artillery support from within the regiment, the gunners of Cannon Company firing over three hundred rounds in support of their infantry brethren that day. During the night, the 3rd Battalion quietly moved back into the line to allow the 2nd to have a rest, although it would be a short one.[59]

American forces continued to move northward trying either to drive the Germans out of the port city of Livorno—which the Americans invariably called Leghorn—or to get around north of the city and cut them off from any support or reinforcement. As a part of this strategy, the 3rd Battalion received orders the next day to take the town of Luciana, lying in the hills east of Leghorn. By this time the Germans were slowly beginning to evacuate the port, but they were by no means withdrawing in a panic. As the Nisei soldiers pressed forward the Germans welcomed them with intense fire from machine guns, tanks, and self-propelled guns. Company L tried to maneuver around the enemy left flank but found it impossible to do so. Company K attacked Luciana directly, with the added support of Company M's 81mm mortars. The end of the day saw the attackers in possession of a small section of the city, and throughout the night American and German patrols bumped into one another in bloody clashes.[60]

The rattle of machine-gun fire was not the only sound that kept soldiers awake that night. General Ryder had ordered forward a battery of 8-inch guns to supplement the fire of Cannon Company's small howitzers. It was late in the day before the big guns arrived at their firing position, just behind Cannon Company and the 442nd headquarters. When these guns finally went to work the concussion of their firing pulled the ceiling down on the heads of the officers in the headquarters, and the ground shook so much that the gunners in Cannon Company gave up even trying to fire their pieces.[61]

The next day Company K continued its house-to-house fight within Luciana. Urban combat, such as this, is much more difficult than meeting an armed foe in an open area, as the 100th Battalion had learned at Cassino. Each house and shop must be cleared of the enemy, block by block and street by street. The sounds of mortars, machine guns, and artillery echo off the rubble and add to the perception of chaos. Late that afternoon all of the divisional and corps artillery assets were allocated to the 3rd Battalion to help it clear the remaining pockets of resistance in the northern part of the city. By the time the sun set on July 17, the

Resting in the shade in the newly liberated Italian city of Leghorn. Signal Corps photo.

Americans controlled Luciana. (It was at Luciana that some 3rd Battalion medics came upon a rather forlorn puppy and adopted it as a mascot. They named her Lucy in honor of the village in which she was found.)[62]

The next day, soldiers of the 135th, along with the 363rd Regiment on temporary loan to the 34th Division from the newly arrived 91st Division, occupied Leghorn, and the 100th Battalion entered the port city on the 19th. The retreating Germans, as was their custom, did a lot of damage to the city's infrastructure before they left. The harbor, one of Italy's best, was the scene of purposely scuttled ships, destroyed piers, and anti-ship mines. Anti-personnel mines throughout the city also inflicted American casualties long after the enemy departed.[63]

The Nisei guarded various installations and served as an ad hoc military police battalion to maintain order in the newly liberated city. Their interaction with the civilians was friendly, and when they discovered that the Italians were willing to trade foodstuffs, they eagerly bartered with them. Rice, a favorite of the Nisei, was often in short supply in their army rations, but they found that civilians readily swapped rice for various components of GI food, such as the chocolate bars. A few of the soldiers also located a brewery and helped themselves to about fifty gallons of beer.[64]

Ironically, it was one of the combat team's chaplains who expressed a decidedly negative opinion of the local populace, holding them at least partially responsible for their country siding with Germany in the first place. "These Italians expect America not only to feed them but to rebuild the darn place for them" he complained in a letter home. "[T]hey must think America is in this [war] for humanitarian purposes. They should suffer through this themselves and perhaps they will eventually learn that warmongering does not pay. Old Mousso [Benito Mussolini] should rebuild it for them, and there is a lot of rebuilding to do." Most of the GIs, however, could not get over how desperately poor the civilians were, and yet how willing they seemed to be to share what little they had. "It's surprising," one man wrote, "how the Italian people take you into their homes and treat you so kindly. They haven't much to offer but what they have they give without holding back."[65]

The 2nd and 3rd Battalions took a bit of a breather as they established a defensive position east of the city and facing north. From there they could look north and distinguish the famed leaning tower in Pisa. Of course, the fact that they could see it so clearly meant that anyone at the top of the tower could also see them. And in fact, enemy observers were using the tower to direct fire onto the advancing Americans. A Cannon Company officer took action by calling in a fire mission directly on the tower. "I realized," he said, "exactly what the Tower meant to the world but I wanted none of our men to die because of it and called the fire order in." Higher authorities, however, aware of the firestorm of protest that accompanied the Allied destruction of the Benedictine monastery at Cassino, refused to authorize the mission.[66]

Sometime around the middle of July, several of the 100th's men were detailed to guard the road entries into Leghorn. These sentries had explicit orders, from the office of General Clark himself, to allow no one to enter the city without the possession of proper authorization. A convoy of trucks from the engineer corps arrived one day to begin the rehabilitation of the port facilities so that American forces could make use of them, and when the sentry refused to wave them on through an unhappy engineer colonel confronted him. "Let us through," he demanded. The GI remained unruffled. "May I see your orders, Sir?" When the officer responded that he had no orders but that he must be allowed into the city anyway, the soldier calmly explained that he was to allow absolutely no one to pass his position without orders. "I can kill you right here," the exasperated officer fumed, "and take my convoy on through." The soldier maintained his composure and, with the toe of his boot, drew the proverbial line in the dirt. "Colonel," he said, "you cross this line, you *make*," using the Hawaiian word for "dead." "We can take you," sputtered the colonel, "you are only one." "Cross the line," the soldier repeated, "and you *make*." The colonel stomped back to his truck and, after some time on his field phone with higher headquarters, reluctantly turned his convoy around and left. When General Clark heard about the incident, he beamed and said: "I selected the 100th [to guard the roads] because I knew my orders would be carried out. I can depend on the 100th to successfully carry out any mission. I have absolute faith in every soldier in the 100th. This private is an example of that trust."[67]

Proving the old adage that you can take the boy out of the country but you cannot take the country out of the boy, many soldiers from rural backgrounds commented on the crops in the surrounding fields. They saw corn and wheat and various fruit orchards with everything from peaches and plums to grapes and olives. Sergeant Morita noted the progress of the local crops in early July. "The alfalfa is ready to cut." About six weeks later he commented on the heat and conjectured that it was undoubtedly much cooler in Colorado. (On the day of his letter, however, the mercury hit 89° in Greeley.)[68]

Typically, an army is only as effective as the intelligence it possesses on the strength and movement of its enemy. To gain this information, three patrols left the 442nd's lines under cover of darkness on July 20. Two twenty-man patrols from Company G got as far as the airfield near the southern outskirts of Pisa, and then

With the city of Leghorn secure, Nisei soldiers enjoy riding in a captured German utility vehicle. Someone has prudently painted American stars on the sides and hood so as not to draw friendly fire. Signal Corps photo.

made it back into friendly lines about midnight the next night. The information they brought back showed that there were still Germans south of the Arno River but suggested that the bulk of the enemy defenses were farther north.

A dozen men from Company L had also gone out, but they did not return until midday on July 22. By that time many of their comrades feared the worst—that they had all been killed or captured. And it had, indeed, almost come to that. Their assignment had been to make contact with a partisan leader in Pisa. He was supposed to have vital information concerning the disposition of enemy troops that he would turn over to the Americans. Having made contact, however, the Americans were almost discovered by a German patrol. They all crowded into the attic of house and sweated it out while the unsuspecting Germans spent time relaxing on the floor below.[69]

General Ryder sent the 133rd and the 135th Regiments to re-lieve the 2nd and 3rd Battalions of the 442nd on July 21, and the Nisei fell back to the 34th Division rest area at Vada for some wel-come rest time. For the greater part of a week, the men spent their time repairing and replacing worn equipment and clothing, reading, writing letters, bathing, and just generally relaxing. In a letter home one of the men wrote, rather wistfully: "The seacoast along here is almost like that of Hawaii." Furthering the feeling of home was a luau that included roast pig and as many other dishes as could be put together using local staples. One erstwhile "chef" came up with some ersatz doughnuts crafted from crackers and dehydrated fruit spread from GI rations, along with soy cereal, sugar, and hot bacon grease. Another experiment yielded pan-cakes made from coarse local flour—sifted through some medical gauze—and tooth powder.[70]

Food has always been a topic of great interest to soldiers. The lack of variety in the combat rations meant that men on a steady diet of them soon grew very tired of their sameness. "It can be said that something is better than nothing, which is true," remem-bered one hungry soldier, "but . . . having fresh chicken or fresh vegetables was a heavenly treat." He described how a head of "lib-erated" cabbage could be made into something wonderful. All one had to do was to remove his helmet and helmet liner, and then break the cabbage up in the steel "pot." Massaging salt and bouillon powder into the leaves resulted in a pretty close approxi-mation of Japanese *oshinko*, or pickled cabbage. "K-rations would keep you alive, I guess," bemoaned a soldier in a Caucasian unit, "but they sure wouldn't keep you happy. I think they use embalm-ing fluid to preserve the stuff." A Nisei GI said that the only reason he ate K-rations was to keep from starving to death and always sought to augment them with items from the local area. Although some men preferred them, one man so despised K-rations that he suggested that the government package a certificate of honorable discharge in every millionth ration as an inducement to the men to eat them.[71]

One attempt to replicate the food of home centered on a popu-lar dish called *hekka,* a sort of sukiyaki dish made with chicken and vegetables. A soldier from the regimental headquarters company scrounged around for suitable ingredients and came up with a fair approximation. He used a goose instead of a chicken and vegetables that were locally grown, but it was pronounced quite tasty. He even offered some to Colonel Pence, but the regimental commander begged off, saying that he was not hungry. Maybe he was not hungry and maybe he just was not sure if he dared to eat this unusual dish, but the "chef" would not take no for an answer. "Sir," he began politely, "I didn't spend two hours cooking this stuff so you could tell me you're not hungry. You eat it." And the colonel did.[72]

As welcome as fresh chicken dinners were to the men, there was at least one occasion when such a repast did not seem all that inviting. A Company I soldier spied several chickens scratching and pecking near the roadside, but any thoughts he might have had of a nicely roasted drumstick vanished when he got a little closer. Unmindful of his presence, they were busy eating the maggots that covered the corpse of a German soldier.[73]

Duty was light, and two officers and seventeen enlisted men from the 100th Battalion received thirty-day passes and were able to go home to Hawaii! For the rest of the regiment, almost all of the men who wanted to were able to obtain passes to visit Rome. Many of those who visited the Eternal City went to USO shows at the Royal Opera House. Popular singer and composer Irving Berlin, who had written such songs as "God Bless America" and "White Christmas," and opera singer Lily Pons were among the headliners who were trying to bring a little bit of happiness to the soldiers far from their homes.[74]

During one of Pope Pius XII's regular visitations with American troops in Rome, half a dozen Nisei soldiers formed part of the honor guard provided by the army. As the pontiff passed by a member of the 442nd's Medical Detachment, the soldier dropped to his knees in reverent respect. The Pope stopped when he saw this and approached the soldier, who then kissed his ring as a further sign of respect. Although it was not unusual for Catholic GIs to react in this way, the number of Nisei Catholics was probably very small.[75]

There was time to interact with the local populace, most of whom made the liberating soldiers feel very welcome. On a reconnaissance in the hills of Italy, a couple of Nisei soldiers came upon a woman and her seventeen-year-old daughter. Neither American could speak Italian, but one was able to converse with the daughter in French. After giving whatever useful information she could, the young girl commented that she thought that the soldier's companion, who was still a teenager himself, was quite handsome. For reasons of his own, the older GI failed to communicate this to his companion until long after any possibility of a romantic connection had disappeared. The younger man never forgave him.[76]

When American soldiers in Italy had any free time, it was not difficult for them to find women willing to satisfy their primal desires for sex. Prostitution, of course, had always existed, but the war-induced economic hardships drove many women to embrace it as a means of basic survival for themselves and, perhaps, their families. A survey conducted at the end of the war found that approximately 75 percent of the American soldiers in Italy admitted to having had sex with Italian women. The last thing that one man's mother told him before he left for the army was: "[W]hen you go in the army don't mess around with the prostitutes." (These words of wisdom, in fact, constituted the totality of his sex education.) The temptation, however, could be difficult to resist. Street hustlers openly approached soldiers on the streets to offer their sisters and even their mothers for sexual pleasure. Sometimes these pimps were little boys or girls. "Want a Signorina?" they would ask. Or "Nice girl of seventeen?" "I went," admitted one Japanese American GI. "We all went! Nobody can deny it!"[77]

The Fifth Army attempted to regulate the sex trade, and the accompanying risk of venereal disease, by keeping one large brothel outside of Naples for military use and placing all others off limits to soldiers; but this measure proved ineffective in preventing the spread of sexually transmitted diseases. By 1944, according to one estimate, virtually all of the prostitutes in Italy, as well as half of the other "available" women, had contracted a venereal disease of some type. Soldiers openly referred to Naples as the "City of Sin" and said that if someone could figure out a way to put a roof over the entire city it would then become the largest whorehouse in the world.[78]

In an effort to prevent venereal infection the army issued six condoms per month to every soldier and encouraged the men to visit the pro—for prophylactic—stations set up in almost every city where there were soldiers. Here they could pick up more free condoms. They were also encouraged to visit a pro station for treatment after having had unprotected intercourse. Treatment consisted of a visual inspection of the genitals, after which a medic injected an antiseptic into the soldier's urethra with instructions to hold it in his bladder for a specified time before urinating. The final step of the treatment was to administer an antiseptic salve externally before wrapping the appendage in gauze. For those too embarrassed to visit the pro station for treatment, the army also provided each soldier with two individual do-it-yourself pro kits per week.

While in Leghorn, the Nisei soldiers had a quasi-official site for the release of pent-up sexual energy. They ran their own whorehouse in a two-story, four-bedroom house. There was one girl for each bedroom, and there were always a couple of armed guards on the premises. It was conveniently located right next door to an army pro station.[79]

Being in a rest area afforded the men such a simple pleasure as a ready supply of clean drinking water. Soldiers on the move could rapidly use up the water in their canteens, especially in warmer weather. Local supplies—in wells or streams—were usually available but the water was not always free of disease-producing organisms. Soldiers therefore carried a supply of halazone tablets—chlorine-based additives for disinfecting drinking water. To be most effective, the soldier was to add the requisite number of tablets to his canteen and then let it set for a half hour. In practice, however, most GIs were thirsty when they added the tablets and often did not wait long enough before drinking the water for the halazone to be effective. And when they did wait long enough they had water that might be safe but very unpleasant in taste. A Company K officer reacted typically when he came upon a clear mountain stream and drank the water before the halazone had had time to work. He moved forward unconcerned until he soon came upon the decomposing corpse of a cow upstream from where he had filled his canteen. "Then," he said, "I swallowed a couple of halizon [sic] tablets in a hurry."[80]

There were sandy beaches near the rest area and army engineers worked to clear anti-personnel mines from the sand to render the area safe for use, although a few men received painful wounds from jellyfish and occasional stingrays. In a perhaps unsporting, but nevertheless very efficient, method of fishing, men used four-ounce blocks of TNT to stun huge numbers of fish. Then, when the fish floated to the surface, the anxious—and hungry—GIs scooped them up and took them back to the beach where fires were ready to roast them into mouth-watering treats.

Sergeant Morita enjoyed the proximity to the beach, and even though the boy from the Rocky Mountains had never learned to swim he found it to be a very enjoyable experience "to go splashing around in salt water." Sadly, the engineer troops missed some of the mines buried in the sand, and as result a Cannon Company soldier lost a leg to one.[81]

Poker remained a popular pastime. Sergeant Morita, a better than average player, made about $170 during his first two months in Italy. German artillery interrupted one game with a few random shells that burst uncomfortably close to the poker players, slightly wounding an onlooker. Morita asked one of his brothers back home to try to find some inexpensive poker chips to send to him. He assured him that "the cheapest you can find will be fine," adding, "We're interested in quantity not quality." Before any stateside poker chips arrived, however, Morita picked some up while on a pass to Rome.[82]

The rest period also allowed time for memorial services for those members of the regiment who had been killed in battle. The survivors, who had previously given little if any thought to their fallen comrades, now had time to reflect on their losses. "When the names of those killed were called," wrote one man, "I tried to shut my eyes but the faces of all my buddies killed, including an awfully good kid whom I had taught in school floated one after another before me. And the tears that rained down my face were as easy to hold back as a 16-inch shell from a battleship. The names and faces appeared endless. It was very painful." And there would be many more before the fighting stopped.[83]

On July 27, Fifth Army commander Mark Clark put in an appearance to personally award the 100th Battalion a Distinguished Unit Citation for its valorous conduct at Belvedere. "All three companies," read the citation,

> went into action boldly facing murderous fire from all types of weapons and tanks and at times fighting without artillery support. Doggedly the members of the 100th Infantry Battalion fought their way into the strongly defended positions. The stubborn desire of the men to close with a numerically superior enemy and the rapidity with which they fought enabled the . . . battalion to destroy completely the right flank positions of a German Army . . . forcing the remainder of a completely disrupted [German] battalion to surrender approximately 10 kilometers of ground."

General Clark then added his personal observation. "All you Americans of Japanese ancestry," he remarked, "should be proud of yourselves! The 34th Division is proud of you! The 5th Army is proud of you! America is proud of you!"[84]

While in the rest area some of the men decided to enter the Allied Mediterranean Theater Swimming and Diving Championships in Rome on August 1 and 2, as representatives of the Fifth Army. One of the medical officers volunteered to coach them. The caliber of swimmers they faced in the tournament was just as good as, or perhaps even better than, those against whom they had competed when they were stationed back at Camp Shelby. These included athletes who had, as civilians, won national championships and had competed in the Olympics. The Nisei athletes acquitted themselves well. A Cannon Company swimmer was selected as the meet's outstanding swimmer, having won the 400-, 800-, and 1,500-meter events and anchoring the 400- and 800-meter relays.

He came away with six wrist watches as prizes, which he sent home to his brother and five sisters.[85]

By the first day of August the rest period was over and it was back to serious training. General Ryder had rotated to the United States a couple of weeks before to take command of the IX Corps, and Major General Charles Bolte, former commander of the 69th Division, replaced him as commander of the 34th Division. Bolte specified that the Nisei troops should get as much training in mountain warfare as time allowed in order to prepare for what lay ahead. This training took on an added, and unfortunate, sense of realism the next day when a truckload of mines blew up. Some combat engineer troops from the 34th Division had been demonstrating to members of the 3rd Battalion how to identify and disarm German mines. When the instruction was over the engineers began loading the mines and various other explosives into their truck when, somehow, a crate of TNT detonated. The truck and ten soldiers standing near it were blown literally to pieces by the blast. Fortunately, most of the 3rd Battalion had already departed the immediate area, but two soldiers from Company M and two from the Combat Team's own 232nd Combat Engineer Company were among the fatalities. Soldiers went over the area picking up anything identifiable as having once been part of a human body and depositing it into an empty mattress cover. It was grisly work. A man detailed to clean up the area described how he "found a small foot from the ankle down, completely blown out of socks and shoe and what looked to be a short shin bone with all the flesh gone. . . . The largest piece I came upon was a small torso with both legs blown off."[86]

On August 15, the entire combat team was removed from the administrative control of the 34th Division and split up, at least temporarily. The 100th Battalion went to the 107th Antiaircraft Artillery Group of Task Force 45 in IV Corps, while the other two infantry battalions went to the 85th Division in II Corps, and the artillery battalion was attached to the 88th Infantry Division near Pisa. General Bolte let it be known to the commander of the 442nd how grateful he was for having had the 442nd under his command. "The 442nd Combat Team came to the 34th Division on 24 June 1944," he recounted, "well trained, capably led, and highly endowed with a spirit and determination to win."

> Immediately, you won the admiration and cordial relationship of your new associates. To have had you earn your battle spurs with us during your introduction into combat from 26 June, near Grossetto, Italy, where you received your first baptism of fire and terminate the period of combat service with your triumphal drive on Pisa on 27 July, has been a distinct pleasure to myself and this command. Hammering the enemy steadily and doggedly pushing obstacles before you, you liberated, in your short time with us, over 10 Italian towns, killed, captured, and wounded over 1000 Germans and captured and destroyed considerable quantities of enemy artillery, tanks, pillboxes and transport. Your performance has been excellent. . . . You have indeed proven to all the world your devotion and loyalty to your country, your willingness and ability to fight alongside your fellow Americans and your gallantry on the field of battle. Now you leave us, to carry on elsewhere with your high ideals and traditional fighting spirits [and it] is with sincere regret that the 34th Division relinquishes command of the 442nd Combat Team, after such a short but efficacious association. We shall watch with interest your continued achievements and victories.[87]

By the next day the 2nd and 3rd Battalions had reached their new home at Castelfiorentino, south of Florence. The men barely had enough time to unload from the trucks before orders arrived re-assigning them to the 88th Division, and they were on the move again on the 19th.

The 100th Battalion, meanwhile, left Vada on August 16 and moved up to the Arno River, just east of Pisa, going into line after midnight. The men they replaced were glad to see them arrive. They were part of a hastily thrown together hodge-podge of British and American antiaircraft artillerists who were doing emergency service as riflemen.[88]

The men of the 232nd Engineers stayed busy as the combat team pushed northward. The Germans had placed mines near two likely approaches to the south bank of the Arno River as they fell back, and it was up to the Nisei engineers to locate and disarm them. Using both the heavy electronic mine detectors and the field expedient of hand-held probes, they removed almost a hundred anti-tank mines as well as some smaller ones. German engineers were just as skilled as the Americans, hiding some of these mines in almost waist-deep water.[89]

On the night of August 20–21, the 2nd and 3rd Battalions took over six miles of front from elements of the British 1st Division. Such a wide sector of responsibility demanded more defenders, so the 232nd Combat Engineers served as a mobile reserve rifle company until a more permanent solution could be found to the manpower shortage. The most immediate danger to the Nisei was a German position in San Columbano, just south of the Arno River and immediately to the left of the 3rd Battalion's area of responsibility.

On August 23, the commander of the 3rd Battalion's heavy weapons company, volunteered to lead a patrol out to destroy this pesky enemy position. In addition to soldiers from his own Company M were others from Company L and a forward observer from Cannon Company. The observer was able to call in accurate fire and the initial enemy position was destroyed. The American patrol then moved beyond San Columbano to locate other targets. Suddenly, German machine-gun fire swept across the patrol, and three men went down. The captain, realizing that drastic action was necessary if his men were to survive, rose up and began returning fire with his submachine gun. The Germans, of course, focused their fire on this obvious target, but the diversion he created was enough for the men to fall back to safer positions whence they could once again call in artillery fire. The captain, unfortunately, paid the ultimate price for securing his men's safety.[90]

The three wounded men were in a difficult situation. Any attempt to rescue or render them first aid necessarily exposed the rescuers to the same deadly fire that had brought them down in the first place. Medics, by virtue of the fact that they were unarmed and wore the red cross insignia, were supposed to be exempt as targets of enemy fire, but this had not always been the case. Still, something had to be done for the wounded men or they would die where they lay. A medic hesitantly raised a small white flag with a red cross in the center over his head and gingerly stood up, waiting to see what the enemy reaction would be. When no gunfire was forthcoming, he slowly led a small team of medics to tend to the wounded Americans. Working hastily, they stabilized the injured men enough to evacuate them on litters. Not only did the Germans respect the red cross and hold their fire during this time, but a German medic approached with information on the condition of a wounded American officer who had been captured.[91]

With the relative positions of the opposing armies changing rapidly, both sides sought information concerning their enemy's intentions, and the best way to obtain it was by capturing and interrogating enemy soldiers. All along the Arno River, patrols from both armies prowled the area, usually at night, for the purpose of capturing enemy soldiers. It was difficult to see enemy positions, and the Germans had planted hundreds, perhaps thousands, of mines along the river. There was frequent contact with enemy patrols, but prisoners were rarely taken.

Finally, on the night of August 28, some men from Company K got lucky. Their patrol started out much like the others. The men moved toward the enemy lines, stumbled into a brief firefight with an enemy patrol, and then headed for home—without any prisoners. Suddenly one of the men saw some movement, or at least thought he did, in an irrigation ditch. The squad leader yelled for whoever was there to come out, but received no reply. One of the men then fired a shot into the ditch, and that drew an immediate response. "Kamerad," called out a frightened German, as he and three others meekly came out of hiding. These soldiers, members of the 71st Panzergrenadier Regiment, had been out seeking to capture some Americans when their luck ran out.[92]

Interrogated by American intelligence officers, the prisoners taken in these forays revealed that German forces were about to pull back to prepared defenses along what was known as the Gothic Line. Consequently, the 100th Battalion began crossing the Arno in the vicinity of Pisa on September 1. To its right, the 2nd and 3rd Battalions also began moving across the river, occupying the towns of Peretola and San Mauro without meeting any resistance. But the fact that the enemy no longer occupied these two villages did not mean that they were safe. Before retreating, the Germans had booby-trapped some of the houses and had sown the roads and adjacent fields with vast numbers of mines. The 3rd Battalion's chaplain was wounded when his jeep ran over one of these mines while he was on the way to recover the body of a Nisei soldier who had been killed earlier.[93]

The next day, patrols from the 2nd and 3rd Battalions probed as far forward as the villages of Sesto and San Martino, respectively. They encountered no enemy soldiers, but the men from the 2nd Battalion did meet a friendly British patrol. About this time, the men of the 442nd noticed a small influx of Japanese-looking soldiers, but these were not replacements sent from Camp Shelby. Instead, they were part of a contingent from the recently arrived 1st Brazilian Division. Allied authorities assigned men from this force to accompany and observe soldiers already in the theater. Just as most of the Japanese Americans spoke English and at least a smattering of Japanese, these Brazilians spoke Portuguese and some Japanese. Because there were no native Portuguese units in Italy, the Japanese Americans offered the best chance for at least some of these South Americans to converse without having to rely on interpreters. During their brief time together, the Americans were chagrined to learn that the pay scale in the Brazilian Army was higher than their own.[94]

Elements of the 88th Division pushed on through the bridgeheads on the night of September 2, and a few days later the 2nd and 3rd Battalion were detached from the division and headed toward the coastal city of Castiglioncello, seventy miles away. At the same time, the 100th Battalion returned from its sojourn with IV Corps, and the 442nd Regimental Combat Team was again back together.

After repairing or replacing clothing and equipment, the combat team embarked on Liberty ships at the port of Piombino on September 10 and sailed south to Naples, arriving around midnight on September 11. At Naples the unit was officially detached from the Fifth Army and assigned to Lieutenant General

Alexander M. Patch's Seventh Army, which was then pushing its way through eastern France toward Germany.

General Mark Clark did not let the 442nd leave his command without a formal farewell. "I desire to commend you," he wrote, in a letter to the regiment's commanding officer,

> on the occasion of your departure from Fifth Army for the superior job you and your troops have done while assigned to Fifth Army. . . . American troops of Japanese Ancestry are well known to the Fifth Army for the splendid showing which had previously been made by the 100th Infantry Battalion during the course of the past year. The conduct of your troops was exemplary both on the battlefield and in rest areas. Your men have demonstrated an eagerness for combat and have proven themselves to be better than anything the enemy has been able to put up against them. The courage and determination which the men of the 442nd Combat Team have displayed during their short time in combat has been an inspiration to us all.[95]

For the next week, members of the regiment relaxed and re-fitted. There were passes into Naples and to nearby Pompeii. By this time the reputation that the Japanese American troops had earned through their hard fighting had spread through most of the Fifth Army—as General Clark had written. But not everyone knew about them. As several Nisei soldiers rounded a corner in Naples they almost ran into a couple of GIs from the 3rd Division, who were also out on the town. "My god," one GI mumbled morosely, "all is lost. The Japs have captured Naples."[96]

But such encounters were rare, and there was again frequent fraternization with the local populace. Some of the GIs got a very jaded look at the seamier underside of Neapolitan society. "I guess about 90% of the people in Napoli," wrote one, "are either prostitutes or pimps." Others, however, reported heartwarming interaction with local families.[97]

On September 18, 672 replacements arrived from the United States and reported to the companies that needed them. The entire regiment then went back into training mode to acclimate the new men as much as possible in the limited amount of time available before the unit went back into the line. Three days later, the men piled into trucks for the short seven-mile drive to the staging area at Bagnoli where they were quartered, out of the rain, in a building that had previously housed part of the University of Naples. At noon on September 27 the combat team, aboard the attack transport ships *Samuel Chase, Thurston, Joseph T. Dickman,* and *Henrico,* set sail from Naples and headed for France.[98]

CHAPTER SEVEN

FIGHTING IN FRANCE

"There's mortars + tanks firing all around me now. . . . I'm keeping my fingers crossed."

The original Allied plan to drive Hitler's German troops out of Western Europe called for two simultaneous invasions in the summer of 1944—one in northwestern France and one in southeastern France. This would require two enormous armies along with the necessary equipment to get them to the invasion sites. One invasion force would stage from Britain, the other from Italy. The plan began to unravel a bit when the German resistance in Italy made that campaign last much longer than had been anticipated. There was also a shortage of ships and landing craft to support two invasions at the same time. Nevertheless, Operation Overlord, the landings on the French beaches of Normandy, went off pretty much as scheduled on June 6, and Operation Dragoon, the assault on the Mediterranean coast, was necessarily delayed until August.

General Patch's Seventh Army drew the assignment to invade France from the Mediterranean. The main infantry assault components that would land across the beaches included the U.S. 3rd, 36th, and 45th Infantry Divisions. The 3rd Division would anchor the American landings on the left, or west, of the landing zone while the 36th would protect the right, or east, flank of the army. The 45th Division would land in the center. The French First Army would follow the 45th Division ashore and had the task of liberating the major port city of Marseilles and the port of Toulon to the west of the invasion beaches while the Americans began moving northward up the Rhone River valley. The assaulting troops were expected to push inland some fifteen to twenty miles by day two of the operation.[1]

227

As with the Normandy operation, this one would also employ paratroopers and glider-borne troops to land behind the beaches to intercept any enemy reinforcements headed for the invasion beaches and to open up strategic roadways for the waves of amphibious landings to come. Both the 82nd and the 101st Airborne Divisions were in Britain recovering from battle losses in Normandy, and were therefore unavailable to General Patch. And since no other complete airborne divisions had yet arrived in the European or Mediterranean theaters, Allied authorities had to cobble together a division-size force—dubbed the First Airborne Task Force—from available assets, chiefly the British Second Independent Parachute Brigade and the U.S. 517th Airborne Regimental Combat Team. Arriving in Italy just a few days after the 442nd, the 517th had been attached to the 36th Division and had received its baptism of fire in the hills northeast of Grosseto. Two American airborne battalions, the 509th and the 551st, helped to fill out the organization. The former had already made two combat jumps and had taken part in the fighting in Tunisia and at Anzio. For the men of the 551st, however, this invasion would be their initiation to combat. Two battalions of parachute field artillery, the 596th and the 463rd, provided extra punch for the paratroopers. Their 75mm howitzers added needed firepower to the airborne formation but would be ineffective against German armor.

The 550th Glider Infantry Battalion, also untested in combat, would come in after the paratroopers had secured landing zones and at about the time that the seaborne troops landed. American planners had a healthy respect for German armor and fully expected that at least four dozen tanks and more than a dozen tank destroyers would be immediately on hand to contest the invasion. Recognizing the threat German armor posed to the lightly armed paratroopers, the planners decided to include an antitank unit in the airborne force. And, since there were no parachute- or glider-qualified antitank units then available in the theater, the call went out to the 442nd's Anti-Tank Company.

Orders arrived on July 14, temporarily detaching the Anti-Tank Company from the regiment and sending it to Gallera Airfield near Rome for a hasty indoctrination into glider warfare. The men arrived the next day and took up residence in tents. Beginning the next day, they spent the next two weeks in glider assault training, with particular emphasis given to learning how to tie down their equipment inside the gliders. The landings would be rough, and it was essential that guns, jeeps, and ammunition trailers not break free when the gliders touched down. One of these large pieces of equipment, if it was not securely fastened might hurtle forward upon landing and crush the pilot and copilot. The Nisei troops soon discovered that their 57mm anti-tank guns were too big to fit into the gliders, so they traded them for British 6-pounder anti-tank guns, which were almost identical but were somewhat lighter and had slightly shorter barrels.

The gliders looked like any other small cargo plane except for the fact that there were no engines on them. The United States had contracted in early 1941 with the Waco Aircraft Company of Troy, Ohio, to design and build cargo gliders capable of being used to deliver supplies and troops to wherever they were needed. The resultant craft, designated the CG-4A by the government, was almost fifty feet long and had a wingspan just short of eighty-four feet. The wings were of plywood and the fuselage was constructed of a heavy-duty cotton fabric stretched tightly over a welded tubular steel framework and then varnished. Each glider could easily carry a dozen soldiers with all of their personal gear, or it could transport various types of equipment such as a jeep or an antitank gun. A single antitank gun team required four gliders to carry the gun, two jeeps, and an ammunition trailer. The soldiers who formed the gun team split up so that a handful of them flew in each of the four gliders.

In use, a 350-foot nylon rope connected an airplane, typically a twin-engine C-47, to the nose of the glider. When the plane began its takeoff run the glider remained motionless as the long nylon tow rope stretched. The taut rope then flung the glider into the air, not unlike the catapults on modern aircraft carriers. (One rumor, current at the time, had it that each of these tow ropes had enough nylon in it to make 150,000 women's stockings.) Usually the glider, because it was so much lighter than the tow craft, got into the air first. The glider pilot then tried to keep his craft a little bit higher than the plane in order to avoid engine turbulence. If he flew too high, however, the tow rope tended to pull the rear of the airplane up, making it that much harder for the plane to get off the ground at all. Sometimes, an airplane pulled two gliders at the same time, splayed out behind on different-length ropes.[2]

As the tandem aircraft neared the designated release point the pilot or copilot of the glider released the tow rope, and the airplane turned to return to its base. The glider then proceeded to as clear and level a field as the pilot could find and landed in what might best be described as a controlled crash. After the pilot and copilot dismounted, the entire front end of the craft, where they had been sitting, hinged upward to allow the passengers to exit and any vehicles to roll forward and out.

The Nisei anti-tankers moved to Marcigilana Airfield, north of Rome, for the final phase of their training. They made two practice flights on August 3 and 4, thus qualifying them for the silver glider badge showing a head-on view of a glider against a large pair of spread wings. The practice flights went smoothly, although one of the gliders came down rather too fast and the weight of the soldiers aboard collapsed the wooden benches upon which they had been seated.[3]

Some of the men enjoyed the experience immensely. After the glider pilots disengaged the tow rope, according to one of them, the glider seemed to soar through the sky like a bird. At about the same time, however, war correspondent Walter Cronkite made a glider flight into Europe from England. His recollection was somewhat different. "Riding in one of those Waco gliders," he wrote many years later, "was like attending a rock concert while locked in the bass drum. . . . Once in the windstream, the canvas [fuselage] beat against the frame with enough decibels to promote permanent deafness." Perhaps the difference in the respective perceptions lay in the fact that it was the first time that most of these soldiers had ever flown in any kind of aircraft, and they likely assumed that the noise was just a normal part of the experience. After this familiarization training, the men then moved south of the city where they were temporarily attached to the 517th Parachute Infantry Regiment.[4]

Pilots and copilots pored over detailed maps of the proposed landing sites that would be available to them. Once committed to a landing they would have no choice but to go through with it. Their unpowered aircraft did not have the capability to pull up and search out alternate sites. The troops also studied the maps to make sure they could orient themselves once they were on the ground and could then proceed to accomplish their tasks in support of the invasion. One vital piece of information, however, was absent from the maps: the name of the country that they were invading! They did not learn—officially—until they were preparing to board the gliders that southern France was their destination.

Not everyone, it seems, was kept in the dark. A *Chicago Tribune* correspondent reported that he heard soldiers in Naples openly talking about the upcoming invasion and even listing the army and navy units that were going to participate. Another reporter, who had been present at an official briefing on the operation, went into a bookstore in Rome to purchase a guide book to southern France to prepare himself. He furtively shielded the book from other shoppers as he went to pay for it. The proprietor noticed and told him that he was being much more careful than several army officers who had recently visited his store. "They come in," he said, "and ask for maps of Southern France and talk of Toulon and Cannes."[5]

Not surprisingly, the Germans were also fairly well informed about the invasion. American soldiers remembered being stunned to hear Berlin Sally, also known to many of them as the Berlin Bitch, address them: "Hello, all you American paratroopers at those airfields around Rome. You parachute boys won't have to worry about bailing out over Southern France in the dark hours of the 15th, because [we] will have it lit up for you boys. We'll have a reception committee waiting for you—and oh, by the way, you will not need those parachutes, our flak will be so thick, you can simply walk down on it!"[6]

Finally, it was August 14, and time for final preparations for the invasion. In the absence of specially prepared camouflage clothing, the paratroopers adopted their own means of making do. Setting their weapons and other gear aside, they lined up by platoons. At the head of each line of soldiers were men with paint spray guns full of black or dark green paint. As each soldier reached the front of the line, he spread his arms out to the sides, and the painter quickly went to work on him. Placing a cardboard box over the soldier's head to protect him from overspray, the painters quickly swung their paint nozzles back and forth over the man, producing an irregular mottled pattern. The anti-tankers apparently saw no need for this, but they did sew small American flag patches onto their left sleeves just as the paratroopers were doing.[7]

A little after midnight, three planeloads of pathfinders took off for France. They were to parachute into the designated landing zones and set up radar devices to help guide the pilots in the main assault force. When they arrived over the French coast the planes encountered heavy fog that obscured visual landmarks. The pilots made several passes, hoping to find a break in the fog, but to no avail. Finally, with no improvement in the weather, the pilots turned on the green jump lights, and the pathfinders bailed out into the dark. When they landed, they discovered that they were fifteen miles west of their drop zones. The main airborne assault force would have to make do without the pathfinders' help.

Some six aircraft dropped their loads near a small village between Toulon and Marseille, but without as much concern about the foggy weather. Flying at an altitude of about six hundred feet, they rapidly discharged clouds of radar-confusing metal chaff and hundreds of dummy parachutists and rifle simulators to confuse the Germans.[8]

At around 1:30 A.M., C-47s at ten different airfields up and down the west coast of Italy began taking off at ten-second intervals. They were filled with British and American paratroopers. Their takeoff times were carefully choreographed, those having the farthest distance to the rendezvous point taking off first. As each plane roared down the dirt runway and into the night sky its twin propellers kicked up small dust storms, blinding the pilots behind them and requiring them to use their instruments to safely navigate into the air. Each "serial"—or group—of about forty-five aircraft required almost an hour to get into its final V-formation. Then, rendezvousing over the island of Elba, scene of Napoleon Bonaparte's exile, they headed west.

The planes were spaced fairly close together—only about a hundred feet apart—and flew at an altitude of about two thousand feet. Their airspeed of 140 miles per hour placed them near the French coast not much more than an hour after leaving the rendezvous point. They dropped down to about fifteen hundred feet, slowed to 125 miles per hour and, a little before 4:30 A.M., the 509th, along with the airborne artillerymen, hit the silk. Within minutes 180 more planes arrived over the drop zones and began discharging the men of the 517th.

The first wave of glider troops—the British 64th Light Artillery—was scheduled to arrive at about 8:00 A.M., just as ground forces began hitting the beaches, but the fog that had played such havoc with the pathfinders also delayed the arrival of the gliders until almost 9:30. Late afternoon saw the arrival of thirty-five more British gliders and forty-one additional planeloads of American paratroopers.[9]

Finally it was the turn of the Nisei glider men. They assembled at two of the many airfields in western Italy that were being used to launch the airborne assault. At four o'clock in the afternoon a C-47 rumbled down the strip towing the first of forty-four gliders that had been allotted to the Anti-Tank Company. Rather inauspiciously, however, the tow rope on the first glider broke, forcing its passengers to find another one to take them to France.[10]

The gliders were finally all airborne and the C-47s headed for their rendezvous point. The force that headed west across the Ligurian Sea toward the coastline of the French Riviera consisted of over three hundred towed gliders filled with soldiers and their equipment. The Nisei passengers, for the most part, seemed to enjoy the ride. Most had never flown at all prior to their training flights in Italy. "We were all happy that we were going to France," remembered one, "and we weren't too concerned over the problems we'd find when we hit the ground. The fellows on my glider sang Hawaiian songs and cheered on the pilot and copilot during most of the flight." He even tore a small hole in the canvas fuselage of his glider so he could see out. The wind immediately began enlarging the tear, and the soldier spent the rest of the flight desperately trying to pinch the fabric together so it would not actually endanger the structural integrity of the aircraft.[11]

Enemy defenses were not as strong as those in Normandy, but the Germans had nonetheless ensured that the invaders would meet with a hostile reception. Correctly guessing that an invasion would likely make use of glider troops, they had carefully prepared many of the prospective landing sites, erecting what was known as "Rommel's asparagus" to hinder the landings. Credited to Field Marshal Erwin Rommel, these consisted of stout poles, perhaps as big as six inches in diameter, planted throughout the field between fifteen and forty feet apart and extending some ten feet in the air. Glider pilots trying to land in these fields risked coming down on top of one of these obstructions. As one OSS (Office of Strategic Services) officer rather indelicately put it, "The barbs ripping through the flimsy floors of the gliders would have torn the balls off of an awful lot of Americans." Another danger was landing between adjacent poles that would shear the wings off. To further cause trouble for any glider assault force, many of these poles were connected by barbed wire and topped with explosive mines.[12]

The carefully choreographed flights came undone early. When the lead glider began to develop problems its tow plane made a 180-degree turn back toward Italy. The pilot, however, neglected to inform the pilots of those planes behind him of the reason for his change of course, and many of them, following his lead, also made the turn. By the time these errant planes returned to the formation they were out of their assigned places, and planes coming up behind them had to abruptly decrease airspeed or climb to avoid collisions.

Some pilots increased speed to regain the proper alignment. Unfortunately, this led to other problems because the Waco gliders were not designed to fly faster than 150 miles per hour. When they did so, they became prone to structural failure. The copilot of one of these speeding gliders contacted the lieutenant colonel who was piloting his tow plane and repeatedly asked him to slow down as their airspeed approached the critical number, but to no avail. Instead, the tow pilot, obviously anxious to catch up with where he thought he should be within the formation, actually *increased* his speed. The glider copilot then looked out his window to the right and watched, horrified, as another glider broke up, hurling its occupants to their deaths below. This time, when he contacted his tow plane pilot, he did away with all the niceties of rank. "Listen, you son of a bitch," he spoke into the phone connecting the two craft, "I'll give you until I count to ten to slow this thing down and then I'm going to shoot your goddam right engine out." And he began to count. "There must have been something in his voice that convinced that 'light' colonel that he meant it," recalled the other occupant of the glider's cockpit, "because before he reached 'eight,' we were below the redlined speed."[13]

As the flights of tow planes and gliders crossed the French coastline some encountered an unforeseen danger. At least one of the Allied warships below opened fire on them, and one round destroyed the right horizontal stabilizer of a glider that carried a jeep and two Nisei anti-tankers. The glider went into a steep dive, and the only thing that kept it from crashing into the sea was its tow rope and the frantic efforts of its pilot and copilot to restore some semblance of control. Remembering his passengers, the pilot turned to shout a warning to them, but he found them seemingly unconcerned, sitting in the jeep and smoking cigarettes. They had heard stories about these crazy glider pilots and must have figured that what they were then experiencing was perfectly normal.[14]

Plans called for each group of gliders to arrive at the landing zones at ten-minute intervals to avoid aerial congestion. Instead, however, four groups of gliders arrived almost simultaneously. This included one element that had overshot the landing zones and was now returning from the opposite direction. There were a couple of mid-air collisions, and one glider pilot later described the near miss he had with a jeep that had fallen free from another glider somewhere overhead. "The air was filled with gliders plunging in for landings from all directions and from all altitudes," remembered one pilot. "You had to weave your way down through a gyrating mass of Wacos [gliders] all intent on getting into a field. You had to select a suitable landing field, watch out for anti-glider obstacles, and keep a sharp eye out for some other glider heading for you on a collision course. It was like Piccadilly Circus at high noon with the traffic being directed by an insane policeman." "Christ, what a mess!" exclaimed another pilot. "Everywhere I looked there were gliders in free flight or still tagging along behind tow planes taking evasive action trying not to run into each other."[15]

Even after a pilot had successfully brought his craft to the ground the chaos continued. "I watched one glider come whistling in at about 100 mph," recalled one man, "hook a wing, and go cartwheeling down the field like a cheerleader at a football game." A paratrooper who had already arrived was stunned by the glider landings. "I've never seen a more awful sight in my life," he said. "[S]ome gliders landed upside down, some came down on one wing only, while others crashed into trees. I saw one jeep being tossed out of a glider, while it was still in the air, and another vehicle crashed through the nose . . . all in all it was a very sickening sight."[16]

"I heard the crashing sound of our glider hitting the trees," recalled one of the amateur glider troops, "and I thought, 'This is it; we are dead!'" Obviously, his assessment of his fate was somewhat premature. In fact, none of the glider passengers were killed, although over a hundred were seriously injured, including six members of the Anti-Tank Company.[17]

The carnage at the landing site was significant. Only two of the gliders were salvageable after the landing. Eleven glider pilots were killed, including two who were transporting a jeep and a handful of Nisei soldiers. Their glider crash-landed with such violence that it snapped all twenty-eight ropes that were meant to secure the jeep to the floor. The jeep then hurtled forward, running over and killing both aviators. "They had got us down safely at the sacrifice of their lives," one anti-tanker recalled. A similarly laden glider was a total wreck after landing, although without the same fatal results. The pilot and copilot of this glider were among the thirty who were seriously injured, each suffering broken legs. One soldier, even decades later, still gets nervous when he is on an airplane that is about to land.[18]

There would likely have been more landing injuries had not paratroopers who had arrived earlier removed many of the pole obstructions before the gliders arrived. And the job was easier than expected in numerous instances. It seems that the Germans had used local Frenchmen to install the poles, and these laborers, either through laziness or out of a patriotic desire to sabotage the effort, had not done a very thorough job. Instead of planting poles deeply and firmly in the ground, they had in several instances simply stood them upright with rocks piled around their bases. According to one man, "[w]e knocked over quite a few of them with just a light push."[19]

In spite of the mishaps, the invasion went well. The German Nineteenth Army, tasked with defending this section of the French coast, did not include the best of the Führer's soldiers. The infantry divisions were not up to full strength and more than a third of the personnel in these units were non-Germans—prisoners of war captured in Russia and in the Balkans—who had traded imprisonment for life in the German Army.[20]

The Anti-Tank Company was split up; one gun section assigned to each battalion of the 517th Parachute Infantry Regiment. With virtually no German tanks to cause them any trouble, the Nisei soldiers acted more as infantrymen than as anti-tankers and captured over a dozen enemy soldiers as the 517th pushed through the villages of Grasse, Col de Braus, Touët de L'Escarène, and others.[21]

Six weeks went by before the rest of the 442nd Regiment sailed through the Tyrrhenian Sea between the islands of Corsica and Sardinia toward France. The voyage was uneventful, although rough seas were encountered in the Strait of Corsica, and the men reached Marseilles at noon on September 29. Disembarking was tricky. Getting ashore was a lot more complicated than simply scrambling over the side of the ship and climbing down the cargo nets into waiting landing craft for the short trip to shore. Even in fairly calm conditions, a careless soldier could easily get crushed between the side of the ship and the boat. First of all, every soldier was loaded down with his rifle, ammunition, grenades, gas mask, pack, and many other items so that simply moving around was difficult. And then, once the soldier had managed to descend the cargo net some twenty or thirty feet he discovered that, due to the curvature of the ship's hull, he was suspended several feet away from the side of the ship. If he was very lucky, he was able to jump the last few feet into a waiting landing craft. In rough seas, however, the landing craft bobbed like a cork. The soldier then tried to time his jump to land when the craft was at the top of its up-and-down cycle. Inevitably some men miscalculated and jumped when the craft was in the trough of a wave rather than at its crest, landing hard and breaking one or both legs as a result.

An artillery officer who was in charge of a jeep-load of instruments had a particularly harrowing experience. Slings were attached to his jeep, with him sitting behind the wheel, and his vehicle was swung over the side and down to the landing craft. Unfortunately, the load shifted, dumping much of what was in the jeep into the craft below and leaving him dangling. The jeep was brought back aboard the ship, and crewmen re-slung it and tried again, this time without incident.[22]

As the men reached the dock they noticed that some of the dockworkers had Asian features. Thinking that they had once again encountered men of Japanese heritage they greeted them in Japanese, but received no response. Each group spoke a language that was unintelligible to the other. One of the chaplains squatted down and, using his finger as a pencil, drew in the dirt the Chinese ideogram for "Japan." The stevedores recognized this and their previously cheerful demeanor turned icy. They wanted no more contact with these men in uniform, for they were Chinese (or perhaps Indo-Chinese) and probably assumed that these soldiers were from the country that was even then waging a vicious war against their people back in Asia.[23]

The war had moved away from the coast well before the arrival of the Nisei infantrymen, and they made an easy, unopposed landing. By the morning of October 1, 1944, they were settling into a tent camp on top of a windswept hill just outside of Septeme. They received new machine guns, mortars, and bazookas and set to work breaking them in as they waited for transportation to take them closer to the action. While they waited, gale force winds ripped through the camp, flattening all of the tents; and then came the rain. They were miserable.

The Seventh Army, meanwhile, had fought its way northward along the Rhone River into northeastern France where the heavily forested Vosges Mountains guarded the German border. Trucks began arriving on October 8 to begin moving the men toward the front lines, by this time several hundred miles away. There were not enough vehicles to transport the entire regiment, so the 3rd Battalion traveled by train. The other units loaded onto the available trucks the next morning and headed up Highway 7, passing through Aix-en-Provence, Avignon, and Valence before halting for the day near Vienne. The next day they repeated the process, traveling through Bourg, Lons le Saunier, and Besancon, and stopping near Vesoul for the night. They reached their destination, Charmois-devant-Bruyères, near Èpinal, at midday on the 11th having covered 450 miles.

The men of the 3rd Battalion boarded boxcars on the afternoon of October 10. These cars, smaller than American rolling stock, were designed to carry either forty men or eight horses, and were therefore called "40 and 8s." The smell of the cars resurrected unpleasant memories among those men who had been incarcerated at the Santa Anita or Tanforan race tracks back in 1942. The trip north was not one of leisure. An officer in Company K was convinced by the bumpy ride that the rail cars must have had square wheels, but the men on the train were better protected against the elements than those traveling in open trucks.[24]

During a short stop in Lyons some of the men spotted an open rail car full of C-rations, which, by most accounts, were much tastier than the K-rations upon which they had subsisted for the past several days. A few soldiers jumped down, scurried over to the unguarded car, and appropriated about twenty cases. They almost made it back without being caught, but a colonel suddenly appeared and threatened to court-martial them all unless they returned the purloined rations. At just about that time, the soldiers' train began to pull out, and one of the men called back to the colonel: "Sorry, these rations are for combat troops."[25]

The train reached Vesoul before dawn of the 13th. The trucks that had carried the rest of the regiment were now empty and waiting near the station. That evening the men detrained and clambered aboard the trucks for the final leg of the trip. They joined the rest of the regiment five hours later, around midnight.[26]

The weather in France at this time made the soldiers long for summer climates. One soldier morosely noted: "The calendar says it's still October, but the freezing weather says it's winter. And it's still raining. When it's not raining, it's drizzling and foggy." A homesick Hawaiian described his new surroundings thus: "It's raining and it's cold, and the rain drops splashing on my tent make me feel very lonesome. I'd like to think of this place in comparison with the area in upper Nuuanu [on Oahu], but this rain and cold makes it impossible for me to picture this place as beautiful." Another man commented that "[a]fter a while every muscle of your body starts to tremble. . . . You can't talk without chattering, you can't hold anything without shaking. You see the muscles quivering under your skin. You're cold and you're sopping wet, and you've been sopping wet from the very first day. After a while, the fact that it's raining doesn't mean anything because you're so wet." No doubt these sentiments were widespread in the regiment.[27]

Sergeant Morita, on the other hand, thought that the French countryside looked a little bit like home. "At first I didn't think much of this country, but now I've changed my mind," he wrote. "[W]ith the trees changing color, and traveling between hills and along a river, it looks just like the country between Loveland [Colorado] and the hills. Of course," he went on, "nothing can beat the height of Colorado mountains."[28]

So many replacements had reached the regiment that the battle losses from Italy were more than made up. In fact, the regiment had the luxury, at least temporarily, of being overstaffed. Orders arrived from Seventh Army headquarters that no unit was to go into combat with more officers and men than what its table of organization called for. In accordance with this directive, twenty-nine officers and three hundred enlisted men were sent to the 2nd Replacement Depot at St. Loup. The remaining officers and men had little time to rest. The combat team was immediately attached to Major General John E. Dahlquist's 36th Division and assigned to cover its new "parent" formation's left flank.[29]

As a prelude to a VI Corps drive on St. Dié, the 442nd's assignment was to seize the crossroads town of Bruyères with a population of about five thousand. Located about midway between St. Die and Épinal, Bruyères was also a regional railroad center. After it cleared Bruyères, the regiment would attempt to do the same at Belmont, a couple of miles to the northeast. Operating on its right, and aiming ultimately at the town of Biffontaine four miles east of Bruyères, was the 36th Division's 143rd Regiment. Early in the afternoon of October 14, the men began moving toward their objective. Hills ringed the town, and although the local citizens undoubtedly had more picturesque names for four of these heights, the American military planners simply dubbed them Hills A, B, C, and D. They ranged in height from fifty-five to three hundred feet. The 2nd Battalion was to take Hill B, immediately north and a little west of the town, while the 100th Battalion would capture Hill A, a little northwest of B. General Dahlquist's intelligence officer had earlier assured the infantrymen that Hill A was only lightly held.[30]

October 15 was a Sunday, and a clearing in the pine forest served as a church. The "congregation" sang "The Church in the Wildwood" and "Sweet Hour of Prayer," and then recited the Twenty-Third Psalm. The psalm's "valley of the shadow of death" was certainly not lost on the men. After a sermon on the meaning of true brotherhood, the assemblage sang "America the Beautiful," "The Battle Hymn of the Republic," and "The Lord's Prayer" before returning to the war.[31]

Intelligence on the strength and location of the enemy forces was sadly deficient, and when the men of the two battalions set out on the morning of October 15 they did not know when or where they would make contact. They quickly learned that the thick pine forests through which they moved would ensure that progress was slow even without enemy troops to oppose them.

Companies E and F led the 2nd Battalion that morning, accompanied by a machine-gun platoon from the heavy weapons company. Company G remained in reserve, ready to be committed whenever it was needed. The soldiers met light resistance at first but made serious contact with the enemy after an hour and a half on the march and spent the next three hours battling against the well-entrenched Germans before digging in during the afternoon.

Like its sister battalion, the 100th also sent two companies forward through the woods at 8:00 A.M. When enemy machine-gun fire halted forward progress, Company B called for tank support and got it. Two medium tanks were available to help out. Enemy machine guns soon fell silent, but as the Nisei moved ahead they encountered a minefield that German tanks had under observation. Bazooka teams soon hit two of the panzers but without crippling results. The tank commanders, however, unwilling to risk further—and perhaps crippling—damage, opted to remove them from harm's way. At the same time, enemy troops knocked out one of the two American tanks present.[32]

Ironically, it was the 100th Battalion's reserve company, Company A—with a mortar platoon from Company D attached—that suffered the heaviest casualties that day. It had moved into a position behind Company B and adjacent to the 45th Division to protect the battalion's flank. When the men learned that they were not to be committed to immediate combat they began digging in to wait for the call to come forward. Suddenly an enemy barrage of mortar shells began exploding in the trees above their position, and lethal fragments rained down upon them. Thirty-two men were hit, and one of them died.[33]

This tragic event had the perhaps beneficial effect of teaching the men how to better protect themselves in the future. They were used to digging two-man foxholes deep enough to shield them from direct fire and nearby explosions on the ground, but this was their introduction into what most referred to as "tree bursts." Whether the enemy gunners fused their rounds to explode at some predetermined elevation above the ground or whether they were using impact fuses that detonated when the rounds hit tree trunks or branches, the effect on the ground below was the same—an unwelcome shower of hot shrapnel. Now merely digging a hole was not enough, and the men began roofing their shelters over with logs, heavy branches, and dirt.

American losses were fairly light, except of course for those in Company A, and the Nisei captured twenty enemy troops during the day. They belonged to the 9th Company of the 19th SS Police Regiment and the 223rd Grenadier Regiment. The SS Police Regiment had arrived in the area from Normandy back in September to provide protection for Marshal Henri Pétain and other officials of the Vichy collaborationist government at Belmont. At least some of the recently captured "German" troops were actually unwilling conscripts from Poland, Russia, and Czechoslovakia who had been forced into the German army when their homelands had been overrun. One of the captives, recognizing that even in a prison camp he at least would not have to dig any more

The occupants of this fighting bunker have provided for a clear field of fire and a substantial roof that will protect them from aerial bursts. Signal Corps photo.

foxholes in the cold, wet earth, joyfully heaved his shovel as far as he could. The prisoners were happy to answer their captors' questions. The Americans learned where 9th Company's ration dump was located, and they were also able to pinpoint the locations of the two enemy units' headquarters. The map coordinates were relayed back to the gun crews of the 522nd Artillery Battalion, which soon had rounds on the way. The prisoners were also very helpful in indicating where and how one of the roads leading out of Bruyères had been mined. This gave the men of the 232nd Engineers some valuable information.[34]

By mid-morning engineers were sweeping the road west of Bruyères for mines when they encountered a major roadblock. The Germans had chopped down dozens, perhaps hundreds, of trees onto the road for a stretch of about a quarter of a mile and placed booby traps among them. When the Americans set to work removing the debris they came under fire from four German machine guns that had been left in place for just such an opportunity. Enemy mortars and artillery also had the roadblock zeroed in and made things very dangerous for those attempting to clear it. And the engineer troops had to resort to hand saws to cut through the tree branches because every time they started up one of their gasoline-powered chain saws the noise alerted the Germans and they again opened fire on the roadway.[35]

The advance continued the next morning, with both battalions clearing the enemy from Hill 555 northwest of Bruyères. As the 2nd Battalion then advanced across a small valley toward Hill B the German defenders unleashed an astonishing volume of fire that effectively halted the advance. Similarly, the 100th Battalion found itself pinned down below Hill A. The situation soon worsened. Toward dusk the Germans launched a counterattack, using artillery, mortars, tanks, and self-propelled guns to assist the infantry. Neither American battalion was able to come to the aid of the other. The 522nd Field Artillery responded with hundreds of rounds from its 105mm guns, and Company D of the temporarily attached 83rd Chemical Mortar Battalion joined in with its big 4.2-inch mortars. By nightfall the enemy attack had fizzled out, and the tired American infantrymen spent a great part of the cold, rainy night digging slit trenches to prepare for whatever the Germans had in store for them on the morrow.

It is likely that soldiers on both sides feared artillery and mortar fire more than anything else. It was so random. So impersonal. So unpredictable. "It's not easy to describe how it feels to be in the middle of an artillery barrage," one Nisei recalled. "It's not knowing what is going to happen from one second to another that is so terrifying. With chunks of jagged steel flying and falling all around us at high velocity, hearing them slamming the ground like buzzing bees . . . not knowing when or where we are going to be hit . . . not knowing whether the wound is going to be serious or not, whether it's going to paralyze or kill us." Another commented that it was times like this that he prayed for safety. "I'm not ashamed to say that I have never prayed so hard in all my life," he admitted. "I prayed in English, I prayed in Japanese, I recited Christian prayers and I recited Buddhist meditations. Had I known other prayers I would have recited them too."[36]

Although soldiers were discouraged from keeping diaries—lest they should fall into enemy hands—many did so anyway. One

Nisei soldier used his diary to describe the misery of the Vosges. "Our wet socks never dry out in our wet boots," he wrote. "Our attempts to keep our extra pair of socks dry by keeping them next to our bodies are unsuccessful. They remain damp. We are never completely dry. We are always cold and shivering. Our teeth chatter. Our fingers are numb and beginning to swell. Our eyes smart from the bitter cold."[37]

Just at light on the 17th, German attacks resumed. After an hour of bitter fighting, the attackers broke off to regroup. Then, at about 9:30, trying to dislodge the Americans from their positions on Hill 555, the enemy attacked again, this time with three tanks. The American regiment was without its anti-tank company, which was still detached to the 517th Parachute Infantry Regiment farther south, but a half-dozen bazooka teams and the fire of the 522nd Artillery Battalion helped to convince the panzer commanders to retreat.

Trying to capitalize on what might understandably be assumed was a degradation of morale among the Germans, both American battalions, the 100th and the 2nd, launched their own counterattacks. But if the Germans were demoralized they did not show it. Once again, as the Americans tried to cross the valley leading up to Hills A and B, the defenders on those hills raked them unmercifully. Not only were the enemy soldiers dug in along the slopes and crests of the hills, they also occupied a number of stoutly built houses near the bases. And these houses made excellent machinegun emplacements. Those facing the 100th Battalion concealed fifteen machine guns and two anti-tank guns. Both American battalions sent out patrols to try to destroy these positions.

On the right flank, four tanks assisted the infantrymen of Company G in clearing some of these houses along the base of Hill 555, but the Americans were unable to move forward toward Hill B. General Dahlquist soon arrived on the scene. Accompanied by only a single aide, he often went forward to see for himself what the tactical situations facing his men were. And when he did, he often issued orders to nearby troops, in complete disregard for the chain of command. This micromanaging was maddening to lower-ranking officers whose authority he thus undermined. And on more than one occasion it led directly to needless deaths.

After observing the results of Company G's unsuccessful effort, Dahlquist spotted a lieutenant and a handful of men from Company C. He immediately ordered them forward toward the base of Hill A to determine the enemy's strength and dispositions. A heavy fog blanketed the valley, allowing these men to reach their objectives undetected. The first house they entered was vacant, and the lieutenant told his men to stay there while he went ahead to check out the next dwelling. Although it, too, was unoccupied, nearby German troops had seen the American officer enter, and they immediately took the house under fire. This revealed what the patrol had set out to find, but in the ensuing firefight the lieutenant was killed.[38]

During the night of October 17–18, reconnaissance patrols brought back information that the Germans were still strongly entrenched on Hill A, but that the village of Bruyères appeared to be more lightly defended. In fact, one of the patrols, guided by a French resistance fighter, even entered the outskirts of the village without encountering any Germans.

The next morning the 3rd Battalion joined the fray, moving into position to the right of the 2nd Battalion. Companies I and L, moving before full light, were able to cross a potentially deadly flat area without being observed. The 522nd Artillery added the noise and destruction of its twelve guns to the cacophony produced when five artillery battalions and two of Cannon Company's platoons let loose at once. The targets this time were the German positions on Hills A and B and the village of Bruyères itself. After half an hour of this, the guns fell silent and Company B, supported by two tanks and a couple of tank destroyers, moved through the rain to attack the house at the base of Hill A. Company A soon followed, while most of Company C, also accompanied by a pair of tanks and a pair of tank destroyers, provided cover fire. The Germans still had a lot of fight in them, and it took the men of the 100th Battalion almost five hours to finally occupy the crest of Hill A.

The other two battalions began the assault on Hill B shortly after 10:00 A.M. Three companies attacked while Company L skirted the base of the hill and headed south for Bruyères. Hill B was finally in American hands by 4:30 that afternoon. Company L then began clearing the village one building at a time. By 6:30, the Nisei infantrymen had linked up with GIs from Company C of the 143rd Infantry, who had entered the town from the south. There were still a few pockets of resistance, but, for the most part, the citizens of Bruyères had been liberated.[39]

Even though much of Bruyères had been reduced to rubble by the artillery fire of the advancing Americans, and then by the retreating Germans, the villagers began to feel as if their day of liberation had indeed arrived. They embraced their liberators, both figuratively and literally. A homemade U.S. flag fluttered outside the second story window of a home directly across the street from the town hall. But the residents also took the opportunity to even some scores within the town itself. They focused their wrath on local women who had been too "friendly" with the occupying enemy. Some were probably prostitutes who simply found the Germans willing to pay for their favors. Others, perhaps, saw such relationships with the Germans to be their only assurance of regular food and shelter. The details did not matter. The townspeople rounded up several of these "collaborators," shaved their heads, and paraded them through town to be cursed and spat upon by the local populace. The chaplain for the 100th Battalion thought such a display distasteful, if not disgraceful, and opined that "grown-up Frenchmen . . . ought to be fighting the Boche instead of taking vengeance on women, be they good or bad."[40]

The men of the 442nd Regiment had killed an unknown number of enemy soldiers and had captured 134. Most of the prisoners talked freely about the activities of their own units, but they had almost no information on overall German strength in the area. American intelligence officers were able to piece together a little more of the German order of battle, however, by identifying the units from which the prisoners came. The enemy units thus identified included a grenadier regiment, a panzer grenadier regiment, an engineer battalion, a fusilier battalion, and a fortress machine-gun battalion.[41]

The rain, which had fallen every day for more than two weeks, continued to make life miserable. The constant downpours had turned the roads into quagmires that trapped men and machines. Three of the artillery battalion's trucks got so deeply mired that the drivers called for a Sherman tank to come pull them out. But even that tracked vehicle got stuck. Engineer troops had to use bulldozers and hand tools to scrape away the wettest mud before dumping truckloads of gravel to provide some traction for the vehicles. And in one mile-long stretch, they used logs and planks to build a wooden roadway.[42]

While the men of the 100th Battalion caught a short breather atop Hill A, and while Company L finished mopping up enemy resistance in Bruyères, the rest of the regiment stepped off at 10:00 A.M. the next day to take Hill D, directly east of the village. Hill D fell within two hours. The GIs then continued toward a railroad track about a half mile east of Bruyères on the edge of the Belmont Forest. The Germans were dug in behind the embankment, and as four rifle companies advanced they also came under the fire of self-propelled guns from near the village of Belmont. The 522nd's howitzers did their best to silence these German guns, and the infantry reached the railroad by six o'clock that evening. They had been so successful, indeed, that the other regiments of the 36th Division, on their right, and the 45th Division, on the left, were nowhere around to support them. They had penetrated two thousand yards into German territory and were in danger of being surrounded and cut off.

At about the same time, the 100th Battalion left Company A atop Hill A and moved down into Bruyères. Late in the afternoon the battalion sent a reconnaissance patrol in the direction of Hill C to try to ascertain whether it was defended or not. Rifle and machine-gun fire from the hill answered the question in the affirmative, and the patrol returned to the village. The Germans shelled the village during the night, but the men were well sheltered.

On the morning of October 20, Company A having rejoined the battalion, all three of the 100th Battalion's rifle companies moved out of Bruyères toward Hill C. General Dahlquist had demanded its capture by noon. The chemical mortars laid down a smoke screen to obscure the movement from German eyes as the Americans moved across an open area toward their objective. By noon, Americans reached the crest of the hill and began mopping up scattered pockets of resistance around its base and preparing for what they believed would be an inevitable counterattack.

By mid-afternoon, with German tanks visible nearby, General Dahlquist inexplicably ordered the battalion back into Bruyères. "That order is screwy," exclaimed one of the officers, "We're still fighting on Hill C." But there was no recourse. The 100th Battalion made its way back into the village while German troops quickly reclaimed Hill C. At about the same time, elements of the 736th Grenadier Regiment launched a vicious, though unsuccessful, attack against the two Nisei battalions dug in near the railroad tracks east of Bruyères.[43]

During the previous night, some Germans had infiltrated back onto Hill D and were making it tough on the troops in that sector, including the men of the 232nd Combat Engineers, who were trying to sweep the road coming out of the village free of enemy mines. The enemy had also ambushed a detachment from the 2nd Battalion headquarters that was bringing much-needed rations forward.[44]

A battalion from the 3rd Infantry Division arrived by mid-afternoon to re-take Hill C, and the 100th Battalion moved across the intervening valley to assist the attack on Hill D, but the Germans were determined not to lose the hill a second time. The next morning someone spotted an American, wounded and unable to move, about fifty yards in front of Company F's position near the base of Hill D. He had apparently been hit the day before and lain there all night. Technical Sergeant Abraham Ohama quickly set out to rescue him. He reached the fallen soldier and hoisted him onto his back. As he started back to safety a German with a submachine gun opened up on him and he fell, wounded. Litter bearers soon arrived to try to evacuate both wounded men. Unlike Ohama, they were wearing the identifying red crosses on their helmets to mark them as noncombatants and, theoretically, to protect them from deliberate enemy fire. But just as they lifted the sergeant onto a litter the Germans fired again. All four litter bearers were hit, and Sergeant Ohama was killed. The soldier whose wounding had initiated this chain of events survived.[45]

Many of Ohama's comrades witnessed his death and were infuriated by the Germans' callous disregard for the fundamentals of human decency. Almost as one they arose and started up the hill, ignoring the fusillade of enemy bullets directed at them. Some who were there later said that they attacked in silence and others were just as certain that at least some of the men screamed the Japanese cry "Banzai" as they fought their way up the hill. It is possible that both were right. It would have been very difficult, over the tremendous noise of gunfire and explosions, to have heard whether a man twenty yards away was shouting or not. Perhaps some did, and others did not. They were angry, and they were relentless, and they killed fifty Germans before reaching the top of the hill. "We had seen Abe killed, and we were real mad," remembered one. "There were so many [dead Germans on the hillside] we had trouble stepping over them, walking around them, back down the hill to rejoin the company."[46]

The Germans sometimes booby-trapped the bodies of fallen Americans, knowing that their comrades would be along to retrieve them. And they sometimes used wounded Americans as bait, shooting anyone who ventured out to help them. Some men were convinced that the Germans used the red crosses painted on the helmets of medics as aiming points so they could kill them. This led some medics to rub mud onto their helmets to hide the red cross markings. They preferred to take their chances like the rest of the soldiers without the prominent marking for enemy riflemen.[47]

While it is true that some Germans disregarded the protocols that were supposed to protect medics and other noncombatants, many others went out of their way to abide by this convention. Back in Italy, for instance, some medics from the 133rd Regiment were looking for wounded men when they suddenly found themselves in the midst of an enemy patrol. "We do not kill or make prisoners of medics," an English-speaking German reassured them. He went on to tell them that the wounded Americans they were seeking were in a German aid station, and that the German medics had almost run out of medicines with which to treat them. He then invited the GIs to come and evacuate their wounded. In another, similar, instance, a German officer initiated a cease-fire so that American wounded could be returned to friendly lines. He apologized for the death of an American medic, explaining that his men had shot him before they saw the red cross on his helmet. He then held five seriously wounded Americans, but said that he must keep one man whose wounds were only superficial. "My colonel," he explained, "would give me hell if the slightly wounded man were returned!" And in southern France an American ambulance driver made a wrong turn and found himself being halted by a German soldier. The enemy soldier politely asked where the ambulance was headed and then spread a map out on the hood of the vehicle so he could show the driver how to return safely to his own lines. As the ambulance turned around to retrace its track it hit a small anti-personnel mine that blew out a tire. German and American soldiers quickly worked together to get the tire changed and the ambulance on its way again.[48]

At mid-morning on October 21, a pair of tanks accompanied German infantry attacking in the 2nd Battalion's sector. A sergeant from Company G tried to knock out one of the tanks with anti-tank grenades, but he might as well have been throwing rocks. Then he grabbed a bazooka and a load of shells and climbed a small elevation to get a better shot. He knew that he had better make his first shot accurate because the telltale flash of his weapon would certainly draw the attention—and the fire—of the enemy tankers. His first round hit the lead tank but did not disable it. The tank's gunners then—as he had expected—gave him their undivided attention. Disregarding the enemy fire as best he could, the sergeant fired four more times before finally disabling the tank. The commander of the second tank apparently decided not to risk being the bazooka's next victim and retreated, along with the infantry.[49]

That afternoon more tanks made their appearance, coming down the road from Belmont. This time bazookas might not be enough to stop them. Colonel Pence had the use of a company of American tanks and a company of tank destroyers, and now he put them to work. Also on hand were four P-47 fighter bombers to provide close air support. The pilots dropped their bombs and fired their machine guns into the enemy column, destroying or damaging seven vehicles and squelching German hopes of a quick victory.[50]

Late that afternoon a copy of the German defensive plans for the area was discovered on the body of a dead officer and immediately relayed to divisional headquarters. General Dahlquist and Colonel Pence quickly put their heads together to try to find, and exploit, a weak spot in the enemy defenses. They hurriedly assembled an ad hoc task force under the command of Major Emmet O'Connor, the executive officer of the 3rd Battalion. O'Connor took Company L from his own battalion and Company F from the 2nd Battalion, along with some communications troops and a mine-sweeping detachment, and led them to a point opposite the southern end of the German-held Hill 505. When the 2nd and 3rd Battalions attacked the west face of the hill the next morning, Task Force O'Connor moved up the southern slope to a position on the enemy's left flank.[51]

A forward observer for the 522nd Field Artillery Battalion accompanied the task force, and when he reached the top of the ridge he wasted no time in earning his pay. He spotted numerous concentrations of enemy soldiers and relayed their locations back to Battery B, and its guns were soon right on target. The Germans had been making it hot for the 2nd and 3rd Battalions, but this unexpected pressure from the left forced them to slowly fall back. By mid-afternoon, Task Force O'Connor had linked up with the other Americans near a cluster of houses called La Broquaime, along the road from Bruyères to Belmont, and the two detached companies returned to battalion control. Enemy casualties included eighty killed and another fifty-four captured, with a loss of only two Americans.[52]

While the 2nd and 3rd Battalions were battling their way up Hill 505, the 100th Battalion moved past them and on toward the hills overlooking the village of Biffontaine, east of Bruyères and southeast of Belmont. After light skirmishing along the way, and an ineffectual strafing attack by two wandering Luftwaffe fighter planes, it reached the village by about the same time that Task Force O'Connor linked up with the rest of the regiment. The 2nd Battalion fell back into a reserve position that night, and the 3rd Battalion pushed toward the northeast, on the 100th's left.

The next day the 2nd Battalion was thrown into the fight in support of the 100th as it fought off several German attempts to dislodge the Americans from their positions. Two men from Company I, one carrying a BAR and the other an M1, surprised an eighteen-man German patrol from ambush. The Germans must have thought there were more than just the two of them because after taking three quick casualties the others quickly dropped their weapons and threw their hands up in surrender. After a while, however, the main American force began to run short of ammunition and drinking water, and it became more and more difficult to evacuate the wounded. There was also some concern that German troops might infiltrate in behind the Americans and cut the battalion off entirely. The battalion was already only barely within the range of friendly artillery and at the extreme range of its radios.[53]

From the direction of Belmont, a reserve platoon from Company A loaded up cases of ammunition and water and mounted five light tanks for a re-supply mission. As the tanks clanked down a road about fifty German infantrymen ambushed them. Rifle and machine-gun fire began sweeping the Americans from their exposed positions atop the tanks. A sergeant, wounded in the initial fusillade, grabbed hold of a machine gun on the last tank in the line and began spraying the enemy position with return fire. He continued shooting until the tanks were out of the ambush zone when, weak from loss of blood, he could no longer hang on and fell from his vehicle. He was later captured by the enemy. The tank drivers, meanwhile, found the hilly terrain too steep for their machines to traverse, so several of the infantrymen carried what supplies they could and set off on foot to locate the 100th Battalion. They were unsuccessful.[54]

General Dahlquist wanted Biffontaine captured as part of a coordinated push with the 3rd Infantry Division to the north. While that division's 7th Infantry Regiment attacked the village of Belmont, and thereby secured the 36th Division's left flank, Dahlquist's troops were to take Biffontaine. The Nisei 3rd Battalion was to cut the road between the two towns; the 100th Battalion, in positions north and west of Biffontaine, was to apply pressure from that direction; the 143rd Regiment of the 36th Division was to move against Biffontaine from the southwest.[55]

As the 3rd Battalion began to move up on the left of the 100th, a patrol from Company L tried to make contact with its sister battalion. The hillside was heavily wooded, and there were footpaths leading in every direction. Nevertheless, relying on dead reckoning and blind luck, the patrol reached the beleaguered battalion without running into any enemy units. Upon learning this, Colonel Pence sent forward a carrying party of men—many of whom had just arrived from the States—with the much-needed supplies, and he sent the 2nd Battalion's Company G along as protection. After a two-hour climb through the forest this relief party reached the 100th Battalion in mid-afternoon, and the battalion's situation became measurably less grim.[56]

As the 3rd Battalion slowly fought in a generally easterly direction along the road between Belmont and Biffontaine, German artillery seemed to be firing at it from three different directions. The 2nd Battalion had moved into the forested hills southwest of Biffontaine and had spent the better part of the day fighting with about a hundred German soldiers who had ridden south out of Biffontaine on bicycles the night before and then climbed into the hills to dispute the battalion's progress.[57]

General Dahlquist sent down orders that the 442nd was to capture Biffontaine the next day! On the morning of the 22nd, Company A occupied an elevated position northeast of the town, Company C was on a hill north of town, and Company B was southwest of the town. Elements of all three companies attacked the town over fairly open and unprotected ground, but still met with quick success. Most of the Germans had already evacuated, but a squad from Company C burst into a house that contained an enemy command post. The GIs captured two German officers and several enlisted men, along with various maps, radios, and weapons. They quickly hustled the captured troops into the cellar where they would be out of the line of fire and also less likely to be able to escape. One of the German officers, however, haughtily insisted that since he was a major he deserved better accommodations than those of his men. The Americans decided that they had more important things to do than to quibble with him and showed him to an upstairs bedroom. Then, through his interpreter, the German officer took great delight in taunting his "hosts" as German tanks and infantry counterattacked the village. Surely, the German gloated, the Americans could see that their situation was hopeless and that surrender was the only thing that would save their lives. But the Americans paid no heed to the obnoxious ramblings of the enemy officer. They were busy fighting, and the major finally retired to his quarters.

Three times that night the Germans tried to retake Biffontaine and three times the Americans pushed them back. The next morning the captured officer, after having spent the night with German shells exploding uncomfortably close to him, demanded that the Americans come and take his mattress and bedding down into the cellar where he would be safer. By now, however, the weary GIs had had enough of his theatrical posturing and told him he was welcome to go sleep in the cellar but that his mattress would stay where it was.[58]

The men from Company A, meanwhile, battled enemy machine-gun fire and entered the town shortly after Company C. The toughest fighting took place on the west side of town where Company B, along with an attached platoon of heavy weapons from Company D fought for three hours to gain a foothold. By dusk, most of the town was under American control, but the GIs had once again run their stocks of ammunition to a dangerously low level. Some of the men took up the rifles and ammunition that they had confiscated from their two dozen prisoners and continued to fight.[59]

During one especially intense German artillery barrage, three men from Cannon Company scrambled under a nearby truck for protection. Of course, if a German round actually hit the truck they might be in danger, but its bulk would protect them from the deadly shrapnel from air bursts overhead. When the enemy fire finally lifted and they ventured out from under their protection they discovered that the truck was loaded with 105mm shells for their own howitzers. A direct hit would likely have vaporized them![60]

The Americans prepared for an enemy counterattack but took advantage of a temporary lull in the action to send some of their more seriously wounded men back to the aid stations for treatment. Every healthy soldier was needed in the defense of the village, so some of the German prisoners were pressed into service to supplement the American litter bearers. The column started for the rear, but the unfamiliar woods, with its dozens of intersecting footpaths, caused considerable confusion. All of a sudden a

German combat patrol seemed to materialize as if by magic from among the surrounding trees. Sometimes fortune favors the bold, and a quick-thinking Nisei soldier called out: "Why don't you put down your guns and come back to America with us? That way you can save your lives." A few of the Germans seemed to waver momentarily and to consider trading their present situation for a well-fed life in an American prisoner-of-war camp in the United States. Their officer, however, curtly responded: "No." Lieutenant Kim, the popular Korean American officer, was one of the litter patients, having suffered wounds to the arm and hand. He did not want to spend the rest of the war in a German prison camp, so he whispered to one of the medics accompanying the column that he was going to attempt to escape. He then rolled off the litter and, along with the medic and another man, dove into the woods and escaped.[61]

The Germans treated their prisoners as well as could be expected, even to the point of helping to carry the American wounded when the Nisei litter bearers appeared exhausted. They were always a little nonplussed, however, when they captured any Nisei soldiers. They just could not understand why these "Japanese" men fought for the United States. "Because of the democratic way of life," explained one of the captives to a puzzled German officer. The officer was still not convinced that merely residing in the United States should make these men consider themselves to be Americans. "Did you know," he asked, "that a cat born in the fish market isn't a fish?" The prisoner agreed with him, but went on to point out that the cat still belonged to the fish market. The prisoners finally wound up in Stalag VII-A in Moosberg, Germany, a little southeast of Munich. The prisoner-of-war facility there was initially designed for ten thousand prisoners, but by late 1944 it held several times that number.[62]

Meanwhile, the 3rd Battalion was busy in the forests east of Belmont and north of Biffontaine clearing out enemy positions in that area. An attached engineer battalion was clearing the road from Belmont to Biffontaine, when the defenders of a German roadblock opened up on them with rifle and machine-gun fire. Accurate fire from the 3rd Battalion's mortars convinced these Germans—eighteen of them—to surrender to the engineers. The

3rd Battalion also liberated a dozen captured British colonial troops from the Germans.[63]

German tanks, meanwhile, appeared at the edge of Biffontaine where their pointblank cannon fire soon reduced the once-sturdy walls of the houses into piles of shattered masonry and dust. The Americans inside moved into the cellars until the tank fire ceased, and then they rushed back up to ground level to drive off the approaching German infantry with small-arms fire. For the rest of the day, the Germans threw themselves at the American defenses, and for the rest of the day, the Americans drove them away.

The next day the 141st and 143rd Regiments from the 36th Division moved up, and the entire 442nd Regiment was pulled out of the line for a rest. The men were ready to stand down after more than a week of almost constant combat. They moved into Belmont where they found warm, dry lodging in private homes. They took turns going to Laval where they were able to shower away some of the accumulated grime on their bodies and to receive clean clothes. A Cannon Company soldier waxed almost poetic remembering the hot showers: "Only someone who has not taken a shower or bath for nine days," he said, "who has lived in damp, filthy clothing and wet boots, exposed to continual, freezing rain, in anxiety under constant danger of death, will appreciate the exalted state a human being can reach."[64]

With the 442nd temporarily removed from combat, the extra soldiers and supernumerary officers who had been sent to the replacement depot on the 16th returned and were distributed among the various companies to make up for recent losses. But manpower shortages continued. Enlisted replacements often arrived from the United States with a minimum of training. The thinking was that these men could—and indeed would have to—learn soldiering on the job. If they kept their heads down and did what they saw the veteran soldiers doing they stood a fair chance of surviving the war. But it was different with officers. By this stage of the war the combat loss of officers was becoming more acute. And since other lives usually depended upon how well a lieutenant, for example, did his job it took longer to train officer replacements. One obvious solution was to promote senior noncommissioned officers—staff sergeants and technical sergeants—to second

lieutenant, and that is what was done. The idea of Nisei officers
was unthinkable back when the 100th Battalion and the 442nd
Regimental Combat Team were being formed. There was just too
much racial prejudice against it. But these men had long since
proven themselves to be the equal of any other American fighting
men. Some had already received field commissions, and the heavy
losses in the Vosges in late 1944 saw many more promotions from
the ranks, including that of twenty-year-old Dan Inouye.[65]

As the war dragged on many infantrymen began to believe
that their chances of returning home unscathed were becoming
infinitesimally small. And worse, perhaps, than a fear of death
was the fear of suffering some horrific wound instead. Sometimes
the men fantasized about receiving a minor wound. Nothing life-
threatening; just something that would allow them to get some
rest in a hospital. Of course, the much talked-about "million-
dollar wound" was also sometimes on their minds. This was a serious injury, one that would require return to the United States
for treatment. It was the type of wound that some men said they
would give a million dollars for, hence the name. Even one of
the regiment's chaplains fantasized about an injury that would
allow him to go home but would not leave him a cripple. When
one of the combat team's medics was wounded late in the war,
he thought: "Oh, boy! I'm gonna' see nurses!" But other medics quickly patched him up, and he stayed on the line. Another
man actually tried for a million-dollar wound during the fighting
in the Vosges. He knew better than to simply expose himself to
enemy fire because there was no way to guarantee that any resulting wound would not be fatal. So instead he lay in his foxhole and
stuck his feet up over the edge, hoping that a German bullet or a
small shell fragment would hit one of them. He was unsuccessful.
When another man tried for a million-dollar wound he found
that the human instinct for self-preservation was too strong. He
put his feet up out of his hole, but as soon as the German mortar
rounds began landing nearby he instinctively pulled them back in
again. And when a man was wounded in the hand while seeking
shelter in his slit trench, his battalion commander good-naturedly
berated him: "Hell, that won't get you home. Stick your foot out
next time."[66]

While the Nisei enjoyed their well-earned rest, the 141st Regiment made good progress southeastward against moderate resistance. In fact, by the afternoon of October 24, Companies A and B, as well as parts of Companies C and D of the 1st Battalion of the 141st, had pushed so far forward that they had lost contact with other American units some three miles to the rear. German troops reacted quickly and closed in behind them, cutting off most of the battalion—about 274 men—on a rise known as Hill 645, located southeast of Biffontaine. When division headquarters learned of the perilous situation it ordered the battalion to fight its way back toward safety and, at the same time, ordered the 2nd and 3rd Battalions of the 141st to move forward until they linked up. All three American battalions fought hard, but the Germans were especially obstinate and denied them the rescue.[67]

The next afternoon the encircled Americans sent a thirty-six-man patrol out from Hill 645 looking for an escape route. Before it reached friendly lines, however, a large enemy force ambushed it, inflicting catastrophic casualties. Only five men were able to make their way back to the surrounded battalion, although somehow they captured a German soldier along the way and brought him back with them.[68]

Efforts to rescue the surrounded troops with tanks met with no success. The Germans had erected strong roadblocks along the way and defended them with numerous automatic weapons and anti-personnel mines. By the end of the day the tactical situation was virtually unchanged, although most of the 141st Regiment was in contact with the enemy. A successful rescue, it now seemed, would require additional forces, and that is how the Nisei GIs became involved.

The welcome rest period for the Nisei then came to an end much too soon as the men of the 2nd Battalion were called upon to aid the 141st Regiment. The predawn hours of October 26 found them groping their way through the pitch dark of the forest to relieve the 3rd Battalion of that regiment. As the men marched in single file they found it necessary to keep one hand on the back or shoulder of the man in front of them to keep from getting lost in the darkness. Some men pinned sheets of white paper to their backs in the hope that they would reflect enough light to help the men behind them to maintain contact. In similar circumstances a practical joker in the 100th Battalion jumped over an imaginary ditch just to see how those walking behind him would react. Sure enough, even though they could not see a ditch of any kind, each man dutifully followed the lead of the man in front of him and jumped forward.[69]

The other two Nisei battalions were alerted to the dire circumstances confronting the beleaguered unit and, late that afternoon, they were ordered to prepare to move out early the next morning in an attempt to break through to what was becoming known—erroneously—as the "lost battalion." It was not an entire battalion and it was not lost at all. The men in it were surrounded and cut off from friendly forces, but they knew precisely where they were, and so did everyone else—including the enemy.

The rescuers would likely need artillery support. With that thought in mind a battery commander from the 522nd Artillery Battalion placed a call to one of his truck drivers, ordering the man to take a forward observer team up to the front in a jeep. The driver rather huffily informed the captain that he had just returned from the front, that he had not had much sleep, and that he was a truck driver not a jeep driver. Another soldier was present and later reported what he heard next. It was the driver saying: "Yes, sir. Yes, sir. Yes, sir. Yes, sir. Immediately, sir. Yes, sir." He then hung the phone up and complained to his friend that the captain had pulled rank on him. How so, his friend wondered. "You're a private, and I'm a captain," quoted the unhappy soldier. "When I tell you to shit, you shit. Now get your God-damned ass out of here, and get in the jeep, and take these guys up." And he did.[70]

Tanks and tank destroyers were available to assist the infantrymen, but the thick forest made vehicle movement extremely difficult. The road was nothing more than a narrow track through the trees, and when a German anti-tank mine blew the tread off one of the tanks there was insufficient room for any following vehicle to maneuver around it.[71]

The surrounded soldiers of the 141st Infantry hung on. They knew that their comrades were making every effort to rescue them. They did not move around much during daylight, not wanting to present targets to any nearby enemy soldiers. "We were just praying, that's all," remembered one man. "We just sat in our foxholes, listening hard, not saying a damn word . . . and we just prayed." Others thought about their lives before the war and what they would do if they got out of it alive. "I kept thinking how wonderful it would be," remarked a father of three, "back on my old job as a street car conductor in Chicago."[72]

Meanwhile shortages were beginning to affect the surrounded soldiers. Food soon began to run out, and this presented a particular hardship for the wounded. One of the machine gunners had a few fruit bars that he had saved from his rations. He gave them to a medic to grind up in water to feed the injured soldiers. Soon food became a favorite topic of conversation among the hungry soldiers. "We concocted in our minds fabulous dishes of T-bone steaks, fried eggs and nice crisp bacon," remembered one man. "Once we spent a whole morning just talking about milk shakes . . . thick and malty ones with double portions of ice cream." Another soldier remembered talking "about chocolate cakes and bacon and eggs and everything that our mothers and wives used to make for us back home. I remember once we spent a whole afternoon just talking about flapjacks . . . golden brown, with butter."[73]

And with more than two dozen men injured, medical supplies were beginning to run short as well. Arrangements were soon made to attempt to resupply the "lost" battalion by air. The plan was for American fighter-bombers to drop a two-day supply of food and water, several cases of small-arms ammunition, and a dozen extra radio batteries to ensure steady communication.

That night General Dahlquist, who was in almost constant contact with the regimental commander of the 141st, urged him to do more to effect a rescue. He wanted action, not excuses for inaction. Even after learning that there were too many wounded men within the trapped battalion to allow it to break out of the German stranglehold, he was adamant. Saying that he certainly did not want the wounded to be abandoned, he nevertheless insisted that the rescue be completed by the next morning. He seemed reluctant to trust the judgment of the men actually trying to accomplish the rescue in the face of determined enemy efforts to prevent it. In fact, by this time every platoon leader and every non-commissioned officer in one of the companies involved had been killed or wounded.[74]

When the soldiers of the 141st Regiment failed to rescue their comrades, General Dahlquist's patience ran out. He relieved the regimental commander, who had only held that position for about three weeks, and he ordered the two uncommitted battalions of the 442nd Regiment—the 100th and the 3rd—to relieve some of the pressure on the exhausted 2nd and 3rd Battalions of the 141st.

On the morning of the 27th, P-47 fighter-bombers arrived overhead to drop supplies to the besieged men, but heavy ground fog made it impossible for the pilots to find the precise clearing in which to release their loads and they were forced to return to their bases without accomplishing their mission. The weather showed no signs of improving so General Dahlquist requested the use of another method of resupply.

Artillery prepared to fire supplies into the men late that afternoon. Both 105mm and 155mm shells existed that were used to deliver propaganda messages over the heads of enemy troops. Armed with only small bursting charges, these thin-walled shells were filled with leaflets. Now, however, instead of leaflets, the available space in these shells contained medical supplies and high-energy chocolate bars. The men took shelter in their foxholes during this "bombardment" because the bursting shells still sent dangerous shards of shrapnel flying outward upon explosion. Some of the shells did not explode and instead buried themselves so deeply in the soft earth as to be all but irretrievable. And there was still a great need for radio batteries, bandages, halazone tablets, and antibiotics.[75]

By early afternoon of the 27th, all three Nisei battalions were on line with the 2nd Battalion on the left, the 3rd Battalion in the center, and the 100th Battalion on the right. The 2nd Battalion's task was to maintain contact with 3rd Division troops to the left so that it did not outpace friendly support and also become a "lost" battalion. The 100th was to attack toward the east while the 3rd advanced from the north.

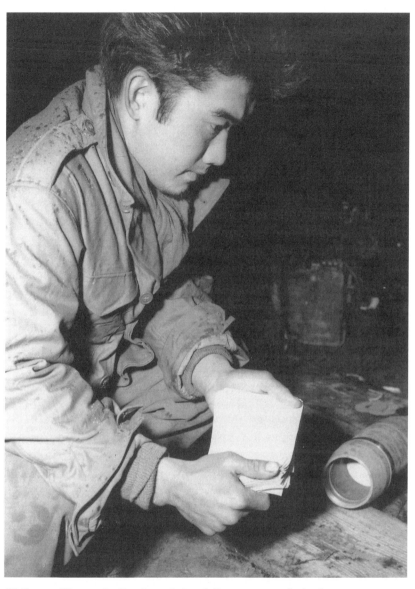

Hollow artillery projectiles, intended to deliver propaganda leaflets over enemy positions, were pressed into use to carry needed food and medical supplies to the "lost battalion." Signal Corps photo.

As the Americans moved forward, a German tank, supported by infantry, rumbled out of the trees toward the 3rd Battalion. It approached to within seventy-five yards and its machine gun and cannon soon began giving the Americans all the fire they could handle. A soldier from Company K worked his way even closer to the enemy vehicle and dispatched it with a well-aimed bazooka shot. He immediately reloaded his launcher, but the tank was finished. Then he noticed a couple of enemy troops preparing to fire the German version of the bazooka—called a *Panzerschreck*. He turned his own weapon on them and fired. His shell hit one of the men, and then he picked up his rifle and killed the other. By then American bazooka fire had also knocked out a German halftrack, and the fighting subsided as darkness fell.[76]

Back in Bruyères more reinforcements arrived, but these were not inexperienced replacements from the States: they were the members of the Anti-Tank Company who had been reassigned from the 517th Parachute Infantry Regiment. And although there was very little room for them to use their anti-tank guns, they were quickly put to good use as litter bearers.[77]

All three Nisei infantry battalions continued moving forward on the morning of October 28, but progress was slow and costly. Mortar and artillery fire rained down on Companies B and C for an hour and resulted in twenty killed and wounded. In the 3rd Battalion's area, well defended roadblocks hindered forward movement until a soldier crept forward with a BAR and wiped out two enemy machine-gun crews. Cannon Company then added its firepower to that of the 522nd to inflict even heavier damage on the enemy. By the time the fighting stopped for the day the 3rd and 100th Battalions had advanced about a quarter of a mile and had captured seventy German soldiers.[78]

On the morning of the 28th, ten P-47s arrived in the vicinity of the lost battalion ready to drop supplies. Visibility was good—although only temporarily—and the pilots commenced their drops, two planes at a time. Pinpoint accuracy was impossible to attain, and none of the precious bundles landed close enough to the stranded men to be of use. German soldiers were able to recover some of the bundles, however, and were very appreciative of the instant coffee contained in them. "Real blended coffee," one

German soldier remembered, "was the high point of that quiet day in our foxhole." The weather closed in again, but shortly after noon, the battalion radioed: "Weather is clear now. Please do something." By late afternoon, supplies of food started to arrive on target, to the great relief of the men. Sadly, one of the first wooden ration crates to fall into the area struck a man in the head and killed him. And there was still a dire need of medical supplies, ammunition, and radio batteries.[79]

The speed at which the P-47s flew made it extremely difficult for them to drop their loads within the relatively small confines of the battalion's space. Troops in a similar situation in Italy some months before had used the artillery spotter planes for this task with very good results. At a cruising speed of seventy-five miles per hour, and at an altitude of only three hundred to four hundred feet, the pilots were able to drop their supplies with great accuracy. These smaller planes were limited in the amount of supplies they could drop at one time, so the supply bundles were slung beneath makeshift parachutes made from GI blankets. That way, when the package hit the ground every bit of it could be put to immediate use. Sixty-five pounds of rations, bundled into an empty 105mm ammunition carton, so altered the flight characteristics of the lightweight craft—it usually only weighed about twelve hundred pounds fully loaded—that great care had to be taken by the pilot when flying such a mission. Perhaps General Dahlquist and the other commanders were not aware of such uses for the small planes. Or perhaps they believed that the greater capacity of the P-47s would allow sufficient supplies to be delivered in fewer sorties, thus diminishing the danger to the pilots.[80]

The 3rd and 100th Battalions continued to work in relatively close proximity to one another and to the two battalions from the 141st Infantry on October 29 as they moved along a steep and narrow ridge. German resistance on that day was the heaviest yet encountered, and the terrain made it even more difficult for the attacking troops. The Germans had had time to position their machine guns so that they provided interlocking fields of fire over much of the area between the two forces. They also seeded the area heavily with mines. Both Nisei battalions sought to bypass these dangers—the 3rd Battalion on the left and the 100th on the right—in order to fall upon the enemy's flanks. Forward progress was almost nonexistent, and enemy fire soon brought Companies I and K to a standstill.

General Dahlquist continued to be impatient with the slow pace of the rescue. "There's a battalion about to die up there," he said, "and we've got to reach them." He surprised one Nisei soldier by bellowing "Why aren't you up out of your foxhole?" And when he observed one of his officers prudently seeking cover behind a nearby tree he came up behind him and physically booted him forward.[81]

Lieutenant Colonel Alfred Pursall, commanding the 3rd Battalion of the 442nd, did not think that General Dahlquist understood the tactical situation facing his men and tried to impress upon him how grim things were. He escorted the general and the general's aide to a position very close to the front, where some of his men were doing their best to stay out of the line of fire. As Pursall gestured toward enemy machine-gun emplacements, the men who were dug in close by urged the officers to seek cover. Dahlquist dismissed the idea and then turned to his aide for a map. The young officer, the son of novelist Sinclair Lewis, reached inside his jacket, pulled out a map, and promptly fell dead from a bullet to his head. The general caught him as he slumped to the ground and then finally took cover.

Colonel Pursall seemed to sense that the only way off the hill they were on was upward, and he decided to lead his men in person. He came up to where some of the men of Company K were hugging the ground for protection from all of the German ordnance that was flying about. "Let's get going, Sergeant," he said to a nearby noncom as he un-holstered his pistol. The sergeant later remembered thinking: "My God! If that dumb son-of-a-bitch is going to walk up into that fire, I guess we better, too!" He called to the other sixteen members of his company still unhurt, and they started up the hill behind the colonel, dodging from tree to tree but never slowing down. When the men of Company I saw what was happening, they, too, rose up. Among the infantrymen scattered on the hill was a lightly armed artillery forward observation team. When Colonel Pursall ordered the men to fix bayonets, the radio operator, armed with only a pistol, felt that the best place for him was behind a nearby rock. Then the colonel looked directly at him and said: "You artillery, you charge too," so up he went.[82]

Casualties mounted, but still the Nisei moved forward using every tree or rock outcropping they could find for temporary cover. A sergeant in Company K, disregarding a painful wound in the arm, used his submachine gun to destroy an enemy machine-gun crew as well as killing several German riflemen. Another soldier in the same company, already burdened with a heavy radio on his back, advanced fearlessly and saved a couple of his fellow soldiers with well-aimed rifle fire before he too was wounded and evacuated.[83]

Perhaps Company I's Barney Hajiro typified the heroism of the men that day, but he seemed an unlikely hero. Originally assigned to Company M back at Camp Shelby, the former dishwasher had developed a reputation as a problem soldier. Some considered him a slacker, one who seemed to spend an inordinate amount of time on sick call. Facing judicial proceedings more than once, his commanding officer managed to get rid of him with a transfer over to Company I. He took a real liking to his new comrades and there was a noticeable change in his demeanor. On this day, he rose up and yelled, "Let's go" and then advanced up the hill, firing from the hip as he attacked enemy machine guns. As he approached one machine gun the two Germans operating the weapon both threw up their hands in surrender, but Hajiro cut them down anyway. He had no time to worry about taking prisoners and continued up the hill firing at individual German riflemen.[84]

Later, in a further effort to put his personal stamp on the rescue effort, General Dahlquist once again ignored the chain of command to directly order a fire mission from the 522nd Artillery Battalion to help relieve some of the German pressure on his isolated infantrymen. When the artillerymen read the target coordinates provided by the general they realized that something was not right. The artillery battalion commander sought confirmation of the target location before firing, and discovered that the coordinates were right on top of Hill 645 and right in the middle of the besieged Americans. Had the gunners fired the mission without double-checking, more Americans would have died. A tragic mistake had been narrowly averted.[85]

Even with accurate target coordinates, the dense forest made it almost impossible for the gunners of the 522nd to ply their trade successfully. Not only did the trees obscure potential targets from ground observation, but the constant rain and overcast skies kept the battalion's observation planes grounded as well. Artillery ammunition was also in short supply and had to be carefully rationed until replenished. The 13th Field Artillery, one of the 522nd's sister battalions in the 36th Division calculated that the ammunition on hand for a ten-day period could probably all be fired away in a brisk ten-minute fire mission.[86]

Sergeant Morita, nevertheless, remained busy. The forward observer teams did not dare to relax their vigilance, but the rugged terrain only made their job more difficult. So many of the hills and trails looked identical that it was no easy chore just to determine one's position in relation to the map coordinates. If they did find likely targets for the howitzers the limited range of their radios made it unlikely that the fire direction center would get them. Sergeant Morita, therefore, grabbed up a radio and headed forward to a position that allowed him to relay information from the observers to the fire direction center and back again. Although he was in between the firing batteries and the infantry, he was in constant danger of German artillery and mortar fire and the possibility of a roaming enemy patrol spotting him.

The 2nd Battalion, meanwhile, had its hands full with a German position atop a hill shown on the maps as Hill 617. While Company G prepared to attack from the west, the other two rifle companies, E and F, maneuvered around to the north so as to catch the enemy in a pincers movement. The enemy concentrated its fire on Company G, and was taken completely by surprise when the other two companies swept down upon them from the north. A hundred German soldiers died defending the hill that day, and forty-one more became prisoners. A platoon in Company E alone captured thirty-four prisoners.[87]

The situation remained grim for the surrounded battalion. It was still too dangerous for the men to leave their foxholes during the day, which made it difficult to heed the call of nature. They could urinate into their helmet shells if they had to and then toss the liquid out of their holes, but defecation was another matter.

Ultimately, many of them deposited their feces into paper bags and pitched these as far from their holes as they could. Sometimes they ventured out at night to refill their canteens from a nearby pool. Even this seemingly mundane chore was not without risk, because the pool was also the source of water for some of the besieging Germans.[88]

Although neither the men of the trapped battalion nor the Nisei rescuers could possibly have known it at the time, the worst was now over. By nightfall, only about seven hundred yards separated the two groups and plans were made to airdrop seven hundred pairs of socks and one hundred cans of foot powder to help the surrounded men fight off the ravages of trench foot. The commander of the trapped soldiers, however, requested that no more supplies be dropped because it made it too easy for the Germans to pinpoint their exact location and subject them to devastating barrages of artillery fire.[89]

The 442nd continued its advance the next day, under the cover of as much artillery and heavy mortar fire as it could command. Resistance was lighter, but there were still casualties to the constant German artillery fire. By about four o'clock in the afternoon, the linkup between the 442nd and the 141st was almost complete. One of the trapped soldiers, alert for any movement by the enemy, glimpsed a soldier slowly working his way through the trees in his direction. He kept his finger on the trigger of his weapon as he strained his eyes for a better look. At about the same time the approaching soldier, Matsuji "Mutt" Sakumoto of Company I, stopped, having seen movement up ahead. Not sure whether or not the person he had seen was a German soldier, he called to his buddy: "Hey . . . there's a guy out there looking at us." As the Nisei soldiers continued cautiously up the hill mutual recognition occurred. Company I had reached the "lost" battalion![90]

Grateful soldiers escorted Sakumoto to a trench where he found First Lieutenant Martin Higgins, the ranking officer of the encircled troops. After thanking the Nisei soldier, Higgins asked if he could spare a cigarette, whereupon Sakumoto generously gave him all that he had. Higgins later recounted that the sight of their rescuers sent chills of relief up his spine. "I can tell you honestly," he said, of the diminutive Japanese American soldiers, "they looked like giants to us." "It was the happiest day of my life," recalled another. "The Japanese Americans were the most pleasing sight in the world—this short, dark-skinned kid coming up, wearing an American helmet several sizes too big. Did that matter? No. Here was a brother of mine coming up to save my life." Another of the rescued soldiers remembered years later that he and his fellow soldiers "were mighty thankful to the brave little men of the 442nd Infantry." Another remarked: "It was really ironical that we were so glad to see Japanese, but, boy, they are real Americans."[91]

Nisei soldiers from Company B soon reached the battalion from another direction. The rescuers offered cigarettes to the rescued men—that was about all the extra provisions of any kind that they had with them. But the mere fact of being rescued was sustenance enough for most of those involved. They jubilantly hugged their rescuers and offered profuse thanks. "We must've looked like zombies," an exhausted Nisei medic recalled, "dragging our feet and delirious from lack of sleep."[92]

Officers at regimental headquarters breathed a hearty sigh of relief when they received a radio message from the no-longer "lost" battalion: "Patrol from 442d here. Tell them we love them." Of the original 274 besieged Americans in the "lost battalion," 211 welcomed rescue that day, although thirty-two of them were wounded and eleven others were suffering from trench foot. Another man from the lost battalion showed up at friendly lines that day but without the benefit of the Nisei's rescue. He had been on the patrol that had been ambushed five days earlier and had wandered lost ever since then, carefully avoiding German probes as he sought friendly lines.[93]

The happy and exhausted Caucasian soldiers were pulled back for rest, but there was no rest for their rescuers. The 2nd Battalion remained on Hill 617 protecting the seam between the 36th Division and the 3rd Division. The other two battalions dug in where the recently rescued soldiers has just spent the last week. "I could never figure out why the Germans never attacked us" that night, remembered one of the men. "They could have run us right off, but they must have been hurt just as bad as we were. We were so tired. The next morning we would have been all dead."[94]

The next morning the 3rd Battalion pushed on down the ridge to reach the position that the "lost battalion" had been originally assigned, overlooking the village of La Houssiere, and the 100th Battalion pulled flank security to the right. As the 3rd Battalion moved forward it called in artillery fire on a German roadblock under construction, and then captured eight enemy soldiers. The 100th faced little resistance, and both battalions reached their objectives before dark on October 31.

The two Nisei infantry battalions that had helped rescue the "lost battalion" suffered significant losses in the process, but much misinformation has attached itself over the years to the issue of casualties. Earlier works cite eight hundred Nisei killed and wounded while rescuing only a fourth of that number. Members of the combat team believed then, and many of the survivors still believe, that the unit was used as cannon fodder. Others take pride in the fact that these heavy casualties were due to the unit's sterling reputation as a fighting outfit, and one that commanders could depend upon in difficult situations. "You can't allow a battalion to get surrounded and not do anything about it," one man declared. "You can't allow them to get wiped out." And although he did believe that there should have been more help from other units of the 36th Division in the rescue of one of its own battalions, "[i]t doesn't make any difference how many people we lost. It had to be done." A former battalion commander believed that being called upon to rescue the surrounded unit was really a backhanded compliment to the men of the 442nd, a tribute to their toughness and ability to accomplish whatever task was set before them. Of course, he ruefully admitted, a "man who is being shot at daily, has a hard time recognizing it as a compliment . . . but it is a compliment, nevertheless."[95]

A close study of the official records of the 442nd Regiment, however, reveals different statistics. They show that for the entire month of October, losses from the combat team amounted to 119 killed or missing and 671 wounded. However, during the period between October 26 and October 30, the two Nisei battalions that played an active role in the rescue, the 100th and the 3rd, lost thirty-seven killed. Determining the number of wounded by date is more difficult, but the number does not exceed 410. Although these numbers still represent heavy losses, they are considerably less than eight hundred. And one can only surmise how many of these casualties might have been incurred in regular combat actions during this time even if there had not been a trapped battalion to rescue.

On November 1, the Germans hit the 3rd Battalion with a heavy concentration of artillery fire, and the men hunkered down into their foxholes and waited for it to end. And when it did end, they fully expected to have to repel an enemy infantry attack. The 100th Battalion, a little to the rear and right of the 3rd, prepared to join the fight if needed, and members of the Anti-Tank Company were doled out to various units. One platoon acted as litter bearers; another, acting as riflemen, guarded the rear of the 100th Battalion, while another guarded a supply route. The German attack did not materialize, so the next day the GIs sent patrols out in all directions to try to find out what the enemy was up to.

On November 3, following a German attack on the 3rd Battalion, an officer left the battalion area to go back and lead a platoon from Company E forward as reinforcement against any further German probes. By the time he had gathered up the men he needed, full dark had fallen over the forest, but he started his little force back anyway. It was almost impossible to see beyond a few feet. The trees were so tall and so close together as to block most light from the forest floor, and the men soon feared that they were hopelessly lost. About that time the lieutenant stumbled against a sleeping soldier lying on the ground. Maybe he could point the patrol in the right direction. "Hey, soldier," the lieutenant inquired, "where's the road?" Becoming slightly exasperated when the man made no reply, he bent down and shook him. "What the hell's the matter," he asked when there was still no answer, "you deaf?" Still there was silence. Determined to elicit a response, the lieutenant risked drawing enemy fire by shining his flashlight at the prostrate figure. It only required a quick look to solve the problem. The "sleeping" soldier was a German sleeping the endless sleep of the dead. The American patrol reached its destination some forty-five minutes later.[96]

The opposing forces traded rifle and machine-gun fire sporadically throughout the next day (November 4), but neither side made a concerted effort to push the other one back. Almost two dozen newly minted officers joined the regiment and were assigned to the companies most in need. Probably more welcome to the men that day than green officers was the issuance of new clothing that included woolen socks. Other clothing arrived— raincoats, for instance—that had been intended for the women of the Women's Army Corps. The men readily accepted the coats, however, as they knew that they might have to wait a long time for men's raincoats in the necessary small sizes. The rain gear was one thing, but they drew the line when their requisitioned undershorts turned out to be women's panties.[97]

The next day, General Dahlquist ordered the 442nd Regiment to move on down to the valley floor in order to get between the two German forces in St. Die and in Gerardmer. German mortar and artillery fire had not amounted to much more than harassment over the last couple of days, and the men hoped that it was a sign of a weakening enemy defense. These hopes were quickly dashed. Almost as soon as they left their foxholes and began moving in a southeasterly direction, enemy gunners went to work. All day long the fire continued, and the men were only able to advance a couple of hundred yards. As the sun began to set, the company commanders ordered their men back up the hill into their previous positions.[98]

On November 6, the men once again climbed out of their holes and went on the offensive. Company G, temporarily attached to the 3rd Battalion and on the right of the line, encountered something that none of the men had seen before—command-detonated mines. As the men approached a minefield, they could see that thin wires ran from each mine back toward the German lines. An enemy soldier simply had to wait until one or more Americans were *near* a mine and then detonate it. The ingenious Germans also attempted to convert an American tank, which a panzerschreck had disabled, into an armored fighting position. Another American tank arrived, however, and pounded it with its 75mm main gun, rendering it of no value to either side.[99]

Cumulative losses were so heavy in the 442nd that on November 6 two platoons from the Anti-Tank Company and the entire 232nd Combat Engineer Company were temporarily employed as infantry. The men in these units performed ably as infantrymen, so much so that all were recommended to receive the Combat Infantryman's Badge, with its accompanying increase in pay; but because they were not *primarily* infantrymen higher headquarters rejected the recommendation.[100]

That night, both sides sent patrols into the darkness to try to get some kind of advantage over their enemies. The Americans finally pushed the Germans off the hill beneath them on November 7, clearing the way into the valley. Heavy mortars from Company M, the 3rd Battalion's weapons company, pounded the enemy positions mercilessly. The mortars dropped over a thousand rounds into the German lines, killing some and driving others to the edge of insanity. Company G led the attack and, as so often happens in war, it took the actions of a handful of brave men to turn the tide. One very determined soldier used hand grenades and submachine-gun fire to neutralize three German machine guns that had been keeping his comrades pinned down. Without these three machine guns, the Germans were unable to stop the oncoming Americans. The rain that had become such a fixture of the fighting front turned to snow that night, adding to the woes of the frontline soldiers on both sides.[101]

Division authorities finally relieved the 442nd Regiment on November 8. It had ceased to be effective as a fighting unit. Not from any lack of bravery or dedication, but simply from a lack of manpower. Whereas the average company strength in the rifle companies three weeks earlier had been180 officers and men, Company I could now put only four riflemen and a light machine gun section into the line. And a sergeant commanded what was left of Company K—seventeen riflemen and part of a weapons platoon. Other companies registered similar strengths. But now the men would get some real rest.[102]

General Dahlquist wanted to honor the men of the 442nd for their heroic efforts and had members of his staff procure a handsome congratulatory plaque for that purpose. The mayor of the town of Besançon recommended a skilled local engraver who, despite being unable to either read, write, or speak English, went right to work. When he proudly presented the finished plaque to the officers of the 36th Division they noticed that it said:

To The
442nd INFANTRY REGIMENT
With Deep Sincerity And Upmost Appreciation
For the Gallant Fight To Effect Our Rescue
After We Had Been Isolated For Seven Days
1st Bn., 141st INFANTRY REGIMENT
Biffontaine, France
From 24th to 30th October
1944[103]

The situation was somewhat salvaged when an officer produced a dictionary that listed "upmost" as synonymous with "utmost." Even so, this gesture was not enough to change the opinion that most members of the 442nd entertained about the general. "I don't know if he was stupid or what," one former officer commented many years later. "How he ever got to be a major general I don't know."[104]

The 2nd Battalion occupied the town of Faye and the 3rd Battalion moved into Lépanges. Regimental headquarters troops and the medical detachment took up residence in Fiménil, and the men of Service Company and the Anti-Tank Company found lodging in a French army barracks in Bruyères. Hot showers and clean clothes were the first things many of the men longed for. Army engineers had even devised mobile showers for troops who were not quartered near a village or town. In these instances, the engineers pulled a shower unit up near a stream and deployed one end of a large hose into the water. A gasoline-powered pump then sucked water out of the stream and into the shower system. Showering, like many other aspects of army life, was highly organized. Four soldiers entered a tent where they removed all of their clothes and placed them into a bag. Then they proceeded into the shower area where they had a prescribed length of time to get wet, lather up, and rinse off. Then it was into another tent where they received freshly laundered clothes—everything from underwear on out—in exchange for the dirty uniforms they had worn only a few minutes before.[105]

Being able to sleep through an entire night, uninterrupted by German shellfire, was also high on everyone's list. The paymaster arrived and paid the men for October. They had access to movies and beer and they slept in houses instead of water-filled holes in the ground.

The 100th Battalion was removed, not only from the 36th Division, but also from the 442nd Regiment on November 8, and attached to the 45th Infantry Division. Its separation was to be only temporary, and it moved back into the Seventh Army rest area at Bains-les-Bains where once again the men were able to enjoy hot baths.[106]

The stay at the rest area was, as always, too brief, and on the morning of November 11 the battalion headed toward Nice, where it was to be attached to the 44th Antiaircraft Artillery Brigade. The weather was very cold, and it took the truck convoy nine hours to cover two hundred miles through heavy snow. That night the men took refuge in vacant houses on the outskirts of Mâcon. The pattern repeated itself the next two days, the trucks averaging only slightly better than twenty miles per hour, and by late on the afternoon of the 13th they arrived at Nice. Here it was back into tents for the next couple of nights, but many of the men got passes to visit the city and sample whatever it had to offer. Then, after a three-hour ride on the 15th, the battalion arrived at St. Martin Vésubie.[107]

On November 17, Brigadier General Walter W. Hess Jr., the artillery commander for the 36th Division, stopped by the battalion command post at Heylles to wish the men of the 522nd luck on their future deployments. The men then loaded onto their trucks and headed, by slow motor marches, toward the Maritime Alps along the French-Italian border. Making overnight halts at Chenimémil, Dijon, and Valence, the battalion reached a position about six miles northwest of Nice on the 21st.[108]

While the 100th Battalion motored southward it was back into the lines for the 2nd and 3rd Battalions as they relieved the 2nd Battalion of the 142nd Infantry Regiment. The 103rd Division had recently arrived from the United States and relieved the 3rd Division. This new arrival, along with the 36th Division, was about to launch a major attack. The Nisei battalions took up a position between the two big divisions just in case they were needed to blunt an enemy counterattack, but their sector remained fairly quiet as

they engaged in active patrolling over the next few days. On November 17, the 143rd Regiment relieved the two Nisei battalions,
and the weary men came off the battle line to a rest area eighteen
miles to the rear. They once again had access to hot showers and
Red Cross doughnuts. The strength of the regiment grew, at least
on paper, with the arrival the next day of 382 officers and men
from the states and sixty-two veterans returning from hospitals.
On that day also, Seventh Army headquarters assigned the 2nd
and 3rd Battalions to join the 100th Battalion near Nice, as part
of the 44th Antiaircraft Artillery Brigade. The next day, all of the
men climbed aboard trucks, including sixty borrowed from the
Seventh Army and VI Corps, and headed for warmer climes.[109]

The trip south took three days, with overnight stops near Dijon
and Valence. The weather remained cold but fairly clear. The
trucks stopped every couple of hours for the men to get out and
stretch their legs and relieve themselves. Then, after ten minutes,
it was back aboard for two more hours on the road. Stops for
midday meals were only slightly longer than the rest stops. These
meals consisted of canned C-rations. They got hot meals for breakfast and supper and spent their nights on the road in tents.[110]

Colonel Pence rejoined the regiment from the hospital on the
23rd, although he still was not entirely recovered from the serious
leg injuries he had suffered from a fall down into a bunker, and
set up his regimental headquarters in the Hotel D'Angleterre in
Nice. He assigned the 3rd Battalion to the northernmost portion
of the regimental line northeast of Sospel, where it relieved the
19th Armored Infantry Battalion, which was headed north to take
part in what was hoped to be the final push into Germany. The
Nisei filled in between the 68th Airborne Infantry Battalion to the
north and the joint U.S.-Canadian 1st Special Service Force to the
south. The battalion's area of responsibility ranged over some four
miles, from Sospel to Moulinet. The 2nd Battalion spent some
time in a reserve area near St. Jeannet in training activities along
with a detachment of officers and men from the all-Puerto Rican
65th Infantry Regiment.[111]

Regimental headquarters assigned a platoon from the Anti-Tank
Company and another from Cannon Company to the 3rd Battalion to give it a little extra firepower. And if more was required, two

batteries of the 522nd Field Artillery were only a phone call away. The 937th Field Artillery Battalion was also in a position to use its bigger 155mm guns if necessary.[112]

The 522nd Field Artillery Battalion went into position near Sospel, in the mountains some forty miles east of Nice near the Franco-Italian border where its three firing batteries covered a front of about thirty miles. The firing batteries set up observation posts while Service Battery took up a position on the outskirts of Nice. There it put together a battalion rest center that offered dances for the enlisted men, with chaperoned local French girls as their dance partners. And when such diversions as these were not sufficient, both officers and men received fairly regular passes to Nice.[113]

From Sospel, the men fanned out to observation posts in the nearby mountains. The lucky ones rode in trucks, the others went by foot, often prodding stubborn mules that carried their supplies along the steep mountain trails. The mules were sometimes fractious and hard to work with, but that was nothing new. Those same characteristics had been encountered in Italy. An army officer almost a century earlier tried to describe to a friend how difficult dealing with these often refractory animals could be:

> It was a puzzle to pack the unfortunate animal destined for our transport. . . . A pack saddle looks like a saw-buck fastened upon the animal like a saddle. To the arms of this saw buck are fastened all those sundry appliances used by 'men of war' on their journeys. Imagine—but you can't imagine—a mule buried in tents, blankets, pots, kettles—pans, Pork, Coffee, Hard Bread, Sugar, 'Jerked beef'. . . . How 'Muley' objects in the most energetic manner to this proceeding; how she elevates her heels toward the skies in deprecation; how she runs side ways[,] bumps her head against the tent poles and how, by skillfull [*sic*] manoeuvre, she often upsets the whole Cargo to the infinite wrath of the packers and the sad demolition of crockery you need not be told.

Another nineteenth-century officer described a similar event. "The mules packed for the first time," he wrote, "scattered in every direction—Some kicking their cargoes off[,] others carried away by the cargoes—Tin pans and camp kettles rattling—mules braying—drunken men singing fighting & swearing—formed as strange a mingling of sweet sounds as one hears generally."[114]

Traversing the sometimes icy mountain roads presented special problems for the artillery battalion. Its men could not rely on the sure-footed mules to pull their howitzers up into the mountains. At one point, on the road from Menton to Sospel, there was a section of road that had thirteen switchbacks that were so tight that the trucks pulling the guns could not maneuver through them. Instead, the men unhitched the guns from the trucks and manually pushed them through the turns after the trucks had worked their way through.[115]

The difficulties presented by the terrain, however, were not insurmountable, and the men enjoyed a respite from heavy campaigning. A noncom from Company A confided to a friend that one of his life's goals was a chance to get drunk on French champagne before he died. Shortly thereafter, a French family provided several bottles of the bubbly liquid to him and his buddies, and he got his wish, passing out after downing two bottles by himself. He awoke the next morning with a clear head and no hint of a hangover. However, as soon as he took a drink of water, he passed out again.[116]

Thanksgiving Day fell on November 23 that year. It was the second one in the war zone for the 100th Battalion, and the first for the rest of the regiment. Ensconced as they were in relatively safe surroundings, the men enjoyed the traditional turkey dinner with all of the usual side dishes. They would later dub operations during this period—December 1944 until mid-March 1945—as the "Champagne Campaign."[117]

A day or two later, headquarters of the 44th Antiaircraft Artillery Brigade ordered the 899th Field Artillery Battalion to relieve the 100th and reattached the latter unit to the 442nd Regiment. The battalion, reinforced with individual platoons from the Anti-Tank Company, Cannon Company, and the 232nd Engineers, moved farther south to relieve most of the 1st Special Service Force at the coastal resort town of Menton. There the battalion took over what had once been a fine resort hotel for its own use.

They did not need all 635 rooms—in fact the rooms on the top three floors were uninhabitable because of artillery damage—but they enjoyed once again such conveniences as soft beds, electric lights, and running water—hot running water. The panoramic view of the coastline was something that peacetime tourists would have paid a good bit to enjoy and, in fact, caused a certain twinge of homesickness in some of the Hawaiians. "No coconut trees," mused one, "but date palms, and that's good enough for me."[118]

By November 28, the 2nd Battalion was almost ready to move up to the line again. To the south of Sospel, Company G, along with a platoon from Company H, relieved a portion of the 1st Special Service Force. The rest of the battalion moved into the village of L'Escarène, slightly to the west, to serve as a reserve force if needed.[119]

Two posts occupied by the 2nd Battalion were stoutly built French forts—part of the much vaunted Maginot Line—Fort La Force and Fort Mille Fourches. Among the weapons left behind were several interesting 81mm mortars that were unlike anything the Americans had seen before. Mortar teams usually operated out in the open where they could adjust the elevation of their weapons and could drop the shells down the barrels. The weapon fired when the shotgun shell-type detonator in the bases of the shells hit the fixed firing pins in the bottoms of the barrels. But these mortars were different. To keep the soldiers from having to expose themselves while loading, these pieces had breeches near the bases where the loaders placed the shells and the detonators. Then the gunner pulled a lanyard to fire the piece, which sent its round through an aperture in the roof of the concrete bunker. The mortars were fixed at 45 degrees elevation, although they could swivel. A gunner adjusted a valve in the base of the piece that vented off gas from the blast to get the desired range to distant targets. The bunkers' most recent occupants had left a supply of shells, but they had removed the detonators. And even though the American detonators were slightly smaller than those designed for the French mortars, the Americans made use of them anyway. They were happy to be able to fire at the enemy from such relatively safe positions.[120]

In the unlikely event that the Germans should attack westward out of Italy, it would be up to the 442nd Regiment to slow them down until more Allied troops could arrive. But such an event did not occur, and even though there was not the daily combat and misery the men had experienced in the Vosges, there were enough reminders that they were, after all, soldiers at war. There were still casualties from occasional sniper fire or artillery bombardments, and British ships regularly patrolled along the coast firing at targets on the Italian side of the border. But the posting of the regiment to the Maritime Alps represented a walk in the park compared to the vicious fighting they had seen in the Vosges country. By December 1, all three battalions were on a line approximately eighteen miles long running northward from the Mediterranean coast. The French 27th Division continued the line on up to the border with Switzerland.[121]

The 232nd Engineers stayed very busy in this relatively quiet sector. During their three-and-a-half-month stay, they planted over forty-two hundred anti-personnel mines in almost a hundred minefields, filled thousands of sandbags, strung more than ten thousand yards of barbed wire, built two steel bridges, and erected a mule shed big enough to shelter more than a dozen of the temperamental beasts. But the job for which the rest of the troops were most thankful was the construction of a shower unit. The finished product would have made Rube Goldberg proud, but it worked, and that was all that mattered. Power for the unit came from an American jeep engine that was hooked up to a German-built 380-volt dynamo. The hot water tank had begun life as a condenser tank in a brewery while an abandoned French fort provided the electric blower. In keeping with the international character of the unit, the fuel pump came from an Italian diesel engine, while a French acetylene torch surrendered its fuel control valve, and Swiss thermometers helped control the water temperature. And, finally, a nearby war-destroyed resort hotel provided the showerheads. The finished contraption could provide fifty gallons of hot water per minute and was a huge success with the men.[122]

Many of the men still wore the painted insignia of the 34th Division on their helmets, but that was about to change. Now they were to replace it with the red, white, and blue insignia of the 442nd Regimental Combat Team. The central device of the insignia is a white hand holding a white torch of liberty, such as is featured on the Statue of Liberty, arrayed on an elongated blue hexagon with an inner border of white and an outer border of red.[123]

As the men settled into their new quarters they had time for some reflection. They certainly appreciated having roofs over their heads that were not the log and dirt covers over the foxholes they had dug in the Vosges country. They may even have mused about how their contribution to the war effort was helping to eradicate anti-Japanese feelings back home. But that enmity still existed in certain parts of the country, as they were soon to learn. For example, in Hood River County, Oregon, citizens had erected a memorial to the local men serving in the armed forces. Members of the local American Legion post, however, decided that the inclusion of the names of sixteen Nisei soldiers from the county was unacceptable and removed them on December 2, 1944. All sixteen had been in the army for almost three years. It seemed inconceivable that even after the great combat record established by the 442nd Regimental Combat Team in Europe and the individual bravery of Japanese American interpreters serving with frontline army and marine units in the Pacific that this organization, made up of former soldiers, should remain so narrow-minded.

Protest letters flooded in, many of them from Caucasian soldiers from Oregon, embarrassed by what was happening in their home state. The national commander of the American Legion urged the members of the post to restore the names and to add the names of thirty-nine other Nisei soldiers from the area who had entered the service since the memorial had been erected. Not only did the leaders of the local post refuse to modify their stance, they announced that they were also removing the name of a seventeenth Nisei whose name they had originally overlooked. Finally, facing the possibility of expulsion by the national organization, the leaders grudgingly had the names restored in March 1945.[124]

On December 7, a nine-man German patrol approached the town of Moulinet. The Germans had been told that very few, if indeed any, Americans were in the town and decided it would be a good time to gather information. How many Americans were in the immediate area? To what unit or units did they belong? How were they deployed? What artillery assets were present? The Germans had been promised that if they succeeded in their mission they would each get a three-week pass back to Germany. Their preliminary information, however, was faulty. There were plenty of Americans in the area. In an effort to capture prisoners, from whom to elicit answers to their questions, the Germans ambushed a group of engineers from a Caucasian engineer battalion as they returned to Moulinet from a mine-sweeping detail. Two of the engineers were hit, one fatally, but the Americans manfully returned fire. The noise alerted the Nisei in Moulinet, and a twelve-man patrol from Company F quickly moved out toward the sound of the guns. The German attackers then became the attacked. The Americans killed one of the enemy soldiers and captured all the rest, including a French civilian who was likely acting as a guide. Now it was the Germans who gave up information. The Americans learned that the 100th Battalion faced two battalions from the 253rd Grenadier Regiment of the German 34th Division. They also learned the location of each battalion's command post and supply dumps. It would be a little longer before the German captives saw their homeland again.[125]

While the regiment's officers had access to the fine Hotel D'Angleterre when they were in Nice, enlisted men could stay at the Hotel Continental if they were lucky enough to get passes to visit the city. A system was set up that, it was hoped, would allow every man in the regiment to spend forty-eight hours in Nice. Each battalion authorized forty-five men at a time to go to Nice for a two-day rest. The officers' rest center was moved to the Hotel Carlton in Cannes. It handled fourteen officers at a time, each on a three-day rotation.[126]

A six-inch snowfall in the 2nd Battalion area on the 11th made travel by mule train especially difficult. On that same day, regimental headquarters moved fifteen miles from Nice to Le Vignal, and a contingent of 275 men, including ten officers, rejoined the regiment from various hospitals.[127]

The relative peace was disrupted ten days before Christmas when the Germans fired a two-hour artillery barrage. One of the

shells started a fire in an ammunition dump, but the quick thinking of a pair of Cannon Company soldiers, who dashed water on
the fire, averted a disaster.[128]

While the men of the 442nd Regiment were enjoying the relative calm of the Champagne Campaign, changes were in the air at
home. A week before Christmas, the Supreme Court announced
its decision in a case involving Mitsuye Endo, a prisoner in one of
the relocation camps. She was a U.S. citizen (as were perhaps two-
thirds of all those incarcerated), had grown up attending Sunday
services in her local Methodist Church, worked for the State of
California, had never visited Japan, and was unable to speak Japanese. Her lawyer had filed a writ of habeas corpus soon after her
arrest, demanding that the government justify her imprisonment
and, by extension, the imprisonment of thousands of other loyal
Nisei. The court, without addressing the legality of the original
incarceration process, ordered her released. "I am of the view,"
wrote one of the justices, "that detention in Relocation Centers of
persons of Japanese ancestry regardless of loyalty is not only unau-
thorized by Congress or the Executive but is another example of
the unconstitutional resort to racism inherent in the entire evacuation program." A day earlier, the army announced that those inmates of the relocation camps who passed army scrutiny for loyalty
would begin to be returned to their homes on the West Coast as
early as January 1945.[129]

On December 19, some anti-tankers noticed something unusual in the waters of the Bay of Menton moving slowly toward the
shore. They notified an officer who, along with four other men
from the company, trundled one of their 57mm guns down to the
beach. The object, whatever it was, had stopped in the shallow
water about fifty yards offshore, so the men, armed with BARs,
waded out to it to investigate. They found, grounded on a sandbar,
a German one-man submarine! The pilot had become disoriented
and believed that he was entering the Italian bay at Ventimiglia,
which was under German control. He hoped that these men could
free his craft from the sandbar and send him on his way, but they,
of course, had other ideas and seized both him and his boat. The
anti-tankers were justifiably proud of their capture and were sorry
to have to turn it over to the U.S. Navy.[130]

Actually, calling this vessel a submarine would be to stretch the definition of such a craft. It was more of a piloted torpedo than anything else, but German industry had manufactured about two hundred of them for the purpose of attacking Allied invasion fleets. Its design was quite simple, consisting of nothing more sophisticated than two torpedoes piggy-backed together. German engineers removed the warhead and most of the internals of the uppermost torpedo and converted it into a compartment for the pilot, adding a plexiglass dome to cover the pilot's compartment and a twelve-horsepower electric motor for propulsion. The pilot wore a compass on his wrist for navigation, and the vessel was unable to fully submerge. An oxygen mask helped the pilot avoid carbon dioxide poisoning, at least theoretically. The pilot, when he located a suitable target, could launch the lower torpedo. In practice, however, those vessels did not prove to be very efficient.[131]

About this time the Nisei went on heightened alert status in response to events farther north. On December 16, the Germans launched what would be their last major offensive of the war in the Ardennes region of Belgium and Luxembourg. In what soon became known as the Battle of the Bulge, the Germans used English-speaking officers and men in American uniforms to cause confusion in the American ranks. Posing as military police, for instance, it was a simple matter for them to misdirect truckloads of American reinforcements away from the scene of fighting. The men of the 442nd captured a number of prisoners during their stay in southern France, but none of them were wearing American uniforms.

That is not to say, however, that they did not encounter enemy soldiers in unusual clothing. One day, while American howitzers were firing at suspected German gun positions, one of the rounds fell short, landing in a field between the lines where some Italian women were working. When the round exploded in their midst, however, these "women" hiked up their skirts, revealing enemy uniform trousers underneath, and scurried for safety.[132]

The German offensive caused considerable excitement among American military planners back in the States. Previously, monthly draft calls had been reduced as it seemed that the end of the war in Europe was fast approaching. In response to the surprise German onslaught, President Franklin Roosevelt instructed Major General Lewis Hershey to once again increase the draft calls. The number of available men under the age of twenty-six, the age group to be targeted by the increased quotas, was almost exhausted by then, so General Hershey proposed dipping into the pool of almost three hundred thousand young men, like Sergeant Morita's brothers, with farm deferments. Early in January 1945 he sent notices to all the draft boards across the nation to begin ordering draft-deferred farmers to take their pre-induction physical examinations. There was an immediate firestorm of protest as congressmen and senators from agricultural districts complained that drafting farmers would result in drastic food shortages on the home front. So intense was the outcry that Hershey found himself backpedaling and saying that he only wanted the young farmers to take their physicals so that if it became necessary to draft them later they would have already completed that necessary step toward induction. There was, therefore, no reclassification of farmers at that time.[133]

Christmas in 1944 was unlike any Christmas most of these soldiers had ever known, but they decided that they would do what they could to bring holiday cheer to those around them. Some speculated that this could very well be the last Christmas they would ever celebrate. And since non-religious, gift-giving aspects of Christmas appealed most to children, the chaplain of the 100th Battalion decided to host a Christmas party for the French children near Monte Carlo on the day before Christmas, a Sunday. For weeks he had accumulated hard candy, chocolate bars, and crackers donated from the men's rations. He had arranged for a local baker to prepare some confections and had the 206th Army Band on hand to provide additional entertainment. At least seven hundred people showed up, half of them adults who pushed and shoved to get whatever largesse was to be had. The chaplain was finally able to maintain some semblance of order that allowed every child under the age of twelve to receive a few crackers, a couple of candy bars, a fig bar, a handful of hard candies, and a few oranges.[134]

The men of the 2nd Battalion staged a similar party in the village of L'Escarène. Planning began well before the big day, and that allowed the men to write home and ask their loved ones to send things that might bring joy to a youngster. And for a month the men hoarded the hard candy that came in their K-rations so they could give it to the kids. When the soldiers told the mayor of the village about their plan he was overwhelmed by their kindness. When the big day arrived almost all the children in the village showed up at the church, where the party was to be held, and a fair number of children from nearby villages were also in excited attendance. No American officers were invited at first, but the mayor thought that at least the battalion commander, Lieutenant Colonel James Hanley, should receive an invitation, and the soldiers relented. Further, the mayor suggested, as soon as the colonel arrived the regimental band, which was providing holiday music for the party, should break into the American national anthem, which he had apparently never heard before, and then follow that up with the French national anthem. Colonel Hanley arrived, coincidentally, just as the band had started to play a popular air called "Donkey Serenade." The mayor and the other town dignitaries immediately jumped to their feet and stood at rigid attention to honor the tune that they mistakenly thought was the American national anthem. No harm was done, however, and the children enjoyed a wonderful respite from their wartime lives, loaded down with candies and small gifts.[135]

Christmas day dawned clear, but cold. There was ice on the mountain trails and snow flurries fell intermittently throughout the day. Another German soldier was captured that day—a former Luftwaffe pilot who, because of the lack of airplanes at this late stage of the war, had been transferred to the infantry. The man who captured him was a mail clerk from the 2nd Battalion.[136]

On clear days observation posts high in the Alps sometimes offered spectacular views. It was on one such day that a sergeant in the artillery battalion noticed what appeared to be a huge German railway gun move out of concealment in a tunnel on the Italian coastline and fire at a pair of Allied warships in the Mediterranean near his position. The artilleryman quickly plotted the position of the enemy gun on his grid map and radioed it to the rear. The coordinates were then quickly relayed to the two ships, which both opened fire. After the ships' second marker round found the target, they fired two salvoes. The sergeant watched with considerable fascination and pleasure as the German gun tumbled into the sea.[137]

On another occasion, a man from the same battery spotted German soldiers walking along the beach on the Italian side of the border. They presented no serious threat, but he was bored and alerted the officer in charge of a forward observation team. "Shoot at 'em," was the officer's response, so he radioed in the grid coordinates and soon heard an outgoing artillery round over his head. It splashed into the Mediterranean about a thousand yards from the beach, so he ordered the appropriate correction and told the gunners to fire for effect. The Germans were soon scampering for safety.[138]

The capture of the German miniature submarine in December surely must have been a first, and during the first week of February the men of Cannon Company did their best to match this feat. Near dusk on February 5, the same Cannon Company officer who had requested a fire mission onto the famous tower in Pisa spotted a small torpedo boat close into shore moving slowly toward the east. It had developed engine trouble while on a reconnaissance mission and had drifted toward the beach. He and some nearby GIs opened fire on it, and it started to come around. Then it changed directions again, so the men again shot at it. This time the two men aboard surrendered their craft rather than risk having it blown to pieces beneath them. The two captives claimed to be German, but when questioned—in German—they did not understand their interrogators. It was determined that they were diehard Italian marines. Thus, for the second time in six weeks, Nisei infantrymen captured an enemy navy vessel.[139]

During the first two-and-a-half months of 1945 the routine of the 442nd remained fairly constant. The 2nd and 3rd Battalions alternated between manning observation posts in the mountains or functioning as a ready reserve force near Sospel. The 100th Battalion spent its time near the coast. The engineers had cleared the beaches of mines, but the damaged sewer systems of the nearby towns so contaminated the water as to make it unsafe for swimming.[140]

One of the reasons for assigning the 442nd Regiment to this relatively quiet sector along the Riviera was so it could build back to something approaching full manpower levels. Veterans of the regiment returned from hospitals and replacements from the States—including Sergeant Morita's younger brother Jack—attended instructional sessions on a variety of topics. The new men learned patrolling techniques in the mountainous region where they were stationed, and even the veterans benefited from lectures and demonstrations on the latest weapons—both American and German.

Patrolling in the snow covered mountains was not as bad as what the men had experienced in the Vosges, but it was still unpleasant. One man listed his winter wardrobe as follows:

[On] top I have a summer undershirt, T-shirt (from home), winter undershirt, sweat shirt (from home), Red Cross knit sweater, wool shirt, fur lined jacket, combat jacket, and if it rains a raincoat on top of all that. On bottom I have, from inside out, summer shorts, long wool shorts, two wool winter pants, and combat pants. On my feet I wear two cotton socks, two heavy wool long socks, and combat shoes (that leak). Around my neck I wear a G.I. towel for a general purpose scarf and mud wiper. On my head I wear a wool knit cap, a hood (that a German girl sewed for me), and a helmet.

Some men warmed their spirits, if not their bodies, with thoughts of home. "Whenever it gets too cold for me," one of the buddhaheads wrote in a letter, "I think of Waikiki Beach, and swear by all the gods that when this war is over, I'll never leave the Islands, that for six months I'm just going to loaf around down at the beaches and get back all the warmth that I have lost since I left the Islands."[141]

While enjoying the relative inactivity of being stationed in the French Alps, the men had time to sample the wine, women, and nightlife of the wartime Riviera. Lucky men got passes to rest centers in Nice or in Cannes where they could relax for a few days. The others usually enjoyed, at the least, day-passes into other coastal cities. Monte Carlo was not far away, and even though it was officially off limits to the soldiers, a few snuck in from time to time. Beausoleil, however, was full of thriving businesses that easily separated the GIs from their money.

One man who spent much of his free time getting acquainted with the local women thought that the women in France were classier than those he had met in Italy. Sergeant Morita thought that the French women he saw in the larger towns were often quite attractive. "However," he confided to one of his brothers back home, "the general run of them are like Japanese women—short with stumpy legs. Me—I'll stick to American women." A couple of weeks later, however, he seemed willing to overlook such shortcomings in French women when he met nineteen-year-old girl who offered to teach him French. "I can't say I learned very much," he reported. "I was interested in other things."[142]

Many of the residents of these seaside towns had evacuated before the Americans arrived. Among those who stayed behind, however, were members of the oldest profession, and, as had been the case in Italy, there were more than enough women willing to sell themselves to the eager GIs. Several of the men "fell in love" and sought approval to marry local girls. One such man made the case at regimental headquarters that his girlfriend was pregnant, and, therefore, marrying her was the "right" thing to do. The regimental commander asked the 2nd Battalion chaplain to meet with the girl to find out as much about her as he could before ruling on the matter. The girl named a local hotel as her place of residence, and when the chaplain arrived there he found numerous soldiers waiting to enter what was obviously a bordello. Still game, however, the chaplain knocked on the girl's door, even though there were murmurings from behind him about rank apparently having privileges, or questioning why he did not have to wait his turn like all the rest of them. The "girlfriend" turned out to be merely one of many prostitutes plying her trade with the soldiers.[143]

Many men found the French civilians to be less friendly than the Italians. The French, according to a Nisei chaplain, were "more receivers than givers," more mercenary. In Italy, many of the suffering populace refused American generosity to keep themselves from being considered beggars, but in France "they would grab the shirt off your back."[144]

There was a shakeup in the command of the regiment. Although Colonel Pence, the regimental commander, had returned to the unit, he was still recuperating from injuries, so command of the regiment passed to Lieutenant Colonel Virgil R. Miller, who had acted as Pence's executive officer. Lieutenant Colonel Gordon Singles was promoted to colonel and transferred out to command the 397th Infantry Regiment in the 100th Division; Major Jack E. Conley replaced him as commander of the 100th Battalion. Lieutenant Colonel Hanley took over from Miller as the regimental executive officer, leaving Major Robert A. Gopel to command the 2nd Battalion.[145]

By this time the rumor mill had started up again in the hills along the Franco-Italian border. (Actually, it is doubtful that an army is ever *without* rumors.) The 442nd was about to move. But where was it headed? Back home, most hoped. After all, they had seen a lot of fighting, particularly the men of the 100th Battalion. Other rumors suggested that the Nisei were going to the Pacific theater to fight the Japanese. Neither rumor was accurate.

Meanwhile, in Italy, rough terrain and torrential rains added to the operational difficulties caused by the transfer of the VI Corps from Italy to southern France. The Fifth Army used this time to build up its inventory of weapons, ammunition, vehicles, and everything else an army needs to function. The veterans were able to spend some time in reserve areas, away from the constant threat of death. Among the many new units arriving that winter was the 92nd Infantry Division, a unit that resembled the 442nd in that its enlisted men were from a racial minority—they were African Americans—while most of the field-grade officers were Caucasian. Unlike the 442nd, however, the 92nd Division did not earn a reputation as a brave and successful unit.

Elements of the 92nd Division attacked German and Italian troops in the hills surrounding Serchio Valley on February 4. For a few days the division made steady overall progress, but fierce enemy artillery barrages and counterattacks soon halted its advance. When a couple of soldiers in one of the regiments broke under the stress and headed for the rear, their panic communicated itself to the entire company and to an adjacent company as well. Soon two hills that had been so recently wrested from enemy control were abandoned by the terrified soldiers. In one week's time the 92nd Division suffered over seven hundred casualties, including forty-seven officers. Of perhaps greater importance, however, was that it had lost the confidence of the army's high command.

In a division-wide reorganization, all of the officers and men of the division's 365th, 370th, and 371st Regiments were evaluated. The underachievers were culled and sent to the 365th and 371st, which were removed from the division, while the most dependable troops were transferred into the 370th Regiment. This process saw 52 officers and 1,264 enlisted men being transferred out of the 370th, and 70 officers and 1,358 enlisted men transferred in. In order to complete the transformation of the 92nd Division and to bring it back up to combat strength, two outside infantry regiments were transferred in. One was the 442nd, and the other was the 473rd. The 473rd Regiment was a recently cobbled together hodgepodge of antiaircraft artillery troops whose initial specialty was no longer needed in view of the virtual non-existence of any further threat from Germany's Luftwaffe.[146]

On March 16, the French 1st Motorized Infantry Division began relieving the 442nd. The Nisei soldiers were heading back to Italy. Or most of them were. The 522nd Field Artillery was going back to the Seventh Army to assist in the attack into Germany. Final preparations for the move included turning in all French francs in exchange for Italian lira. The men were a little more flush with cash than the finance officers had planned on, however, and they did not have enough lira to complete the exchange. Some men would have to wait.[147]

Army authorities did not want the Germans to learn of the redeployment to Italy, so the men were told to remove all identifying insignias from their uniforms in case some curious observer might report their presence to the enemy. This included removing their distinctive shoulder patches from their uniforms and scraping off the same insignia painted on their helmets. This requirement was probably unnecessary, because as soon as the unit was back in Italy it would be very obvious to even a casual observer that these were the men of the 442nd. After all, there was no other unit like it in the American army.[148]

On March 9, the 522nd Field Artillery Battalion, which had relocated to Menton a couple of months earlier, began moving out to rejoin the Seventh Army. The rest of the combat team reached the docks of Marseilles on March 17, 18, and 19 and boarded LSTs for the trip to Italy. Departure was also staggered, the ships setting sail on the 20th, 21st, and 22nd.[149]

CHAPTER EIGHT

FINAL BATTLES

"The way the Germans are quitting . . . we just say, 'good, it won't be long now.'"

It took four days for the artillerists of the 522nd Field Artillery Battalion to cover just over six hundred miles to the Saarland village of Ipplingen where it joined the XXI Corps. Their new assignment was to support the drive of the 63rd Infantry Division for the final push into Germany. Shortly before noon on March 13, a howitzer from the 522nd's Battery A fired the battalion's first round on German soil.[1]

As the rest of the combat team sailed toward Italy, someone on one of the LSTs spotted the telltale wake of a torpedo bearing down on the port side of the ship. "Everyone was just dumfounded," recalled one of the men. "Some just stood there where they were. Some just hit the deck, for there was no shelter topside. We could clearly see a streak in the water where the torpedo was making its way. For a long silence the clock stood still. Then we looked at the right side of the ship and we could see the device just went under the ship. What a lucky day."[2]

The LSTs docked at the heavily damaged port of Leghorn a little before noon on the 25th. Sunken ships clogged the harbor and reminded some of the men of when they first landed at Naples. Trucks took the men to a temporary staging area near Pisa. No passes were issued because the arrival of the 442nd back in Italy was supposed to be a secret from the Germans. Efforts to mask their arrival soon proved fruitless, however, as any casual observer near the docks could easily have noticed these men with Asian features debarking. And since the combat record that the 100th Battalion and the 442nd Regimental Combat Team had established the first time they were in Italy was well known, it did not take much in the way of deductive reasoning to determine that they were back.

The infantrymen of the 442nd did not have the artillery support of the 522nd anymore, but were duly served by two other field artillery battalions, a company from a tank destroyer battalion, a company of 4.2-inch mortars, and a platoon of assault guns from a tank battalion. And, of course, the 442nd's own Cannon Company was ready with its howitzers.[3]

The men drew new equipment for the campaign ahead. This included rifles, machine guns, clothing, vehicles, radios, and even six new howitzers for Cannon Company. There were also changes within the three heavy weapons companies of the combat team (Companies D, H, and M). They replaced their heavy, water-cooled machine guns with the lighter air-cooled models, and reduced the number of 81mm mortars from six to only two or three per company. That allowed the other mortar teams, as well as many support troops, to carry more ammunition for those mortars still in use.[4]

Drawing new clothing always presented problems for the Nisei GIs because of the difficulty of obtaining proper sizes. A couple of men in Cannon Company were each down to their last pair of shoes when they returned to Italy, and it seemed that there were none to be had in the necessary small sizes. Their company's supply sergeant was used to dealing with these sorts of problems and decided that the best approach to a solution was sometimes the direct approach. He somehow talked his way in to see the brigadier general who was in charge of supply and logistics for the 92nd Division. "General," he began, "two of my boys needed shoes but no one seemed to know where to get them, because we needed three-and-a-half size shoes." These soldiers were, he continued, "big men with small feet." The general laughed heartily. "They're big men with small feet, all right. The 442nd has all big men. They deserve three pairs." And about ten days later six pairs of size 3½ shoes arrived, three for each of the men.[5]

On the evening of the 28th, trucks moved the men to an area just west of San Martino. There was no immediate combat assignment for them so they went on road marches, zeroed in their newly issued weapons, attended demonstration lectures on the latest German land mines, and engaged in other training exercises.[6]

A few days later, General Clark visited the camp of the 100th Battalion with a welcome message full of praise and admiration. He told the assembled troops that he had regretted having to send them to France several months earlier, even though it was militarily necessary. "I have followed closely your splendid record," he told them. "I have seen you in action and know your ability. . . . You of all battalions, I pledge, will share in the great victory ahead."[7]

There had been changes in Italy since the 442nd had left for France the previous fall. The invasion of southern France left the Fifth Army with only one armored and four infantry divisions, and by November even these few units showed a combined manpower shortage of about seven thousand men. Supplies of ammunition and other necessities with which to carry on operations in western Italy had also fallen to dangerously low levels. During the winter of 1944–45, however, these shortages were erased. Fresh new divisions arrived and thousands of individual replacements brought existing units back up to almost full strength.[8]

As the Fifth Army's situation improved over the winter, that of the Germans facing it worsened. Virtually all German units suffered manpower shortages, and it was increasingly difficult to keep them supplied. Allied bombers and fighter-bombers had destroyed all of the bridges across the Po River in northern Italy, hindering the flow of supplies from Germany. With the Luftwaffe almost impotent, Allied planes were free to attack enemy targets wherever they might find them. By the spring of 1945, it had become extremely dangerous for German units to move except at night. In fact, by the first of April, Allied planners estimated that the Germans were down to about two weeks' worth of supplies of all classes, with resupply down to a trickle.[9]

April 1 was Easter Sunday, and half a world away, while U.S. Marines and soldiers were going ashore on Okinawa to begin the last major land campaign against Japan, the Nisei troops in Italy had the opportunity to attend church services in the morning. But in the afternoon, it was back to training.

As wounded men continued to recover and return to the 442nd, and as more replacement troops arrived from the States, it became necessary to work out a more efficient means of assigning them to tasks than had been followed in the past. An officer and ten enlisted men were thus formed into an ad hoc Provisional Company to absorb all of the reinforcements and to put them to temporary use bringing food, water, and ammunition to the front-line troops and evacuating the dead and wounded to the rear.[10]

By the time the LSTs weighed anchor for Italy, the 522nd was shuffled over to the 45th Infantry Division of the XV Corps, which began crossing the Rhine River at the ancient city of Worms on March 21. By this time American forces were moving so fast that the men of the 522nd were often unable to identify their parent organization. For example, near the end of March, a couple of officers took a battalion spotter plane up one morning to scout for potential enemy targets, and when they landed they learned that the battalion, which had been attached to the 45th Division when they lifted off, had been assigned to the 44th Division by the time they landed.[11]

Shortly after midnight on March 27, Headquarters Battery and the three firing batteries of the 522nd crossed the Rhine on a treadway bridge. Service Battery crossed the next day, and then it was back to the 63rd Division for the last two days of the month. The battalion was almost never in the same place two nights in a row for the final two months of the war.

While the bulk of the battalion reverted to Division Artillery control, Battery A was assigned to work with the 116th Cavalry Squadron on April 5. Two days later, the rest of the battalion joined Battery A. From the 8th to the 14th, the battalion supported the 4th Reconnaissance Troop before being shifted over to help the 42nd Field Artillery Battalion of the 4th Infantry Division.

German resistance continued to crumble, and the victorious GIs pressed forward rapidly. At one point, near Neumehlerhof, a retreating German artillery unit abandoned one of its big 150mm guns. The Nisei gunners were delighted to see that the Germans, in their haste to get away, had left a fair supply of ammunition for this gun. So the commander of Battery B of the 522nd rounded

This soldier's drying laundry will go with him if he receives a sudden order to move. Signal Corps photo.

up a scratch crew including a mess sergeant and some other men not usually assigned to the guns. They gathered up the abandoned ammunition, turned the gun toward the Siegfried Line, and used it to hasten the flight of the retiring enemy.[12]

In Italy, Allied plans called for a coordinated attack by both the American Fifth Army and the British Eighth Army to begin on April 9, 1945. The immediate objective of the Fifth Army was the ancient Italian city of Bologna, an important transportation hub and a gateway to the Po River Valley. The II Corps was to advance almost due north up Highway 65 and IV Corps was to attack along Highway 64, from the southwest. The IV Corps line extended some seventy miles inland from the Ligurian Sea, with the 92nd Division anchoring the western end of the line. Its part in the overall scheme of maneuver was to help break the western end of the German Gothic Line a few days in advance of the major attack. The division was to move northward on a front that stretched from the coast on the west all the way to the Serchio Valley and drive the enemy from Mount Belvedere and Mount Brugiana preparatory to seizing the port city of La Spezia. The 442nd Regiment's role in this campaign was to move along the mountains east of Highway 1, against a seemingly more determined foe than the Nisei artillery battalion encountered in Germany.

The enemy's Gothic Line seemed almost impregnable. German engineers had blasted bunkers out of the rugged mountains and had made use of reinforced concrete to further strengthen them. They positioned machine guns such that the area covered by each one usually overlapped the coverage of those adjacent to it. Observation posts high in the mountains allowed German artillery observers to call in fire missions on a wide range of target areas. And although Allied forces had cracked this line farther east, the coastal sector remained as formidable as ever.

Allied planners did everything they could to take advantage of the weakened condition of the enemy forces opposing them. For example, they embarked upon a deception plan to make the Germans think that the American II Corps was going to move eastward to reinforce the British Eighth Army for a final push in that sector. The hope was that the Germans would shift their own forces eastward to meet this presumed threat, thereby making it easier for the American Fifth Army in the west. Both American corps headquarters stopped all radio communications, relying instead on the more secure telephone lines, while they each set up dummy headquarters locations farther east. The mock headquarters personnel then carried on a "usual" amount of authentic-sounding radio communications designed to enhance the ruse.[13]

Their training period at an end, the Nisei soldiers received orders to move closer to the front. The movement was to be made as secretively as possible just in case there were still a few Germans who did not know that they had returned to Italy. So at 7:30 in the evening of April 3, they climbed into trucks headed out of San Martino. They reached the outskirts of Pietrasanta about an hour and a half later, where the trucks stopped. The men got out and began the final leg of their journey on foot. The 100th Battalion and the regimental headquarters stopped in the village of Vallecchia, and the 2nd Battalion settled in nearby. The 3rd Battalion, however, kept moving, headed for the mountain village of Azzano.

Shell craters occasionally marked the otherwise smooth road toward Azzano, and the men were warned to stay off the shoulders for fear of mines. They spread out, trying to keep at least five yards between them so that a single enemy mortar shell or artillery round could not kill more than a few of them, and started forward. For a while, the road was fairly level, but after passing through Seravezza it began to climb into the hills and quickly deteriorated into not much more than a rocky mountain trail with a steep drop along one side. Each man's burden included his weapon, a full field pack, a sleeping back, and two days' worth of rations, so the uphill march began to take its toll. It was dark and raining and hard to see where the edge of the road dropped off. During the course of the march, some two dozen men lost their footing and tumbled down the slopes. Most only suffered minor bumps and bruises, but two men were injured seriously before the battalion reached Azzano after midnight.[14]

It had been difficult, in the dark, rainy night, to maintain contact along the entire line of march. In fact, seventy men at the rear of the column got separated and lost. Rather than continue along unfamiliar ground, and risk possible capture by the enemy, they sought cover in nearby farmhouses until it was just light enough to see. They then located the communication wire stretched alongside the road and hurriedly followed it into Azzano before full light revealed their presence to any Germans. They spent the daylight hours of April 4 inside the buildings of Azzano and out of sight of German observers on the surrounding hills.

That night, Companies I and L, along with the machine-gun platoons from Company M and some Ammunition and Pioneer troops from Headquarters Company, slipped out of the village toward the northwest and followed an Italian partisan down into a valley. They waded a small creek and then, after a brief rest, they began to climb Mount Carchio-Mount Folgorito Ridge to get behind German positions on top of the ridge. Movement up the slope on that clear, moonless night was slow and fraught with danger. Silence, although almost impossible, was essential. "If you fall," cautioned Colonel Pursall, "don't cry out!" In many places the ascent was so steep that the men had to look for shrubs or tree trunks by which to pull themselves upward. It was nearly impossible to remain upright for most of the way, and the men crawled upward on their hands and knees. There were lots of bruised knees and shins, and when one man accidentally dislodged a large rock, it bounded down the slope until it hit another man and knocked him off his feet and twenty feet down the side of the mountain. The Germans recognized that it would be rather unlikely that a body of American soldiers would ascend this path, but they took no unnecessary chances, seeding it with mines and booby traps. The pioneer troops found and disarmed almost all of them. The one that did detonate did not hurt anyone, but the soldiers were sure that the noise of the explosion must have alerted the Germans on top of the hill. But it did not.[15]

Finally, at 6:00 A.M. on April 5, the soldiers reached the top of the ridge, eight hours after having left Azzano and an hour later than they had planned to arrive. The sun had not yet risen, and they caught the Germans completely by surprise. Only one enemy sentinel was even awake, and he was quickly captured before he could sound an alarm. He then indicated the location of a bunker where his comrades were sound asleep. As the GIs moved toward the dugout they passed right by three machine guns aimed in the direction from which they had just come. Had the Germans been more alert, these three guns might well have held off the entire 3rd Battalion. Instead, however, a burst of BAR fire into the bunker's entrance brought seven sleepy, scared, and half-dressed German soldiers out waving a white rag of surrender.[16]

By 7:30, the 3rd Battalion had secured the ridgeline between Mount Folgorito and Mount Carchio, but the two mountain peaks remained in enemy hands, and they would not be given up without a fight. Company L fought its way toward the top of Folgorito, but Germans there called in fierce artillery fire on the slopes below. Gradually, however, the Americans pushed onward until they engaged the defenders in hand-to-hand combat and forced those they did not kill or capture to retreat down the western side of the mountain.

Back at Azzano, meanwhile, Company K, along with a mortar platoon from Company M, started down and across the valley in the daylight. Perhaps, with many of the German observation posts now in American hands, they could cross without being subjected to devastating shellfire. In this they were disappointed. Enemy mortars and howitzers pounded the advancing infantrymen, causing heavy casualties. Men of the Provisional Company, along with soldiers from the Anti-Tank Company, quickly moved forward to help evacuate the wounded.[17]

While the 3rd Battalion worked its way up the mountain that night, the 100th Battalion, with two platoons from the Anti-Tank Company attached, relieved the 371st Infantry Regiment, formerly of the 92nd Division, at a position that the Americans had dubbed Hill Florida. Florida was one of a series of hills leading northward to Folgorito. They included Hills Georgia, Ohio 1, Ohio 2, Ohio 3, and Mount Cerretta. The 100th Battalion's goal for the day was the adjacent hill, Hill Georgia, and there was no mistake about it. For ten minutes, beginning at 4:55 A.M., American artillery blasted the hills in preparation for Company A's assault, which cleared the hill by 5:30.

The ridge along which the 100th moved toward its next objective was only wide enough to deploy one company at a time and with Company C in reserve, Companies A and B alternated leading the way. The Germans, dug into stout bunkers on the reverse

slope of the hill, watched the Americans warily advancing, waiting for them to get closer. Within sixty yards of the defenses the
GIs hit a minefield, and when the mines started exploding the
Germans further welcomed them with grenades and machine-gun
fire. The Germans were so well supplied with grenades that they
began to tie them together in clusters of six to increase their le-
thality. Nevertheless, the defenders soon abandoned the hill in
the face of the spirited American advance.[18]

After a Company A squad leader was wounded, one of his
men stepped in to replace him, but the going was slow. Crawling carefully to avoid mines, he got near enough to a German
machinegun nest to toss a grenade into it. As soon as the grenade
exploded he rose up and rushed the emplacement firing bursts
from his submachine gun, killing one of the gunners and forcing the other to surrender. Moving on to another enemy machine
gun, he flushed the crew from their position with a hand grenade
and then mowed them down with his Thompson. His actions took
the fight out of the enemy in the immediate area and inspired his
fellow soldiers, many of whom were recent replacements.[19]

Other heroic efforts were playing out in another Company A
squad nearby when another man rushed two successive machine-
gun emplacements with grenades, knocking out both. But other
enemy guns took him under fire and German grenades began
to rain down around him. Spying a shell crater occupied by two
other GIs, he made for its safety. Just as he reached the hole, an
enemy grenade bounced off his helmet and rolled toward the
other two soldiers. He instinctively dove onto the grenade, absorb-
ing its blast with his body. This selfless act saved the lives of the
other two men, but at the cost of his own.[20]

The fighting lasted all day and into the night as the GIs cleared
the enemy bunkers one at a time with tank-busting bazookas and
hand grenades. After a failed German counterattack just before
midnight, the fighting stopped for the day. But it had been costly.
The battalion had lost seventy men, including fourteen killed.[21]

Early the next morning, Company C attacked Hill Ohio 1. Once
again, however, the Americans faced positions that the Germans
had had months to prepare, and progress once again seemed gla-
cially slow. A smoke screen was laid down to shield the advance

from German eyes while the infantry slowly dug the defenders out of one position after another. By nine o'clock the wind had blown the smoke screen away and German artillery commenced plastering the attackers. Individual heroism was commonplace as the GIs closed to within hand-grenade range of the many bunkers on the forward slopes of the hill.

Jack Conley, the new commander of the 100th Battalion and newly promoted to lieutenant colonel, requested close air support for his men and four fighter bombers—P-47s—soon arrived on station. The first time around the planes dropped their ordnance too close to the Nisei, but ground-to-air liaison was cumbersome. The battalion commander had the targets under direct visual observation, but he could not communicate directly with the pilots. Instead, he had to telephone his request back through regimental headquarters. Headquarters had a direct line to a mobile ground radio, which, in turn, could communicate directly with the pilots. But the system worked! Conley was able to get the pilots to suspend their attacks until he could arrange for the artillery to fire some smoke rounds to mark the targets effectively. The pilots then made three or four more bombing and strafing runs on enemy positions on the three "Ohio" hills. Standing in full view of the Germans, the infantrymen gleefully watched the progress of the bomb runs, heedless of the danger of drawing fire upon themselves. After the planes departed, the American artillery took over again and blasted the hillsides for ten more minutes.[22]

Companies B and C brushed aside the defenders at the top of Ohio 1 and then pushed on toward Ohio 2. The German defenders were reported to be "stunned and dazed," and surrendered in droves. In very short order, Ohio 2 was also in American hands. While most of the GIs there stopped to catch their breath, one platoon headed for Ohio 3 and by midday had knocked out three machine-gun nests and captured fourteen more prisoners. Among the materiel that fell into American hands at this time, in addition to the usual German rifles, machine guns, and mines, was an American field radio and enough food and ammunition to sustain an entire company for a week.[23]

Next, Company B assaulted a hill that jutted toward the west, called Rocky Ridge. With the support of 155mm howitzers, and despite German minefields, the Nisei infantrymen reached the top by noon. Along the way they added another thirty-one prisoners to the battalion's total for the day, but it had not been without cost. Eight soldiers from Company B died that morning, and seventeen more were wounded.[24]

The other battalions were also busy. The 2nd Battalion, after leaving its reserve position at about midnight, finally completed the climb and linked up with the 3rd Battalion at Mount Carchio by noon on April 6. While the 2nd Battalion's Company F moved west toward Mount Belvedere,[25] the 3rd Battalion focused its attention toward the southeast where the 100th Battalion was fighting its way northward. As the 3rd Battalion approached Mount Cerretta from the north, the fighting was just as fierce as elsewhere, but by three o'clock that afternoon these soldiers linked up with their comrades from the 100th Battalion. Here they found more evidence of what appeared to be a German army that was losing its fighting spirit. Among the growing number of German prisoners were those who voiced their opinion that the war in Italy could not last much longer. The GIs had also captured a significant amount of supplies, including dozens of rifles, a light mortar, sixteen machine guns, almost a hundred bazooka rounds, more than a hundred of the dreaded mines, and over two thousand hand grenades and rifle grenades. A bigger surprise was the large amount of American supplies that the GIs discovered. Not only were there American rifles and ammunition, but also blankets, sleeping bags, and even rations. The rations were particularly welcome because the hundred Italian civilians who had contracted to carry food, ammunition, and other supplies to the battalion that night had all deserted. But the 442nd had paid a high price for their gains. Nineteen Nisei died that day and another sixty-five were wounded. The last time the regiment had suffered battle losses of this magnitude was in the rescue of the "lost battalion" in France.[26]

The 2nd Battalion had been unable to gain control of Mount Belvedere before the sun set on April 6 and renewed its attack the next morning. The Americans had their hands full dealing with troops of the defending Kesselring Machine Gun Battalion until one of the men became a one-man attack unit after

German machine guns pinned down his company. Crawling to within thirty yards of one of the pesky emplacements, he tossed a pair of grenades, killing both gunners. He then jumped to his feet and rushed the second position, hurling another well-placed grenade that wounded two Germans and convinced two more that their survival depended upon them surrendering, which they did. There was yet another nearby machine gun, and this heroic soldier then set out to neutralize it. He was momentarily stunned when a bullet hit his helmet, denting but not penetrating it. In the meantime, several German riflemen had interposed between him and this third machine gun. Before he could take it out he had to do something about them. This time his submachine gun fire forced them back and allowed him time to rush the machine gun. He did, and captured all four of its crewmen. His platoon was then free to continue its advance. He and his company were responsible for killing twenty enemy soldiers, capturing twenty-six more, and destroying a total of six German machine-gun positions. By 8:30 on the morning of April 8, Mount Belvedere was finally in American hands.[27]

The men of the 100th Battalion spent April 7 cleaning out small pockets of resistance, consolidating their positions atop Mount Cerreta, the Ohio hills, and Rocky Ridge, and trying to close the gaps between themselves and the neighboring 370th Infantry Regiment. That regiment, arrayed on the 442nd's left, had made impressive initial gains that day, but was unable to resist a strong German counterattack and was forced to give ground. Its leaders planned to renew the push the next day, but postponed it because there were so many stragglers that any kind of cohesive forward movement was impossible. The 370th's lack of success endangered the men of the 442nd. Higher headquarters pulled the 370th out of the line late in the morning of April 8, and put the 473rd Regiment into its place with orders to drive northwestward toward Massa. The 100th Battalion went into regimental reserve while the 2nd Battalion maintained its position on the right flank of the regiment, ready to react to the changing conditions of the battlefield. Regimental reinforcements arrived that day—250 of them—and were temporarily assigned to the Provisional Company. They were needed to fill the gaps in the line companies caused by death and serious wounds.[28]

At noon, Company G moved off of Mount Belvedere toward the west. It met determined resistance but reached its objective, Mount Tecchioni by nightfall and began to dig in. But the Americans got little sleep that night. About ten o'clock the Germans hit the American position with intense mortar and small-arms fire, then staged a brief counterattack at midnight. The GIs forced the Germans back, but mortar fire kept them awake until two in the morning.[29]

Companies E and F waited until early evening to leave Mount Belvedere. Their respective goals were the villages of Altagnana and Pariana about a half mile to the north along the Frigido River. Company E moved, without opposition, into Altagnana by 6:00 P.M. Company F, meanwhile, sent a reconnaissance patrol farther west toward Pariana to see if there were any Germans occupying that town. There were, but enfilading fire from Company E helped drive them off for the night. German artillery pounded the village throughout the night, forcing the Americans to seek shelter away from the center of town.[30]

The 3rd Battalion moved down toward the village of Montignoso on the 8th. Resistance was negligible, but the GIs found the town in ruins when they entered about 3:30 that afternoon. Nevertheless, with Montignoso in friendly hands, Highway 1 was clear almost all the way to Massa and regimental headquarters moved up from Vallecchia.[31]

The 2nd Platoon of Company F continued its attack on Pariana early on the morning of April 9, but the 150 veterans of the Kesselring Machine Gun Battalion who had been driven off Mount Belvedere offered stout resistance. In addition to the usual assortment of machine guns and mortars, the Germans had at their disposal a tank, a self-propelled gun, and an armored car. The American riflemen had the support of some of Company H's machine guns, and by mid-afternoon had established a lodgment on the edge of town. They then added to their firepower by employing eight German mortars and seventy-five cases of projectiles that they had captured. As dark settled over the village there were only a few German holdouts. The Kesselring Machine Gun Battalion had virtually ceased to exist.[32]

The men of the 3rd Battalion enjoyed a hot breakfast that morning, their first in several days, before moving out of Montignoso to cross the ridge between Belvedere and Tecchioni. In keeping with standard tactical procedures, two companies—K and I—took the lead while the third company—L—stayed back as a reserve force, ready to be committed wherever needed. Flanking fire from a nearby hill brought the advance to a halt. With the riflemen pinned down, Company M's mortars went to work. For three hours they hammered the enemy positions along with the heavier fire of the artillery. Finally able to advance again, Company L moved up to replace Company K, which had taken the brunt of the German fire so far. The battalion reached the ridge by early evening and relieved Company G before moving on down to the Frigido River. Battalion casualties were light—four men wounded. The Germans facing the 3rd Battalion that day did not fare as well, losing sixty killed. They also lost ten machine guns and a truckload of ammunition.[33]

The Germans appeared to be retreating as there was no visible evidence of enemy activity across the Frigido River from the 3rd Battalion's position. It was imperative, however, for the Americans to know how far back the Germans had fallen and into what type of defensive works they might have moved. Patrols moved out at first light the next morning and crossed the river to learn the answers. Partisan guides led them to several towns along the river, and the results were the same everywhere. The Germans had definitely pulled back and the local inhabitants welcomed their American liberators with open arms.[34]

Company L of the 442nd entered Carrara the next day to find all of the Germans gone and the city under the control of anti-German Italian partisans. Company K then pushed forward into the mountains north of the city and captured the villages of Gragnana and Sorgnano without a fight, and the 100th Battalion took control of the marble quarries at the Cave of Colonnata. It might have moved even farther north if the roads had not been choked with civilians returning to Carrara. But it was just as well, because the Americans had already made such rapid progress that they were about to outrun their supplies and supporting artillery. The bulk of the 100th Battalion marched northward toward Colonnata, using local mules to carry some of its baggage. The men reached their objective after a twelve-hour road march. The handful of Germans who still occupied the town gave up without a fight.[35]

April 10 was uncharacteristically quiet in the 442nd's sector. The 100th Battalion remained in reserve most of the day, while Companies E and F moved out in the morning. By early afternoon they had reached Mount Brugiana against negligible resistance. From Mount Brugiana's twenty-nine-hundred-foot peak they could look down onto the city of Carrara. The 473rd Regiment, in the meantime, captured Massa without a fight.[36]

In spite of the successes enjoyed by American troops pushing rapidly north, the Germans left enough reminders behind them to assure that the pursuing troops did not get too overconfident. On some of the roadways, German engineers planted huge artillery shells, equipped with detonators, about eighteen inches below the surface of the road. They had then very carefully completely resurfaced the roadways to erase any evidence of recent excavation. A man, or even a column of men, walking over the road could not exert enough downward pressure to detonate these devices. These mines were designed to destroy heavy American vehicles, tanks or trucks, which passed over them. Nisei engineers of the 232nd Engineer Company discovered these devices the hard way, losing four bulldozers in the process.[37]

While the engineer troops worked to clear the road from Massa to Carrara supplies were unable to get through. The mountainous terrain made man-powered supply caravans almost impossible, and attempts to drop food to the troops in the city from the air also failed. The engineers opened the road by late afternoon on the 12th, but jeeps carrying hot food to some of the outlying villages still found it safer to drive on the railroad crossties than on roads.[38]

Company G led the 2nd Battalion out of Carrara on the morning of April 13, heading north toward Mount Pizzacuto five miles away. The Americans had almost reached the base of the mountain when the Germans opened up on them. Artillery airbursts, those reviled reminders of the Vosges, began tearing holes in the formation, and direct fire from self-propelled guns added their destructive power. Only one American field artillery battalion was close enough to provide counter-battery fire, at Gragnana, but the artillerymen were subjected to the same fierce shelling as the infantry. The 2nd Battalion dug in and waited, and prayed, for relief.[39]

Relief was not immediately forthcoming. The 100th Battalion, scheduled to follow the 2nd toward Mount Pizzacuto at a twenty-five-hundred-yard interval, found itself pinned down in the village of Gragnana by the same firestorm that engulfed the friendly artillery battalion. The 3rd Battalion, back in Carrara, was immobilized by huge coastal guns firing from several miles away.[40]

Word arrived that day that President Franklin Roosevelt had died of a stroke, the day before, at his vacation home in Warm Springs, Georgia. Americans all over the world mourned the death of the president. The Nisei soldiers remembered him as the man who, when responding to those who questioned the loyalty of the Japanese American soldiers in early 1943, said: "Americanism is a matter of the mind and heart; Americanism is not, and never was, a matter of race or ancestry." But they also remembered him as the man who, only a year before that, had signed Executive Order No. 9066 that sent many of them into the internment camps, where some of their families still resided.[41]

That night, Company B moved forward under cover of darkness to reinforce 2nd Battalion headquarters in the town of Castelpoggio and took up a position at the northern edge of the town. Its presence there soon proved of great value. A German battalion from the 361st Panzer Grenadier Regiment, equipped with rifles, machine guns, and panzerschrecks, and using the early morning fog as cover, had moved up to within thirty yards of the American position and launched an attack from there. The assault was coordinated with self-propelled guns stationed farther away and made good initial progress, ten of the attackers actually getting into the town. The addition of Company B's riflemen to the town's defenders came as quite a surprise to the assault troops and, after thirty minutes of intense fire, the Germans retreated. Unfortunately for them, however, their line of retreat placed them directly into the gunsights of Companies F and G and within range of Company H's

81mm mortars. American losses were relatively light, but German casualties included a company commander among the thirty-five killed, while another 150 surrendered. As the smoke cleared from these early morning exertions, Company G was already on the move toward Mount Pizzacuto. Friendly artillery support had finally arrived.[42]

Just before the German assault on Castelpoggio that morning, a half dozen newly arrived replacements from the States left the village loaded down with water and food for Company G. They believed their route to be safe and had therefore left their rifles behind so they could carry additional supplies for their comrades. A roving German patrol spotted them, however, and captured them. The Germans relieved them of all their supplies and equipment and took them into Fort Bastione for additional questioning. Failing to get any information of value from the prisoners, three German soldiers began escorting them toward the rear. As they passed through a small village on the way to the rear of the German position they were caught in an American artillery barrage. When an exploding shell killed one of their guards, the prisoners jumped the other two, killed them, and made their escape.[43]

That same day, April 14, the twice-postponed Fifth Army offensive began in earnest as hundreds of bombers and thousands of artillery pieces pounded the German lines all across Italy. On the far western end of the Fifth's line four army air force P-47s attacked Fort Bastione the next day. Each of the planes fired rockets into the target and dropped a pair of 500-pound bombs. This was sufficient, along with artillery fire, to soften up the position so Company G could attack. Still, it took three hours before the fort was in American hands. After a brief rest, Company F and a platoon from Company G, took the peak of Mount Grugola to the northwest.[44]

German troops had gotten in behind the left rear of the regiment, and severe fighting again broke out near Castelpoggio. The regiment's engineer troops put aside their minesweepers, their shovels, and other such equipment and grabbed up their rifles. They served as riflemen this day, as they so often did and, along with Company C, fought off a determined German attack throughout the afternoon along La Bandita Ridge northwest of

Carrara. The composition of the attacking force was indicative of how close the German army was to final defeat. Fighting side by side with a battalion of the 286th Panzer Grenadier Regiment was a contingent of German sailors and marines.[45]

In Carrara that evening, several 3rd Battalion men prepared to depart for a much deserved leave at home. That afternoon there had been a brief awards ceremony, and their officers had presented them with various decorations. German artillerists spoiled any celebratory mood, however, when a shell hit the battalion command post. Five of the eight men wounded were among those slated to go home.[46]

American forces, including the 442nd Regiment, steadily pushed toward the northwest and the important road center at Aulla. If the Germans lost Aulla, their forces along the coast, particularly at La Spezia, would be cut off from retreat into the Po River Valley. Both sides knew this, and the German resistance remained an important consideration. The constant stress of combat was beginning to tell on the Nisei. "For two weeks," one man recalled, "we had been fighting our way up and down three thousand-foot mountains and the men were walking zombies, marching, firing, hitting the ground, marching some more and hitting the ground again, only out of some instinctive memory of what they were supposed to do."[47]

On the morning of April 17, Company B sent a ten-man reconnaissance patrol toward the village of Gignago, and a similar patrol toward Casale. The men sent to Casale had a rather uneventful experience, but those dispatched to Gignago stirred up quite a bit of excitement. They had approached within fifty yards of a German position without being aware of its existence. Nor were the Germans cognizant of the close proximity of these Americans until after they had moved into a farmhouse and established an observation post. The Germans then sent a soldier to demand surrender, but the Americans, probably not completely aware of the gravity of their situation, made him their prisoner instead and opened fire on the Germans.

When the Company B men had still not returned by the next day, Company C sent out a patrol to locate and, if necessary, rescue them. Following a telephone wire, and then following the sound of gunfire, the rescuers soon came upon the missing men. Their arrival surprised the Germans, but they quickly adjusted to this new threat, and the fighting continued throughout the night before the Americans—after suffering two killed and seven wounded—were able to extricate themselves and return to friendly lines.[48]

By April 20, the Germans had destroyed their big, long-range coastal guns at Punta Bianca, near La Spezia. Moving them northward along with retreating German forces was impractical and letting them fall into Allied hands was unthinkable. Two days later, Polish troops from the British Eighth Army entered Bologna, followed closely by the Nisei's former parent division, the 34th.[49]

Final victory in Italy now was only a matter of time, but that did not mean that the Germans were willing to concede, and the men of the 442nd continued to fight, and to die. On April 21, Lieutenant Dan Inouye led his Company E platoon in an attack across an area near San Terenzo that offered practically no natural concealment, and was swept by the ever-present interlocking fields of fire of German machine guns. The platoon was able to silence an enemy mortar observation post, but it was soon pinned down by the ubiquitous machine guns. Armed with a Thompson submachine gun and a load of grenades, Inouye inched forward. When he got close enough to the first machine-gun emplacement, he pulled the pin on a grenade but took a bullet in the midsection before he could throw it. He quickly regained his balance and threw the grenade into the enemy bunker. A burst from his Tommy gun finished off the occupants. Loss of blood soon made it difficult for him to remain standing so he lurched forward on his knees and took out a second gun position with a pair of grenades. With one grenade left, he staggered toward the final enemy machine gun. Just as he drew his arm back to throw it a German rifle grenade hit his elbow and exploded, leaving what was left of his arm hanging uselessly by his side—and still clutching the sputtering grenade. Somehow he had the presence of mind to grab the grenade with his left hand and fling it toward the bunker, where it exploded. Another bullet in his right leg finally ended his fight, but he refused evacuation until his platoon had cleared the enemy position.[50]

Such heroism was almost routine in this phase of the war. On April 22, a private led a squad from Company K in an attack on the village of Tendola. He neutralized an enemy machine gun with a hand grenade and then noticed four more machine guns raking his platoon. He could not get close enough to throw hand grenades so he attached a grenade launcher onto the end of his M1 rifle and fired a grenade into one of the positions. He then crawled near enough to another to kill its inhabitants with rifle fire. But then his luck ran out. As he rose up to shoot at some fleeing Germans a burst of fire killed him. But the advancing Americans had made Tendola too hot to hold, and the Germans began evacuating the next day.[51]

By April 23, German resistance in front of the Fifth Army in northern Italy was beginning to melt away. The U.S. 34th Division was moving rapidly northward and was in fair position to cut off a large segment of the enemy at Parma. The 100th Battalion faced little serious opposition on this day and by early afternoon it was headed back to Carrara and regimental reserve. Companies L and I of the 3rd Battalion occupied Mount Nebbione and Mount Carbolo, respectively. Companies E and G captured San Terenzo after a five-hour fire fight with Italian Bersaglieri troops, and then Company G advanced toward La Piastra. The GIs counted almost fifty German bodies on the battlefield when the fighting was over, and they bagged 125 prisoners. And in addition to the usual amount of captured rifles and machine guns, the Nisei also took two motorcycles, a half dozen artillery radios, twenty-five horses and mules, and thirty bicycles.[52]

Captain Mitsuyoshi Fukuda, meanwhile, assembled a task force made up of Companies B and F, a platoon from the Anti-Tank Company, and some communications troops to attack toward Aulla from the south. The 3rd Battalion was poised to follow up on any success by the task force. Task Force Fukuda set out early in the afternoon of April 23 to chase down the retreating Germans and force them to either fight or surrender. The men reached Mt. Grosso by noon the next day and then moved rapidly northeast through the towns of Vecchietto and Bibola before arriving directly south of Aulla. To the east, the 2nd Battalion moved forward as if on a training march. The enemy was gone from its front.

The 2nd Battalion reached the village of Pallerone, also just south of Aulla, by late afternoon, where it came upon another American battalion pinned down by German fire.[53]

German defenses in Italy, and in fact everywhere, were crumbling fast by this time. On April 25, the American 88th Infantry Division captured the city of Verona, the last important obstacle before reaching the Brenner Pass through the Alps to Austria. Task Force Fukuda and the 2nd Battalion brushed aside slight resistance on the outskirts of Aulla and entered the city by 9:00 A.M. They found it completely free of enemy troops, except for the bodies of those recently killed. So instead of having to face machine guns and grenades, the American liberators faced flowers and vino.[54]

The mission envisioned for Task Force Fukuda was the capture of Aulla, and now that that had been accomplished the component parts of the task force reverted back to their original parent units. The 3rd Battalion of the 370th Infantry Regiment relieved the Nisei 2nd Battalion, allowing the tired soldiers to move back to an area near Sarzana where they could rest with the rest of the regiment.[55]

The regiment's rest period was, as was so often the case, too short. Trucks soon arrived to transport it northward toward the port city of Genoa. Riding was, of course, much better than walking, and the men enjoyed the relative luxury of motor transport. Their progress was slowed by roadways that were pockmarked by explosions and by bridges that had been destroyed. In some places, trucks had to be pulled across some of the streams by winches set up on the opposite sides. As they rolled through the numerous small villages they were welcomed by appreciative crowds of cheering Italians.[56]

On April 27, a reconnaissance patrol penetrated the outskirts of Genoa without encountering the enemy and, in fact, the men began to hear more and more rumors of German intentions of surrendering. On that same day the 473rd Infantry Regiment was the first American unit into the city. The Nisei of the 3rd Battalion reached the southern outskirts of Genoa the next day, where they boarded trolley cars, trucks, taxicabs, and any other sort of motorized conveyance and rolled through the city to their assigned position on high ground just to the northwest of the city. The 2nd Battalion followed by truck and arrived at the city after dark that night.[57]

On the 29th, the 2nd Battalion reached Allessandria in early afternoon. A patrol from the 100th Battalion had been there earlier that day and presided over the surrender of over three hundred German soldiers and officers. And surrender was contagious. Approximately a thousand Germans surrendered to the 2nd Battalion in nearby towns. Two rifle companies brought in seventeen hundred prisoners. "They're giving up by the thousands," one Hawaiian happily wrote home, "and it's good to see them come dragging their tails in with that lost defeated look so very evident on their faces."[58]

The progress through Germany for the artillery battalion was quite rapid. For at least part of the time the troops moved along modern, high-speed, divided highways. What an improvement over the mountain roads of Italy! As the GIs whipped along these highways they saw ever more evidence of the Nazi collapse. Parked along the highway were German fighter planes. Some had apparently suffered battle damage, but others were brand new and still crated. Among them were several Messerschmitt Me 262s, among the first operational jet fighter planes. The once much-vaunted Luftwaffe had run out of capable pilots, mechanics, and fuel.

Many German soldiers saw the inevitable end to Adolf Hitler's hoped-for Thousand-Year Reich and surrendered. In one instance, a couple of enlisted men from Battery C of the 522nd came upon a German house in the woods. Knocking on the door brought the woman of the house, who told the GIs that there were twenty or thirty German soldiers inside. Thinking quickly, one of the GIs told her that American soldiers had the place surrounded and that the Germans had better give themselves up. She relayed the message to the German major who was in charge, and he ordered his men to stack their weapons inside the house and then march into the yard with their hands up. There is no record of their reaction when they learned that only two American soldiers had "surrounded" the house. That late in the war, however, it might not have mattered to them.[59]

Late in April, the fast moving artillery battalion crossed the Danube River at Lauingen-Dillingen in Bavaria and turned toward the southeast. A four-man forward observation team pulled their jeep into the village of Wasseralfingen and discovered a large man-made hill nearby, covered with grass and artificial trees to camouflage it from the air. Circling it, they came upon a gated entrance leading to a tunnel in the hillside. Inside the tunnel was a fairly sophisticated facility for manufacturing 88mm antiaircraft guns, complete with living quarters for the slave laborers from Bulgaria, Poland, and other German-occupied countries.[60]

An officer and a noncom, scouts from the 522nd, were roving far ahead of the main body of the Seventh Army in a jeep when they made a truly gruesome discovery. They beheld a fairly large cluster of barracks buildings, all enclosed by a barbed wire fence. Inside the fence, standing around listlessly or lying in the snow, were dozens of emaciated people wearing striped pajama-like clothing with triangular patches on the breast. These patches were color-coded so the guards could quickly identify an inmate's "crime." A yellow triangle signified a Jew, while brown indicated a gypsy, and violet was for Jehovah's Witnesses. Political prisoners wore red patches, habitual criminals wore green, and homosexuals wore pink.[61]

The Americans had discovered one of the sub-camps of the Dachau prison facility. One of the GIs used his carbine to shoot the lock off the gate, and some of the inmates began, very tentatively, to shuffle out of the camp. At about the same time, two more members of the battalion, temporarily on loan to an armored battalion, found another one of the sub-camps. Dispensing with anything as mundane as a carbine bullet through the lock, a tank destroyer simply bulled its way through the fence.[62]

One of the Nisei observers recalled that the inmates "were so emaciated and pathetic, and they just stared at us, still inside the enclosure with the death ovens behind them." He could not even tell which of the cadaverous inmates were men and which were women. "It was a sight that burned in our minds," remembered another. "Skin and bones that once were men. I wondered if they could ever recover." The inmates reminded yet another man of zombies, "expressionless and disoriented." A Headquarters

Battery noncom described the prisoners as looking "like walking skeletons with sunken eyes, dressed in dirty blue-and-white prison garb." "The faces" of the inmates "were skulls," recalled a surgeon from an armored division, "bones painted brown, and the fingers . . . were thick wires that crooked with enormous effort, moved by muscles that must have been mere wisps." He later commented that nothing "in all the lexicon of medical horrors could have so shriveled the flesh from around the bones and from under the skin, leaving those varnished skeletons, those incredible painful bird's eyes, those unearthly nasal screams."[63]

Mainland Nisei who had come from the internment camps found added reason to pause. "When I saw the temporary barracks and barbed wire fences," one remembered, "it reminded me of the Poston [relocation] camp from which I volunteered. It is ironic," he continued, "that many of us who came from the relocation camps in the US would come to Germany to help release the Jewish victims. While the scope and purpose of the Japanese Americans and the Jews were different, the reason for incarceration was the same: racial discrimination."[64]

Some of the recently liberated prisoners came upon the body of a horse or cow that had apparently been killed by stray bullets. They set upon it ravenously, tearing the flesh with their bare hands and wolfing down the raw meat. Others were so close to complete starvation that they could not keep solid food down. At first GIs gave them their own rations, but were soon ordered to stop. It quickly became apparent that the inmates' digestive systems could not handle the relatively rich food contained in C- and K-rations and that the soldiers should not attempt to feed them such food. Some of the Nisei mixed up a thin gruel with powdered eggs and water in the hopes that they could thus provide nourishment to the inmates, but many of them were already so weak and starved that they were even unable to swallow water.[65]

A forward observer team from Battery B came upon another sub-camp in the same general area but was naturally wary about approaching it. From a distance, the Americans could see no evidence of a German military presence and decided to investigate. The prisoners were French and, generally, not as emaciated as the "walking skeletons" that others had described. When they were finally convinced that the Americans were there to free them they asked in which direction France lay. The Nisei officer pointed his finger and they immediately set off on foot for home.[66]

The Nazis had opened the prison camp at Dachau in 1933. Over the course of the next twelve years, it became home to over two hundred thousand prisoners. Dachau was not a death camp per se, but a slave labor camp where the inmates were forced to work in factories producing goods for the German war machine. Nevertheless, thousands died there. Some from starvation. Some from the cruel medical experiments that Nazi doctors carried out on them.

After the Allied invasion of Normandy on June 6, 1944, Germany subjected even more prisoners to the cruelty of forced labor in an effort to produce enough materiel to hold back the Allies. Thus, Dachau officials opened some thirty outlying camps—sub-camps—that housed about thirty thousand prisoners. At the time that the troops of the Seventh Army approached Dachau, it and its sub-camps held 67,665 prisoners. Most were categorized as political prisoners but 22,100 Jews were also incarcerated there.[67]

Most American soldiers had had no inkling of the Holocaust. "Everyone was strictly horrified," recalled a GI from a different unit when he witnessed these camps.

> We were sick to our stomachs! And we were pretty callous people. You know, we had gone through a war, for many, many months we were in battle, and we had seen a lot of things, we had seen a lot of hands and heads blown off, and buildings shattered, and people killed, and so on and so forth. But something like this, we had never seen, we could never imagine anything like this.[68]

Over the next few days, elements of the 522nd passed by, or within a few miles of, many other such sub-camps. Only a few days before the Americans arrived and shot the locks off the gate of one of the sub-camps, prison officials had sent seven thousand inmates marching south to keep them from being liberated. They were probably the hardiest of the prisoners, although they were far from healthy. Many died of exhaustion or succumbed to the cold along the way, and German guards quickly shot any who could not keep up with the marching column. Finally, on the night of May 1, near Waakirchen, the guards herded the prisoners into a deep ravine and set machine guns up along the rim. One of the prisoners recalled that they were "in a perfect spot for [the] Nazi National Pastime, the Execution of Jews." But the guns remained silent. The next morning, the prisoners awoke to find that the guards—and the machine guns—were gone, and American troops were marching along the road nearby. Among them were members of the 522nd Field Artillery Battalion. These men, recalled one of the former inmates, "were like angels of mercy, who descended from Heaven to lift me out of my Hell."[69]

Sergeant Morita apparently never talked about Dachau and did not mention it in any of his surviving letters home. Perhaps he did not witness its horrors or, and this seems more likely, perhaps the memories were so awful that he did not want to relive them. When another man from Headquarters Battery was asked if he had ever shared his feelings about what he saw at Dachau he replied: "No, I didn't talk about it. How could anyone understand who didn't see it? It's not that easy to talk about. It affected all of us. It took us a long time to get over that. . . . We couldn't understand why people had to go and do things like that to other human beings."[70]

These horribly emaciated political prisoners were not the only ones who gained their freedom from German imprisonment. As American and other Allied forces advanced into Germany from the west in early 1945, the Soviets pushed in from the east. In order to prevent the Red Army from liberating German prisoner-of-war camps in Poland and eastern Germany, the Germans emptied the camps in its path and sent thousands of Allied prisoners on a forced march westward. Among them were a score or so of Nisei prisoners, some of whom had languished in captivity since the previous June. Like the Dachau prisoners, many of the marchers died from exposure or starvation along the way. A soldier from the 1st Infantry Division remembered that all he had to eat for nine days on the march was one raw potato, and the only way he quenched his thirst was by eating snow.[71]

Many of these marching prisoners headed toward Stalag III-A at Luckenwalde, about thirty miles south of Berlin. This prison camp, like all the others by this time, was seriously overcrowded. Approximately four thousand of the new arrivals were forced to shelter in several large circus-type tents, each of which housed several hundred hungry, filthy American prisoners. In late April, a Soviet tank unit on its way to Berlin liberated Stalag III-A.

On May 2, 1945, the fighting in Italy ceased, and on the 8th Germany unconditionally surrendered. Standing in formation, the men of the infantry battalions received great news: the war in Europe was over! The reactions of the American soldiers were subdued. True, there were some boisterous celebrations, but for the most part the men expressed feelings of relief rather than jubilation. They were glad, of course, that they could finally look forward to returning home, but they could not help thinking of their many comrades who would not be going with them. Tears rolled down many cheeks as thoughts turned to those comrades who had not lived to see this day. And even though the war against Germany was finally over, the fighting in the Pacific continued.[72]

With the war against Japan still to be won, army officials scoured the ranks of the Nisei veterans in Europe for volunteers for language training. The prospect of leaving their buddies in Europe and being sent, ultimately, to the Pacific theater did not appeal to most of the men. They had fought their war—and survived. Many did not want to tempt fate by volunteering for what amounted to another combat assignment. A few of the mainlanders, however, succumbed to the promise of a quick trip back to the United States for training. They would be able to leave Europe right away and have some leave time at home before reporting to Camp Savage. Four officers and 194 enlisted men from the infantry battalions and eighty-nine men from the artillery battalion soon bade goodbye to their comrades and prepared to ship out for the States. A fifty-six-man contingent of artillery volunteers did not even make it out of Germany before hearing about the Japanese surrender, thereby negating the need for a large number of additional Japanese linguists in the army.[73]

CHAPTER NINE

PEACE

"If everything goes okay you can expect me in Denver about the 15th of November."

On May 16, orders arrived that attached the 442nd Regiment, for administrative purposes, to the 71st Antiaircraft Artillery Brigade at Ghedi airfield, south of Brescia in northern Italy. There the Nisei helped disarm and process tens of thousands of German and Italian prisoners of war. Each prisoner had to be searched for weapons and other contraband material and subjected to a thorough delousing with DDT. The Nisei had instructions to allow the prisoners to keep personal items, such as wristwatches or small pocket knives, but they were to confiscate pistols, daggers, cameras, binoculars, and many other such items. And although all of the confiscated items were supposed to be turned in to army authorities, a lot of them found their way into the hands of the GIs and, eventually, home to the States or to Hawaii.

Among the most popular souvenirs were German and Italian pistols. Perhaps the favorites were the venerable Lugers, which had been around since before the First World War, and the more modern P-38s. One man "liberated" a German officer's sword from its owner but had no interest in bringing home a pistol. He said he was "sick of guns." Unfortunately, because rear-area soldiers and sailors aboard ships had virtually no chance of obtaining such souvenirs from the defeated foe, some stole them from the baggage of combat soldiers. One Nisei soldier who had considered himself quite lucky to have acquired both a P-38 and an Italian Beretta discovered that the German handgun had disappeared from his baggage by the time he arrived home.[1]

The eighty-five thousand prisoners vastly exceeded the number of GIs on hand to guard them, but most seemed reconciled to the fact that the war was over and made no effort to escape. They were, after all, probably eating better as prisoners of war than would have been the case if they were still fighting the Americans.

By the middle of June, the number of German prisoners entering the prison compound at Ghedi had slowed to a trickle, and the 442nd Regiment was on the move again. The 206th Army Band went to Milan, the 232nd Engineer Combat Company to Florence, and the infantry battalions relocated about sixty miles to the scenic lakes area near Lecco. For the infantrymen, the stay was a short one. The 442nd had been assigned to continued service in the Mediterranean theater, but after less than a week the designation was changed. It was slated to transfer to the Pacific theater. The men were soon in the midst of rigorous training exercises to prepare them for this deployment. By mid-July, however, they had joined their comrades in the band and engineer company in the Pisa-Leghorn-Florence area guarding prisoners of war again.

Guard duty was much less stressful than combat and there was time at the end of the day for the men to take showers, change into clean clothes, and amuse themselves in any number of ways. There were still duties to be performed, but for the most part these consisted of guarding prisoners of war and other such routines. There was plenty of free time for letter writing, card playing, or just relaxing without fear of imminent combat.

The situation was different for the men of the artillery battalion. They were in Germany, the heart of recent resistance. Army officials were greatly concerned that the German people would resist occupation by the American soldiers and warned the GIs that these civilians were not to be trusted. At first there were very strong prohibitions against GIs having any social contact with the German people. A pamphlet produced and issued by the Twelfth Army Group included this stern warning: "Most . . . German civilians deny being Nazis. They are all 'good' Germans. . . . [Y]ou won't find any German—man, woman or child—who will admit to ever having been a Nazi." "Don't believe there are any 'good' Germans in Germany. . . . Only a few people bucked the Nazis. You won't meet them; the Nazis purged them long ago." This warning was based on more than just speculation. A medic from another

unit wrote to his wife just a few days after the war against Germany
ended. "The people," he wrote, "are typically German—although
they insist as they all do everywhere—they never favored Hitler
and his actions. I'm beginning to wonder," he mused, "where all
his support came from."[3]

In light of these concerns, the army banned all social fraternization between occupying troops and the German people. The GIs,
however, sought out civilians with whom to converse, barter, and
engage in the simplest and most innocent of social interaction.
And some not so innocent. These were, after all, young men in
the prime of their lives, and they craved female companionship
after having been separated from home for, in some cases, several years. One high-ranking officer had proposed that the army
transport as many American women as it could into Germany so
the soldiers would not have any excuse for seeking out German
women. Officials did not follow through on this suggestion, and
one must wonder how many women might have volunteered for
such an "assignment."[4]

In spite of the order against fraternization, it was obvious to
most that the men were going to ignore it. "Soldiers are going to
have their fling," wrote an officer of the 28th Infantry Division,
"regardless of rules or orders. If they are caught they know what
the punishment will be." A soldier caught conversing with a German girl, for example, could be fined as much as a month's pay.
"However," the officer continued, "that is not stopping them."
And he was correct. Many soldiers decided that the risk of facing
a court-martial was small as they sought sexual liaisons with German women. But even the curmudgeon George Patton seemed to
wink at these rules; or, perhaps he simply recognized the purely
commercial nature of some of these encounters, when he said:
"Copulation without conversation is not fraternization."[5]

Such trysts were often with German prostitutes or other women
who had contracted various sexually transmitted diseases. And
since GIs were not reporting their assignations to the pro stations
because they did not want to get into trouble for violating the
ban on fraternization, the rate of venereal disease skyrocketed.
By the end of the summer it had nearly quadrupled to a rate of
190 cases per thousand troops. When the strictures were removed

After Germany's surrender, GIs had time to meet and interact with the civilian population. Here, a Nisei GI enjoys some leisure time with his pretty German girlfriend. Private photo.

Americans and Germans interacted enthusiastically on several social levels.[6]

One member of the artillery battalion was smitten by a local girl, and it seems that this was not a mere physical relationship—not Patton's "copulation without conversation." Even though after October 1 there was no longer a rule against GIs and German girls dating, they were still not allowed to marry. But he could not forget this girl when he returned to the States so he reenlisted in the army, went back to Germany as part of the long-term occupation force, and in 1952 married his German sweetheart.[7]

The various elements of the 522nd Field Artillery Battalion were dispersed, with each of the batteries occupying a different German village. By mid-July, Sergeant Morita's Headquarters Battery, along with Battery C, took up residence in the village of Donauworth, on the Danube River. The men found that good German beer was plentiful and relatively inexpensive. The men from Battery C hung a twenty-five gallon rubberized canvas bag full of beer in the patio of their quarters. Any time of the day or night that a thirsty artilleryman wandered by he could fill his canteen cup from any of the four spigots.[8]

The artillerists found time to produce a mimeographed weekly battalion newsletter that contained information of current interest to the men as well as articles on the battalion's war record. There were several suggestions for a name for the publication—*Muzzle Blast, Cannon Report, Fire Mission, High Explosive,* and *Muzzle Flash* were some that referenced the unit's particular function. One wag suggested *Scars and Gripes* to parody the army's *Stars and Stripes.* Ultimately, however, the name chosen was *High Angle,* a reference to the type of indirect fire that was often employed by the battalion. The newsletter was such a success that beginning with the seventh edition, on July 27, a local civilian print shop was employed to produce a very professional-looking publication on better-quality paper. Everyone in the battalion chipped in a little from each monthly paycheck to cover the cost of production.[9]

The battalion took over the second floor of the Café Engel for use as a clubhouse. Enlisted men used one room and noncommissioned officers used the other. They hired civilian waitresses to serve beer, coffee, and tea in the evenings, and ice cream was also available for those with a sweet tooth.[10]

The men of Battery C finally moved into quarters that were decidedly more comfortable than the leaky tents in which they had been living. The four-story building called the Wagner House was evacuated and turned over to the battery. The mess hall and other administrative offices were on the ground floor, while senior sergeants and officers occupied the second floor. Corporals and fifth grade technicians were on the third floor, and privates moved into the top floor. The permanent roof over their heads, however, was not enough to squelch all of the complaints, particularly those who had to climb the stairs to the top floor several times a day. One suggested remedy was that since privates were at the bottom of the order of rank, they should also be at the bottom level of housing with noncommissioned officers above them and officers on the top floor. Needless to say, this suggestion was not implemented.[11]

The men of the battalion served as military policemen while they were in Donauworth, and one of their tasks was to be alert for fleeing Nazi officials. Headquarters received word that a high-ranking official named Frederick Kops had left Berchtesgaden and was thought to be headed toward Donauworth with a lot of stolen artwork. It was a sharp-eyed (and suspicious) soldier from Headquarters Battery who apprehended a man fitting the general description of Kops, but who claimed that his name was Richard Kopf.[12]

Another time, four of these Special Police, as they were designated, exhibited considerable bravery. The bridge over the Danube near their headquarters was a temporary structure with no guardrails. While crossing this bridge in a small truck some GIs maliciously swerved toward a group of children who were walking across the bridge. Although there was probably no intent to do the children any harm, one little girl lost her balance and fell into the turbulent river below. Two nearby artillerymen were off duty and enjoying the fine summer weather in shorts when the accident occurred. They immediately jumped into the river to save her. They had a difficult time against the swift current, so two more men quickly shucked off their outer garments and joined them in the water. Finally, the four men were able to get the child to shore. Authorities awarded each man the Soldiers' Medal for heroism.[13]

There was also time for sightseeing. Army officials opened up the French Riviera, with segregated facilities for eighteen thousand officers and men. The officers' accommodations were at Cannes, while the enlisted men enjoyed Nice. One of the medics recalled attending the opera in Nice and watching *Carmine* from a plush velvet-curtained box seat that he would never have been able to afford during peacetime. Back in Milan, even though the major opera house was temporarily unusable because of bomb damage, Beniamino Gigli, widely acclaimed as the greatest tenor of his time, sang in such Verdi operas as *Masked Ball* and *La Forza del Destino*. Italy's many historic sites also beckoned. Italian tour guides eagerly showed GIs the reputed birthplace of Christopher Columbus in Genoa, the tomb of Elizabeth Barrett Browning in Florence, and the rebuilt balcony in Verona that was said to have been William Shakespeare's inspiration for one of the scenes in *Romeo and Juliet*.[14]

Soldiers applying for leave usually had to take whatever destination was offered so as not to overwhelm the facilities of the more popular sites. Some lucky troops got five-day visits to Switzerland. A member of Cannon Company spent part of his leave visiting his sister, an army nurse, in a field hospital near Nuremberg. By the time of his visit most of the injured and sick GIs had been sent home, and there were a lot of empty beds. He took advantage of the surplus of beds by sleeping in a different, clean bed every night of his stay there.[15]

Some members of the regiment, such as the regimental chaplain, perhaps had a little more luck than others. In late August he flew to Palestine and spent a week visiting as many biblical locations as time would allow. He found the water in the River Jordan to be a rather dirty green, but he enjoyed the beauty of the Sea of Galilee. Like more recent tourists, he was hounded by souvenir vendors and local guides, many of whom offered competing versions of biblical events. Still, he felt genuinely enriched by the experience and even managed to scoop up a bit of water from the Jordan River into a small bottle that he had brought along for that purpose. "[S]ome day," he wrote in a letter to his wife, "I'll bust it over some converts [*sic*] head and really baptize him."[16]

It is unlikely that very many others in the unit shared the chaplain's enthusiasm for these Middle Eastern sights. Perhaps the most popular destination was Paris, where the American Red Cross took over the management of several hotels for the exclusive use of soldiers. So many soldiers wanted to visit the renowned City of Light that for the first few months after the end of the war in Europe, GIs were restricted to two-day passes.[17]

Sergeant Morita was able to wrangle a three-day pass to Paris by early August, and his experience is probably typical of those who visited the French capital. The train ride from Munich to Paris took the better part of two days. The trains were crowded, accommodations nonexistent. A Headquarters Battery soldier from another battalion found it almost impossible to sleep along the way. "Sleep came on with night," he wrote home, "but there was no room for it. Wedged into a corner next to the window, I tried every move known to contortionist and GI traveler to make myself available to Morpheus—all in vain. When morning came I was still trying to adjust to the unadjustable, and when we entered Paris I was far from feeling healthy and wise."[18]

Morita's original plans called for a room at the Lafayette Club Hotel at 39 Avenue de l'Opera, but instead he checked into Room 35 in the annex of the Garde du Nord at 33 Rue de St. Quentin. Like countless sightseers before him he visited the usual sights— Notre Dame Cathedral, the Eiffel Tower, and the Arc d'Triomphe. He found the price of souvenirs very high, but he did have enough money to take in the show at the Folies Bergère and to visit the Casino de Paris.[19]

Licensed prostitutes made a practice of hanging around outside these Red Cross hotels where they found a ready supply of prospective customers, young men who had been denied female companionship of any kind for many months. In fact, these women of the street often provided soldiers with their first sexual experience. "Solicitation by these rather pathetic girls happened everywhere I went," reported a Caucasian medic to his wife. "It is commonplace in Paree. No embarrassment—hard to believe, but true." While it is not known whether Sergeant Morita patronized such women, it is certain that the opportunity presented itself.[20]

General George Marshall, the army's chief of staff, instructed famed movie director Frank Capra, who was serving as a colonel in the signal corps, to prepare a film to be shown to all troops as soon as possible after the war ended in Europe. The resulting movie, titled *Two Down and One to Go*, was meant to be a boost to soldiers' morale as they contemplated the fact that they had indeed defeated two of the Axis powers, Italy and Germany, and had one more, Japan, to go. Marshall was so anxious for every soldier to see this film that he authorized the use of an airplane to deliver copies of it to garrisons on the Aleutian Islands. Between 80 and 90 percent of all soldiers in the European and Mediterranean theaters saw the film, but gave it mixed reviews. Some saw the movie as an attempt to build up a desire among the recently victorious GIs to join their brethren in the Pacific and help defeat Japan. "But if they think a movie is going to pep this outfit up & make them wildeyed [sic] to go after Tojo," a Caucasian soldier wrote, "they're nuts. Let some of the stateside boys get him." Another man thought that it suggested that since the troops in Europe had done such a good job in defeating Italy and Germany, they would now be sent to help do the same to Japan. As he saw it, "*Two Down and One to Go* probably even had somewhat of a depressing effect—here was a threat to that newly-found security which V-E day had promised." With the war in Europe over, the American soldiers there were anxious to return home and resume their civilian lives. The vast majority of the Nisei soldiers and their officers were glad to leave the military behind them. One perhaps summed up the common soldiers' reactions to peace as eloquently as most when he declared: "Two and a half years of Army life—bivouac fields in Mississippi heat, Louisiana's frost and cold, Italy's dust, vino and Mama mia, the snow and cognac and Oo la la in France, and Schnapps and Deutsch talk in Germany—has been quite tough and strenuous for me and I think I'll live in solitary for a while."[21]

At the end of the First World War, Americans were brought home by unit, but this method had certain built-in problems. It meant that soldiers who were recent replacements went home with their units, while men who had been in other units and overseas longer had to wait until their units' time for redeployment came. Not wanting to repeat this system, the War Department had announced its plan to prioritize the demobilization of soldiers several months before the war in Europe even ended. Because of the length of this war, the often high casualties in certain units, and the fact that such units had large numbers of recently arrived replacement troops, officials in Washington opted for a plan of individual return. This was meant to ensure that the men with the most service would be released first. The system assigned point values for different aspects of service such as longevity, overseas time, and decorations. This way, theoretically at least, the men with the most time overseas in combat would amass enough points to be sent home early. Likewise, the army, aware of the hardships suffered by the families of servicemen, also awarded points to men who were fathers.

Specifically, for each month in the service after September 16, 1940 (the date that the draft was established), a man received one point. He received an additional point for every month he was overseas. (The Hawaiians in the 442nd Combat Team were allowed to count their months at Camp McCoy and Camp Shelby as overseas time.) He earned five points toward discharge for every combat decoration he received. This included the obvious awards like the Purple Heart, the Bronze Star and Silver Star, and the Distinguished Flying Cross (but not the much-coveted Combat Infantry Badge), and it also counted the battle stars awarded by the army for having participated in specific campaigns. And finally, a soldier-father earned twelve points for each child under the age of eighteen (up to a maximum of three children).[22]

On May 10, the army set the minimum number of points necessary for discharge at eighty-five. Men with that many points would receive priority in release from the service unless they possessed some essential skill necessary to prosecute the war against Japan. In that case, they had to remain in the army until a suitable replacement arrived. Sergeant Morita, and virtually every other soldier in the European and Mediterranean theaters counted, and then recounted, his points toward discharge. In addition to the points awarded him because of his length of service and the amount of overseas time he had accumulated, Morita also received five points for his Bronze Star and five points each for having participated in the Rome-Arno Campaign, the Northern Apennine Campaign in Italy, and the Rhineland Campaign in France. His total was seventy-three. He would not be among the first ones going home, but three dozen infantrymen from the 442nd left for home by the end of May.[23]

Then, a few days later, an announcement was made that men with certain military occupational specialties, or MOSs, might have to remain in service beyond the time at which they reached the magic number of discharge points. One of these was Sergeant Morita's MOS 648, radio repairman.[24]

There was some grousing about the system from some infantrymen who believed that air force personnel were awarded a disproportionally high number of decorations, making some of them eligible for return to the States even though they had spent much less time overseas than most of the foot soldiers. An infantry officer in a Caucasian unit claimed that the army air force accounted for more than 83 percent of the decorations in the European theater but only about 9 percent of the casualties. On the other hand, he continued, the infantry took 75 percent of the casualties but received only 9 percent of the decorations. For example, among the decorations awarded to a twenty-six-year-old fighter pilot, each of which earned him five more points, was the Air Medal with thirty-five oak leaf clusters! This man undoubtedly performed heroically, but it was virtually impossible for a foot soldier to amass the same number of discharge points—180—from decorations.[25]

There seemed to be some disparity even within the air force. Air force mechanics who kept the airplane engines running smoothly, for example, were considered part of the Service Group and therefore ineligible for any five-point battle stars. The drivers of the fuel trucks for the bombers, however, were part of the Bomb Group and *did* rate the battle stars.[26]

Many GIs in the Pacific theater were undoubtedly envious of the good fortune of the men in Europe. Their war was over, and they were going home. The point system, however, was intended to apply also to those men still fighting the Japanese. A soldier in the 7th Infantry Division on Okinawa, for example, whooped with joy when he learned that he also had enough points to go home. "That damn point system really worked!" he rejoiced. He was one of thirty high-point soldiers who were notified to leave their foxholes—under cover of darkness—and gather up their gear for the trip home. This contingent of veterans had seen combat! Most were veterans of Attu, Kwajalein, Leyte, Guam, and Okinawa, and none had fewer than 120 discharge points.[27]

The men in Italy spent three weeks at Lecco, which sat upon Y-shaped Lake Como north of Milan—one of the most beautiful locales in northern Italy. The War Department had designated the 442nd Regiment as a Category I unit, slated to remain in Europe on occupation duty instead of being shipped to the Pacific theater. This idyll came to a sudden end on June 19 when the ruling was reversed and the regiment assigned to Category II for use in combat against the Japanese. And although the men remained in their scenic surroundings, they began a vigorous conditioning regimen to get back into combat shape when orders arrived transferring the men back to the region around Pisa and Florence for more guard duty.

There were lots of ways for the soldiers to burn off any excess energy while they waited to go home. There were, of course, the athletic events: baseball, softball, swimming, basketball, and even horseshoes and ping pong. The Fifth Army held swimming competitions and, once again, as at Camp Shelby, the men of the 442nd shone. They captured every first place ribbon but one.

Much had happened while Sergeant Morita was on leave to Paris. On August 6, the day that he caught the train in Munich, a B-29 bomber dropped an atomic bomb over the Japanese city of Hiroshima, obliterating much of the city in an instant. During his first full day in Paris another bomber dropped a second atomic bomb on the Japanese city of Nagasaki. Then, only a day or so after his return from leave, Japan accepted Allied surrender terms and the war was over. No longer was there any need to postpone the return of soldiers from Europe because of their MOSs. The list of such specialties was reduced to three: orthopedic mechanic, fixed station transmitter attendant, and electroencephalographic specialist (whatever that was).[28]

Now the biggest obstacle to complete demobilization was the relative availability of shipping. To move the personnel and equipment of one armored division from Europe to the United States required seventy-five trains just to transport everything to the port of embarkation. Fifteen Liberty ships were then required for the trans-Atlantic voyage.[29]

By September 1, the army newspaper *Stars and Stripes* announced that all men with at least eighty-five points would be back in the United States within sixty days. A week later, the army reduced the "magic number" to eighty, and a week after that to seventy. Sergeant Morita, along with many of his fellow soldiers with the requisite number of points, welcomed the announcement. In the four months between the German surrender and the end of September he had accumulated eight more points for service time and five more for participation in the Central European Campaign. His total thus stood at ninety-one.[30]

As men from particular units began to rotate home, their departure often left these units considerably under their authorized strength, so the low-point men who remained transferred into other units until their turn to go home. For example, in mid-September, 113 men of the 522nd Field Artillery Battalion with fewer than sixty-four points transferred to the 53rd Quartermaster Base Depot, and twenty-eight more went to the 215th Quartermaster Salvage Repair Company. By the first week of October, the 522nd Field Artillery Battalion was officially deactivated.[31]

Traveling USO shows continued to entertain troops who were waiting for their orders home. Soldiers were able to hear the latest music from stateside bands such as that of Les Brown; they could laugh at the antics of comedians like Bob Hope and Phil Silvers; they could ogle Hollywood starlets such as sultry Spanish-born Jinks Falkenberg; and they could sing the latest songs with entertainers like the popular Andrews Sisters or Frank Sinatra. Many soldiers resented Sinatra. They called him "4-F Frankie" because of his 4-F draft status exempting him from military service. (This was due to a punctured eardrum.) To the soldiers, however, he was a seemingly healthy young man who spent the war singing to adoring female fans while they dealt with all the hazards of warfare. The singer, obviously not wanting to alienate a large potential audience for his postwar career, often sought to smooth things over by making some self-deprecating comment about his nickname as soon as he came onstage.[32]

As summer turned to fall, the Nisei in Italy formed a regimental football team, counting on their speed and agility to make up for what they might have lacked in size. Their team finished third in the "Leghorn League," but then went on to play two post-season games against the champion team from the 88th Division. This team, the Blue Devils, had not allowed any points to be scored against them during the regular season, and because of that, perhaps, they did not take the challengers very seriously. But the competitive spirit was extremely strong among the Nisei and they upset the mighty Blue Devils 7–6 on Christmas Day. A rematch a week later resulted in a 13–13 tie.[33]

A year before Germany's capitulation, President Roosevelt had signed into law the Servicemen's Readjustment Act, a measure designed to ease the transition of returning veterans back into civilian life. Perhaps the most important long-term effect of this legislation was that it put higher education within the reach of American men and women who would otherwise not have been able to afford the cost of attending a college or university. Sergeant Morita was one of the many servicemen from that era who planned to use the GI Bill to further his education when they returned home.[34]

The army also arranged for soldiers to take classes at universities in Europe while they waited to go home. These classes provided healthy outlets for the men's energy and helped many of them to begin to prepare for life as civilians. Since no one could know how long they would be in Europe, the courses were necessarily of short duration. Some ran for three weeks, some longer. Courses were soon being offered in a wide variety of subject areas. Theater-level schools opened at Biarritz, on the southwestern coast of France near the Spanish border, and had room for twelve thousand students; and at Shrivenham, England, some seventy miles northwest of London, which could accommodate four thousand more. Each offered university-level courses in eight fields of study, all taught by army officers with advanced college degrees or by American university professors. The abbreviated two-month semesters offered over 250 courses in agriculture, commerce, education, engineering, fine arts, journalism, liberal arts, and science. The army established a third school, also in England, for soldiers seeking more practical training. It offered courses in aircraft and engine repair, auto mechanics, cabinet making, carpentry, construction maintenance, drafting, electrical trades, heavy equipment operator, instrument repair, machine shop, mechanical refrigeration, painting and decorating, plumbing and heating, radio repair, surveying, and welding.[35]

It was impossible to meet the demand for classes in just these three institutions, so army officials quickly arranged for the establishment of other facilities. In Italy, for example, the University of Florence was re-opened with academically qualified American military personnel as instructors. By the middle of August, the Seventh Army in Germany operated over 130 such schools. One of these, operating under the auspices of the XX Corps, was the

Weihenstephan Agricultural and Technical College, about twenty-five miles north of Munich. Subjects there included mathematics and science courses that one would expect to find in almost any university, but also specialized courses such as Beef Production, Successful Poultry Management, Vegetable Growing Business, Marketing Farm Products, Dairy Cattle Selection, and Livestock Production. And at the battalion level the men could sign up for Algebra, Radio for Beginners, Electricity for Beginners, Spoken German, Bookkeeping and Accounting, Introduction to Business Law, Crop Management and Soil Conservation, Elementary Photography, and Auto Mechanics.[36]

The campus contained about two dozen buildings, most of which were put to use by the soldier-students and their instructors. A large operating creamery building provided housing for the Americans, which was particularly handy for those studying courses related to the dairy industry. The ad hoc mess hall contained a section where the men could relax at the end of the class day and drink beer from the nearby Bavarian State Brewery, which had been in continuous operation for almost eight hundred years. The chemistry building did double duty by becoming a movie theater in the evenings where GIs could see different first-run movies every other day. There were no classes on Sunday, so students could patronize an American Red Cross facility on the shore of Würmsee. Boats were available for use on the lake and there was a golf course and tennis courts, all fully stocked with all of the required equipment. Visitors could swim in the lake, go horseback riding, or spend time at a bowling alley.[37]

Sergeant Morita was one of five men from the 522nd Field Artillery Battalion (three of whom were fellow Coloradans) sent to Weihenstephan Agricultural and Technical College for eight weeks beginning in late August. He signed up for a course in college chemistry, no doubt preparing to continue his college education in pursuit of a degree in pharmacy after his military service was completed.[38]

Sergeant Morita finally received travel orders on October 31, directing him to report to a huge staging area at Le Havre, France. This and other port staging areas were beehives of activity as personnel checked rosters to make sure that soldiers presenting themselves for shipment home had the requisite number of points. Then those who needed booster shots or delousing were taken care of. Other personnel ensured that all baggage was properly tagged, and no soldier was allowed to bring home more than twenty-five pounds of baggage in excess of his military issued gear. Those bringing home captured enemy weapons, like Sergeant Morita's .32-caliber Walther semi-automatic pistol, had to have all of the proper clearances. It was also here that the soldiers converted their foreign currency into American dollars, although many, like Sergeant Morita, held on to a few souvenir bills.

And then, finally, it was time to board a ship and go home. After the Japanese surrender there was no more need to employ ships to supply the troops in the Pacific, and every ship imaginable was pressed into duty bringing troops home from all theaters. The ships that brought the soldiers home from Europe made considerably better time than when they had sailed in the other direction. These included Victory Ships, bigger and faster than the earlier Liberty Ships, converted passenger liners, and two captured enemy ships, the German *Europa* and the Italian *Vulcania*, were even pressed into service. The giant British liners *Queen Elizabeth* and *Aquitania* were each big enough and fast enough to bring home twenty thousand soldiers per month, but the British government laid claim to them again, and they became unavailable. Even the battleship USS *Washington* and three heavy cruisers ferried soldiers back to the States, and some even came home on an aircraft carrier. No longer was it necessary for American ships to travel in large convoys, protected by warships against the threat of German submarine wolfpacks.[39]

"It seemed unreal," recalled one homeward-bound Nisei soldier, "so unreal that most of us got on the troopship . . . bound for New York as if we were heading for another campaign. But once on the ship, we knew this one was different." It had begun to sink in that the war was truly over. The celebratory mood that soon enveloped these vessels included "a lot of singing—mostly off-key." It did not matter; they were going home.[40]

Even with no German submarines to worry about, Mother Nature sometimes provided some added excitement on the voyage across the Atlantic. One ship developed engine trouble on the way and spent five days dead in the water in the Azores. The *Zanesville Victory*, carrying Sergeant Morita among its anxious passengers, faced rough seas and stormy weather, but still managed to make it to New York City in eight-and-a-half days. The SS *Sheepshead Bay* ran into a violent winter storm in December 1945 that caused the ship's anchor to break loose from its position on deck and clatter around and finally punch a hole in the gunwale, at which point it disappeared over the side. A radar mast also fell victim to the howling winds, and when the ship entered New York Harbor in the midst of a blizzard on New Year's Day, the men on board could barely make out the form of the Statue of Liberty.[41]

Eight hundred military aircraft were also pressed into service in hopes that they could bring home fifty thousand men per month from Europe. A few even came home on one of the B-17 bombers that were put to such use. It was too long of a trip to fly nonstop without refueling, so they flew from Italy to Casablanca to Dakar to Brazil to Miami. But even with all these intermediate stops it got the men home a lot faster than those traveling by ship.[42]

The last contingent of the 442nd Regimental Combat Team still active in Europe finally headed home under the command of Lieutenant Colonel Alfred Pursall, who had commanded the 3rd Battalion during most of the fighting. These soldiers lined the rails of the SS *Wilson Victory* as it entered New York harbor on July 4, 1946. Crowds on the docks cheered and whistled, and New York City fire boats arched streams of water into the air in welcome. Lady Liberty stood with her welcoming torch held high, the same torch that was emblazoned on the shoulder patches of these Nisei soldiers. Once on dry land again, it was off to Camp Kilmer, New Jersey, for a week and a half, and then on to the nation's capital for a welcome-home visit by President Harry Truman.

It was hot on July 15 as the soldiers stepped smartly along Constitution Avenue on the way to the White House. Government workers had extended lunch hours that day so they could watch the parade. A summer storm came up and dampened clothing, although probably not the enthusiasm showered upon the veterans. The parade ended at the grassy Ellipse near the White House, and the soldiers stood at ease until the arrival of the chief executive, at which time Colonel Pursall brought his men smartly to attention.

The president congratulated the soldiers for having "fought for the free nations of the world" along with all the others who had shared that duty. "You fought not only the enemy, but you fought prejudice—and you have won. Keep up that fight, and we will continue to win—to make this great Republic stand for just what the Constitution says it stands for: the welfare of all the people all the time." The color guard then stepped forward as Truman, the old artillery captain from World War I, crisply saluted and then affixed yet another citation streamer to the regimental flag. Upon the conclusion of the ceremony these men, like those who had returned before them, were ready to put the military behind them.[43]

Returning GIs reported to one of two dozen separation centers for final processing. Upon arrival at one of these, usually one closest to a soldier's home, they were assigned temporary housing and began filling in what must have seemed like an endless number of forms. They turned in all excess clothing and underwent physical and psychiatric examinations to determine whether they were healthy enough to return to civilian society. Another reason for these examinations was to document all of a soldier's health problems so he could not later submit claims for pensions based upon injuries received in the service.

Next, each soldier's record was examined to determine what medals and decorations he had earned. Because the metal that was used to manufacture the medals was still on the list of strategic materials, even though hostilities had completely ended, most soldiers being separated from the service received only a small ribbon for each medal they were to receive. When manufacture of the medals commenced, in the not too distant future, the government would mail them to the deserving veterans.

Sergeant Morita qualified for the American Defense Service Medal, which was awarded to all members of the armed forces who had any active duty time before December 7, 1941; the American Campaign Medal, which was awarded to all service members with at least one year of service within the continental United States between December 7, 1941 and March 2, 1946; the European-African-Middle Eastern Campaign Medal, which recognized any service within those areas between December 7, 1941 and March 2, 1946; the World War II Victory Medal, which went to every member of the armed forces who had served between December 7, 1941 and December 31, 1946; the Good Conduct Medal, for having had a clean record with no important infractions; and the Bronze Star Medal for his performance during the fighting in the Vosges Mountains of France.

Other decorations (such as battle stars) were awarded for participation in specific campaigns. These were small metal stars, about three-sixteenths of an inch across, that a recipient would affix to the appropriate ribbon bar on his uniform. Sergeant Morita earned four such awards: Rome-Arno, which covered service in Italy between January 22, 1944 and September 9, 1944; Northern Apennines, which covered service in Italy any time between September 10, 1944 and April 4, 1945; Rhineland, which covered service in France and Germany between September 15, 1944 and March 21, 1945; and Central Europe, which covered service in Germany between March 22, 1945 and May 11, 1945. Members of the infantry battalions of the combat team, because they went back to Italy instead of into Germany with the artillery battalion, did not merit the Central Europe battle star. Instead, they received a star for service in the Po Valley Campaign in northern Italy between April 5, 1945 and May 8, 1945. The men of the original 100th Battalion also earned a campaign star for the Naples-Foggia Campaign in Italy, covering service there between August 18, 1943 and January 21, 1944, and one for the Anzio Campaign, covering service between January 22, 1944, and May 24, 1944.

American soldiers also sometimes received decorations from grateful foreign countries for particularly valorous actions. One such medal, the Italian Cross for Military Valor, left its Nisei recipient at a loss to explain how he had earned it. He was not a combat soldier at all, but rather the regiment's public relations officer. The accompanying certificate praised him for having processed more than twenty-seven hundred stories that focused attention on the bravery and dedication of his fellow soldiers. "How a noncombatant won the Italian medal for military valor," he later mused, "I do not know."[44]

Infantrymen who had performed satisfactorily in actual combat—and this was the huge percentage of them—received the Combat Infantryman Badge to wear on their uniforms above their

Hula dancers entertain the returning Hawaiian soldiers. Signal Corps photo.

other decorations. This badge, highly prized by all who wear it, consists of a blue enameled rectangle about three inches long. On the rectangle, and facing the wearer's right, is a silver flint-lock musket encircled by a silver wreath. Members of the Anti-Tank Company earned two other distinctive awards. One was a pair of silver wings with a head-on view of a glider emblazoned on them. These, similar to the wings worn by paratroopers signifying completion of parachute training, likewise denoted the completion of glider infantry training. Then, when the anti-tankers rode the gliders into southern France they earned the right to wear a small bronze arrowhead on their European-African-Middle Eastern Campaign Medals to show that they had participated in an actual invasion.

Finally, it was time to go home. The soldiers paraded for one last ceremony, where officers addressed them, praising them for their valor, thanking them for their service, and urging them to return to civilian life as good, productive citizens. Each man then

Home at last, these happy GIs disembark from the transport ship Waterbury Victory *in Honolulu. Signal Corps photo.*

filed past an officer and picked up his discharge certificate. For Sergeant Morita, this took place on November 27, 1945, and then it was just a short trip home from the separation center at Fort Logan in Denver, Colorado, to his father's farm.

Some men never got past the feeling of bitterness and betrayal caused by the government's relocation policy, but few took it to the extreme that Shinkichi George Tajiri did. Most of the men on the combat team had two given names. There might be a Japanese first name and an American middle name, or the other way around. Sergeant Morita's full name, for example, was Carl Katsumi Morita, although he almost always went by Carl. Tajiri, on the other hand, was so incensed by the relocation camps that he insisted on using only his Japanese name. After the war was over, he returned to the United States for a few years but then moved to Europe where he became a highly celebrated artist. Uetaro

Sammonji was also bitter. He had let it be known to his comrades that if he should be killed fighting in Europe that they should bury his body there rather than return it to the United States. The Europeans, he believed, would show more respect to his memory than the government that had imprisoned so many of his kind. And when he was killed in action on October 28, 1944, he got his wish and was buried in France.[45]

Some returning veterans still occasionally encountered racism. In a small town near San Francisco, Lieutenant Inouye, still wearing his uniform with an empty sleeve where his right arm had been, stopped at a barber shop for a trim. But before he could even enter the shop, an employee met him at the door. "You're a Jap," he informed the soldier, "and we don't cut Jap hair." Another veteran, also in uniform, had a similar experience in another California barber shop. The Caucasian barber asked him if he was Hawaiian, probably having heard of the war record of the "Hawaiian" 442nd Regiment. When he replied that no, he was Japanese, the barber refused to cut his hair.[46]

Sometimes these encounters ended on more positive notes. Proudly wearing his uniform, with a chest full of ribbons, a Nisei veteran boarded a bus in his hometown of Los Angeles just after the war. As he stepped onto the vehicle, a woman passenger in the front seat loudly muttered, "Damn Jap." Before the soldier could even react to this rude comment, the driver, who had only recently returned from military service himself, stopped the bus. "Lady," he said as he turned to the outspoken passenger, "apologize to this American soldier or get off my bus." She could not bring herself to apologize and quickly became a pedestrian.[47]

Some men remained in uniform. Not a few company-grade officers—and this included enlisted men who had earned field promotions—found life in the postwar army appealing and made careers in it. Many saw service in Korea and even Vietnam before retiring. Young Oak Kim, the popular Korean American officer, left the army at the end of the war, but reenlisted when war broke out again in Korea in 1950. He ultimately commanded a battalion in the 7th Infantry Division during this conflict and retired as a colonel in 1972. Hiroshi Miyamura, who joined the 442nd in Europe too late to see any action against the Germans, later served in

Korea where he was awarded the Medal of Honor for outstanding heroism.[48]

Some veterans of the 442nd found that the recognition of their contributions to the American character helped to open doors to various civilian pursuits, including politics. The high percentage of Hawaii's population that was of Japanese ancestry probably made it a little easier for Hawaiian Nisei to enter politics than might have been the case on the mainland, and quite a few did so, both at the territorial level and, after statehood in 1959, the state level. One such man was Daniel Inouye, whose dreams of becoming a doctor were shattered along with his right arm in 1945. After the war, Inouye, like John F. Kennedy, Richard M. Nixon, and many other veterans, went into politics. When Hawaii became a state Inouye was its first representative to the U.S. Congress. He was then elected to the U.S. Senate in 1962 where he served until his death in 2012. Other men went on to distinguished careers in the law, science, academia, and the arts.

Almost half of the sixteen million men and women in the service took advantage of the educational opportunities offered by the Servicemen's Readjustment Act of 1944—or GI Bill—to earn college degrees, and that included many of the Nisei veterans. Some earned doctoral degrees and became renowned experts on such topics as entomology, plant and animal physiology, and virology. Others became successful medical doctors, engineers, or lawyers. But the GI Bill was not just for those wanting to earn advanced degrees or, indeed, for those attending college classes at all. It also provided financial assistance for veterans who wanted to obtain technical training to prepare them for any number of jobs.

Carl Morita was one such veteran. Even though he had earned some college credits before the war and had expressed a desire to return to college to earn a degree in pharmacy, he returned to farming instead. Perhaps he felt an obligation to help his father on the farm, since he was the oldest son who was not already married and raising a family. He did, however, use some of his GI Bill benefits to achieve his long-held desire to learn to fly. He had applied for flight training almost as soon as he entered the army back in 1941, but nothing came of that. But in 1948 he signed up for lessons at Modern Air Service. Ultimately, he obtained a commercial pilot's license, and although he never flew for a major airline, he was able to augment his farm income by flying crop dusters.[49]

Although the 442nd Regimental Combat Team produced its share of scientists, politicians, engineers, and professors, Carl Morita's experience was probably characteristic of the vast majority of World War II veterans. They returned to the United States and soon were immersed in efforts to make their livings in a wide variety of occupations. Morita married Tachi Uno, the younger sister of his wartime buddy, Tomoji "Moe" Uno, and began raising a family that included two daughters and a son.

"I just wanted to make a living[,] get married[,] and have a family," Morita responded to a question about what he expected to achieve as a civilian. And then, when asked if those expectations had been realized, he answered: "100%."[50]

Epilogue

Did these Japanese American soldiers defeat Nazi Germany all by themselves? Of course not. Were they all heroes? No. Did any of them ever actually shirk their duty by feigning injury? Yes. Did any of them kill German prisoners? Yes. In other words, the individual members of this unit were in almost every respect much like all the other GIs of World War II. The medals they earned represented the tangible rewards for what the Nisei soldiers had accomplished while fighting their nation's enemy. Less easily measured is the impact that their service had on convincing their fellow citizens to accept them as loyal Americans, regardless of their ancestry. One indicator of their success in this regard was their employment in racially integrated units in America's next war, in Korea. The bravery and the patriotism exhibited by Japanese Americans—both in and out of uniform—went a long way toward dispelling racial animosity toward them from other Americans and were undoubtedly in the minds of at least some congressmen and senators when they passed the Immigration and Nationality Act of 1952. The law finally allowed Japanese immigrants, including the parents of many of these soldiers, to apply for U.S. citizenship.

Some will argue that the 442nd Regimental Combat Team was the most highly decorated unit of its size and length of service in the entire U.S. Army in World War II. Not everyone agrees. But it is undeniable that the 442nd Regimental Combat Team was certainly *one* of the army's most highly decorated units. Its members were awarded almost every decoration for valor that existed, including more than fifty Distinguished Service Crosses, hundreds of Silver Stars, and thousands of Bronze Stars and Purple Hearts (but no Medals of Honor). The family of Sadao Munemori, who had thrown himself onto an enemy grenade to save the lives of two other men, received, in his honor, the Distinguished Service Cross, the nation's second-highest award. It required the postwar effort of U.S. Senator Albert Thomas (D-Utah) to get Munemori's award upgraded to the Medal of Honor.

Many years after the war, interested persons discovered that not only had Sadao Munemori been the only Nisei to receive the Medal of Honor, but no African Americans had been awarded the medal in *either* of the two world wars, even though there were several instances of extreme heroism exhibited by men from both racial groups. A committee investigated the possibility that such lack of recognition might have been racially motivated and set about reviewing the applicable records. Thus, in April 1991, President George H. W. Bush presented a posthumous Medal of Honor to the elderly sister of an African American soldier who had earned it by virtue of his heroic performance in World War I. Subsequently, after further investigation, President William J. Clinton, on January 13, 1997, presented seven Medals of Honor to black soldiers from World War II who had received the Distinguished Service Cross.

Seeing the successful outcome in recognizing the bravery of African American soldiers in the world wars, U.S. Senator Daniel Akaka (D-Hawaii) asked for a review of the records of Japanese American soldiers who had received lesser decorations for valor. After rigorous study, twenty more veterans of the 442nd Regimental Combat Team were presented with the Medal of Honor. Among these were U.S. Senator Dan Inouye and Company I's heroic BAR man Barney Hajiro, the former misfit from Company M. President Clinton made the formal awards at the White House on June 21, 2000. After reading the list of names to receive the medal, Clinton said: "They left a lasting imprint on the meaning of America. They didn't give up on our country, even when too many of their countrymen and women had given up on them. They deserve, at the least, the most we can give—the Medal of Honor." It is unfortunate that it took more than half a century for this recognition. Most of those so honored were not present at the ceremony. Some, like Private Munemori, gave their lives during the events for which they received the medal. Others died later during the war. Still others have since passed away.[1]

By August 15, 1946, the men of the 442nd Regimental Combat Team had all returned home, except for those who decided to stay in the army for a career, and the unit was officially inactivated on that day in Honolulu. It was reactivated as an army reserve unit the following year and is now designated as the 100th Infantry Battalion of the 442nd Regiment. In fact, this unit is not only the 442nd's only infantry battalion, it is the only infantry battalion in the entire force structure of the army reserve.

It did not see any active service during the Korean War, but in 1968 the army activated it in response to the Tet Offensive in South Vietnam. The battalion remained in the islands, however, and was inactivated again nineteen months later.

The army called the 100th Battalion to active service a second time on August 16, 2004, but this time, after some intense stateside training, it deployed to the seat of war—Iraq. There, the battalion faced a different kind of war than had its parent organization: urban warfare against a non-uniformed enemy that relied heavily on ambush and remotely triggered explosives. According to one man, the time spent overseas was a time of "constantly worrying about where the next mortar round or rocket attack will come from or even if my fellow soldiers will be all right during their patrols outside the wire." Stationed near Balad, north of Baghdad, the battalion helped train Iraqi military and police forces and provided security to Iraqi voters as they went to the polls to validate a national constitution and, later, to elect members to a new national parliament. A possible result of the security was the fact that voter turnout in the battalion's area of responsibility was more than 80 percent. During a second deployment, in 2008, the battalion provided security for convoys heading into Iraq from Kuwait.[2]

The composition of today's battalion is very different than it was during World War II. The men are no longer all of Japanese heritage nor are they all from Hawaii. Most, in fact, are from American Samoa, Guam, and Saipan. And during the battalion's first deployment to Iraq there were almost as many from the mainland to bring the unit up to full strength as there were from

Hawaii. And, as of September 16, 2010, women were members of the battalion. On that date the 740th Combat Support Company was activated and attached to the 100th Battalion, and about fifty of its soldiers are women who specialize in maintenance, transportation, supply, and food services. Upon learning of this change, a ninety-eight-year-old veteran of the original unit said: "That's progress, I guess."[3]

Regardless of the sex or place of birth of the soldiers in today's 100th Battalion, there is still great unit pride among its members. "The best part of being here," declared a young soldier whose grandfather was an original member of the battalion during World War II, "is being in this unit and wearing this patch," adding: "If my grandfather was still alive I'd want him to be as proud of me as I am of him."[4]

Participation in a war, any war, leaves most men with a greater appreciation for life. "War is ugly," is the way a Company I soldier summed it up. "One sees the destruction of bodies, of homes, of villages and cities, and maiming of people, children and adults. I would not recommend or encourage anyone to volunteer his services to engage in such carnage. But, for me," he continued, as if wanting to leave no misunderstanding of his sentiments, "if it is for the defense and freedom of our great nation, I would not hesitate to live my life again as a soldier."[5]

The proud men who served in the various components of the 442nd Regimental Combat Team during World War II, like the millions of other men and women who served in that conflict, will soon all be gone.

Former Staff Sergeant Carl K. Morita, Headquarters Battery, 522nd Field Artillery Battalion, 442nd Regimental Combat Team, died on September 7, 1998.

NOTES

Preface

1. The men who are the main focus of this work considered themselves to be Americans of Japanese descent. They do not, nor therefore do I, use the hyphenated term Japanese-Americans. They are Japanese Americans.

Introduction

1. Thomas D. Murphy, *Ambassadors in Arms: The Story of Hawaii's 100th Battalion* (Honolulu: University of Hawaii Press, 1954), 39 (quotation); J. Garry Clifford and Samuel R. Spencer, Jr., *The First Peacetime Draft* (Lawrence: University Press of Kansas, 1986), 221.

2. "The Draft: Fine Points for Eligibles," *Time*, October 14, 1940, 33; "The Draft: How it Works," *Time*, September 23, 1940, 19–20; "The Draft: Behind the Schedule," *Time*, November 25, 1940, 18 (first quotation); "The Draft: First Conscript," *Time*, October 21, 1940, 23; "The Draft: The Day," *Time*, October 28, 1940, 18 (second quotation).

3. Clifford and Spencer, *Peacetime Draft*, 2.

4. "Jon Blackwell, "1940: You're in the Army Now," *The Trentonian*, 1998–1999, http://www.rootsweb.com/~pasulliv/Draft1940.htm; "The Draft: Only the Strong," *Time*, November 11, 1940, 24; "Draft Lottery Turns Up All Kinds of Americans," *Life*, November 11, 1940, 36–37.

5. "The Draft: How It Works," *Time*, September 23, 1940, 20 (first quotation); Albert A. Blum, *Drafted or Deferred: Practices Past and Present* (Ann Arbor: Bureaus of Industrial Relations, Graduate School of Business Administration, The University of Michigan, 1967), 93–94 (second quotation).

6. This was Tomaru Honda. Interview with Tomaru Honda, May 1, 2000, by the Go For Broke Educational Foundation, http://www.goforbroke.org/oral_histories/oral_histories_hanashi.asp.

7. "Three-Power Pact Between Germany, Italy, and Japan, Signed at Berlin, September 27, 1940," The Avalon Project at Yale Law School, http://www.yale.edu/lawweb/avalon/wwii/triparti.htm (quotation).

8. Carl Morita, "Recollections of Carl Morita"; Army Service Experiences Questionnaire, Department of the Army, U.S. Army Military History Institute, Carlisle Barracks, Pennsylvania.

9. John D. Kenderline, *Your Year in the Army: What Every New Soldier Should Know* (New York: Simon and Schuster, 1940), 19–22; J. A. Power, *You're In the Army Now!* (New York: Paramount, 1940), 15.

10. Carl Morita to his father, July 16, 1941; California Center for Military History, *Camp Roberts*, 21; Marston, "Camp Roberts," 179; Davis says the hospital could only handle 750 patients, "Camp Roberts."

11. Power, *You're In the Army Now!*, 59.

12. Institute of Military Studies, University of Chicago, *A Manual of Basic Military Training*, 10e (Harrisburg, Pa.: The Military Service Publishing Company, 1942), 94; Lee Kennett, *G.I.: The American Soldier in World War II* (New York: Charles Scribner's Sons, 1987), 32 (quotation).

13. Service Record of Carl K. Morita; Marston, "Camp Roberts," 179.

14. War Department, *Basic Field Manual: Soldier's Handbook, July 23, 1941* (Washington, D.C.: Government Printing Office, 1941), 80; Service Record of Carl K. Morita.

15. War Department, *Basic Field Manual, July 23, 1941*, 83–84.

16. Institute of Military Studies, University of Chicago, *A Manual of Basic Military Training*, 680.

17. "World War II—Louisiana Maneuvers," http://www.beau.org/~velmer /local/ww2.html, accessed July 17, 2008; Ricky Robertson, "More Stories of the Great Louisiana Maneuvers," http://www.crt.state.la.us/tourism/lawwii/maneu vers/Robertson/Maneuvers_Stories.htm, accessed July 17, 2008.

18. Frederick Simpich, "Around the Clock With Your Soldier Boy," *National Geographic Magazine* 80, no. 1 (July 1941), 2 (first quotation); Carl K. Morita to his father, September 22, 1941 (second quotation).

19. United States Army, *The New Infantry Drill Regulations* (Harrisburg, Pa.: Military Service Publishing Company, 1943), 223.

20. Douglas E. Wilson, "Remarks on 'Glossary of Army Slang,'" *American Speech* 17, no. 1 (February 1942), 68.

21. Carl Morita to his father, September 22, 1941.

22. William H. Baumer, Jr., *He's In the Army Now* (New York: Robert M. McBride and Company, 1941, 1943), 64.

1. Pearl Harbor and After

1. David M. Kennedy, *Freedom From Fear: The American People in Depression and War, 1929–1945* (New York: Oxford University Press, 1999), 499.

2. Gordon W. Prange, *At Dawn We Slept: The Untold Story of Pearl Harbor* (New York: Penguin Books, 1981), 480, 493.

3. The witness to the attack on Pearl Harbor was Samuel Sasai. Hawaii Nikkei History Editorial Board, comp., *Japanese Eyes American Heart: Personal Reflections of Hawaii's World War II Nisei Soldiers* (Honolulu: Tendai Educational Foundation, 1998), 86 (first quotation); The soldier was Akiji Yoshimura. Bill Hosokawa, *Nisei: The Quiet Americans* (New York: William Morrow and Company, 1969), 229 (second quotation); Ralph Tempuku in Tomi Kaizawa Knaefler, *Our House Divided: Seven Japanese American Families in World War II* (Honolulu: University of Hawaii Press, 1991), 89 (third quotation).

4. Conrad Tsukayama was the one with the close-up view of the Japanese pilot. *Japanese Eyes American Heart*, 13 (first quotation), 16; Tom Mizuno was the civilian who was spared that day. *Japanese Eyes American Heart*, 33.

5. Interview with Nelson Akagi, August 15, 2002, by the Go For Broke Educational Foundation, Tape #2. All of the interviews by the Go For Broke Educational Foundation cited in this chapter may be found at: http://www.goforbroke.org/oral_histories/oral_histories_hanashi.asp. Lawson Fusao Inada, ed., *Only What We Could Carry: The Japanese American Internment Experience* (Berkeley, Calif.: Heyday Books and San Francisco: California Historical Society, 2000), 59; Thomas K. Walls, *The Japanese Texans* (San Antonio: University of Texas Institute of Texas Culture at San Antonio, 1987), 13.

6. *Japanese Eyes American Heart*, 95; the scared Guardsman was Ted Tsukiyama. Knaefler, *Our House Divided*, 35 (first quotation); Lyn Crost, *Honor by Fire: Japanese Americans at War in Europe and the Pacific* (Novato, Calif.: Presidio Press, 1994), 10; the guardsman who had not yet learned to load his rifle was Conrad Tsukayama. *Japanese Eyes American Heart*, 17 (second and third quotations).

7. Ronald G. Follows, "Monarchs to Missiles: A 75-Year History of Hawaii's National Guard," The National Guard Endowment Foundation, http://www.ngef.org/custom/hing.asp; Murphy, *Ambassadors in Arms*, 44.

8. Hosokawa, *Nisei*, 463.

9. The president of the JACL was Saburo Kido. Hosokawa, *Nisei*, 225 (first quotation); the student was Shig Wakamatsu. Hosokawa, *Nisei*, 231 (second quotation); the Japanese Texan was Henry Kawahata. Walls, *The Japanese Texans*, 16 (third quotation).

10. Greg Robinson, *By Order of the President: FDR and the Internment of Japanese Americans* (Cambridge, Mass., and London: Harvard University Press, 2001), 84–87.

11. Robinson, *By Order of the President*, 67–69.

12. Dorothy Matsuo, *Boyhood to War: History and Anecdotes of the 442nd Regimental Combat Team* (Honolulu: Mutual Publishing, 1982), 22.

13. This was Akiji Yoshimura. Hosokawa, *Nisei*, 230.

14. Hosokawa, *Nisei*, 259; Betty E. Mitson, "Looking Back in Anguish: Oral History and Japanese-American Evacuation," *The Oral History Review* 2 (1974), 36, 40 (quotation).

15. Eric L. Muller, *Free to Die for Their Country: The Story of the Japanese American Draft Resisters in World War II* (Chicago and London: University of Chicago Press, 2001), 24–25.

16. "How to Tell Japs From the Chinese," *Life* (December 22, 1941), 81–82 (first quotation); Milt Caniff, "How to Spot a Jap," *A Pocket Guide to China* (Special Services Division, Services of Supply, United States Army: Washington, D.C.: 1942), 68 (second quotation).

17. Thelma Chang, *"I Can Never Forget": Men of the 100th/442nd* (Honolulu: Sigi Productions, 1991), 89.

18. Hosokawa, *Nisei*, 266 (first quotation); William Dudley, ed., *Japanese American Internment Camps* (San Diego: Greenhaven Press, 2002), 49 (second quotation); Arvarh E. Strickland, "Remembering Hattiesburg: Growing Up Black in Wartime Mississippi," in Neil R. McMillen, ed., *Remaking Dixie: The Impact of World*

War II on the American South (Jackson: University Press of Mississippi, 1997), 91 (third quotation); Dudley, *Internment Camps*, 50.

19. Muller, *Free to Die for Their Country*, 25 (first quotation), 23 (second quotation).

20. Executive Order No. 9066, as reproduced in Wendy Ng, *Japanese American Internment During World War II: A History and Reference Guide* (Westport, Conn. and London: Greenwood Press, 2002), 155 (quotation); Roy Ito, *We Went to War: The Story of the Japanese Canadians Who Served During the First and Second World Wars* (Stittsville, Ontario: Canada's Wings, Inc., 1984), 147.

21. Ito, *We Went to War*, 124–25, 147–48.

22. Earl Warren's testimony before the House Select Committee Investigating National Defense Migration on February 21 and 23, 1942, as reported in Dudley, *Internment Camps*, 24–29.

23. Ellen Eisenberg, "'As truly American as your son': Voicing Opposition to Internment in Three West Coast cities," *Oregon Historical Quarterly* (December 2003): http://www.accessmylibrary.com/coms2/summary_0286-2854550_ITM.

24. Hosokawa, *Nisei*, 271–72.

25. Muller, *Free to Die for Their Country*, 176; Minoru Kiyota, *Beyond Loyalty: The Story of a Kibei*, trans. Linda Klepinger Keenan (Honolulu: University of Hawaii Press, 1997), 62.

26. Muller, *Free to Die for Their Country*, 27–28.

27. Muller, *Free to Die for Their Country*, 30; this was Ernest Uno's recollection. Inada, *Only What We Could Carry*, 40, 70 (first quotation); this was Yoshiko Uchida's recollection. Inada, *Only What We Could Carry*, 71 (second quotation).

28. Muller, *Free to Die for Their Country*, 28–29.

29. Jack Morita to Carla Morita, March 27, 2000.

30. Murphy, *Ambassadors in Arms*, 52; Katsugo Miho remembers that it was about March 1942. Knaefler, *Our House Divided*, 35; this was Ralph Yempuku. Franklin Odo, *No Sword to Bury: Japanese Americans in Hawai'i During World War II* (Philadelphia: Temple University Press, 2004), 127 (first quotation); this was Ted Tsukiyama. John Tsukano, *Bridge of Love* (Honolulu: Hawaii Hosts, Inc., 1985), 54 (second quotation).

31. This was Wallace Nunotani in Chang, *"I Can Never Forget,"* 98 (quotation).

32. Odo, *No Sword to Bury*, 97; Yutaka Nakahata and Ralph Toyota, "Varsity Victory Volunteers: A Social Movement," *Social Process in Hawaii* 8 (1943), 30 (quotation).

33. Nakahata and Toyota, "Varsity Victory Volunteers," 31; this was Ralph Yempuku. Knaefler, *Our House Divided*, 89 (quotation), 96.

34. The man who designed the emblem was Junichi Buto Odo, *No Sword to Bury*, 173, 175, 178, 196.

35. Odo, *No Sword to Bury*, 207–208; Nakahata and Toyota, "Varsity Victory Volunteers," 32; Odo, *No Sword to Bury*, 202; this was Richard Chinen. Odo, *No Sword to Bury*, 201.

36. Nakahata and Toyota, "Varsity Victory Volunteers," 31–33.

37. Nobo Ikuta, "My Many Steps From Childhood to Adulthood," The Men of I Company 442nd Regimental Combat Team, *And Then There Were Eight* (Honolulu: 442nd Veterans Club, 2003), 157.

38. Service Record of Carl K. Morita; Carl Morita, "Recollections of Carl Morita."

39. Susumu Ito was the unhappy soldier at Fort Sill; Chang, *"I Can Never Forget,"* 94 (first quotation). Yuki "Uke" Minaga was the goldbrick; "Chronicles of My Lifetime," *And Then There Were Eight*, 89. The engineer was Kenneth Otagaki. Chang, *"I Can Never Forget,"* 99. The 7th Division soldier was Tadashi Sakai. Matsuo, *Boyhood to War*, 37–38 (second quotation).

40. Matsuo, *Boyhood to War*, 39; Ronald Oba, *The Men of Company F, 442nd Regimental Combat Team* (Honolulu: 1993), 13; Tanaka, *Go For Broke: A Pictorial History*, 19 (quotation); Tanaka, *Go For Broke: A Pictorial History*, 18.

41. Interview with Norman Ikari, June 27, 1999, by the Go For Broke Educational Foundation, Tape #2; William K. Emerson, *Chevrons: Illustrated History and Catalog of U.S. Army Insignia* (Washington, D.C.: Smithsonian Institution Press, 1983), 190; Carl Morita to his brother, August 18, 1942 (quotation).

42. Murphy, *Ambassadors in Arms*, 41–42, 60.

43. This was Rev. Masao Yamada. Tsukano, *Bridge of Love*, 65.

44. The soldier who thought he was destined for a labor battalion was Spark Matsunaga. Matsuo, *Boyhood to War*, 32 (quotation).

45. Murphy, *Ambassadors in Arms*, 62.

46. Murphy, *Ambassadors in Arms*, 60.

47. Murphy, *Ambassadors in Arms*, 69–70.

48. Matsuo, *Boyhood to War*, 32; Masayo Umezawa Duus, *Unlikely Liberators: The Men of the 100th and 442nd*, trans. Peter Duus (Honolulu: University of Hawaii Press, 1987), 25; Richard Halloran, *Sparky: Warrior, Peacemaker, Poet, Patriot: A Portrait of Senator Spark M. Matsunaga* (Honolulu: Watermark Publishing, 2002), 39.

49. Murphy, *Ambassadors in Arms*, 71.

50. Murphy, *Ambassadors in Arms*, 71 (quotation), 73.

51. http://www.globalsecurity.org/military/facility/fort-mccoy.htm; http://www.mccoy.army.mil/FactsSheets/index.asp?id=wwii; Kazuo Sakamaki, *I Attacked Pearl Harbor*, trans. Toru Matsumoto (New York: Association Press, 1949), 57.

52. Murphy, *Ambassadors in Arms*, 76.

53. Murphy, *Ambassadors in Arms*, 75–76.

54. Tanaka, *Go For Broke*, 25.

55. This was Tsuyoshi Furukawa. Thomas Taro Higa, *Memoirs of a Certain Nisei, 1916–1985*, trans. Mitsugu Sakihara, ed. Elsie Higa Taniguchi (Kaneohe, Hawaii: Higa Publications, 1988), 44.

56. Murphy, *Ambassadors in Arms*, 78.

57. Samuel Hideo Yamashita, "The Aloha Team, 1942–1943," *More Than a Game: Sport in the Japanese American Community*, ed. Brian Niiya (Los Angeles: Japanese American Museum, 2000), 165; Steering Committee, *The Boys of Company "B"* (Honolulu: Hawaii Hochi, 1981), 14.

58. The "Four Musketeers," all from Company B, were: Fred Kanemura, James Komatsu, Isao Nadamoto, and Richard Oguro. Steering Committee. *The Boys of Company "B,"* 14.

59. Murphy, *Ambassadors in Arms*, 81.

60. Higa, *Memoirs of a Certain Nisei*, 40–41.

61. Interview with Robert Aoki, August 24, 2000, by the Go For Broke Educational Foundation, Tape #1; Murphy, *Ambassadors in Arms*, 83.

62. Murphy, *Ambassadors in Arms*, 78.

63. The officers were Maj. James Lovell, 1st Lts. Rocco Marzano and Ernest Tanaka. Tanaka, *Go For Broke*, 14. According to one of these men, Raymond R.

Nosaka, the members of this detail were Robert Goshima, Masao Hatanaka, Noburo Hirasuna, Masao Koizumi, Herbert Ishii, Fred Kanemura, James Komatsu, Masami Iwashita, John Kihara, Katsumi Maeda, Koyei Matsumoto, Toshio Mizusawa, Taneyoshi, Nakano, Tokujii Ono, Tadao Hodai, Seiji Tanigawa, Yasuo Takata, Robert Takashige, William Takaezu, Seiei Okuma, Patrick Tokushima, Takeshi Tanaka, Mack Yazawa, Yukio Yokota, and Raymond R. Nosaka. *Japanese Eyes American Heart,* 156. The inquisitive passenger was Tokuji Ono; interview with Tokuji Ono, September 27, 2003, Tape #4, the Go For Broke Educational Foundation; "Fort Massachusetts," http://www.nps.gov/guis/extended/MIS/M History/Forts.htm, accessed January 2, 2006.

64. The dog lover was Raymond Nosaka. *Japanese Eyes American Heart,* 157.

65. Duus, *Unlikely Liberators,* 49.

66. Interview with Tokuji Ono, Tapes #4 and #5.

67. Duus, *Unlikely Liberators,* 48–49.

68. This was Yasuo Takata. Tanaka, *Go For Broke,* 14.

69. This was Hajime Yamane. Interview with Hajime Yamane, August 23, 2000, by the Go For Broke Educational Foundation, Tape #2.

70. http://www.globalsecurity.org/military/facility/camp-shelby.htm, accessed December 28, 2005.

71. Wayne Kirby, "Memories That Won't Fade," in Morris Courington, ed., *Cruel Was the Way: Memories of Combat Infantrymen in World War II* (Park Forest, Ill.: Velletri Books, 2000), 221.

72. This was Neil Nagareda in Hawai'i Holocaust Project, *Days of Remembrance: Hawai'i Witnesses to the Holocaust* (Manoa: Center for Oral History, Social Sciences Research Institute, University of Hawai'i at Manoa, 1991), II, 513.

73. Murphy, *Ambassadors in Arms,* 91.

74. Murphy, *Ambassadors in Arms,* 96.

2. Birth of the 442nd

1. Duus, *Unlikely Liberators,* 56.

2. Muller, *Free to Die for Their Country,* 33 (first quotation); Ed Quillen, "Honor Carr Somehow," *Denver Post,* August 14, 2007 (second quotation); http://www.denverpost.com/quillen/ci_6613908; Jason Morgan Ward, "'No Jap Crow': Japanese Americans Encounter the World War II South," *Journal of Southern History* 73, no. 1 (February 2007), 85 (third quotation).

3. Hosokawa, *Nisei,* 225; Colorado Historical Society, Historic Marker Program, http://www.coloradohistory.org/RIPsigns/show_markertext.asp?id=811 (quotations).

4. Toyo Suyemoto, "Another Spring," *Last Witnesses: Reflections on the Wartime Internment of Japanese Americans,"* ed. Erica Harth (New York: Palgrave, 2001), 31 (quotation); Kiyota, *Beyond Loyalty,* 76.

5. Interview with Joe Inami, March 6, 2004, by the Go For Broke Educational Foundation, Tape #4. All of the interviews by the Go For Broke Educational Foundation cited in this chapter may be found at: http://www.goforbroke.org/oral_histories/oral_histories_hanashi.asp. Inada, *Only What We Could Carry,* 161–62.

6. Murphy, *Ambassadors in Arms,* 106.

7. Murphy, *Ambassadors in Arms,* 106–107.

8. Murphy, *Ambassadors in Arms*, 56; Hosokawa, *Nisei*, 260 (quotation).

9. Chang, *"I Can Never Forget,"* 102; Duus, *Unlikely Liberators*, 59.

10. *Pacific Citizen*, May 12, 1945 (first quotation); the World War I veteran was Joe Kurihara. Hosokawa, *Nisei*, 361–62 (second quotation); Crost, *Honor by Fire*, 65.

11. Interview with Mitsuru Doi, June 7, 1999, by the Go For Broke Educational Foundation, Tape #1; Murphy, *Ambassadors in Arms*, 112.

12. The 4'9" soldier was Takeshi Kazumura. Crost, *Honor by Fire*, 152; the man who memorized the eye chart was Joe Tanaka. Matsuo, *Boyhood to War*, 53; the man who doubted the validity of the medical examinations was Karou Watanabe. Matsuo, *Boyhood to War*, 48 (quotation); the soldier was Bill Mauldin. Albert E. Cowdrey, *Fighting for Life: American Military Medicine in World War II* (New York: The Free Press, 1994), 22.

13. Oral history of Ray Nosaka, Center for Oral History, University of Hawaii, http://nisei.hawaii.edu/object/io_1153256822062.html. Interview with George Ishihara, February 6, 2000, by the Go For Broke Educational Foundation, Tape #3; interview with Henry Yoshitake, April 30, 2001, by the Go For Broke Educational Foundation, Tape #3; interview with Susumu Ito, January 23, 2000, by the Go For Broke Educational Foundation, Tape #7; the wounded seninbari-wearer was Mickey Akiyamna. Carol Lynn Akiyama, "Mickey Makio Akiyama: A Brief History," http://www.javadc.org/MICKEY%20MAKIO%20AKIYAMA.htm.

14. Daniel K. Inouye with Lawrence Elliott, *Journey to Washington* (Englewood Cliffs, N.J.: Prentice-Hall, 1967), 82–86 (Daniel Inouye quotations); Matsuo, *Boyhood to War*, 47 (last quotation).

15. Oral history of Ronald Oba, Center for Oral History, University of Hawaii, accessed February 16, 2009. The oral histories from the University of Hawaii cited in this and subsequent chapters may be found at: http://nisei.hawaii.edu/object/io_1160629851328.html.

16. Robert Sasaki was the man who enlisted out of monotony. Matsuo, *Boyhood to War*, 52 (first quotation); Takao Ito was the man who enlisted to get out of the pineapple fields. Matsuo, *Boyhood to War*, 53 (second quotation); Charles Shigeru Ota, "A Tale of One Soldier and His Best Friend," *And Then There Were Eight*, 274 (third quotation).

17. Oba, *The Men of Company F*, 9; Crost, *Honor by Fire*, 152; interview with Tomaru Honda, May 1, 2000, by the Go For Broke Educational Foundation, Tape #2.

18. Interview with Tadashi Tojo, January 21, 2002, by the Go For Broke Educational Foundation, Tape #4.

19. The reluctant volunteer was Charlie Higuchi. Oral history of Ronald Oba, University of Hawaii.

20. Hiroshi Aruga, "It Began in Civilian Clothes At the Iolani Palace Grounds," *And Then There Were Eight*, 130; Sadaichi Kubota, *"Esprit de Corps* In The Second Platoon, I Company," *And Then There Were Eight*, 197–98; Tsukano, *Bridge of Love*, 115 (quotation).

21. "Maritime Matters: Ocean Liner History and Cruise Ship News," http://www.maritimematters.com/matsonliners1.html (quotation); Oral history of Katsugo Miho, Center for Oral History, University of Hawaii, http://nisei.hawaii.edu/object/io_1206614351937.html.

22. Oral history of Katsugo Miho.

23. Interview with Joe Inami. Victor Izui was the man who had had second thoughts about enlisting. Interview with Victor Izui, April 29, 2000, by the Go For Broke Educational Foundation, Tape #2 (quotation); Kobe Shoji was the former teacher. Matsuo, *Boyhood to War,* 57.

3. Training

1. James M. Hanley, *A Matter of Honor: A Mémoire* (New York: Vantage Press, 1995), 10.
2. Hanley, *A Matter of Honor,* 12–13; "Charles W. Pence, '18," DePauw University Intercollegiate Athletics, http://www.depauw.edu/ath/hallfame/bios/pence.asp.
3. Takeo Susuki, "Early History of the 522nd Field Artillery Battalion," in The Historical Album Committee of the 522 Field Artillery Battalion of the 442 Regimental Combat Team, *Fire for Effect: A Unit History of the 522 Field Artillery Battalion* (Honolulu, Hawaii: 522nd Field Artillery Battalion Historical Album Committee, 1998), 80 (hereinafter cited as *Fire for Effect*).
4. Chang, *"I Can Never Forget,"* 110.
5. "Troops From Hawaii Formally Welcomed," *Hattiesburg* (Miss.) *American,* April 15, 1943, 7; "Shelby Briefs," *Hattiesburg* (Miss.) *American,* May 10, 1943, 3.
6. From an address by Sherwood Dixon, July 21, 1953, cited in Tsukano, *Bridge of Love,* 318.
7. "Alaskan Members of 442nd Find The South Different," *Hattiesburg* (Miss.) *American,* August 27, 1943, 9.
8. The actual amount was $101,550. "Troops From Hawaii Heavy Bond Buyers," *Hattiesburg* (Miss.) *American,* April 23, 1943, 4; 2,686 according to Orville C. Shirey, *Americans: The Story of the 442d Combat Team* (Nashville: Battery Press, 1946, 1998), 20.
9. The artilleryman was Manabi Hirasaki. Interview with Manabi Hirasaki, April 17, 1999, by the Go For Broke Educational Foundation, Tape #2. All of the interviews by the Go For Broke Educational Foundation cited in this chapter may be found at: http://www.goforbroke.org/oral_histories/oral_histories_hanashi.asp. The surgical technician was Yeechi Kuwayama, Rudi Williams, "Japanese American War Hero Recalls Life During World War II" American Forces Information Service News Article, May 25, 2000. Online at http://www.defenselink.mil/news/May2000/n05252000_20005252.html.
10. *Japanese Eyes American Heart,* 224; War Department, *Technical Manual: The Army Cook* (TM 10-405) (Washington, D.C.: April 24, 1942), 97 (quotation); oral history of Ronald Oba, University of Hawaii.
11. Chang, *"I Can Never Forget,"* 120; Richard Masaichi Oshiro, "The Road Back to Lanai," *And Then There Were Eight,* 269.
12. Rudi Williams, "Japanese American War Hero Recalls Life During World War II"; this was Yutaka "Henry" Ikemoto. Interview with Henry Ikemoto, February 25, 2001, by the Go For Broke Educational Foundation, Tape #2. Tadashi Tojo's family name was originally Iwata. Interview with Tadashi Tojo, January 21, 2002, by the Go For Broke Educational Foundation, Tape #1.
13. "Name Problems Acute in Combat Team," *Hattiesburg* (Miss.) *American,* July 15, 1943, 7; the Caucasian officer was Christopher Keegan. Interview with

Christopher Keegan, June 7, 1999, by the Go For Broke Educational Foundation, Tape #3.

14. "Whitey" was George Oiye. Tara Shioya, "The Conflict Behind the Battle Lines: The Japanese Americans who fought in World War II were engaged in another, private battle, against prejudice and misunderstandings," *The San Francisco Chronicle*, September 25, 1995, 4/Z1, at http://www.sfmuseum.org/war/issei.html (first quotation); the artilleryman was Tadashi Tojo. Shioya, "Conflict Behind the Battle Lines," 4/Z1 (second quotation).

15. Elizabeth Ball Carr, *Da Kine Talk: From Pidgin to Standard English in Hawaii* (Honolulu: The University Press of Hawaii, 1972), 3.

16. Carr, *Da Kine Talk*, 4–6.

17. Carr, *Da Kine Talk*, 150, 131, 4; Allen Okamoto, "It Was Rough Being a 'Penna Kotonk,'" *And Then There Were Eight*, 254–55.

18. Some have suggested that the name comes from the Japanese word *buta*, which means pig, although such a characterization would seem to have been better applied to the seemingly pig-headed mainlanders.

19. Ernest N. Uno, "A 'Kotonk's Welcome Into the 442nd RCT," *And Then There Were Eight*, 329. The corporal, later sergeant, who intervened was Thomas Tamotsu Tamashiro, KIA on July 9, 1944.

20. Matsuo, *Boyhood to War*, 71.

21. Duus, *Unlikely Liberators*, 65; this was George Goto. Chang, *"I Can Never Forget,"* 113 (quotation).

22. Interview with Susumu Ito, January 23, 2000, by the Go For Broke Educational Foundation, Tape #4; interview with Yoshio Kinoshita, July 13, 2001, by the Go For Broke Educational Foundation, Tape #1.

23. Chang, *"I Can Never Forget,"* 117; Oral history of Ronald Oba, University of Hawaii; the man receiving food from home was Susumu Ito. Chang, *"I Can Never Forget,"* 25.

24. The cook was Frank Dobashi. *Japanese Eyes American Heart*, 224.

25. The man who felt like a zoo resident was Neil Nagareda. Interview with Neil Nagareda, June 2, 1988, in *Days of Remembrance: Hawai'i Witnesses to the Holocaust*, vol. 1, 506; Maurice Zolotow, "The Man Who Astonished Hattiesburg," *Saturday Evening Post* 218, no. 19 (November 10, 1945), 94, 96; John Howard, *Concentration Camps on the Homefront: Japanese Americans in the House of Jim Crow* (Chicago: University of Chicago Press, 2008), excerpt at http://www.press.u chicago.edu/Misc/Chicago/354767.html (quotations).

26. "Bogalusans Entertain Soldiers From Hawaii," *Hattiesburg* (Miss.) *American*, June 7, 1943, 4; "442nd Group Visits New Orleans," *Hattiesburg* (Miss.) *American*, July 26, 1943, 6.

27. Strickland, "Remembering Hattiesburg," 93; Mike Masaoka and Bill Hosokawa, *They Call Me Moses Masaoka: An American Saga* (New York: William Morrow and Company, 1987), 143; William T. Schmidt, "The Impact of Camp Shelby in World War II on Hattiesburg, Mississippi," *The Journal of Mississippi History* 39 (February 1977), 47.

28. Inouye and Elliott, *Journey to Washington*, 97 (quotation); Strickland, "Remembering Hattiesburg," 153; *Days of Remembrance*, vol. 1, 125.

29. Chang, *"I Can Never Forget,"* 124; reporting the episode was Mike N. Tokunaga. *Japanese Eyes American Heart*, 373 (first quotation); the officer was Maj.

Emmet O'Connor. Mitsuo Oshiro, "At War's End, Four Things Stood Out in My Mind," *And Then There Were Eight*, 263 (second quotation).

30. Cpl. Bill Hajikawa was the organizer. George M. Tanna, "The 522nd Baseball Team at Shelby," in *Fire for Effect*, 100.

31. Tsukano, *Bridge of Love*, 178; Howard, *Concentration Camps on the Home Front*, 86. The pitcher was Mitsuo "Lefty" Higuchi; the pinch hitter was Duke Wataya; the home run hitter was Goro Kashiwaeda. "442nd Holds Official Shelby Baseball Title," *Hattiesburg* (Miss.) *American*, October 26, 1943, 6.

32. Henry Oshiro was the bantamweight champ and Tsugio Tsukano was the welterweight. Tsukano, *Bridge of Love*, 152; Tommy Umeda, "Hawaiian Nisei Boxer: Yukito 'Tommy' Umeda," *Journal of Combative Sport* (March 2001), http://ejmas.com/jcs/jcsart_umeda_0401.htm, accessed March 10, 2009.

33. Tsukano, *Bridge of Love*, 141.

34. Strickland, "Remembering Hattiesburg," 156 (quotation); obituary for Herbert Masaru Sasaki in *JAVA* [Japanese American Veterans' Association] *Newsletter* 13, no. 2 (April–June 2005); "Hawaiian Troops Start Work After 1st Open House," *Hattiesburg* (Miss.) *American*, May 3, 1943, 9.

35. Howard, *Concentration Camps on the Home Front*, 137.

36. Howard, *Concentration Camps on the Home Front*, 136.

37. "232nd Engineers Group Visits Arkansas Relocation Camp," *Hattiesburg* (Miss.) *American*, August 4, 1943, 5; "442nd Engineers Plan Big Week-End," *Hattiesburg* (Miss.) *American*, September 16, 1943, 9.

38. The thoughtful drinker was Lloyd Onoye. Tanaka, *Go For Broke: A Pictorial History*, 141.

39. Inouye and Elliott, *Journey to Washington*, 88–89, 100.

40. The "stripper" was Noble Taziri. "Shelby Briefs," *Hattiesburg* (Miss.) *American*, June 3, 1943, 3; the emcee was Sgt. Charles Tanaka, the harmonica virtuoso was Tsugio Mizota, Stanley Hashimoto was the jitterbugger, and Lt. Edward H. Graham played the trumpet. "Shelbyettes," *Hattiesburg* (Miss.) *American*, May 26, 1943, 3; "Shelby Briefs," *Hattiesburg* (Miss.) *American*, May 21, 1943, 7 (quotations).

41. The two former band leaders were Herbert Odagawa and Paul Higaki. "442nd Band Toots Into Shape," *Hattiesburg* (Miss.) *American*, June 19, 1943, 8.

42. These were Harold Fukunaga and Robert Kuniyuki, respectively. Matsuo, *Boyhood to War*, 68.

43. John Sloan Brown, *Draftee Division: The 88th Infantry Division in World War II* (Lexington: University Press of Kentucky, 1986), 42.

44. Interview with Michael Akamine. *Days of Remembrance*, vol. 2, 600; interview with Barney Hajiro, June 10, 2000, by the Go For Broke Educational Foundation, Tape #1; the quick-thinking soldier was Ernie Makita. Harold Joji Watase, "Personal Encounters," *And Then There Were Eight*, 36 (quotations).

45. Oral history of Ronald Oba, University of Hawaii.

46. Kiyoshi Harry Shimizu, *Proving Our Loyalty: The World War II Story of a Young Nisei Infantryman Fighting for His Country in the Hundredth Battalion* (ca. 1995), 6.

47. Sherwood Dixon in a speech on July 21, 1953 and cited in Tsukano, *Bridge of Love*, 318.

48. The left-handed shooter was Stanley Akita. Interview with Stanley Akita, October 29, 2001, by the Go For Broke Educational Foundation, Tape #3.

49. Leon C. Standifer, *Not in Vain: A Rifleman Remembers World War II* (Baton Rouge and London: Louisiana State University Press, 1992), 50–51.

50. Hanley, *A Matter of Honor*, 18.

51. Shirey, *Americans*, 21.

52. Takashi Matsui, "Teaching at the Military Intelligence Service Language School." Stanley L. Falk and Warren M. Tsuneishi, eds. *American Patriots: MIS in the War Against Japan* (Washington, D.C.: Japanese American Veterans Association of Washington, DC, 1995), 4.

53. This would-be translator was Kaname Takemoto. Paul Howard Takemoto, *Nisei Memories: My Parents Talk about the War Years* (Seattle and London: University of Washington Press, 2006), 73–74.

54. This would-be translator was Frank Fukuzawa. Interview with Frank Fukuzawa, February 24, 2001, by the Go For Broke Educational Foundation, Tape #3.

55. Enlistment papers of Carl Morita.

56. Murphy, *Ambassadors in Arms*, 117; Joe Sekine has the flag presentation occurring on July 20, 1943, in *The Boys of Company "B,"* 33.

57. Murphy, *Ambassadors in Arms*, 118.

58. Shirey, *Americans*, 21.

59. W. Stanley Hoole, ed., *And Still We Conquer: The Diary of a Nazi Unteroffizier in the German Africa Corps Who Was Captured by the United States Army, May 9, 1943 and Imprisoned at Camp Shelby, Mississippi*, trans. Irving Shater (University, Alabama: Confederate Publishing Company, 1968), entry for September 5, 1943, 37.

60. Hanley, *A Matter of Honor*, 19–20.

61. Hoole, *And Still We Conquer*, entry for September 8, 1943, 39 and September 2[5], 1943, 40.

62. Oral history of Shiroka "Whitey" Yamamoto, University of Hawaii, Oral history of Stanley Masaharu Akita, Center for Oral History, University of Hawaii, http://nisei.hawaii.edu/object/io_1158860760392.html.

63. Interview with Barney Hajiro, June 10, 2000, by the Go For Broke Educational Foundation, Tape #1.

64. Hanley, *A Matter of Honor*, 20–21.

65. Warren Nishimoto interview with Stanley Akita, December 16, 2005, The Hawaii Nisei Project, University of Hawaii, http://nisei.hawaii.edu/page/home; George Joji Miyashiro, "So Much Still Remembered," *And Then There Were Eight*, 218.

66. Warren Nishimoto interview with Stanley Akita, December 16, 2005.

67. The traffic accident fatalities were Cpl. Katsumi Miho and Pvt. Shosei Kutaka.

68. The six member organizations were: Salvation Army, Young Men's Christian Association (YMCA), Young Women's Christian Association (YWCA), National Jewish Welfare Board, National Catholic Community Service, and Travelers Aid Association. Jennifer Wilding, "Warriors in Greasepaint," http://www.onwar.com/articles/0201.htm.; Howard, *Concentration Camps on the Home Front*, 140.

69. The company commander was Captain Edwin Shorey and the experienced enlisted man was Sgt. Masami S. Yoshinari. Tooru Joe Kanazawa, *Close*

Support: A History of The Cannon Company of the 442nd Regimental Combat Team (1993), 2.

70. Kanazawa, *Close Support*, 3–4.

71. "Combat Team Promotions," *Hattiesburg* (Miss.) *American*, September 11, 1943, 6; "Combat Team Promotions," *Hattiesburg* (Miss.) *American*, September 7, 1943, 6.

72. Ted Tsukiyama, "The 522nd Field Artillery Battalion," in *Fire for Effect*, 14.

73. A Thanksgiving menu in Carl Morita's effects listed, in addition to roast young turkey and giblet gravy, such other delectable items as: cranberry sauce, nut dressing, snowflake potatoes, candied yams, garden fresh peas, lettuce and sliced tomatoes with thousand island dressing, sweet mixed pickles, spice cake, apple pie, ice cream, mixed nuts, assorted fruits, hot rolls and butter, and coffee with milk and sugar; Shirey, *Americans*, 25; Kanazawa, *Close Support*, 8.

74. *History of the Field Artillery School, Volume II, World War II.* (Fort Sill, Okla., 1946), 105–10.

75. N. S. P. Stitt, ". . . in Italy," *The Field Artillery Journal* 34, no. 5 (May 1944), 280.

76. Tsukiyama, "The 522nd Field Artillery Battalion," in *Fire for Effect*, 14–15; Roy S. Okubo, "Louisiana and D-Series Maneuvers," in *Fire for Effect*, 153.

77. Yuki "Uke" Minaga, "Chronicles Of My Lifetime," *And Then There Were Eight*, 89.

78. Melvin H. Harter, "Aloha Service Center For Combat Team," *Hattiesburg* (Miss.) *American*, December 24, 1943, 2nd section, 15.

79. A Christmas menu from Fort Sill in Carl Morita's effects.

80. Thomas Clayton Quigley, "My War: The Family Version," http://www.1jma .dk/articles/MyWar-text%20only.pdf, accessed March 2, 2008.

81. Interview with Robert Ichikawa, February 25, 2001, by the Go For Broke Educational Foundation, Tape #3.

82. Shirey, *Americans*, 27; Kanazawa, *Close Support*, 5 (first quotation); Hiro Higuchi to his wife, November 25, 1943, Hiro Higuchi Papers, Japanese American Veterans Collection, University of Hawaii (second quotation).

83. Hanley, *A Matter of Honor*, 22.

84. *Japanese Eyes American Heart*, 25–26.

85. Tsukano, *Bridge of Love*, 156.

86. Army Service Forces, Office of the Quartermaster General, *U.S. Army Rations and Supplements* (QMC 17-3, 1945), reprint, no page number.

87. Army Service Forces, Office of the Quartermaster General, *Rations and Supplements*, no page number; Franz A. Koehler, "Special Rations for the Armed Forces, 1946–53" (QMC Historical Studies, Series II, No. 6, Historical Branch, Office of the Quartermaster General, Washington, DC, 1958), excerpted at http://www.qmfound.com/army_rations_historical_background.htm, accessed 1/26/2010.

88. George Oiye, *Footprints In My Rearview Mirror: An Autobiography and Christian Testimony* (Xulon Press, 2003), 125 (first quotation); Susumu Ito and George Oiye, *Charlie Battery 522 FABN 1943–1945: A Legend* (Los Angeles: Robert Press, 2003), [30], [37] (second quotation).

89. Address by Sherwood Dixon, July 21, 1953, in Tsukano, *Bridge of Love*, 318–19.

90. Inouye and Elliott, *Journey to Washington*, 98–99; the amateur strategist was Thomas Saito Espineda. Interview with Thomas Saito Espineda, January 30, 1999, by the Go For Broke Educational Foundation, Tape #3 (quotation).

91. "Gypsy Rose Lee Leaves Shelby A-gog," *Hattiesburg* (Miss.) *American*, February 1, 1944.

4. Trial by Fire

1. Matsuo, *Boyhood to War*, 89.

2. "How to Behave in North Africa," *Life*, January 11, 1943, 59–60 (second quotation); John H. Hougen, *The Story of the Famous 34th Infantry Division* (1949; reprint, Nashville: The Battery Press, 1979), 31 (second quotation).

3. Interview with Seitoku Akamine, October 20, 1998, by the Go For Broke Educational Foundation, Tape #3. All of the interviews by the Go For Broke Educational Foundation cited in this chapter may be found at: http://www.gofor broke.org/oral_histories/oral_histories_hanashi.asp. Hanley, *A Matter of Honor*, 37–38.

4. Higa, *Memoirs of a Certain Nisei*, 58.

5. This was Col. Ray C. Fountain. Murphy, *Ambassadors in Arms*, 121.

6. Murphy, *Ambassadors in Arms*, 122.

7. Martin Blumenson, *The United States Army in World War II: The Mediterranean Theater of Operations: Salerno to Cassino* (Washington, D.C.: Office of the Chief of Military History, United States Army, 1969), 124, 133–34.

8. Blumenson, *Salerno to Cassino*, 137.

9. Blumenson, *Salerno to Cassino*, 156–57, 166.

10. Blumenson, *Salerno to Cassino*, 159; Lucian K. Truscott, Jr., *Command Missions: A Personal Story* (New York: E. P. Dutton and Company, 1954), 259.

11. Blumenson, *Salerno to Cassino*, 160–61.

12. Members of the 34th Infantry Division, *The Story of the 34th Infantry Division: Book I: Louisiana to Pisa* (Information and Education Section MTOUSA, 1944) 34th Infantry Division Association, http://www.34infdiv.org/history/34narrhist.html; Homer R. Ankrum, *Dogfaces Who Smiled Through Tears: The 34th Red Bull Infantry Division and Attached 100th (Hawaiian) Battalion And 442nd "Go For Broke" Regimental Combat Team in World War II: A Chronicle of Heartbreaks, Hardships, Heroics, and Humor of the North African and Italian Campaigns* (Lake Mills, Iowa: Graphic Publishing Company, 1987), 313.

13. Interview with Tokuji Ono, September 23, 1903, by the Go For Broke Educational Foundation; interview with Roy Honbo, June 19, 2000, by the Go For Broke Educational Foundation; interview with Edward Ikuma, June 20, 2000, by the Go For Broke Educational Foundation; Murphy, *Ambassadors in Arms*, 125.

14. Interview with Edward Ikuma, June 20, 2000, by the Go For Broke Educational Foundation, Tape #4.

15. Members of the 34th Infantry Division, *The Story of the 34th Infantry Division*, http://www.34infdiv.org/history/34narrhist.html.

16. Blumenson, *Salerno to Cassino*, 161–62.

17. Murphy, *Ambassadors in Arms*, 127; Ankrum *Dogfaces Who Smiled Through Tears*, 321.

18. This was Sgt. Conrad Tsukayama.

19. Blumenson, *Salerno to Cassino*, 162.

20. Murphy, *Ambassadors in Arms*, 128; Ankrum says Takata was carrying a Thompson submachine gun. *Dogfaces Who Smiled Through Tears*, 321.

21. Tanaka, *Go For Broke: A Pictorial*, 79.

22. Ankrum, *Dogfaces Who Smiled Through Tears*, 322.

23. Interview with Young Oak Kim, May 12, 2001, by the Go For Broke Educational Foundation, Tape #2.

24. Blumenson, *Salerno to Cassino*, 165, 170.

25. Hougen, *Famous 34th*, 70–71; Ankrum, *Dogfaces Who Smiled Through Tears*, 326 (quotation).

26. Blumenson, *Salerno to Cassino*, 183.

27. Blumenson, *Salerno to Cassino*, 197–99.

28. Murphy, *Ambassadors in Arms*, 131–32; the designer was Marvin D. Cone. Ankrum, *Dogfaces Who Smiled Through Tears*, vi.

29. Hougen seems to place this event a day earlier, on October 20. *Famous 34th*, 79; Murphy, *Ambassadors in Arms*, 134–35.

30. Blumenson, *Salerno to Cassino*, 213; Murphy, *Ambassadors in Arms*, 135; Roger Fazendin, *The 756th Tank Battalion in the Battle of Cassino, 1944* (New York, Lincoln, and Shanghai: iUniverse, 1991), 45 (quotation).

31. The Nisei bazooka men were Pvts. Masao Awakuni and Ichiro Obara. Ankrum, *Dogfaces Who Smiled Through Tears*, 336; Hougen, *Famous 34th*, 79.

32. Murphy, *Ambassadors in Arms*, 136.

33. Hougen, *Famous 34th*, 79; Murphy, *Ambassadors in Arms*, 137.

34. Murphy, *Ambassadors in Arms*, 137–38.

35. Ankrum, *Dogfaces Who Smiled Through Tears*, 340 (quotation); Blumenson, *Salerno to Cassino*, 222; Murphy, *Ambassadors in Arms*, 142.

36. Blumenson shows Pozzilli to be well within the 45th Division's area of operations. *Salerno to Cassino*, 227; Murphy, *Ambassadors in Arms*, 144–45.

37. This was Lt. Lewis Key.

38. Murphy, *Ambassadors in Arms*, 145.

39. Murphy, *Ambassadors in Arms*, 146.

40. These were Lt. Neill Ray and Cpls. Bert Higashi and Katsushi Tanouye. Murphy, *Ambassadors in Arms*, 146–47.

41. Murphy, *Ambassadors in Arms*, 149.

42. Margaret Bourke-White, *They Called It "Purple Heart Valley": A Combat Chronicle of the War in Italy* (New York: Simon and Schuster, 1944), 116.

43. This unfortunate soldier was Terumi Kato. Terumi Kato, "Two Presidents (Then and To-Be) Shook My Hand," *And Then There Were Eight*, 381.

44. Morris J. Leslie, "Evacuation in Mountain Fighting," attachment to "133rd Infantry Regiment, Narrative History 34th Infantry Division From 1 January 1944 to 31 January 1944, inclusive," 34th Infantry Division Association, http://www.34infdiv.org/history/133inf/4401.txt; This soldier was Henry S. Kuniyuki. *Japanese Eyes American Heart*, 222.

45. Cowdrey, *Fighting for Life*, 156–57; Paul Fussell, *The Boys' Crusade: The American Infantry in Northwest Europe, 1944–1945* (New York: Modern Library Paperback Edition, 2003), 118; Richard Tregaskis, *Invasion Diary* (New York: Random House, 1944), 219–20 (quotation).

46. The mortally wounded soldier was Hachiro Ito. The man who tried to help him was Jesse Hirata. *Japanese Eyes American Heart*, 61–62.

47. Blumenson, *Salerno to Cassino*, 233, 256, 249 (quotation).

48. Murphy, *Ambassadors in Arms*, 151.

49. Murphy, *Ambassadors in Arms*, 152.

50. Murphy, *Ambassadors in Arms*, 152.

51. The heroic soldier was Pvt. Shizuya Hayashi, and many years after the war his Distinguished Service Cross was upgraded to the Medal of Honor. Murphy, *Ambassadors in Arms*, 154; Ankrum, *Dogfaces Who Smiled Through Tears*, 360; interview with Tokuji Ono, June 11, 2000, by the Go For Broke Educational Foundation.

52. These soldiers were Pvt. Mikio Hasemoto and Sgt. Allan M. Ohata. Medal of Honor citations are at http://www.history.army.mil/html/moh/wwII-g-l.html.

53. Murphy, *Ambassadors in Arms*, 157.

54. This was Sam Sasai. Matsuo, *Boyhood to War*, 111.

55. Roland Shaw Pruette, *Memories of an Infantryman From World War II* (n.p., 1994), 17.

56. Pruette, *Memories of An Infantryman*, 19–20; interview with Susumu Ito, January 23, 2000, by the Go For Broke Educational Foundation, Tape #6; Cowdrey, *Fighting for Life*, 267.

57. *Honolulu Star-Bulletin*, January 5, 1944, as quoted in Murphy, *Ambassadors in Arms*, 197 (first quotation); the morale officer was Capt. Katsumi Kometani. *Honolulu Star-Bulletin*, February 10, 1944, as quoted in Murphy, *Ambassadors in Arms*, 198 (second quotation).

58. Blumenson, *Salerno to Cassino*, 269; Ankrum, *Dogfaces Who Smiled Through Tears*, 367 (quotation).

59. Murphy, *Ambassadors in Arms*, 158–59.

60. Murphy says there were three field promotions, *Ambassadors in Arms*, 161–62; Ankrum says there were seven, Ankrum, *Dogfaces Who Smiled Through Tears*, 383.

61. Israel A. S. Yost, *Combat Chaplain: The Personal Story of the World War II Chaplain of the Japanese American 100th Battalion*, ed. Monica E. Yost and Michael Markrich (Honolulu: University of Hawaii Press, 2006), 100–101.

62. Murphy, *Ambassadors in Arms*, 162–163; Blumenson, *Salerno to Cassino*, 307.

63. Fred Sheehan, *Anzio: Epic of Bravery* (Norman: University of Oklahoma Press, 1964), 22–24; Blumenson, *Salerno to Cassino*, 358–59.

64. Ankrum, *Dogfaces Who Smiled Through Tears*, 389 (first quotation), 388 (second quotation); this was Maj. Gen. Fred L. Walker. Blumenson, *Salerno to Cassino*, 346 (third quotation); Blumenson, *Salerno to Cassino*, 351 (fourth quotation).

65. This one-man mine sweeper was Sgt. Calvin Shimogaki. Murphy, *Ambassadors in Arms*, 169.

66. Murphy, *Ambassadors in Arms*, 169–70.

67. Commanding Company A was Capt. Mitsuyoshi Fukuda. Murphy, *Ambassadors in Arms*, 170.

68. Ankrum, *Dogfaces Who Smiled Through Tears*, 392.

69. Blumenson, *Salerno to Cassino*, 369–70.

70. Blumenson, *Salerno to Cassino*, 370–71.

71. Blumenson, *Salerno to Cassino*, 372–73.

72. Murphy, *Ambassadors in Arms*, 173, 171, 175 (quotation).

73. Company I with a few men from Company K. Blumenson, *Salerno to Cassino*, 378.

74. Blumenson, *Salerno to Cassino*, 378–79.

75. Blumenson, *Salerno to Cassino*, 401.

76. Blumenson, *Salerno to Cassino*, 383.

77. This was Sgt. Gary Hisaoka. Murphy, *Ambassadors in Arms*, 173.

78. The bazooka man was Masao Awakuni. Murphy, *Ambassadors in Arms*, 173; Ankrum, *Dogfaces Who Smiled Through Tears*, 416.

79. 133rd Infantry Regiment, "Narrative History 34th Infantry Division From 1 February 1944 to 29 February 1944, inclusive," 34th Infantry Division Association, http://www.34infdiv.org/history/133inf/4402.txt.

80. According to Blumenson there were 142 B-17s and 114 B-25s and B-26s. *Salerno to Cassino*, 411, 413; this was Archbishop Don Gregorio Diamare. Blumenson, *Salerno to Cassino*, 414 (quotation).

81. Murphy, *Ambassadors in Arms*, 175; another estimate places the losses of the 100th Battalion much higher, Blumenson, *Salerno to Cassino*, 383.

82. Warren Nishimoto interview with Stanley Akita, http://nisei.hawaii.edu/page/home.

83. Interview with Masaru Abe, October 19, 1999, by the Go For Broke Educational Foundation, Tape #3 (quotation); interview with Warren Takaji Iwai, January 28, 2007, by the Go For Broke Educational Foundation, Tape #8.

84. Blumenson, *Salerno to Cassino*, 441–45.

85. Murphy, *Ambassadors in Arms*, 178.

86. Dennis A. Connole, *A "Yankee" in the "Texas Army"* (Lanham, Md.: Hamilton Books, 2008), 42 (quotation), 158.

87. Ankrum, *Dogfaces Who Smiled Through Tears*, 464.

88. Murphy, *Ambassadors in Arms*, 179.

89. Yost, *Combat Chaplain*, 55–56.

90. Dale P. Harper, "American-Born Axis Sally," *World War II*, November 1995, and online at http://historynet.com/wwii/blaxissally/index1.html; Ankrum, *Dogfaces Who Smiled Through Tears*, 465 (quotation); Yost, *Combat Chaplain*, 139.

91. The account of the prisoner capture comes from interviews with Kim and Akahoshi conducted by the Go For Broke Educational Foundation, http://www.goforbroke.org/oral_histories/oral_histories_video_list.asp.

92. The surgeon was Capt. John J. Dahl and the chaplain was Rev. Israel Yost. Murphy, *Ambassadors in Arms*, 184.

93. Murphy, *Ambassadors in Arms*, 187.

94. Ankrum, *Dogfaces Who Smiled Through Tears*, 524; the man from Company C was Pfc. Robert H. Yasutake, and the man from Company B was S/Sgt. Yeiki "Lefty" Kobashigawa. Murphy, *Ambassadors in Arms*, 188–89; Ankrum, *Dogfaces Who Smiled Through Tears*, 524.

95. The other components of the task force were the 125th and the 151st Field Artillery Battalions, Company C of the 191st Tank Destroyer Battalion, Company A of the 804th Tank Destroyer Battalion, and Company C of the 84th Chemical Mortar Battalion. Murphy, *Ambassadors in Arms*, 189.

96. Murphy, *Ambassadors in Arms*, 189.

97. Ernest F. Fischer, Jr., *United States Army in World War II: The Mediterranean Theater of Operations: Cassino to the Alps* (Washington, D.C.: Center of Military History, United States Army, 1977, 1993), 201–202.

98. Ankrum, *Dogfaces Who Smiled Through Tears*, 526.

99. Fischer, *Cassino to the Alps*, 204–205.

100. Ankrum *Dogfaces Who Smiled Through Tears*, 533.

101. Stephen E. Ambrose, *D-Day June 6, 1944: The Climactic Battle of World War II* (New York: Simon and Schuster, 1994), 490.

102. Members of the 34th Infantry Division, *The Story of the 34th Infantry Division*, http://www.34infdiv.org/history/34narrhist.html.

5. Going Overseas

1. Carl Morita to Stoke, Carrie, and Eddie Morita, April 16, 1944; Carl Morita to ?, April 16, 1944 (quotations); Morita's two assistants were T/4 Masaru Fujimoto and T/4 Herbert Kumabe. S. Don Shimazu, "Headquarters Battery," in *Fire for Effect*, 122.

2. Shirey, *Americans*, 26–28.

3. Hosokawa, *Nisei*, 364–65; Minoru Kiyota, from *Beyond Loyalty*, in Inada, *Only What We Could Carry*, 306–307 (quotation).

4. K. George Hachiya and Andrea Wood Cranford, *Love of Country: A Story About An American Who Gave His Life for His Country* (Lincoln, Neb.: 2003), 29n; 267, according to Masaoka and Hosokawa, *They Call Me Moses Masaoka*, 179; Muller, *Free to Die for Their Country*, 125–26 (quotations).

5. Muller, *Free to Die for Their Country*, 129.

6. Muller, *Free to Die for Their Country*, 142–43.

7. Bell I. Wiley, "The Preparation of Units for Overseas Movement," in Robert R. Palmer, Bell I. Wiley, and William R. Keast, *United States Army in World War II: The Army Ground Forces: The Procurement and Training of Ground Combat Troops* (Washington, D.C.: Historical Division, Department of the Army, 1948), 597.

8. Shirey, *Americans*, 28.

9. The officer was Lt. Edwin Ratcliffe. Ito and Oiye, *Charlie Battery*, [2].

10. Shirey, *Americans*, 28.

11. The despondent soldier was James Mukai, and his rescuer was Richard Nishioka. Elizabeth Nishioka, "He Never Stopped Caring," *And Then There Were Eight*, 248.

12. Carl Morita to ?, April 16, 1944.

13. Hiro Higuchi to his wife, February 4, 1944, Hiro Higuchi Papers, Japanese American Veterans Collection, University of Hawaii.

14. These were Yukito "Tommy" Umeda, the winner, and Walter Watanabe, the loser. Yukito "Tommy" Umeda, "And in This Corner—Tommy Wong," *And Then There Were Eight*, 328.

15. According to Richard Nishioka in Matsuo, *Boyhood to War*, 86.

16. Hanley, *A Matter of Honor*, 33; a copy of the letter is reproduced at: http://www.ccsu.edu/uploaded/websites/Veterans_History_Project/Vets_Photos/Bensh,_Richard_O_/Publication_1943.pdf, accessed 2/1/2010.

17. Raymond Gantter, *Roll Me Over: An Infantryman's World War II* (New York: Ivy Books, 1997), 1.

18. Hanley, *A Matter of Honor,* 34; Tsukiyama, "The 522nd Field Artillery Battalion," in *Fire for Effect,* 31; Florida International University, "Liberty Ships, Master List of Names," http://www.fiu.edu/~thompsop/liberty/liberty_listJ.html.

19. Bill Mauldin, *The Brass Ring* (New York: W. W. Norton, 1971), 133.

20. Hanley, *A Matter of Honor,* 34–35.

21. Tanaka, *Go For Broke: A Pictorial History,* 50.

22. Kanazawa, *Close Support,* 12–13; the Caucasian officer was Captain Ralph J. Graham. Shirey, *Americans,* 29–30.

23. Oral history of Ronald Oba, University of Hawaii; Carl Morita to his father, May 30, 1944 (quotation).

24. This was Daniel Inouye. Inouye and Elliot, *Journey to Washington,* 102 (first quotation); Brown, *Draftee Division,* 76 (second quotation).

25. This was Norman Sato. Kanazawa, *Close Support,* 13.

26. This was Daniel Inouye. Inouye and Elliot, *Journey to Washington,* 102 (first quotation); Matsuo, *Boyhood to War,* 87; Mauldin, *The Brass Ring,* 133 (second quotation); Asaya Naguwa, "Monte's Life," *And Then There Were Eight,* 242; Curly Muraoka in Matsuo, *Boyhood to War,* 88.

27. This was Ronald Oba. Matsuo, *Boyhood to War,* 87.

28. George W. Neill, *Infantry Soldier: Holding the Line at the Battle of the Bulge* (Norman: University of Oklahoma Press, 2000), 50.

29. This was Wilfred Taira. Dorothy Matsuo, comp., *Silent Valor: The Story of the 442nd Medics* (Honolulu: Honolulu Chapter of the 442n Medics, 2002), 24.

30. Neill, *Infantry Soldier,* 50 (first quotation); Kanazawa, *Close Support,* 13 (second quotation); this was Curly Muraoka, of Cannon Company, Matsuo, *Boyhood to War,* 88.

31. Inouye and Elliot, *Journey to Washington,* 102.

32. Interview with George T. Sakato, September 25, 2000, by the Go For Broke Educational Foundation, Tape #2, http://www.goforbroke.org/oral_histories/oral_histories_hanashi.asp; Tsukiyama, "522nd Field Artillery," in *Fire for Effect,* 31 (quotation); Mauldin, *The Brass Ring,* 133; Inouye and Elliot, *Journey to Washington,* 102.

33. Kanazawa, *Close Support,* 15; Inouye and Elliott, *Journey to Washington,* 103; Oiye, *Footprints In My Rearview Mirror,* 130; Connole, *A "Yankee" in the "Texas Army",* 26; Army Information Branch. Information and Education Division, A.S.F. United States Army, *Pocket Guide to Italian Cities* (Washington, D.C.: War Department, 1944), iii (quotation).

34. Oba, *The Men of Company F,* 28, 40.

35. Chang, *"I Can Never Forget,"* 144; Tsukiyama, "522nd Field Artillery," in *Fire for Effect,* 31.

36. Department of the Navy, Naval Historical Center, "Naval Armed Guard Service: Tragedy at Bari, Italy on 2 December 1943," http://www.history.navy.mil/faqs/faq104-4.htm, accessed 12/28/2007.

37. Oba, *The Men of Company F,* 40.

6. The 442nd in Italy

1. This was Hiroshi Sakai. 442nd Regiment's "Unit Journal" for April 22, 1944 to June 2, 1944, 1.

2. Ito and Oiye, *Charlie Battery,* [3].

3. Peter Kawahara quoted in Franz Steidl, *Lost Battalions: Going for Broke in the Vosges, Autumn 1944* (Novato, Calif.: Presidio Press, 1997), 31.

4. Oral history of Stanley Masaharu Akita, Center for Oral History, University of Hawaii.

5. The gunner was Cpl. Katsugo Miho. Matsuo, *Boyhood to War*, 206.

6. Dorothy Matsuo, "Flunking the Demonstration Fire for General Ryder," in *Fire for Effect*, 88–89.

7. Letter from Pvt. George Otsubo, *Pacific Citizen*, September 2, 1944, 6.

8. Letter from Pvt. George Otsubo, *Pacific Citizen*, September 2, 1944, 6 (first quotation); *Pocket Guide to Italian Cities* (1944), iv; Minoru Masuda to his wife, June 22, 1944, in Minoru Masuda, *Letters from the 442nd: The World War II Correspondence of a Japanese American Medic*, ed. Hana Masuda and Dianne Bridgman (Seattle and London: University of Washington Press, 2008), 39 (second quotation); Carl Morita to Stoke, Carrie, and Eddie Morita, July 1, 1944 (third quotation).

9. Murphy, *Ambassadors in Arms*, 192; "Unit Journal," 3.

10. Murphy, *Ambassadors in Arms*, 203; Americans of Japanese Ancestry World War II Memorial Alliance (hereinafter, AJA Alliance), "European Campaigns-Rome to Arno," June 24, 1944, http://www.ajawarvets.org/campaigns/campaign_05_rome_arno.htm.

11. Christopher R. Keegan, "The Operations of the 2nd Battalion, 442nd Infantry (attached to the 34th Infantry Division) in the pursuit to the Arno in the vicinity of Suvereto, Italy, 26th June 1944 (Rome-Arno Campaign) (Personal Experience of a Heavy Weapons Company Commander)," (Fort Benning, Ga.: The Infantry School, 1949–1950), 8.

12. Keegan, "Operations of the 2nd Battalion," 10; Victor Izui, "Becoming a Medic, Being a Medic," *And Then There Were Eight*, 167 (quotation).

13. Hiro Higuchi to his wife, July 8, 1944, "Chaplain Higuchi Wartime Correspondence," Japanese American Veterans Collection of Digital Resources, University of Hawaii Libraries. http://libweb.hawaii.edu/libdept/archives/mss /aja/higuchi/index.htm; Kanazawa, *Close Support*, 20 (quotation).

14. Keegan, "Operations of the 2nd Battalion," 9.

15. Keegan, "Operations of the 2nd Battalion," 13.

16. The company commander was Capt. Thomas Akins. Keegan, "Operations of the 2nd Battalion," 18–19.

17. The grenadier was Henry Oyasato. Keegan, "Operations of the 2nd Battalion," 20–21.

18. Keegan, "Operations of the 2nd Battalion," 23–24.

19. Medal of Honor citation for Kiyoshi K. Muranaga, http://www.history .army.mil/html/moh/wwII-m-s.html; Kanazawa, *Close Support*, 21; Shirey says that Muranaga's third round hit just in front of the enemy gun, Shirey, *Americans*, 33.

20. The man wielding the hammer was Pfc. Roy Fujii. Tsukiyama, "The 522nd Field Artillery Battalion," in *Fire for Effect*, 35; the man who pulled the lanyard was Pfc. Larry Nakahara. Ito and Oiye, *Charlie Battery*, 137.

21. Capt. Sakae Takahashi commanded Company B. Murphy, *Ambassadors in Arms*, 205–206.

22. Shirey, *Americans*, 34; Murphy, *Ambassadors in Arms*, 206.

23. Murphy, *Ambassadors in Arms*, 206–207.

24. The bazooka man was Henry Nakamura, the BAR man was Taneoshi Nakano, and the rifleman who was killed was Grover Nagaji. Shirey, *Americans*, 35.

25. Murphy, *Ambassadors in Arms*, 207, 211 (quotation).

26. Murphy, *Ambassadors in Arms*, 208.

27. Shirey, *Americans*, 35; Murphy credits the 100th Battalion alone with 178 German deaths by the end of June 27. Murphy, *Ambassadors in Arms*, 210.

28. Kanazawa, *Close Support*, 23.

29. The sergeant who was killed was Tami Takemoto. Matsuo, *Silent Valor*, 28.

30. Murphy, *Ambassadors in Arms*, 209.

31. Murphy, *Ambassadors in Arms*, 209.

32. Murphy, *Ambassadors in Arms*, 210; Shirey, *Americans*, 35.

33. Warren Nishimoto interview with Herbert Isonaga, March 9, 2005, The Hawaii Nisei Project, University of Hawaii, http://nisei.hawaii.edu/page/home; interview with Masato Doi, September 26, 2003, by the Go For Broke Educational Foundation, Tape #3. All of the interviews by the Go For Broke Educational Foundation cited in this chapter may be found at: http://www.goforbroke.org /oral_histories/oral_histories_hanashi.asp.

34. N. S. P. Stitt, ". . . in Italy," *The Field Artillery Journal* 34, no. 5 (May 1944), 280.

35. Edward A. Raymond, "Air OPs. . . .," *The Field Artillery Journal* 34, no. 5 (May 1944), 276.

36. Tanaka, *Go For Broke: A Pictorial History*, 132.

37. Shirey, *Americans*, 36.

38. Carl Morita to Stoke, Carrie, and Eddie Morita, July 1, 1944.

39. The erstwhile traffic cop was Fred Ida. Hachiya and Cranford, *Love of Country*, 39.

40. Oral history of Shiroka "Whitey" Yamamoto, Center for Oral History, University of Hawaii, http://nisei.hawaii.edu/object/io_1149140408406.html.

41. Tanaka, *Go For Broke*, 127.

42. One of the soldiers was Robert Iwamoto; the other was not identified. "Japanese American [*sic*] Drive Nazis Crazy With Languages," *Pacific Citizen*, October 14, 1944, 3; Tanaka, *Go For Broke*, 28 (quotation).

43. Fischer, *Cassino to the Alps*, 265; Members of the 34th Infantry Division, *The Story of the 34th Infantry Division*, http://www.34infdiv.org/history/34narrhist .html.

44. The BAR man was Frank Ono. Shirey, *Americans*, 36–37.

45. Shirey, *Americans*, 37.

46. The mortar man was Kazuo Masuda. Shirey, *Americans*, 37.

47. This heroic soldier was Ted Tanouye. Shirey, *Americans*, 37–38.

48. The battalion commander was Lt. Col. James Hanley. Matsuo, *Boyhood to War*, 102. Another source says that the artillery only fired about a dozen rounds before wiping out German resistance on Hill 140. S. Don Shimazu, "Headquarters Battery," in *Fire for Effect*, 118.

49. George M. Tanna, "Outbreak of the War and Induction," in *Fire for Effect*, 144; *High Angle*, 1, no. 4 (July 7, 1945), 2 in Ito and Oiye, *Charlie Battery*, [142]; *High Angle*, 1, no. 5 (July 14, 1945), 2 [146].

50. Tsukiyama, "*522nd Artillery Battalion*," in *Fire for Effect*, 35; Carl Morita to Stoke, Carrie, and Eddie Morita, July 1, 1944 (quotation).

51. Hiro Higuchi to his wife, July 20, 1944, in *Japanese Eyes American Heart*, 235–36.

52. The Nisei rifleman was Kazuo Masuda. Shirey, *Americans*, 45.

53. This heroic officer was Lt. Takeishi Miyashiro. Shirey, *Americans*, 38; Murphy, *Ambassadors in Arms*, 214.

54. The bazooka man was Richard Okazaki. Murphy, *Ambassadors in Arms*, 214; Shirey, *Americans*, 38; Murphy, *Ambassadors in Arms*, 214; this was Masaichi Miyahsiro. Murphy, *Ambassadors in Arms*, 214–15.

55. The brave grenadier was Pfc. Kiichi Koda. Shirey, *Americans*, 39; Murphy, *Ambassadors in Arms*, 215.

56. Hiro Higuchi to his wife, July 8, 1944, Hiro Higuchi Papers, Japanese American Veterans Collection, University of Hawaii (first quotation); the forthright soldier was Takashi Kitaoka. Warren Nishimoto interview with Takashi Kitaoka, March 11, 2005, The Hawaii Nisei Project, University of Hawaii, http://nisei.hawaii.edu/page/home (second quotation).

57. This was Koichi Koda. Takemoto, *Nisei Memories*, 142 (quotation); this was Yoshiharu M. Aoyama. Kanazawa, *Close Support*, 25.

58. Shirey, *Americans*, 40.

59. Shirey says 350 in *Americans*, 40; Kanazawa says 339 in *Close Support*, 27.

60. Shirey, *Americans*, 40–41.

61. Shirey, *Americans*, 41.

62. Shirey, *Americans*, 42; Matsuo, *Silent Valor*, 99.

63. Fischer, *Cassino to the Alps*, 276–77.

64. Murphy, *Ambassadors in Arms*, 216.

65. Hiro Higuchi to his wife, July 22, 1944 in *Japanese Eyes American Heart*, 238 (first quotation); Murphy, *Ambassadors in Arms*, 218 (second quotation).

66. The officer was Lt. George Buirkle. Kanazawa, *Close Support*, 29.

67. Tanaka, *Go For Broke*, 63.

68. Letter from Pfc. Andrew Kawamoto, *Pacific Citizen*, August 19, 1944; Carl Morita to Stoke and Carrie Morita, July 7, 1944 (quotation); Carl Morita to Carrie Morita, August 17, 1944; *Greeley Daily Tribune*, August 18, 1944.

69. Shirey, *Americans*, 43.

70. Murphy, *Ambassadors in Arms*, 217 (quotation); Yost, *Combat Chaplain*, 143.

71. Samuel Sasai in *Japanese Eyes American Heart*, 89–90 (first quotation); Henry Giles, *The G.I. Journal of Sergeant Giles*, comp. and ed. Janice Holt Giles (Boston: Houghton Mifflin, 1965), 31 (second quotation); Yost, *Combat Chaplain*, 11; William Shinji Tsuchida, *Wear It Proudly: Letters by William Shinji Tsuchida* (Berkeley and Los Angeles: University of California Press, 1947), 58.

72. The soldier chef was Francis Sakai. Shirey, *Americans*, 45.

73. Takashi Aragaki, "What Can An Army Cook Do?," *And Then there Were Eight*, 123.

74. Tsukiyama, "*522nd Artillery Battalion*," in *Fire for Effect*, 38.

75. The medic was William Yasutake. Carol Lynn Akiyama, "Mickey Makio Akiyama: A Brief History," http://www.javadc.org/MICKEY%20MAKIO%20AKIYAMA.htm.

76. The older man was Tadao Beppu. His younger companion was Frank Nomura. Matsuo, *Boyhood to War*, 197.

77. Peter Schrijvers, *The Crash of Ruin: American Combat Soldiers in Europe during World War II* (New York: New York University Press, 1998), 179; the soldier with

the rudimentary sex education lecture was Robert Ichikawa. Interview with Robert Ichikawa, February 25, 2001, by the Go For Broke Educational Foundation, Tape #2 (first quotation); interview with Victor Izui, April 29, 2000, by the Go For Broke Educational Foundation, Tape #3; Yost, *Combat Chaplain*, 102 (second quotation). The forthright soldier was Fred Hirayama; interview with Fred Hirayama, March 31, 2003, by the Go For Broke Educational Foundation, Tape #5 (third quotation).

78. Schrijvers, *The Crash of Ruin*, 180–81.

79. Tanaka, *Go For Broke*, 61.

80. The thirsty officer was Lt. Robert H. Foote. Robert Hutchinson Foote, *A Connecticut Yankee in Nisei King Company's Court: With the Japanese American 442nd RCT in World War II* (Ithaca, N.Y.: The Internet-First University Press, 2005), 12.

81. Oiye, *Footprints In My Rearview Mirror*, 137–38; Carl Morita to Stoke, Carrie, and Eddie Morita, July 27, 1944 (quotation); the unfortunate swimmer was George Komoto. Kanazawa, *Close Support*, 30.

82. Carl Morita to Stoke, Carrie, and Eddie Morita, September 1, 1944; Carl Morita to Stoke, Carrie, and Eddie Morita, August 9, 1944 (quotation); Carl Morita to Carrie Morita, August 17, 1944.

83. Murphy, *Ambassadors in Arms*, 219.

84. Murphy, *Ambassadors in Arms*, 211 (first quotation), 219 (second quotation).

85. The coach was Capt. Katsumi Kometani. The outstanding swimmer was Charles Oda. Kanazawa gives the date of the swim meet as July 23 in *Close Support*, 29. Other members of the team were: T/5s Itsuhi Oshita and Thomas Tanaka, Pfcs. Yujiro Takahashi, Robert Iwamoto, and Asami Higuchi, and Pvts. John Tsukano, Kenneth Oshima, Mike Mizuki, and Joseph Yasuda. Shirey, *Americans*, 47.

86. The fatalities included Cpl. Chikao Nishi, S/Sgt. Katsuhiro Kanemitsu of Company M, and Cpl. Masao Iha and Sgt. Daniel Betsui of the engineer company. Shirey, *Americans*, 45; Frank Shimada, "What Price Equality?," *And Then There Were Eight*, 292 (quotation).

87. Extract of official narrative, September 10, 1944, http://ajawarvets.org/campaigns/campaign_06_bruyeres.htm.

88. Shirey, *Americans*, 47.

89. George Goto, "Brief History of the 232nd Engineer Combat Company," http://www.katonk.com/442nd/232nd.html.

90. This was Capt. Robert Hempstead. Shirey, *Americans*, 48.

91. The American medic was James Kanaye; the officer was Lt. Ralph Potter. Shirey, *Americans*, 48.

92. Shirey, *Americans*, 49.

93. This was Rev. Masao Yamada. Extract of official narrative, September 1, 1944.

94. Extract of official narrative, September 2, 1944; Tsukiyama, "*522nd Artillery Battalion*," in *Fire for Effect*, 38–39; Oba, *The Men of Company F*, 71.

95. Extract of official narrative, September 10, 1944.

96. Audie Murphy, *To Hell and Back* (1949; New York: Henry Holt and Co., 2002), 79.

97. Murphy, *Ambassadors in Arms*, 223.

98. Shirey, *Americans*, 50; extract of official narrative, September 18, 1944.

7. Fighting in France

1. Connole, *A "Yankee" in the "Texas Army,"* 178.
2. Interview with Hiroshi Kaku, August 8, 2004, by the Go For Broke Educational Foundation, Tape #3. All of the interviews by the Go For Broke Educational Foundation cited in this chapter may be found at: http://www.goforbroke. org/oral_histories/oral_histories_hanashi.asp. Interview with Dave Kawagoye, January 13, 2001, by the Go For Broke Educational Foundation, Tape #3.
3. Interview with Dave Kawagoye, January 13, 2001, by the Go For Broke Educational Foundation, Tape #3.
4. Interview with Hobi Fujiu, March 24, 2001, by the Go For Broke Educational Foundation, Tape #3; Walter Cronkite in foreword to John L. Lowden, *Silent Wings of War: Combat Gliders in World War II* (Washington and London: Smithsonian Institution Press, 1992), x–xi (quotation); Jimmy Sakimoto, *Company History Antitank Company 442d Infantry Regimental Combat Team* (1945), 8.
5. Robert H. Adelman and George Walton, *The Champagne Campaign* (Boston and Toronto: Little, Brown and Co., 1969), 64.
6. Michel De Trez, *First Airborne Task Force: Pictorial History of the Allied Paratroopers in the Invasion of Southern France* (Belgium: D-Day Publishing, 1998), 178. Recent research indicates that a large percentage of quotations attributed to Axis Sally and other enemy radio personalities are fictitious. This might be one of them. Ann Elizabeth Pfau and David Hochfelder, "'Her Voice a Bullet': Imaginary Propaganda and the Legendary Broadcasters of World War II," *Sound in the Age of Mechanical Reproduction*, ed. David Suisman and Susan Strasser (Philadelphia: University of Pennsylvania Press, 2010), 47–68, 252–58.
7. De Trez, *First Airborne Task Force*, 333, 445.
8. Harris V. Hollis, "The Operations of the First Airborne Task Force in the Invasion of Southern France 15–20 August 1944," (Fort Benning, Ga.: Academic Department, The Infantry School, Advanced Infantry Officers Course, 1948–1949), 14–15; Adelman and Walton, *The Champagne Campaign*, 87.
9. Lowden, *Silent Wings at War*, 83–87.
10. Toro Hirose, "Go For Broke," http://www.thedropzone.org/Europe /Southern%20France/hirose.html.
11. This was Yukio Nakahira. Adelman and Walton, *The Champagne Campaign*, 104–105.
12. This was OSS Captain Geoffrey M. T. Jones. Adelman and Walton, *The Champagne Campaign*, 43 (quotation); Hirose, "Go For Broke."
13. Milton Dank, *The Glider Gang: An Eyewitness History of World War II Glider Combat* (Philadelphia and New York: J. B. Lippincott, 1977), 151.
14. Dank, *Glider Gang*, 152.
15. Dank, *Glider Gang*, 156 (first quotation); Lowden, *Silent Wings at War*, 89–91 (second quotation).
16. Lowden, *Silent Wings at War*, 89–91 (first quotation); De Trez, *First Airborne Task Force*, 345 (second quotation).
17. Takash "Tak" Hattori, "AWOL From the Hospital," *517th Parachute Regimental Combat Team* (Paducah, Ky.: Turner Publishing Company, 1998), 52 (quotation); Dank, *Glider Gang*, 164; Sakimoto, "Antitank Co. 100/442 RCT," *517th Parachute Regimental Combat Team*, 37.
18. Dank, *Glider Gang*, 164; Gerard M. Devlin, *Paratrooper! The Saga of U.S. Army and Marine Parachute and Glider Combat Troops During World War II* (New York: St.

Martin's Press, 1979), 455; interview with Hobi Fujiu, March 24, 2001, by the Go For Broke Educational Foundation, Tape #3; Wallace K. Kagawa, "Memories of August 15, 1944," *517th Parachute Regimental Combat Team*, 66 (quotation); Devlin, *Paratroopers!*, 455. The man who still gets nervous when flying is Frank Seto. Interview with Frank Seto, August 2, 1998, by the Go For Broke Educational Foundation, Tape #2.

19. This was OSS Capt. Geoffrey M. T. Jones. Adelman and Walton, *The Champagne Campaign*, 59.

20. Devlin, *Paratrooper!*, 445.

21. Sakimoto, "Antitank Co.," 37.

22. The man in the swaying jeep was George Oiye. Ito and Oiye, *Charlie Battery*, [38].

23. Duus, *Unlikely Liberators*, 160.

24. Kanazawa, *Close Support*, 36. This was 1st Lt. Robert Foote. Foote, *A Connecticut Yankee in Nisei King Company's Court*, 13.

25. Tanaka, *Go For Broke: A Pictorial History*, 74.

26. Shirey, *Americans*, 51; "442d Regimental Combat Team, Narrative of Events, 1–31 October 44," http://www.army.mil/CMH/topics/apam/442.htm.

27. This was John Tsukano in *Japanese Eyes American Heart*, 191 (first quotation); Murphy, *Ambassadors in Arms*, 226 (second quotation); Tanaka, *Go For Broke*, 77 (third quotation).

28. Carl Morita to Stoke, Carrie, and Eddie Morita, October 12, 1944.

29. "Narrative of Events," October 16, 1944.

30. Kanazawa, *Close Support*, 40; interview with Young Oak Kim, May 12, 2001, by the Go For Broke Educational Foundation, Tape #8.

31. Murphy, *Ambassadors in Arms*, 226.

32. These tanks were from Company B of the 752nd Tank Battalion; Murphy, *Ambassadors in Arms*, 227.

33. Shirey, *Americans*, 54; Murphy, *Ambassadors in Arms*, 228.

34. Hanley, *A Matter of Honor*, 64; Murphy, *Ambassadors in Arms*, 237; "Narrative of Events," October 15, 1944.

35. Goto, "Brief History of the 232nd Engineer Combat Company."

36. Tsukano, *Bridge of Love*, 247 (first quotation); Mich Takada in Oba, *The Men of Company F*, 58 (second quotation).

37. Tsukano, *Bridge of Love*, 237.

38. This was 2nd Lt. Masanao Otake. Murphy, *Ambassadors in Arms*, 230.

39. Shirey, *Americans*, 56; Murphy, *Ambassadors in Arms*, 231.

40. Tsukano, *Bridge of Love*, 232; Duus, *Unlikely Liberators*, 175; Yost, *Combat Chaplain*, 188 (quotation).

41. The German units were the 192nd Panzer Grenadier Regiment, the 736th Grenadier Regiment, the 716th Engineer Battalion, the 198th Fusilier Battalion, and Fortress Machine Gun Battalion 49; "Narrative of Events," October 18, 1944; Shirey also identifies the 19th SS Police Regiment and the 223rd Grenadier Regiment, *Americans*, 54.

42. "Narrative of Events," October 18, 1944; Oiye, *Footprints In My Rearview Mirror*, 141; Goto, "Brief History of the 232nd Engineer Combat Company."

43. Duus, *Unlikely Liberators*, 179. This was Young Oak Kim. Duus, *Unlikely Liberators*, 180 (quotation); Murphy, *Ambassadors in Arms*, 231–32; "Narrative of Events," October 20, 1944.

44. "Narrative of Events," October 20, 1944.

45. The wounded man was Pfc. Minoru Oshima. Matsuo, *Boyhood to War*, 108.

46. Crost, *Honor by Fire*, 193; Tsukano, *Bridge of Love*, 265–66; Masao Yamada to his wife, October 30, 1944, in *Japanese Eyes American Heart*, 259; Shirey, *Americans*, 58. James M. Hanley puts the number of slain Germans at eighty-seven. Hanley, *A Matter of Honor*, xii; commenting on the dead Germans was Sgt. Kenji Ota. Kanazawa, *Close Support*, 46 (quotation).

47. Takemoto, *Nisei Memories*, 140; Brendan Phibbs, *The Other Side of Time: A Combat Surgeon in World War II* (Boston and Toronto: Little, Brown and Company, 1987), 138; interview with Kune Hisatomi, January 13, 2000, by the Go For Broke Educational Foundation, Tape #5; interview with Yuke Iguchi, February 25, 2001, by the Go For Broke Educational Foundation, Tape #4.

48. Ankrum, *Dogfaces Who Smiled Through Tears*, 415 (first quotation), 517 (second quotation); Adelman and Walton, *The Champagne Campaign*, 214.

49. The heroic bazooka man was S/Sgt. Yoshimi Fujiwara. Shirey, *Americans*, 58.

50. The tanks were from Company B of the 752nd Tank Battalion, and the tank destroyers were from Company C of the 636th Tank Destroyer Battalion. Shirey, *Americans*, 58.

51. Hanley says it was Company I. Hanley, *A Matter of Honor*, 67.

52. The observer officer was 1st Lt. Albert Binotti. Shirey, *Americans*, 59; Hanley, *A Matter of Honor*, 68; "Narrative of Events," October 20, 1944 puts the cost at three Americans wounded.

53. Medal of Honor citation for Pvt. Barney Hajiro, http://www.history.army .mil/html/moh/wwII-g-l.html.

54. The captured soldier was S/Sgt. Itsumu Sasaoka. Shirey, *Americans*, 61.

55. Murphy, *Ambassadors in Arms*, 233.

56. Shirey, *Americans*, 61; "Narrative of Events," October 23, 1944; Murphy says that the supplies were abandoned and that scouting parties found them the next day about 350 yards from their position. Murphy, *Ambassadors in Arms*, 236.

57. Murphy, *Ambassadors in Arms*, 234.

58. Murphy, *Ambassadors in Arms*, 236.

59. Murphy, *Ambassadors in Arms*, 233–34; Shirey, *Americans*, 61–62.

60. Kanazawa, *Close Support*, 49.

61. Stanley Akita in *Japanese Eyes American Heart*, 206; Duus, *Unlikely Liberators*, 186 (quotation). The medic was T/4 Richard Chinen, and the other man was Sgt. George Hajiwara. Duus, *Unlikely Liberators*, 186.

62. Oral history of Stanley Masaharu Akita, University of Hawaii.

63. "Narrative of Events," October 23, 1944.

64. Kanazawa, *Close Support*, 51.

65. "Narrative of Events," October 25, 1944.

66. Israel Yost to his wife, March 19, 1944, Yost, *Combat Chaplain*, 132. The slightly wounded medic was Victor Izui. Interview with Victor Izui, April 29, 2000, by the Go For Broke Educational Foundation, Tape #4 (first quotation); interview with George T. Sakato, September 25, 2000, by the Go For Broke Educational Foundation, Tape #3. This was Kats Nakamura in Oba, *The Men of Company F*, 64. The wounded man was Rudi Tokiwa, the officer was Lt. Col. Alfred Pursall. Tsukano, *Bridge of Love*, 265 (second quotation).

67. Shirey, *Americans*, 63; Kanazawa, *Close Support*, 51–52; another source puts the number of men in this position at 241. Jeffrey J. Clarke and Robert Ross Smith, *United States Army in World War II: The European Theater of Operations: Riviera to the Rhine* (Washington, D.C.: Center of Military History, United States Army, 1993), 329.

68. Clarke and Smith, *Riviera to the Rhine*, 329; Jack Wilson, "My Twelve Months, Year 1944, with the 36th Infantry Division," *And Then There Were Eight*, 97.

69. *Japanese Eyes American Heart*, 64–65.

70. The commander of Battery C was Capt. William Ratcliffe, the driver was Pfc. Stanley Sakai, and the third soldier was Pfc. Edward Ichiyama. Interview with Edward Ichiyama, January 22, 2000, by the Go For Broke Educational Foundation, Tape #6.

71. Murphy, *Ambassadors in Arms*, 240; the tanks were from the 752nd Tank Battalion, and the tank destroyers were from the 636th Tank Destroyer Battalion. Shirey, *Americans*, 64.

72. The man who talked about praying was Howard Jessup, and the former street car conductor was William Murphy. John A. Hyman, ed., *From the Riviera to the Rhine* (1945), http://www.texasmilitaryforcesmuseum.org/36division/ar chives/france/hyman4.htm.

73. The soldier who shared his fruit bars was Arthur Rodgers. Steidl, *Lost Battalions*, 82; Clifford H. Peek, Jr., ed., *Five Years—Five Countries—Five Campaigns: An Account of the One-Hundred-Forty-First Infantry in World War II* (Munich, Germany: 141st Infantry Regiment Association, 1945), 72 (first quotation); the soldier who craved flapjacks was William Bandorick. Hyman, *Riviera to the Rhine* (second quotation).

74. The decimated company was Company E of the 141st Infantry Regiment. After Action Report, 141st Infantry Regiment, October 1944, 36, 44.

75. After Action Report, 141st Infantry Regiment, October 1944, 36, 38, 40, 44; Duus, *Unlikely Liberators*, 201.

76. The bazooka man was Pfc. Matsuichi Yogi. Shirey, *Americans*, 64.

77. "Narrative of Events," October 27 and 28, 1944.

78. The BAR man was S/Sgt. Gordon Yamashiro. Shirey, *Americans*, 64.

79. The German soldier was Joseph Schwieters. Steidl, *Lost Battalions*, 83 (quotation); Chang, *"I Can Never Forget,"* 52.

80. Edward A. Raymond, "Air OPs. . . . ," *The Field Artillery Journal* 34, no. 5 (May 1944), 277.

81. Duus, *Unlikely Liberators*, 202 (first quotation). The surprised soldier was Pfc. Henry Nakada, and the officer was 2nd Lt. Richard Hayashi. Duus, *Unlikely Liberators*, 195 (second quotation).

82. The noncom was T/Sgt. Chester Tanaka. Crost, *Honor by Fire*, 192–93 (first quotation); the radio operator was Yuki Minaga. Chang, *"I Can Never Forget*, 49 (second quotation).

83. The Company K men were S/Sgt. Fujio Miyamoto and Pfc. Jim Tazoi, respectively. Shirey, *Americans*, 65, 67.

84. Interview with Barney Hajiro, June 10, 2000, by the Go For Broke Educational Foundation, Tapes #1 and #2.

85. Crost, *Honor By Fire*, 191.

86. Clarke and Smith, *Riviera to the Rhine*, 311.

87. Shirey, *Americans*, 67; "Narrative of Events," October 28, 1944.

88. Yuki Minaga, "Chronicles of My Lifetime," *And Then There Were Eight*, 90.

89. After Action Report, 141st Infantry Regiment, October 1944, 43, 44.

90. Matsuji "Mutt" Sakumoto. "'Sir, This Is The First Man Who Came To Us,'" *And Then There Were Eight*, 75.

91. Sakumoto, "'Sir, This Is The First Man,'" 75; Martin Higgins, "Message from the Battalion Commander," *And Then There Were Eight*, 93–94 (first quotation); Buck Glover was the soldier who remarked that it was the happiest day of his life. Steidl, *Lost Battalions*, 95 (second quotation); the second thankful soldier cited was Clifford Peek. Peek, *Five Years—Five Countries—Five Campaigns*, 75 (third quotation); "Japanese Americans Rescue 'Lost Battalion,'" *Pacific Citizen* November 11, 1944, 7 (fourth quotation).

92. Victor Izui, "Carnage in the Vosges, A Medic's Story," *And Then There Were Eight*, 72.

93. After Action Report, 141st Infantry Regiment, October 1944, 45 (quotation), 44; Clarke and Smith give the number of wounded as twenty-six. *Riviera to the Rhine*, 329.

94. John Tateishi, ed., *And Justice for All: An Oral History of the Japanese American Detention Camps* (New York: Random House, 1984), 166.

95. Dorothy Matsuo wrote that the "casualty rate of the 442nd was four times more than the 211 men rescued," in *Boyhood to War*, 114; according to Lyn Crost the Nisei "suffered more than 800 casualties" in *Honor By Fire*, 197; Douglas Sterner said that the rescuers "lost 800 men in five days," in *Go For Broke: A Tribute to the Nisei Warriors of World War II* (A HomeOfHeroes.com Electronic Book, 2001), 44; and Bill Yenne reported 140 killed and "many times that number wounded," in *Rising Sons: The Japanese American GIs Who Fought for the United States in World War II* (New York: Thomas Dunne Books, 2007), 172; Rudi Tokiwa was the soldier who said that you cannot allow another battalion to get wiped out. Tsukano, *Bridge of Love*, 263 (first quotation); Col. Sherwood Dixon saw the use of the 442nd as rescue troops as a compliment. *Bridge of Love*, 270 (second quotation).

96. The surprised officer was 1st Lt. George Stairs. Shirey, *Americans*, 68.

97. Tanaka, *Go For Broke*, 79.

98. Shirey, *Americans*, 68–69.

99. Steidl, *Lost Battalions*, 124; Shirey, *Americans*, 69.

100. Kanazawa, *Close Support*, 59; Hanley, *A Matter of Honor*, 73.

101. Hanley puts this date as November 8. Hanley, *A Matter of Honor*, 73; this was Pfc. Joe Nishimoto. Shirey, *Americans*, 71.

102. Clarke and Smith, *Riviera to the Rhine*, 313; Shirey, *Americans*, 71.

103. Matsuo, *Boyhood to War*, 118.

104. Ben Wilson, Jr., "Memories Never Forgotten: Upmost Was the Utmost," 36th Infantry Division Association http://kwanah.com/36division/ps/ps98942 htm; Christopher Keegan was the former officer quoted. Interview with Christopher Keegan, June 7, 1999, by the Go For Broke Educational Foundation, Tape #5 (quotation).

105. Hiroshi Aruga, "It Began in Civilian Clothes at the Iolani Palace Grounds," *And Then There Were Eight*, 131.

106. "Narrative of Events," 442nd Regimental Combat Team, November 1944.

107. "Narrative of Events," 442nd Regimental Combat Team, November 1944.

108. "522nd Fought Five Months in France," *High Angle* 1, no. 11 (August 25, 1945), 4, as reproduced in Ito and Oiye, *Charlie Battery*, [167].

109. "Narrative of Events," 442nd Regimental Combat Team, November 1944.

110. "Narrative of Events," 442nd Regimental Combat Team, November 1944.

111. "Narrative of Events," 442nd Regimental Combat Team, November 1944.

112. "Narrative of Events," 442nd Regimental Combat Team, November 1944.

113. Tsukiyama, "The 522nd Field Artillery Battalion," in *Fire for Effect*, 55; William P. Wright, Jr., "My Story," in *Fire for Effect*, 79.

114. Albert J. Myer to James Walden, August 13, 1855, in Albert J. Myer, "'I Am Already Quite a Texan': Albert J. Myer's Letters from Texas, 1854–1856," ed. David A. Clary, *Southwestern Historical Quarterly* 82, no. 1 (July 1978), 62–63 (1st quotation); Leo E. Oliva, *Fort Union and the Frontier Army in the Southwest* (Santa Fe, N.M.: National Park Service, 1993), 221 (2nd quotation).

115. Oiye, *Footprints In My Rearview Mirror*, 148.

116. The drinker was T/Sgt. Masaru Abe. Interview with Masaru Abe, October 19, 1999, by the Go For Broke Educational Foundation, Tape #3.

117. "Narrative of Events," 442nd Regimental Combat Team, November 1944.

118. "Narrative of Events," 442nd Regimental Combat Team, November 1944; Murphy, *Ambassadors in Arms*, 248–49.

119. "Narrative of Events," 442nd Regimental Combat Team, November 1944.

120. Hanley, *A Matter of Honor*, 77; "81 mm mortar, model 1932," http://www.fortweb.net/photos/maginot/81mm.htm.

121. Hanley, *A Matter of Honor*, 79.

122. Goto, " Brief History of the 232nd Engineer Combat Company," http://www.katonk.com/442nd/232nd.html.

123. AJA Alliance, "Champagne Campaign," January 21, 1945.

124. Tamotsu Shibutani, *The Derelicts of Company K: A Sociological Study of Demoralization* (Berkeley, Los Angeles, London: University of California Press, 1978), 65–66.

125. AJA Alliance, "Champagne Campaign," December 6–7, 1944.

126. AJA Alliance, "Champagne Campaign," December 8, 1944.

127. AJA Alliance, "Champagne Campaign," December 11, 1944.

128. They were Sgt. Tsuyoshi Shintani and Cpl. Fred Kinoshita. Kanazawa, *Close Support*, 64.

129. Denshō, "The Japanese American Legacy Project." http://www.densho.org/archive/default.asp?path=fromthearchive/200812-fromthearchive.asp.

130. Shirey, *Americans*, 76; Murphy, *Ambassadors in Arms*, 247; the men who spotted the craft were Pvts. Yoshio Hikichi and Donald Nakamura; the officer was 1st Lt. Alvin Meier, Hanley, *A Matter of Honor*, 81.

131. Most of the information on these submarines comes from Paul Kemp, *Midget Submarines of the Second World War* (London: Caxton, 2003), 42–45. Also consulted was "Neger Human Torpedoes" at http://www.uboatwar.net/neger.htm.

132. Murphy, *Ambassadors in Arms*, 248.

133. George Q. Flynn, "Drafting Farmers in World War II," *At Home on the Range: Essays on the History of Western Social and Domestic Life*, ed. John R. Wunder (Westport, Conn.: Greenwood Press, 1985), 166–68.

134. Yost, *Combat Chaplain*, 212.

135. Tsukano, *Bridge of Love*, 334; Chaplain Hiro Higuchi, in a letter to his wife, relates a slightly different version. He told her that the village priest requested the national anthem, and when the band began to play a tune called "Sweet Susie Brown," the priest had everyone rise to respectful attention. Hiro Higuchi to his wife, December 19, 1944, in *Japanese Eyes American Heart*, 252–53.

136. AJA Alliance, "Champagne Campaign," December 25, 1944.

137. The sharp-eyed artilleryman was S/Sgt. George Oiye. George Oiye, "My Life With Charlie Battery," in *Fire for Effect*, 168.

138. The soldier who spotted the Germans was T/5 Yuki Minaga; the officer in charge of the observation team was 1st Lt. Doyle Briner. Yuki Minaga, "My Experiences of World War II," in *Fire for Effect*, 176.

139. The keen-eyed officer was 1st Lt. George Buirkle. Hanley, *A Matter of Honor*, 81–82; AJA Alliance, "Champagne Campaign," February 5, 1945.

140. Hanley, *A Matter of Honor*, 80.

141. Tsuchida, *Wear It Proudly*, 103–104 (first quotation); Murphy, *Ambassadors in Arms*, 247 (second quotation).

142. The soldier with the high opinion of French women was Hobi Fujiu. Interview with Hobi Fujiu, March 24, 2001, by the Go For Broke Educational Foundation, Tape #4; Carl Morita to Fred Morita, October 18, 1944 (first quotation); Carl Morita to Stoke, Carrie, and Eddie Morita, November 6, 1944 (second quotation).

143. Murphy, *Ambassadors in Arms*, 249; Schrijvers, *The Crash of Ruin*, 185; interview with Hajime Yamane, August 23, 2000, by the Go For Broke Educational Foundation, Tape #4; Duus, *Unlikely Liberators*, 221.

144. Hiro Higuchi to his wife, December 24, 1944, Hiro Higuchi Papers, Japanese American Veterans Collection of Digital Resources, University of Hawaii Libraries, http://libweb.hawaii.edu/libdept/archives/mss/aja/higuchi/index.htm.

145. Shirey, *Americans*, 77; Murphy lists Conley as Lt. Col. James E. Conley. Murphy, *Ambassadors in Arms*, 248.

146. Paul Goodman, *A Fragment of Victory in Italy: The 92nd Infantry Division in World War II* (1952; Nashville: The Battery Press, 1993), 193. The 473rd was created on January 14, 1945, from the 434th Antiaircraft Artillery (Automatic Weapons) Battalion, the 435th Antiaircraft Artillery (Automatic Weapons) Battalion, and the 900th Antiaircraft Artillery (Automatic Weapons) Battalion, as well as headquarters troops from the 2nd Armored Group. Fischer *Cassino to the Alps*, 418n.

147. AJA Alliance, "Champagne Campaign," March 19, 1945.

148. Murphy, *Ambassadors in Arms*, 251; Masashi Kobashigawa, "So Much To Be Thankful For," *And Then There Were Eight*, 189.

149. Shirey, *Americans*, 77.

8. Final Battles

1. Chang, *"I Can Never Forget,"* 161.

2. Shirey, *Americans*, 77; "Champagne Campaign" says they cleared port at 4:00 P.M. on March 23. AJA Alliance, "Champagne Campaign," March 23, 1945, March 24, 1945, http://www.ajawarvets.org/campaigns/campaign_09_champagne.htm, quotation.

3. These were the 325th and the 599th Field Artillery Battalions, Company B of the 895th Tank Destroyer Battalion, Company B of the 84th Chemical Mortar Battalion, and the 758th Tank Battalion. Kanazawa, *Close Support*, 72.

4. James M. Hanley, "Operational Report [of the 442nd Regimental Combat Team]: 5 April 1945 to 2 May 1945," 1.

5. The supply sergeant was Hideao Noguchi. The two soldiers who needed shoes were Clarence Achiu and Vincent Ninomiya. Kanazawa, *Close Support*, 69–70.

6. AJA Alliance, "Champagne Campaign," March 28–30, 1945.

7. Murphy, *Ambassadors in Arms*, 253.

8. These were the 1st Armored Division, the 34th, 85th, 88th, and 91st Infantry Divisions. Truscott, *Command Missions*, 449, 456; Thomas R. Brooks, *The War North of Rome, June 1944–May 1945* (Edison, N.J.: Castle Books, 2001), 305; newly assigned units included the American 10th Mountain Division and 92nd Infantry Division, the 6th South African Armored Division, the Brazilian Expeditionary Force, and the British-equipped Italian Legnano Group (about half the size of an American infantry division); *19 Days from the Apennines to the Alps: The Story of the Po Valley Campaign* (Milan, Italy: 1945), 11.

9. *19 Days*, 14–15.

10. AJA Alliance, "Po Valley Campaign," April 2, 1945, http://www.ajawarvets.org/campaigns/campaign_10_po_valley.htm.

11. *High Angle*, 1, no. 5, July 14, 1945, 1,4, as reproduced in Ito and Oiye's *Charlie Battery*, [145].

12. The battery commander was Capt. Ivan Johnson. *Pacific Citizen*, May 19, 1945, 6; "52 Displacements Made in Germany," *High Angle* 1, no. 12, September 1, 1945, 4, as reproduced in *Charlie Battery*, [172]; Tsukiyama, "The 522nd Field Artillery Battalion," in *Fire for Effect*, 57.

13. *19 Days*, 26–27.

14. AJA Alliance, "Po Valley Campaign," April 3, 1945; Hanley, "Operational Report," 2.

15. Kanazawa, *Close Support*, 71 (quotation); AJA Alliance, "Po Valley Campaign," April 4, 1945; Shirey says the man fell sixty feet, *Americans*, 82.

16. Hanley, "Operational Report," 3; AJA Alliance, "Po Valley Campaign," April 5, 1945; Hanley says that there was only one machine gun and that there were sixteen German prisoners.

17. Hanley, "Operational Report," 3.

18. Hanley, "Operational Report," 3–4; Murphy, *Ambassadors in Arms*, 255.

19. This heroic soldier was Pfc. Henry Arao. Shirey, *Americans*, 83.

20. This heroic soldier was Pfc. Sadao Munemori. Shirey, *Americans*, 83.

21. Kanazawa, *Close Support*, 72.

22. Hanley, "Operational Report," 4–5; Murphy, *Ambassadors in Arms*, 259.

23. Hanley, "Operational Report," 5 (quotation); Murphy, *Ambassadors in Arms*, 259–60.

24. Murphy, *Ambassadors in Arms*, 260.

25. This Mount Belvedere had no connection to the village of Belvedere that the 442nd had liberated farther south in June 1944.

26. Hanley, "Operational Report," 5–6; Shirey says the linkup came at 7:00 P.M., *Americans*, 84; Murphy says the linkup came at 9:00 P.M., *Ambassadors*

in Arms, 260–62. Hanley's figures on American losses are inconsistent. In the battalion sections of his report, the numbers add up to nineteen killed and sixty-five wounded. He then lists regimental losses as thirteen killed and fifty-three wounded.

27. This heroic soldier was T/Sgt. Yukio Okutsu. Shirey, *Americans*, 85; Hanley, "Operational Report," 8.

28. Murphy, *Ambassadors in Arms*, 261; AJA Alliance, "Po Valley Campaign," April 7, 1945.

29. Hanley, "Operational Report," 8–9; Shirey, *Americans*, 85.

30. Hanley, "Operational Report," 8–9.

31. Hanley, "Operational Report," 8.

32. Hanley, "Operational Report," 10; Shirey, *Americans*, 85–86.

33. Hanley, "Operational Report," 10; Shirey, *Americans*, 86.

34. Hanley, "Operational Report," 12.

35. Kanazawa, *Cannon Company*, 75.

36. Hanley, "Operational Report," 11.

37. Hanley, "Operational Report," 12; Shirey lists only three bulldozers lost, *Americans*, 87.

38. Shirey, *Americans*, 87.

49. Shirey, *Americans*, 87, 89.

40. Murphy, *Ambassadors in Arms*, 265; Shirey, *Americans*, 89.

41. Shirey, *Americans*, 89.

42. Murphy, *Ambassadors in Arms*, 266; AJA Alliance, "Po Valley Campaign," April 14, 1945; Hanley, "Operational Report," 15.

43. Shirey, *Americans*, 89.

44. Brooks, *The War North of Rome*, 371; Hanley, "Operational Report," 16.

45. Hanley, "Operational Report," 16; AJA Alliance, "Po Valley Campaign," April 15, 1945.

46. AJA Alliance, "Po Valley Campaign," April 15, 1945.

47. Inouye and Elliott, *Journey to Washington*, 147.

48. Murphy, *Ambassadors in Arms*, 267.

49. Shirey, *Americans*, 90.

50. Inouye and Elliott, *Journey to Washington*, 150–52.

51. This was Pvt. Joe Hayashi. Shirey, *Americans*, 90–91.

52. Hanley, "Operational Report," 22–23; Shirey, *Americans*, 91.

53. Hanley, "Operational Report," 23–24; Murphy, *Ambassadors in Arms*, 268.

54. Murphy, *Ambassadors in Arms*, 268–69.

55. Hanley, "Operational Report," 24.

56. Hanley, "Operational Report," 25; AJA Alliance "Po River Campaign," April 27, 1945; Murphy, *Ambassadors in Arms*, 269.

57. Hanley, "Operational Report," 26.

58. Murphy, *Ambassadors in Arms*, 269 (quotation); Hanley, "Operational Report," 26–27.

59. These GIs were T/4 Yuki Minaga and Cpl. Warren Tanaka. Yuki Minaga, "My Experiences of World War II," in *Fire for Effect*, 177.

60. Transcription of an oral history given by Clarence Matsumura in Solly Ganor, "Light One Candle," Inada, *Only What We Could Carry*, 380.

61. United States Holocaust Memorial Museum, Frequently Asked Questions, http://www.ushmm.org/research/library/faq/details.php?topic=02#04.

62. They were Capt. Billy Taylor and Sgt. Shozo Kajioka. It was probably Sgt. Kajioka who shot the lock off. Tsukiyama, "522nd Artillery," in *Fire for Effect*, 62; Knaefler, *Our House Divided*, 40; they were T/4 Tadashi Tojo and T/5 Robert Sugai. Matsuo, *Boyhood to War*, 208.

63. This was Pfc. Neil Nagareda. Matsuo, *Boyhood to War*, 209 (first quotation); Cpl. Katsugo Miho doubted if the prisoners could recover. Knaefler, *Our House Divided*, 40 (second quotation); these were T/5 Tadashi Tojo and S/Sgt. Don Shimazu thought the prisoners looked like skeletons. Tsukiyama, "522nd Artillery Battalion," in *Fire for Effect*, 65 (third and fourth quotations, respectively); Dr. Brendan Phibbs was the doctor. Phibbs, *The Other Side of Time*, 317, 319 (fifth quotation).

64. The former Poston inmate was T/4 Joseph Ichiuji. "Nisei Veterans Participate in Houston JACL Tribute to Japanese Americans in WWII," http://www.javadc.org/Press%20release%2005-06-05%20NISEI%20VETERANS%20PARTICIPATE%20IN%20HOUSTON%20JACL%20TRIBUTE%20.HTM.

65. Transcription of an oral history given by Clarence Matsumura in Ganor, "Light One Candle," Inada, *Only What We Could Carry*, 382.

66. This was Lt. James Mizuno. Chang, *"I Can Never Forget,"* 171, 174.

67. *Holocaust Encyclopedia*, http://www.antiochian.org/souls-aflame.

68. Schrijvers. *The Crash of Ruin*, 255.

69. Tsukiyama, "522nd Artillery Battalion," in *Fire for Effect*, 66 (first quotation), 68 (second quotation).

70. This was Clarence Matsumura in Ganor, "Light One Candle," Inada, *Only What We Could Carry*, 382.

71. This POW was Arthur F. Gage. Arthur F. Gage, "My Army & POW Experience," *World War II Stories in Their Own Words*, http://carol_fus.tripod.com/army_hero_arthur_gage.html.

72. Tanaka, *Go For Broke: A Pictorial History*, 144.

73. Shirey, *Americans*, 97; Ito and Oiye, *Charlie Battery*, [157], [161].

9. Peace

1. The man who was "sick of guns" was Masaru Abe. Interview with Masaru Abe, October 19, 1999, by the Go For Broke Educational Foundation, Tape #4 (quotation); the man who had had his baggage pilfered was Tetsuo Asato. Interview with Tetsuo Asato, November 29, 2002, by the Go For Broke Educational Foundation, Tape #6. All of the interviews by the Go For Broke Educational Foundation cited in this chapter may be found at: http://www.goforbroke.org/oral_histories/oral_histories_hanashi.asp.

2. Shirey, *Americans*, 97; Ito and Oiye, *Charlie Battery*, [157], [161].

3. 12th Army Group, *Don't Be a Sucker in Germany!* (12th Army Group, 1945, reproduced at http://www.3ad.com/history/ww11/feature.pages/occupation.booklet.htm (first quotation); the medic was Keith Winston. Keith Winston, *V...-Mail: Letters of a World War II Combat Medic*, ed. Sarah Winston (Chapel Hill, N.C.: Algonquin Books of Chapel Hill, 1985), 241 (second quotation).

4. The officer was Lt. Gen. Frederick Morgan, on August 24, 1944. Earl F. Ziemke, *The U.S. Army in the Occupation of Germany, 1944–1946* (Army Historical Series, Washington, D.C.: Center of Military History, United States Army, 1975), 98.

5. The 28th Division officer was Maj. William Hill. Ziemke, *The U.S. Army in the Occupation of Germany*, 324 (first quotation); Kennett, *G.I.: The American Soldier in World War II*, 211–12 (second quotation).

6. Ziemke, *The U.S. Army in the Occupation of Germany*, 332.

7. Mitsuo Sakamoto, *My Best World War II Souvenir: Chronicles of One Man's Experiences in the United States Army* (Hawaii: 1995), 38.

8. Oiye, *Footprints In My Rearview Mirror*, 157.

9. *High Angle* 1, no. 1 (June 16, 1945), 3, as reproduced in Ito and Oiye, *Charlie Battery*, [131].

10. *High Angle* 1, no. 7 (July 27, 1945), 1, as reproduced in Ito and Oiye, *Charlie Battery*, [153].

11. Sakamoto, *My Best World War II Souvenir*, 6–7; *High Angle* 1, no. 7 (July 27, 1945), 3, as reproduced in Ito and Oiye, *Charlie Battery*, [155].

12. This was Tamotsu Fukuoka. Lyn Crost, "They Stop the Escape of a Nazi Art Collector," in *Fire for Effect*, 96.

13. They were Pfcs. Torao Nitta, Robert Yutaka, Shunro Nomura, and T/4 Tadashi Tojo. Tadashi Tojo, "Experiences and Reflections of the War," *Fire for Effect*, 135–36.

14. The medic was Herbert Akamine. Matsuo, *Silent Valor*, 134.

15. This was Norman Ugai and his sister Marguerite. Kanazawa, *Close Support*, 53.

16. The chaplain was Hiro Higuchi. Hiro Higuchi to Hisako Higuchi, September 2, 1945, Chaplain Higuchi Wartime Correspondence, Japanese American Veterans Collection Digital Resources, University of Hawaii at Manoa, http://libweb.hawaii.edu/libdept/archives/mss/aja/higuchi/hiro.htm.

17. Ziemke, *The U.S. Army in the Occupation of Germany*, 332.

18. Raymond McNabney to his family, May 1945, Raymond McNabney, *War Notes: From the Letters of Sgt. Raymond McNabney, 1942–1945* (Tulsa, Okla.: Cock-a-hoop Publishing, 1994), 175.

19. Pass in the belongings of Carl Morita; Carl Morita to Stoke, Carrie, and Eddie Morita, August 14, 1945; souvenir programs in the belongings of Carl Morita.

20. The medic was Keith Winston. Winston, *V...- Mail*, 184–85.

21. John C. Sparrow, *History of Personnel Demobilization in the United States Army* (CMH PUB 104-8, DA Pam 20-210, July 1952; reprint Washington, D.C.: Center of Military History, United States Army, 1994), 118–23; the first GI quoted was Henry Giles. Henry Giles, *The G.I. Journal of Sergeant Giles*, 359 (first quotation); the second GI quoted was James A. Huston. James A. Huston, *Biography of a Battalion: The Life and Times of an Infantry Battalion in Europe During World War II*, ed. James W. Huston (Mechanicsburg, Pa.: Stackpole Books, 2003), 270 (second quotation). The Nisei soldier was Edward Nakagawa. *High Angle* 1, no. 8 (August 3, 1945), 2 as reproduced in Ito and Oiye, *Charlie Battery*, [158] (third quotation).

22. Joseph R. Itagaki to Charles R. Hemmenway, June 3, 1945, in *Japanese Eyes American Heart*, 357–58.

23. Associated Press, "Army to Let 1,300,000 Go on Credits for Service, Combat, Overseas Duty and Parenthood," *Greeley* [Colorado] *Daily Tribune*, May 10, 1945; Shirey, *Americans*, 93.

24. Sparrow, *Personnel Demobilization*, 175.

25. This commentator was James A. Huston. Huston, *Biography of a Battalion,* 284; Associated Press, "Flying Colonel Has 312 on Point System," *Greeley* [Colorado] *Tribune,* June 18, 1945.

26. Letter from an air force staff sergeant to his U.S. Senator, cited in Sparrow, *Personnel Demobilization,* 127.

27. This was 1st Sgt. Charles W. Laird of Company H, 32nd Infantry Regiment. "30 Veterans Summoned from Fox Holes of Okinawa, Told They Are Discharged," Associated Press, *Greeley* [Colorado] *Daily Tribune,* May 18, 1945; Henry Yeo and Heather Reifsnyder, "Same Family, Different Sides," *Scope* (Spring 2007) http://www.llu.edu/news/scope/documents/scopespr07.pdf.

28. Sparrow, *Personnel Demobilization,* 175.

29. Sparrow, *Personnel Demobilization,* 309.

30. *High Angle* 1, no. 12 (September 1, 1945), 1, as reproduced in Ito and Oiye, *Charlie Battery,* [169]; *High Angle* 1, no. 13 (September 8, 1945), 1, as reproduced in Ito and Oiye, *Charlie Battery,* [173]; *High Angle* 1, no. 14 (September 15, 1945), 4, as reproduced in Ito and Oiye, *Charlie Battery,* [182]. Service Record of Carl Morita.

31. *High Angle* 1, no. 15 (September 22, 1945) and 1, no. 16 (September 29, 1945).

32. Interview with Gerald Gustafson, May 14, 2005, by the Go For Broke Educational Foundation, Tape #4. All of the interviews by the Go For Broke Educational Foundation cited in this chapter may be found at: http://www.goforbroke .org/oral_histories/oral_histories_hanashi.asp.

33. Murphy, *Ambassadors in Arms,* 271.

34. Carl Morita to Stoke, Carrie, and Eddie Morita, August 9, 1944.

35. Ziemke, *The U.S. Army in the Occupation of Germany,* 330; Hervie Haufler, "The Most Contented G.I.s in Europe," *American History* (October 1999) at http://www.historynet.com/the-most-contented-gis-in-europe-october-99 -american-history-feature.htm; *High Angle* 1, no. 7 (July 27, 1945), 2, as reproduced in Ito and Oiye, *Charlie,* [154].

36. Ziemke, *The U.S. Army in the Occupation of Germany,* 330; *High Angle* 1, no. 11 (August 25, 1945), 1, as reproduced in Ito and Oiye, *Charlie Battery,* [165]; *High Angle* 1, no. 7 (July 27, 1945), 2, as reproduced in Ito and Oiye, *Charlie Battery,* [154].

37. "Third Group of Students Arrives to Begin Study at Weihenstephan A and T," *The Reaper* 1, no. 3 (September 28, 1945), 1; "Fun and Recreation Offered at Red Cross Club on Würm See," *The Reaper* 1, no. 3 (September 28, 1945).

38. *High Angle* 1, no. 12 (September 1, 1945), 1, as reproduced in Ito and Oiye *Charlie Battery,* [169].

39. Ziemke, *The U.S. Army in the Occupation of Germany,* 335; interview with Mark Hashimoto, April 29, 2000, by the Go For Broke Educational Foundation, Tape #4; interview with Virgil William Westdale, June 30, 2002, by the Go For Broke Educational Foundation, Tape #6; interview with Yoshimi Hiraoka, May 27, 2000, by the Go For Broke Educational Foundation, Tape #7.

40. This happy soldier was Katsugo Miho. Knaefler, *Our House Divided,* 41.

41. George Oiye, "My Life With Charlie Battery," in *Fire for Effect,* 171; interview with Yoichi Ichikawa, March 25, 2001, by the Go For Broke Educational Foundation, Tape #3.

42. Sparrow, *Personnel Demobilization*, 309; interview with Tetsuo Tokita, June 8, 1999, by the Go For Broke Educational Foundation, Tape #6; interview with Edward Ikuma, June 20, 2000, by the Go For Broke Educational Foundation, Tape #5.

43. Crost, *Honor by Fire*, 305–306.

44. Masaoka and Hosokawa, *They Call Me Moses Masaoka*, 178.

45. Kanazawa, *Close Support*, 12, 71.

46. Crost, *Honor by Fire*, 301 (quotation); the second soldier was Kune Hisatomi. Interview with Kune Hisatomi, January 13, 2000, by the Go For Broke Educational Foundation, Tape #6.

47. This soldier was Mitsuo Usui. Crost, *Honor by Fire*, 301.

48. Kanazawa, *Close Support*, 98–99.

49. Carl Morita to his father, September 22, 1941.

50. Carl K. Morita's Army Service Experiences Questionnaire.

Epilogue

1. "President William Jefferson Clinton's Comments Honoring Asian American Medal of Honor Recipients," U.S. Army Center of Military History, http://www.history.army.mil/html/moh/clinton_apmoh.html.

2. This was Sgt. 1st Class Ryan Matsumoto. Gregg K. Kakesako, "100th Battalion assesses gains in Iraq. Soldiers due home starting today aided security forces and detained insurgents," *Honolulu Star Bulletin*, December 29, 2005, http://archives.starbulletin.com/2005/12/29/news/story03.html.

3. William Cole, "Hawaii Guard unit commander removed," *Army Times* (March 17, 2005), http://www.armytimes.com/legacy/new/1-292925-728015.php; Gregg K. Kakesako "100th Battalion assesses gains in Iraq. Soldiers due home starting today aided security forces and detained insurgents," *Honolulu Star Bulletin*, December 29, 2005, http://archives.starbulletin.com/2005/12/29/news/story03.html; the quoted former soldier was Takashi Kitaoka. William Cole, "Women join ranks of the 100th," *Honolulu Star Advertiser*, October 3, 2010, http://www.staradvertiser.com/news/20101003_Women_join_ranks_of_the100th.html.

4. This was Spec. Len Tanaka. Chuck Prichard, "100th Infantry Battalion soldier carries pride and family tradition with him into Iraq campaign," http://findarticles.com/p/articles/mi_m0KAB/is_2_51/ai_n27864353/.

5. Sadaichi Kubota, "War is Hell, But the Good Things Count," *And Then There Were Eight*, 202.

BIBLIOGRAPHY

Books

Adleman, Robert H., and George Walton. *The Champagne Campaign.* Boston: Little, Brown, 1969.

And Then There Were Eight: The Men of I Company, 442nd Regimental Combat Team, World War II. Honolulu: Item Chapter 442nd Veterans Club, 2003.

Ankrum, Homer R. *Dogfaces Who Smiled Through Tears: The 34th Red Bull Division, and attached 100th (Hawaiian) Battalion, and 442nd "Go For Broke" Regimental Combat Team in World War II: A Chronicle of Heart Breaks, Hardships, Heroics, and Humor of the North African and Italian Campaigns.* Lake Mills, Iowa: Graphic, 1988.

Asahina, Robert. *Just Americans: How Japanese Americans Won a War at Home and Abroad: The Story of the 100th Battalion/442d Regimental Combat Team in World War II.* New York: Gotham Books, 2006.

Astor, Gerald. *"Battling Buzzards": The Odyssey of the 517th Parachute Regimental Combat Team, 1943–1945.* New York: Donald I. Fine, Inc., 1993.

Axford, Roger W. *Too Long Silent: Japanese Americans Speak Out.* New York: Media Publishing and Marketing, 1986.

Baker, Vernon J., with Ken Olsen. *Lasting Valor.* Columbus, Miss.: Genesis Press, 1997.

Baumer, William H., Jr. *He's in the Army Now.* New York: R. M. McBride, 1941.

Blum, Albert A. *Drafted or Deferred: Practices Past and Present.* Ann Arbor: Bureau of Industrial Relations. Graduate School of Business Administration. The University of Michigan, 1967.

Blumenson, Martin. *The United States Army in World War II: The Mediterranean Theater of Operations: Salerno to Cassino.* Washington, D.C.: Office of the Chief of Military History, United States Army, 1969.

Blunt, Roscoe C., Jr. *Foot Soldier: A Combat Infantryman's War in Europe.* Rockville Centre, New York: Sarpedon, 1994, 2001.

Bonn, Keith E. *When the Odds Were Even: The Vosges Mountains Campaign, October 1944–January 1945.* Novato, Calif.: Presidio Press, 1994.

Bourke-White, Margaret. *They Called It "Purple Heart Valley": A Combat Chronicle of the War in Italy.* New York: Simon and Schuster, 1944.

Brager, Bruce L. *The Texas 36th Division: A History.* Eakin, 2002.

Brooks, Thomas R. *The War North of Rome, June 1944–May 1945.* Edison, N.J.: Castle Books, 2001.

Brown, John Sloan. *Draftee Division: The 88th Infantry Division in World War II.* Presidio Press, 1998.

Burton, Jeffrey F., Mary M. Farrell, Florence B. Lord, and Richard W. Lord. *Confinement and Ethnicity: An Overview of World War II Japanese American Relocation Sites.* Seattle and London: University of Washington Press, 2002.

California Center for Military History. *Images of America: Camp Roberts.* San Francisco: Arcadia Publishing, 2005.

Carr, Elizabeth Ball. *Da Kine Talk: From Pidgin to Standard English in Hawaii.* Honolulu: University of Hawaii Press, 1972.

Chang, Thelma. *"I Can Never Forget": Men of the 100th/442nd.* Sigi Productions, 1991.

Charles, Roland W. *Troopships of World War II.* Washington, D.C.: Army Transportation Association, 1947.

Clark, Mark W. *Calculated Risk.* New York: Harper and Brothers, 1950.

Clarke, Jeffrey J. and Robert Ross Smith. *Riviera to the Rhine: The European Theater of Operations.* Washington, D.C.: Center of Military History, United States Army, 1993.

Clifford, J. Garry and Samuel R. Spencer, Jr. *The First Peacetime Draft.* Lawrence: University Press of Kansas, 1986.

Combat History of the Second Infantry Division in World War II. Baton Rouge: Army and Navy Publishing Company, 1946.

Connole, Dennis A. *A "Yankee" in the "Texas Army."* Lanham, Md.: Hamilton Books, 2008.

Courington, Morris, ed. *Cruel Was the Way: Memories of Combat Infantrymen in World War II.* Velletri Books: 2000.

Cowdrey, Albert E. *Fighting for Life: American Military Medicine in World War II.* New York: The Free Press, 1994.

Crost, Lyn. *Honor By Fire: Japanese Americans at War in Europe and the Pacific.* Presidio, 1994.

Daniels, Roger, ed. *Prisoners Without Trial: Japanese Americans in World War II.* New York: Hill and Wang, 1993.

Dank, Milton. *The Glider Gang: An Eyewitness History of World War II Glider Combat.* Philadelphia and New York: J. B. Lippincott, 1977.

DeTrez, Michel. *First Airborne Task Force: Pictorial History of the Allied Paratroopers in the Invasion of Southern France.* Belgium: D-Day Publishing, 1998.

Devlin, Gerard M. *Paratrooper! The Saga of U.S. Army and Marine Parachute and Glider Combat Troops During World War II.* New York: St. Martin's Press, 1979.

Dudley, William, ed. *Japanese American Internment Camps.* San Diego: Greenhaven Press, 2002.

Duus, Masayo Umezawa. *Unlikely Liberators: The Men of the 100th and 442nd.* Translated by Peter Duus. Honolulu: University of Hawaii Press, 1987.

Ellis, John. *The Sharp End: The Fighting Men in World War II.* New York: Charles Scribner's Sons, 1980.

Falk, Stanley and Warren Tsuneishi. *American Patriots: MIS in the War Against Japan*. Washington, D.C.: Japanese American Veterans Association of Washington, D.C., 1995.

Fazendin, Roger. *The 756th Tank Battalion in The Battle of Cassino, 1944*. New York, Lincoln, and Shanghai: iUniverse, 1991.

Field Artillery School. *Field Artillery Fundamentals*. Fort Sill, Okla.: 1942.

Fisher, Ernest F., Jr. *The United States Army in World War II: The Mediterranean Theater of Operations: Cassino to the Alps*. Washington, D.C.: Center of Military History. United States Army. 1977, 1993.

The 517th Parachute Regimental Combat Team. Paducah, Ky.: Turner Publishing, 1998.

Flynn, George Q. "Drafting Farmers in World War II," *At Home on the Range: Essays on the History of Western Social and Domestic Life*, edited by John R. Wunder. Westport, Conn.: Greenwood Press, 1985.

Foote, Robert H. *A Connecticut Yankee in Nisei King Company's Court: With the Japanese American 442nd RCT in World War II*. Ithaca, N.Y.: The Internet-First University Press, 2005. http://ecommons.cornell.edu/bitstream/1813/3717/3/A%20Connecticut%20Yankee.pdf.

Fussell, Paul. *The Boys' Crusade: The American Infantry in Northwest Europe, 1944–1945*. New York: Modern Library Paperback Edition, 2003.

Gantter, Raymond. *Roll Me Over: An Infantryman's World War II*. New York: Ivy Books, 1997.

Goodman, Paul. *A Fragment of Victory in Italy: The 92nd Infantry Division in World War II*. 1952; Nashville: The Battery Press, 1993.

Hachiya, K. George and Andrea Wood Cranford. *Love of Country: A Story About an American Who Gave His Life for His Country, Americans Who Proved Their Loyalty on Battlefields, A University That Never Doubted Their Loyalty*. Lincoln, Neb.: 2003.

Halloran, Richard. *Sparky: Warrior, Peacemaker, Poet, Patriot: A Portrait of Senator Spark M. Matsunaga*. Honolulu: Watermark Publishing, 2002.

Hanley, James M. *A Matter of Honor: A Mémoire*. New York: Vantage Press, 1995.

Harth, Erica, ed. *Last Witnesses: Reflections on the Wartime Internment of Japanese Americans*. New York: St. Martin's Press, 2001.

Hata, Donald Teruo and Nadine Ishitami Hata. *Japanese-Americans and World War II*. Wheeling, Ill.: Harlan Davidson, 1995.

Hawaii Nikkei History Editorial Board, ed. *Japanese Eyes, American Heart: Personal Reflections of Hawaii's World War II Nisei Soldiers*. Honolulu: Tendai Educational Foundation, 1998.

Hawaii, University of, Hawaii War Records Committee. *In Freedom's Cause: A Record of the Men of Hawaii Who Died in the Second World War*. Honolulu: University of Hawaii Press, 1949.

Hawai'i Holocaust Project. *Days of Remembrance: Hawai'i Witnesses to the Holocaust*. Vol. 1. Mānoa: Center for Oral History, Social Sciences Research Institute, University of Hawai'i at Mānoa, 1991.

Higa, Thomas Taro. *Memoirs of a Certain Nisei, 1916–1985*. Edited by Elsie Higa Taniguchi. Translated by Mitsugu Sakihara. Kaneohe, Hawaii: Higa Publications, 1988.

Hirasaki, Manabi, and Naomi Hirahara. *A Taste for Strawberries: The Independent Journey of Nisei Farmer Manabi Hirasaki.* Los Angeles: Japanese American National Museum, 2003.

Historical Album Committee of the 522 Field Artillery Battalion of the 442 Regimental Combat Team. *Fire for Effect: A Unit History of the 522 Field Artillery Battalion.* Honolulu: 1998.

Hoole, W. Stanley, ed. *And Still We Conquer: The Diary of a Nazi Unteroffizier in the German Africa Corps Who Was Captured by the United States Army, May 9, 1943 and Imprisoned at Camp Shelby, Mississippi.* Translated by Irving Shater. University, Alabama: Confederate Publishing Company, 1968.

Hosokawa, Bill. *Nisei: The Quiet Americans.* Boulder: University Press of Colorado, 2002.

———. *Out of the Frying Pan: Reflections of a Japanese American.* Niwot: University Press of Colorado, 1998.

———. *Colorado's Japanese Americans: From 1886 to the Present.* Boulder: University Press of Colorado, 2005.

Hougen, John H. *The Story of the Famous 34th Infantry Division.* San Angelo, Texas: 1949.

Howard, John. *Concentration Camps on the Home Front: Japanese Americans in the House of Jim Crow.* Chicago and London: University of Chicago Press, 2008.

Huebner, Klaus H. *Long Walk Through War: A Combat Doctor's Diary.* College Station: Texas A&M University Press, 1987.

Huston, James A., *Biography of a Battalion: The Life and Times of an Infantry Battalion in Europe During World War II.* Edited by James W. Huston. Mechanicsburg, Pa.: Stackpole Books, 2003.

Inada, Lawson Fusao, ed. *Only What We Could Carry: The Japanese American Internment Experience.* Berkeley, Calif.: Heyday Books, 2000.

Inouye, Daniel K., and Lawrence Elliott. *Journey to Washington.* Englewood Cliffs, N.J.: Prentice-Hall, 1967.

Institute of Military Studies, The University of Chicago. *A Manual of Basic Training.* Harrisburg, Pa.: The Military Service Publishing Company, 1942.

Ito, Roy. *We Went to War: The Story of the Japanese Canadians Who Served During the First and Second World Wars.* Stittlsville, Ontario: Canada's Wings, Inc., 1984.

Ito, Susumu, and George Oiye. *Charlie Battery 522 FABN 1943–1945: A Legend.* Honolulu: Robert Press, 1991; reprint 2003.

Jones, Wilbur D., and Carroll Robins Jones. *Hawaii Goes to War: The Aftermath of Pearl Harbor.* Shippensburg, Pa.: White Mane Books, 2001.

Kanazawa, Tooru J. *Close Support: A History of the Cannon Company of the 442nd Regimental Combat Team.* Cannon Company, 442nd RCT, 1993.

Kaneshiro, Takeo, comp. *Internees: War Relocation Center Memoirs and Diaries.* New York: Vantage Press, 1976.

Kashiwagi, Hiroshi. *Swimming in the American: A Memoir and Selected Writings.* San Mateo, Calif.: Asian American Curriculum Project, 2005.

Kemp, Anthony. *The Maginot Line: Myth and Reality.* New York: Military Heritage Press, 1988.

Kemp, Paul. *Midget Submarines of the Second World War.* London: Chatham, 1999.

Kenderdine, John D. *Your Year in the Army: What Every New Soldier Should Know.* New York: Simon and Schuster, 1940.

Kennedy, David M. *Freedom From Fear: The American People in Depression and War, 1919–1945*. New York: Oxford University Press, 1999.

Kennett, Lee. *G.I.: The American Soldier in World War II*. New York: Charles Scribner's Sons, 1987.

Kirby, Wayne. "Memories That Won't Fade," in Courington, Morris, ed. *Cruel Was the Way: Memories of Combat Infantrymen in World War II*. Velletri Books: 2000.

Kitagawa Daisuke. *Issei and Nisei: The Internment Years*. New York: Seabury Press, 1967.

Kiyota, Minoru. *Beyond Loyalty: The Story of a Kibei*. Translated by Linda Klepinger Keenan. Honolulu: University of Hawaii Press, 1999.

Knaefler, Toni Kaizawa. *Our House Divided, Seven Japanese American Families in World War II*. Honolulu: University of Hawaii Press, 1991.

Kreidberg, Marvin A., and Merton G. Henry. *History of Military Mobilization in the United States Army, 1775–1945*. Department of the Army Pamphlet No. 20-212. Washington, D.C.: Government Printing Office, 1955.

Lee, Ulysses. *The Employment of Negro Troops*. Washington, D.C.: Office of the Chief of Military History. United States Army, 1966, 1982.

Lewis, Norman. *Naples '44*. New York: Avalon, 1978; New York: Carroll and Graf, 2005.

Litwak, Leo. *The Medic: Life and Death in the Last Days of WWII*. New York: Penguin, 2001.

Lockhart, Vincent M. *T-Patch to Victory: The 36th Infantry Division from the Landing in Southern France to the End of World War II*. Staked Plains Press, 1981.

Lowden, John L. *Silent Wings at War: Combat Gliders in World War II*. Washington and London: Smithsonian Institution Press, 1992.

Mandelbaum, David G. *Soldier Groups and Negro Soldiers*. Berkeley and Los Angeles: University of California Press, 1952.

Martin, Ralph G. *Boy from Nebraska*. New York and London: Harper Brothers, 1946.

Masaoka, Mike. *They Call Me Moses Masaoka: An American Saga*. New York: 1987.

Masuda, Minoru. *Letters from the 442nd: The World War II Correspondence of a Japanese American Medic*. Seattle and London: University of Washington Press, 2008.

Matsuo, Dorothy. *Boyhood to War: History and Anecdotes of the 442nd Regimental Combat Team*. Honolulu: Mutual Publishing, 1982.

———. *Silent Valor: The Story of the 442nd Medics*. Honolulu: Honolulu Chapter of the 442nd Medics, 2002.

Mauldin, Bill. *The Brass Ring*. New York: W. W. Norton, 1971.

McNabney, Raymond. *War Notes: From the Letters of Sgt. Raymond McNabney, 1942–1945*. Tulsa, Okla.: Cock-a-hoop Publishing, 1994.

Moenk, Jean R. *A History of Large-Scale Army Maneuvers in the United States, 1935–1964*. Fort Monroe, Va.: Headquarters, USCAC, 1969.

Moore, Christopher Paul. *Fighting for America: Black Soldiers—the Unsung Heroes of World War II*. New York: Ballantine Books, 2005.

Morisawa, Jackson S. *Fabled Facts of the 442nd RCT: Recollections of Some Humorous Situations Amidst the Horrors of War*. 1993.

Motley, Mary Penick, ed. and comp. *The Invisible Soldier: The Experience of the Black Soldier, World War II*. Detroit: Wayne State University Press, 1975.

Moulin, Pierre. *U.S. Samurais in Bruyeres: People of France and Japanese Americans: An Incredible Story.* Translated by David Guinsbourg, Luc Pétry, and Françoise Bock. France: Peace and Freedom Trail, 1993.

Mrazek, James E. *The Glider War.* New York: St. Martin's Press, 1974.

Muller, Eric L. *Free to Die for Their Country: The Story of the Japanese American Draft Resisters of World War II.* Chicago: University of Chicago Press, 2001.

Murphy, Thomas D. *Ambassadors in Arms: The Story of Hawaii's 100th Battalion.* Honolulu: University of Hawaii Press, 1954.

Nakagawa, Kerry Yo. *Through a Diamond: 100 Years of Japanese American Baseball.* San Francisco: Rudi Publishing, 2001.

National Historic Landmarks of Arkansas: Rohwer Relocation Center. Little Rock, Ark.: Arkansas Historic Preservation Program.

Neill, George W. *Infantry Soldier: Holding the Line at the Battle of the Bulge.* Norman: University of Oklahoma Press, 2000.

Nelson, Kevin. *The Golden Game: The Story of California Baseball.* Heyday Books and the California Historical Society Press, 2004.

Ng, Wendy. *Japanese American Internment During World War II: A History and Reference Guide.* London and Westport, Conn.: Greenwood Press, 2002.

Niiya, Brian, ed. *More Than a Game: Sport in the Japanese American Community.* Los Angeles: 2000.

19 Days from the Apennines to the Alps: The Story of the Po Valley Campaign. Milan, Italy: 1945.

Nishimuta, Juli Ann. *The Nishimutas: An Oral History of a Japanese and Spanish Family.* New York: iUniverse, 2006.

Oba, Ronald, ed. *The Men of Company F, 442nd RCT.* Honolulu: 1989, 1993.

Odo, Franklin. *No Sword to Bury: Japanese-Americans in Hawaii During World War II.* Philadelphia: Temple University Press, 2004.

Oiye, George. *Footprints In My Rearview Mirror: An Autobiography and Christian Testimony.* Xulon Press, 2003.

Oliva, Leo E. *Fort Union and the Frontier Army in the Southwest.* Santa Fe, N.M.: National Park Service, 1993.

Osgood, Charles. *Kilroy Was Here: The Best American Humor from World War II.* Hyperion, 2000.

Palmer, Bennet J., Sr. *The Hunter and the Hunted.* 1999.

Palmer, Robert R., Bell I. Wiley, and William R. Keast. *The Procurement of Ground Combat Troops.* Washington, D.C.: Historical Division, Department of the Army, 1948.

Peek, Clifford H., Jr., ed. *Five Years—Five Countries—Five Campaigns: An Account of the One-Hundred-Forty-First Infantry in World War II.* Munich, Germany: 141st Infantry Regiment Association, 1945.

Pfau, Ann Elizabeth, and David Hochfelder. "'Her Voice a Bullet': Imaginary Propaganda and the Legendary Broadcasters of World War II." *Sound in the Age of Mechanical Reproduction.* Edited by David Suisman and Susan Strasser. Philadelphia: University of Pennsylvania Press, 2010.

Phibbs, Brandon. *The Other Side of Time: A Combat Surgeon in World War II.* Boston: Little, Brown, 1987.

Power, J. A. *You're in the Army Now!* New York: Paramount Press, 1940.

Prange, Gordon. *At Dawn We Slept: The Untold Story of Pearl Harbor.* New York: Penguin Books, 1981.

Pruette, Rowland Shaw. *Memories of an Infantryman from World War II*. 1994.

Robinson, Greg. *By Order of the President: FDR and the Internment of Japanese Americans*. Cambridge, Mass., and London: Harvard University Press, 2001.

Saiki, Patsy Sumie. *Ganbare! An Example of Japanese Spirit*. Honolulu: Kisaku, Inc., 1982.

Sakamaki, Kazuo. *I Attacked Pearl Harbor*. Translated by Toru Matsumoto. New York: Association Press, 1949.

Sakamoto, Mitsuo. *My Best World War II Souvenir: Chronicles of One Man's Experiences in the United States Army*. Hawaii, 1995.

Schaps, Ralph B. *500 Days of Front Line Combat: The WWII Memoir of Ralph B. Schaps*. Edited by Theresa M. Deane and Joseph E. Schaps. Lincoln, Neb.: iUniverse, Inc., 2003.

Schetter, Charles, Akira Sunshine Fukunaga, and Jimmy Sakimoto, comp. *Company History Antitank Company 442nd Infantry Regimental Combat Team*. 1945.

Schrijvers, Peter. *The Crash of Ruin: American Combat Soldiers in Europe during World War II*. New York: New York University Press, 1998.

Sevareid, Eric. *Not So Wild a Dream*. New York: Knopf, 1946.

Sheehan, Fred. *Anzio: Epic of Bravery*. Norman: University of Oklahoma Press, 1964.

Shibutani, Tamotsu. *The Derelicts of Company K: A Sociological Study of Demoralization*. Berkeley: University of California Press, 1978.

Shimizu, Kiyoshi Harry. *Proving Our Loyalty: The World War II Story of a Young Nisei Infantryman Fighting for his Country in the Hundredth Battalion*. Aurora, Colo.: 1995.

Shirey, Orville C. *Americans: The Story of the 442d Combat Team*. Washington, D.C.: Infantry Journal, 1946, 1947.

Sone, Monica. *Nisei Daughter*. Little, Brown and Company, 1953; Seattle and London: University of Washington Press, 1998.

Sparrow, John C. *History of Personnel Demobilization in the United States Army*. CMH PUB 104-8, DA Pam 20-210, July 1952; reprint Washington, D.C.: Center of Military History, United States Army, 1994.

Staff of the *Field Artillery Journal*. *Field Artillery Guide*. Washington, D.C.: U.S. Field Artillery Association, 1942.

Standifer, Leon C. *Not in Vain: A Rifleman Remembers World War II*. Baton Rouge and London: Louisiana State University Press, 1992.

Stanton, Shelby L. *World War II Order of Battle*. New York: Galahad Books, 1984.

Steidl, Franz. *Lost Battalions: Going for Broke in the Vosges, Autumn 1944*. Novato, Calif.: Presidio Press, 1997.

Steering Committee, Company B and others. *The Boys of Company "B."* Honolulu: Hawaii Hochi, 1981.

Sterner, C. Douglas. *Go For Broke: A Tribute to the Nisei Warriors of World War II*. A HomeOfHeroes.com Electronic Book, 2001.

Stouffer, Samuel A. "The Point System for Redeployment and Discharge." In Stouffer, et al., *The American Soldier: Combat and its Aftermath*. Princeton University Press, 1948; reprint, New York: John Wiley & Sons, 1965.

Strickland, Arvarh E. "Remembering Hattiesburg: Growing Up Black in Wartime Mississippi." in Neil R. McMillen, ed., *Remaking Dixie: The Impact of World War II on the American South*. Jackson, Miss.: 1997.

Stuart, Colburn Cox. *Inside View Japanese American Evacuee Center at Rohwer, Arkansas, 1941–1945. Programs of Desha County Historical Society.* McGehee, Ark.: Desha County Historical Society, 1979.

Takemoto, Paul Howard. *Nisei Memories: My Parents Talk About the War Years.* Seattle and London: University of Washington Press, 2006.

Tanaka, Chester. *Go For Broke: A Pictorial History of the Japanese American 100th Infantry Battalion and the 442nd Infantry Regimental Combat Team.* Richmond, Calif.: Go For Broke, Inc., 1982; Novato, Calif.: Presidio Press, 1997.

Tateishi, John. *And Justice for All: An Oral History of the Japanese-American Detention Camps.* New York: Random House, 1984.

Tregaskis, Richard. *Invasion Diary.* New York: Random House, 1944.

Truscott, L. K., Jr. *Command Missions: A Personal Story.* New York: E. P. Dutton and Company, 1954.

Tsuchida, William Shinji. *Wear It Proudly: Letters by William Shinji Tsuchida.* Berkeley and Los Angeles: University of California Press, 1947.

Tsukano, John. *Bridge of Love.* Honolulu: Hawaii Hosts, Inc., 1985.

U. S. Department of the Interior. War Relocation Authority. *Nisei in Uniform.* Washington, D.C.: Government Printing Office, 1944.

Wagner, Robert L. *The Texas Army: A History of the 36th Division in the Italian Campaign.* State House Press, 1991.

Wakamatsu, Jack K. *Silent Warriors: A Memoir of America's 442nd Regimental Combat Team.* Los Angeles: JKW, 1992; New York: Vantage, 1995.

Walls, Thomas. *The Japanese Texans.* San Antonio: University of Texas Institute of Texan Cultures, 1987.

War Department. *Pocket Guide to the Cities of Southern France.* Washington, D.C., 1944.

———. *Pocket Guide to Italian Cities.* Washington, D.C., 1944.

———. *Technical Manual: The Army Cook (TM 10-405).* Washington, D.C.: April 24, 1942.

Wheeler, Robert Reginald, ed. *The Road to Victory: A History of Hampton Roads Ports of Embarkation in World War II.* 2 vols. Newport News, Va.; New Haven, Conn.: Yale University Press, 1946.

Whitlock, Flint. *The Rock of Anzio: From Sicily to Dachau: A History of the 45th Infantry Division.* Boulder, Colo.: Westview Press, 1998.

Wiley, Bell I. "The Preparation of Units for Overseas Movement." In Robert R. Palmer, Bell I. Wiley, and William R. Keast *United States Army in World War II. The Army Ground Forces. The Procurement and Training of Ground Combat Troops,* 561–618. Washington, D.C.: Historical Division. Department of the Army, 1948.

Wilson, Joe W., Jr. *The 761st "Black Panther" Tank Battalion in World War II.* Jefferson, N.C.: McFarland, 1999.

Wilt, Alan F. *The French Riviera Campaign of August 1944.* Carbondale: Southern Illinois University Press, 1981.

Winston, Keith. *V…-Mail: Letters of a World War II Combat Medic.* Chapel Hill, N.C.: Algonquin, 1985.

Woods, Imogene, and Twelve WWII Infantrymen. *The Ordinary Infantrymen: Heroes Then, Heroes Again.* Springfield, Mo.: Imogene Woods, 2003.

Yamashita, Samuel Hideo. "The Aloha Team, 1942–1943." In Brian Niiya, ed., *More Than a Game: Sport in the Japanese American Community*. Los Angeles: Japanese American Museum, 2000.

Yarrison, James L. *The Modern Louisiana Maneuvers*. Center of Military History, 1999.

Yenne, Bill. *Rising Sons: The Japanese American GIs Who Fought for the United States in World War II*. New York: Thomas Dunne Books, 2007.

Yoshida, Jim, with Bill Hosokawa. *The Two Worlds of Jim Yoshida*. New York: William Morrow and Company, 1972.

Yost, Israel A. S. *Combat Chaplain: The Personal Story of the World War II Chaplain of the Japanese American 100th Battalion*. Edited by Monica E. Yost and Michael Markrich. Honolulu: University of Hawaii Press, 2006.

Ziemke, Earl F. *The U.S. Army in the Occupation of Germany, 1944–1946*. Army Historical Series. Washington, D.C.: Center of Military History, United States Army, 1975.

Articles

Bearden, Russell E. "Life Inside Arkansas's Japanese-American Relocation Centers." *Arkansas Historical Quarterly* 48 (Summer 1989): 169–96.

Bittner, Eric. "Loyalty . . . Is a Covenant: Japanese-American Internees and the Selective Service Act." *Prologue* 22 (Fall 1991): 248–52.

Blackwell, Jon, "1940: You're in the Army Now." *The Trentonian*, 1998–1999, http://www.rootsweb.com/~pasulliv/Draft1940.htm.

Chermol, Brian H. "Wounds Without Scars: Treatment of Battle Fatigue in the U.S. Armed Forces in the Second World War." *Military Affairs* 49, no. 1 (January 1985): 9–12.

Clark, Thomas Blake, and O. D. Russell. "Hail Our Japanese-American GIs." *The Reader's Digest* XLVII (July 1945): 65–67.

Colvin, Christopher Scott. "Our Rohwer Home: From California to Arkansas." Research Paper. Ouachita Baptist University, 1996.

Coggins, Cecil Hengy. "The Japanese-Americans in Hawaii." *Harper's Magazine*, June 1943, 75–83.

Cramer, Douglas. "Dachau 1945: The Souls of All Are Aflame." *Again* 1, no. 26 (2004). http://www.antiochian.org/souls-aflame.

"The Draft: How It Works." *Time*, September 23, 1940, 20.

"The Draft: Only the Strong." *Time*, November 11, 1940, 24.

"Draft Lottery Turns Up All Kinds of Americans." *Life*, November 11, 1940, 36–37.

Eisenberg, Ellen. "'As truly American as your son": Voicing Opposition to Internment in Three West Coast cities." *Oregon Historical Quarterly* 104, no. 4 (December 2003): 542–65. http://www.accessmylibrary.com/coms2/summary_0286-2854550_ITM.

Erlanger, Alene. "The Truth About War Dogs." *Quartermaster Review*. March-April, 1944. http://www.qmfound.com/dog_truth.htm.

Foster, G. B. "Leaflet Shells." *The Field Artillery Journal* 35, no. 4 (April 1945): 195–97. http://sill-www.army.mil/firesbulletin/archives/1945/APR_1945/APR_1945_FULL_EDITION.pdf.

"Germany's Rocket and Recoilless Weapons." *Intelligence Bulletin*, March 1945. http://www.lonesentry.com/articles/rocket/index.html.

Glasgow, Matt. "Go For Broke: The 442d Combat Team Story." *Soldiers* 33 (November 1978): 6–12.

Hadley, Arthur. "An Artilleryman Looks at Propaganda." *The Field Artillery Journal* 35, no. 4 (April 1945): 197–98. http://sill-www.army.mil/firesbulletin /archives/1945/APR_1945/APR_1945_FULL_EDITION.pdf.

Hansen, Arthur A., and David A. Hacker. "The Manzanar Riot: An Ethnic Perspective." *Amerasia Journal* 2 (Fall 1974): 112–57.

Harper, Dale P. "Mildred Elizabeth Sisk: American-Born Axis Sally." *World War II* (November 1995). http://www.historynet.com/mildred-elizabeth-sisk-amer ican-born-axis-sally.htm/3.

Haufler, Hervie. "The Most Contented G.I.s in Europe." *American History* (October 1999) at http://www.historynet.com/the-most-contented-gis-in-europe -october-99-american-history-feature.htm.

Headquarters 34th Infantry Division. "Lessons Learned in Combat 8 November 1942 to 1 September 1944," 1944. Charles L Bolte papers, Box 6, at the U.S. Army Military History Institute Library, Carlisle Barracks, Pennsylvania. Transcribed by Patrick Skelly, 2006. http://www.34infdiv.org/history/34div /LessonsLearned.pdf.

Hollis, Harris W. "The Operations of the First Airborne Task Force in the Invasion of Southern France 15–20 August 1944 (Personal Experience of an Assistant G-2)." Monograph in the Library of the Advanced Infantry Officers' Training Course, Fort Benning, Ga., 1948–1949.

Holt, Thaddeus. "'Relax—It's Only a Maneuver.'" *MHQ: The Quarterly Journal of Military History* 4 (Winter 1992): 30–41.

"Japanese in America: The Problem and the Solution," by an Intelligence Officer. *Harper's Magazine* CLXXXV (October 1942): 489–97.

Jennings, Gary. "Pidgin: No Laughing Matter." *Harper's Magazine* (July 1963): 69–73.

Kurashige, Lon Yuki. "America's Concentration Camps: Remembering the Japanese American Experience." *Journal of American History*, June 1996, 160–62.

Marston, O. F. "The Camp Roberts Replacement Center." *The Field Artillery Journal* 31, no. 3 (March 1941): 178–79. http://sill-www.army.mil/firesbulletin /archives/1941/MAR_1941/MAR_1941_FULL_EDITION.pdf.

Marston, O. F., and W.J. Egan. "Two Replacement Centers." *The Field Artillery Journal* 31, no. 6 (June 1941): 373–78. http://sill-www.army.mil/firesbulletin /archives/1941/JUN_1941/JUN_1941_FULL_EDITION.pdf.

Menton, Linda K. "Research Report: Nisei Soldiers at Dachau, Spring 1945." *Holocaust and Genocide Studies* 8, no. 2 (Fall 1994): 258–74.

Mitson, Betty E. "Looking Back in Anguish: Oral History and Japanese-American Evacuation." *Oral History Review* 2 (1974): 24–51.

Mohler, Henry K. "The Therapeutic Use of Sulfanilamide and Related Compounds." *The Military Surgeon* 88 (May 1941): 473–86.

Nakahata, Yutaka, and Ralph Toyota. "Varsity Victory Volunteers: A Social Movement." *Social Process in Hawaii* VIII (November 1943): 29–35.

Okihiro, Gary Y. "Japanese Resistance in America's Concentration Camps: A Reevaluation." *Amerasia Journal* 2 (Fall 1973): 20–34.

Pallister, Casey J. "George 'Montana' Oiye: The Journey of a Japanese American from the Big Sky to the Battlefields of Europe." *Montana: The Magazine of Western History* 57, no. 3 (Autumn 2007): 21–33.

Quillen, Ed. "Honor Carr Somehow." *Denver Post,* August 14, 2007. http://www.denverpost.com/quillen/ci_6613908.

Reinecke, John E., and Aiko Torimasa. "The English Dialect of Hawaii." *American Speech* 9, no. 1 (January 1934): 48–58, and 9, no. 2 (April 1934): 122–31.

Rowntree, Leonard G., Kenneth H. McGill, and Thomas I. Edwards. "Causes of Rejection and the Incidence of Defects in 18 and 19 Year Old Selective Service Registrants." *Journal of the American Medical Association* 123 (September 1943): 181–85.

Schlenker, Gerald. "The Internment of the Japanese of San Diego County During the Second World War." *The Journal of San Diego History* 18, no. 1 (Winter 1972): 1–9. http://www.sandiegohistory.org/journal/72winter/interment.htm.

Schmidt, William T. "The Impact of Camp Shelby in World War II on Hattiesburg, Mississippi." *Journal of Mississippi History* 39 (February 1977): 41–50.

Shioya, Tara. "The Conflict Behind the Battle Lines: The Japanese Americans who fought in World War II were engaged in another, private battle, against prejudice and misunderstandings." *The San Francisco Chronicle,* September 25, 1995, 4/Z1, at http://www.sfmuseum.org/war/issei.html.

Simpich, Frederick. "Around the Clock with Your Soldier Boy." *National Geographic* 80, no. 1 (July 1941): 1–36.

Skates, John Ray. "German Prisoners of War in Mississippi, 1943–1946." *Mississippi History Now: An online publication of the Mississippi Historical Society.* 2001. http://mshistory.k12.ms.us/index.php?id=233.

"Soldier of 1940 is 15 lb. Heavier, 2 in. Taller." *Life* 9, no. 17 (October 21, 1940): 57–60

Umeda, Tommy. "Hawaiian Nisei Boxer: Yukito 'Tommy' Umeda." *Journal of Combative Sport,* March 2001. http://ejmas.com/jcs/jcsart_umeda_0401.htm.

Wagner, Robert L. "The Odyssey of a Texas Citizen Soldier." *Southwestern Historical Quarterly* 72, no. 1 (1968): 60–87.

Ward, Jason Morgan. "'No Jap Crow': Japanese Americans Encounter the World War II South." *Journal of Southern History* 73, no. 1 (February 2007): 75–104.

Williams, Rudi. "Japanese American War Hero Recalls Life During World War II." American Forces Information Service News Article, May 25, 2000. http://www.defense.gov/news/newsarticle.aspx?id=45179.

Zolotow, Maurice. "The Man Who Astonished Hattiesburg." *Saturday Evening Post* 218, no. 19 (November 10, 1945): 37, 94, 96.

Theses

Morimoto, Patricia. "The Hawaiian Dialect of English: An Aspect of Communications During the Second World War." M.A thesis, University of Hawaii, 1966.

Watanabe, Nathan K. "The 100/442d Regimental Combat Team's Rescue of the Lost Battalion: A Study in the Employment of Battle Command." M.A. Thesis. U.S. Army Command and General Staff College, 2002. Combined Arms

Research Library Digital Library. http://cgsc.cdmhost.com/cdm/single
item/collection/p4013coll2/id/298/rec/5.

Online Sources

Akiyama, Carol Lynn. "Mickey Makio Akiyama: A Brief Life History." 2006.
http:www.javadc.org/MICKEY%20MAKIO%20AKIYAMA.htm.

Anderson, Rich. "The United States Army in World War II." 2000. http://www
.militaryhistoryonline.com/wwii/usarmy/artillery.aspx.

Archer, Clark L., Sr., ed. *Paratroopers' Odyssey: A History of the 517th Parachute
Combat Team.* Hudson, Florida: 517th Parachute Regimental Combat Team
Association, 1985. See also: http://www.517prct.org/documents/odyssey
/odyssey_history.htm.

Born, K. M. "Quartermaster War Dog Program." 2007. http://www.qmfound
.com/K-9.htm

Davis, Al. "Historic California Posts: Camp Roberts." http://www.military
museum.org/campbob.html.

Department of the Navy. Naval Historical Center. "Naval Armed Guard Service:
Tragedy at Bari, Italy on 2 December 1943." 2006. http://www.history.navy
.mil/faqs/faq104-4.htm.

Follows, Ronald G. "Monarchs to Missiles: A 75-Year History of Hawaii's National
Guard." The National Guard Educational Foundation. 2011. http://www
.ngef.org/custom/hing.asp

"Fort Massachusetts." http://www.nps.gov/guis/extended/MIS/MHistory/Forts
.htm, accessed January 2, 2006.

Goto, George. *History of the 232d Engineer Combat Company.* http://www.katonk
.com/442nd/232nd.html.

Harrington, Charles Lee, Jr. "My Father's Journey: The Life and Times of my
fat[h]er from 1922 until the present." http://www.archive.org/stream/My
FathersJourney/TheJourney.wps.txt, accessed 3/2/2008.

Higuchi, Hiro. "Chaplain Higuchi Wartime Correspondence." Japanese American Veterans Collection of Digital Resources. University of Hawaii Libraries.
http://libweb.hawaii.edu/libdept/archives/mss/aja/ higuchi/index.htm.

Hyman, John A., ed. *From the Riviera to the Rhine.* 1945. http://www.texasmilitary
forcesmuseum.org/36division/hyman.htm.

Keegan, Christopher R. *The Operations of the 2nd Battalion, 442nd Infantry (Attached
to the 34th Infantry Division) in the Pursuit to the Arno in the Vicinity of Suvereto,
Italy, 26th June 1944 (Rome-Arno Campaign).* Fort Benning, Ga., The Infantry
School 1949. https://www.infantry.Army.mil/monographs/content/wwii
/STUP2/KeeganChristopherR %20%20CPT.pdf.

"Maritime Matters: Ocean Liner History and Cruise Ship News." http://www
.maritimematters.com/matsonliners1.html, accessed March 17, 2009.

Members of 34th Infantry Division. *The Story of the 34th Infantry Division. Book 1.
Louisiana to Pisa.* Information and Education Section, MTOUSA, 1944.
http://www.34infdiv.org/history/34narrhist.html.

———. *The Story of the 34th Infantry Division. Book II. Pisa to Final Victory.* Public
Relations Section at Archetipografia di Milano, 1945. http://www.34infdiv
.org/history/34narrhist.html.

Nilges, T. M., comp. "Captain Edward J. Nilges." http://www.acuity4u.net/ED
   /HOME_PAGE.html, accessed March 10, 2007.
Noack, William R. "Avocation—Soldiering: A Way of Life." 2004. http://archiver
   .rootsweb.ancestry.com/th/read/NOACK/2004-07/1089839080.
O'Donnell, Patrick. "Go For Broke: Toro Hirose of the 442nd RCT." http://www
   .Thedropzone.org/europe/Southern%20France/hirose.html, accessed
   February 11, 2006.
Porter, John D. *The Operations of the 442d Regimental Combat Team in the Vosges
   Mountains, 29 Sept–20 Nov 1944 (Rhineland Campaign).* Fort Benning, Ga.:
   The Infantry School, 1947. https://www.infantry.army.mil/monographs
   /content/wwii/STUP2/Porter,%20%20Johnn%20D,%20%20201LT.pdf.
Quigley, Thomas Clayton, "My War. The Family Version." 2001. http://www.1jma
   .dk/articles/MyWar-text%20only.pdf.
Robertson, Ricky. "More Stories of the Great Louisiana Maneuvers." http://web
   .archive.org/web/20080227004508/http://www.crt.state.la.us/tourism
   /lawwii/maneuvers/Robertson/Maneuvers_Stories.htm, accessed July 17,
   2008.
Stabrowski, Sayuri. "Filling in the Holes: A Kibei's Recounting of the Japanese
   American Experience." 2003. http://bancroft.berkeley.edu/ROHO/educa
   tion/docs/filling_in_the_holes.doc.
34th Infantry Division Association. "History, 133rd Infantry Regiment, 34th
   Infantry Division." http://www.34infdiv.org/history/133narrhist.html.
12th Army Group. *Don't Be a Sucker in Germany!* 12th Army Group, 1945. http://
   3ad.com/history/wwll/feature.pages/occupation.booklet.htm.
Woodward, A. "United Service Organizations." http://www.answers.com/topic
   /united-service-organizations.
United States Department of Veterans Affairs, "GI-BILL History." http://www
   .gibill.va.gov/benefits/history_timeline/index.html.
Waller, Anna M. *Dogs and National Defense.* Department of the Army. Office of the
   Quartermaster General. 1958. http://www.uswardogs.org/id24.html.
Wilding, Jennifer. "Warriors in Greasepaint." 2002. http://www.onwar.com/ar
   ticles/0201.htm.
Wilson, Ben, Jr. "Memories Never Forgotten: Upmost Was the Utmost." 36th
   Infantry Division Association. http://kwanah.com/36division/ps/ps98942
   htm.
"World War II—Louisiana Maneuvers." http://www.beau.org/~velmer/local
   /ww2.html.

INDEX

Page references to illustrations are in italic type.